CRIMINAL DEFINITIONS

CRIMINAL DEFINITIONS

By

Tim Bracken

CLARUS
PRESS

Published by
Clarus Press Ltd,
Griffith Campus,
South Circular Road,
Dublin 8.

Typeset by
Compuscript Ltd,
Shannon Industrial Estate,
Shannon,
Co. Clare.

Printed by
Eprint Ltd
35 Coolmine Industrial Estate,
Dublin 15

ISBN
978-1-905536-29-0

PREFACE

I have been practising law for more years than I care to think about and one thing that always struck me, particularly in the days before electronic tools such as the internet, the time and effort it took sometimes to find a particular source or a particular point. I find this more so in an area of law which is almost completely statutory based and sometimes searching for the exact definition that you need can take a substantial amount of time. In the Criminal Law Code there are hundreds of definitions, some of which are particular to a section of an Act and some which are particular to the whole Act. The definitions by and large are not generic so a definition in one Act will not be applicable in another Act.

The purpose of this book is to provide the practitioner with instant access to definitions, be it Counsel in Court who requires a definition at the drop of a hat or the Solicitor in his office who is discussing a matter with a client on the telephone and needs to find a definition at the turn of a page.

I hope this work fulfils this need. It is set out in a simple, user friendly style which will make access and sourcing definitions in the Criminal Code easy and efficient.

TIM BRACKEN
Barrister-at-Law
April 2010

CONTENTS

BAIL

A

“A BROADCAST”

(5) In this section—

“a broadcast” means the transmission, relaying or distribution by wireless telegraphy of communications, sounds, signs, visual images or signals intended for direct reception by the general public whether such communications, sounds, signs, visual images or signals are actually received or not.

Bail Act 1997, s 4(5)

"APPLICANT" (SEE THE APPLICANT)

"AUTHORISED PERSON"

"'authorised person' means a person who is appointed in writing by the Minister, or a person who is one of a prescribed class of persons, to be an authorised person for the purposes of sections 6B and 6C.

Bail Act 1997, s 1(1) inserted by Criminal Justice Act 2007, s 5

B

"BAIL"

(1) Where the District Court remands a person or sends him forward for trial or sentence, the Court may—

(*a*) commit him to prison or other lawful custody, or
(*b*) release him conditionally on his entering into a recognisance, with or without sureties.

In this Part, references to "custody" are to a committal under paragraph (*a*) and references to "bail" are to a conditional release under paragraph (*b*).

(2) The Court may, instead of taking a recognisance from a person in accordance with subsection (1), fix the amount of the recognisance in which he and his sureties, if any, are to be bound with a view to their being subsequently taken in accordance with subsection (3) and in the meantime commit him to custody in accordance with subsection (1) (*a*).

(3) Where the Court fixes the amount of a recognisance under subsection (2), the recognisance may thereafter be taken by a justice of the Court or by a peace commissioner.

(4) Where a person is brought before the Court after remand under subsection (1) the Court may further remand him.

Criminal Procedure Act 1967, s 22(1)

"BROADCAST"

"a broadcast" means the transmission, relaying or distribution by wireless telegraphy of communications, sounds, signs, visual images or signals intended for direct reception by the general public whether such communications, sounds, signs, visual images or signals are actually received or not.

Bail Act 1997, s 4(5)

C

"COURT"

"court" means any court exercising criminal jurisdiction but does not include court martial.

Bail Act 1997, s 1(1) 16/97

"CRIMINAL RECORD"

"criminal record", in relation to a person, means a record of the previous convictions of the person for offences (if any).

Bail Act 1997, s 1(1) 16/97

"CUSTODY"

(1) Where the District Court remands a person or sends him forward for trial or sentence, the Court may—

(*a*) commit him to prison or other lawful custody, or
(*b*) release him conditionally on his entering into a recognisance, with or without sureties.

In this Part, references to "custody" are to a committal under paragraph (*a*) and references to "bail" are to a conditional release under paragraph (*b*).

Criminal Procedure Act 1967, s 22(1) 12/67

P

"PARENTS"

"parents", in relation to a child, means—

(*a*) in case one parent has the sole custody, charge or care of the child, that parent,
(*b*) in case the child has been adopted under the Adoption Acts, 1952 to 1998 (or, if adopted outside the State, his or her adoption is recognised under the law of the State), the adopter or adopters or the surviving adopter, and
(*c*) in any other case, both parents.

Children Act 2001, s 3

"PERSON X 2" (SEE THE)

"PRESCRIBED"

'prescribed' means prescribed by regulations made by the Minister.".

Bail Act 1997 (1) Inserted by Criminal Justice Act 2007 s 5

"PROPERTY"

In this section 'property' means—

(*a*) cash, money in an account in a financial institution, cheques, bank drafts and transferable securities (including shares, warrants and debentures),
(*b*) land,
(*c*) mechanically propelled vehicles, and
(*d*) any other asset exceeding €3,000 in value.".

Bail Act 1997, s 1a(16) inserted by Criminal Justice Act 2007, s 6

"PROSECUTOR"

In this Act 'the prosecutor' means, in relation to an offence—

(*a*) in Part IA and section 13, the Director of Public Prosecutions, and
(*b*) in Parts II and III, other than section 13—

(i) the Director of Public Prosecutions,
(ii) a person prosecuting the offence at the suit of the Director of Public Prosecutions, or
(iii) a person authorised by law to prosecute the offence.

(2) Notwithstanding subsection (1), references to the prosecutor in Parts IA, II and III shall be construed, in relation to offences for which proceedings may not be instituted or continued except by, or on behalf or with the consent of, the Attorney General, as references to the Attorney General.".

Criminal Procedure Act 1967 s 4 substituted by Criminal Justice Act 1999, s 8

"PUBLISH"

'publish' means publish to the public or a portion of the public.

Criminal Procedure Act 1967 s 4j(5) inserted by Criminal Justice Act 1999, s 9

S

"SENTENCED TO IMPRISONMENT"

The expression "sentenced to imprisonment" shall include cases where imprisonment is imposed by a court on any person either with or without the option of a fine, or in respect of the non-payment of any sum of money, or for failing to do or abstaining from doing any act or thing required to be done or left undone, and the expression "sentence of imprisonment" shall be construed accordingly.

Criminal Justice (Amendment) Act 1914, s 41(1)

(*c*) in the Schedule to the Act by—
(i) the insertion after paragraph 7 of the following paragraph:
"7A. Any offence under section 3 of the Criminal Justice Act 1990 (certain murders and attempts).",
(ii) the substitution in paragraph 28 of the following subparagraphs for subparagraph (*c*):
"(*c*) section 16 (affray), and
(*d*) section 17 (blackmail, extortion and demanding money with menaces).",
(iii) the substitution of the following paragraph for paragraph 28A (inserted by section 79 of the Criminal Justice Act 2006):
"*Offences under the Criminal Justice Act 2006.*

28A. Any offence under the following provisions of the Criminal Justice Act 2006 —

(*a*) section 71, 72 or 73 (organised crime);
(*b*) section 176 (reckless endangerment of children);
(*c*) section 183 (possession of article intended for use in connection with certain offences);
(*d*) section 183A (possession of monies intended for use in connection with certain offences).",

and

(iv) the insertion after paragraph 33 of the following paragraph:
"*Offences under the Prisons Act 2007.*
34. Any offence under section 36 of the Prisons Act 2007.".

Criminal Justice (Miscellaneous Provisions) Act 2009, s 48 amending Bail Act 1997

"SERIOUS OFFENCE"

The list of offences which constitute **serious offences** is set out in the schedule to the Bail Act 1997. However this schedule has been heavily amended and where there is an amendment to one of numbered offences in the schedule this is set out directly under that number.

Common law offences

1. Murder.

2. Manslaughter.

3.

4.

5.

6. Rape.

Definitions 3, 4 and 5 deleted by **Non-Fatal Offences Against the Person Act, 1997, s 30(a)(b)(c)**

Offences against the person

7. Any offence under the following provisions of the *Non-Fatal Offences against the Person Act, 1997*—

(*a*) *section 3* (assault causing harm);
(*b*) *section 4* (causing harm);

(*c*) *section 5* (threats to kill or cause serious harm);
(*d*) *section 6* (syringe, etc. attacks);
(e) *section 7* (1) (offence of possession of syringe, etc. in certain circumstances);
(*f*) *section 8* (placing or abandoning syringe);
(*g*) *section 9* (coercion);
(*h*) *section 10* (harassment);
(*i*) *section 13* (endangerment);
(*j*) *section 14* (endangering traffic);
(*k*) *section 15* (false imprisonment);
(*l*) *section 16* (abduction of child by parent, etc.);
(*m*) *section 17* (abduction of child by other persons).".

7 substituted by the Non-Fatal Offences Against the Person Act 1997, s 30(d)

7A. Any offence under section 3 of the Criminal Justice Act 1990 (certain murders and attempts)

7A inserted by the Criminal Justice (Miscellaneous Provisions) Act 2009, s 48

1. Any offence under the provisions of the Criminal Justice (Public Order) Act 1994:—

(*a*) Section 18 (assault to cause bodily harm or commit indictable offence);
(*b*) Section 19 (assault or obstruction of peace officer)

Sexual offences

2. Any offence under section 1 (incest by males) and section 2 (incest by female of or over 17 years) of the Punishment of Incest Act 1908.

3. Any offence under section 1 (defilement of girl under fifteen years of age) and section 2 (defilement of girl between fifteen and seventeen years of age) of the Criminal Law Amendment Act, 1935

4. Any offence under the following provisions of the Criminal Law (Rape) (Amendment) Act 1990;

(*a*) Section 2 (sexual assault);
(*b*) Section 3 (aggravated sexual assault);
(*c*) Section 4 (rape under section 4);

5. Any offence under the following provisions of the Criminal Law (Sexual Offences) Act, 1993—

(*a*) Section 3 (buggery of persons under 17 years of age);
(*b*) Section 5 (protection of mentally impaired persons);
(*c*) Sections 9 and 11 (organisation etc. of prostitution).

"12A. Any offence under the following provisions of the *Child Trafficking and Pornography Act, 1998* —

(*a*) *section 3* (child trafficking and taking, etc., child for sexual exploitation);
(*b*) *section 5* (producing, distributing, etc., child pornography).".

12 A inserted by the Child Trafficking and Pornography Act 1998, s 12

Explosives

6. Any offence under the following provisions of the Explosives Substances Act, 1883—

(*a*) Section 2 (causing explosions likely to endanger life or damage tom property)
(*b*) Section 3 (possession etc. of explosive substances);
(*c*) Section 4 (making or possessing explosives in suspicious circumstances)

Firearms

7.
Any offence under the following provisions of the Firearms Act 1925:

(*a*) section 2 (restrictions on possession, use, and carriage of firearms);
(*b*) section 3 (applications for, and form and effect of, firearm certificates);
(*c*) section 4A(18) (authorisation of rifle or pistol clubs or shooting ranges);
(*d*) section 10A (reloading of ammunition);
(e) section 15 (possession of firearms with intent to endanger life);
(*f*) section 25 (punishments).".

14 substituted by the Criminal Justice Act 2007, s 17

8. Any offence under the following provisions of the Firearms Act, 1964—
(*a*) Section 26 (possession of firearm while taking vehicle without authority);
(*b*) Section 27 (use of firearm to resist arrest or aid escape);
(*c*) Section 27A (possession of firearm or ammunition in suspicious circumstances);
(*d*) Section 27B (carrying firearm with criminal intent).

9. 1
Any offence under the following provisions of the Firearms and Offensive Weapons Act 1990:

(*a*) section 7 (possession, sale, etc., of silencers);
(*b*) section 8 (reckless discharge of firearm);
(*c*) section 9 (possession of knives and other articles);
(*d*) section 10 (trespassing with a knife, weapon of offence or other article);

(e) section 11 (production of article capable of inflicting serious injury);
(*f*) section 12 (power to prohibit manufacture, importation, sale, hire or loan of offensive weapons);
(g) section 12A (shortening barrel of shotgun or rifle).",
(*c*) by the insertion of the following paragraph after paragraph 16:

"16A. Any offence under section 3 of the Firearms (Firearm Certificates for Non-Residents) Act 2000 (prohibition of false information and alteration of firearm certificates).".

16 substituted and 16A inserted by the Criminal Justice Act 2007, s 17

Robbery and burglary

10. Any offence under the *Criminal Justice (Theft and Fraud Offences) Act, 2001*

17 amended by the Criminal Justice (Theft and Fraud Offences) Act, 2001 section 64

11. Any offence under the following provisions of the Criminal Damage Act, 1991—:

(*a*) Section 2 (damaging property);
(*b*) Section 3 (threat to damaging property);
(*c*) Section 4 (possessing any thing with intent to damage property)

Road traffic offences

12. Any offence under the following provisions of the Road Traffic Act, 1961:—

(*a*) Section 53 (dangerous driving causing death or serious bodily harm);
(*b*) Section 112 (taking vehicle without authority)

Offences in relation to aircraft and vehicles

13. Any offence under section 11 of the Air Navigation and Transport Act, 1973 (unlawful seizure of aircraft).

14. Any offence under section 3 of the Air Navigation and Transport Act 1975 (unlawful acts against the safety of aviation)

15. Any offence under section 10 of the Criminal Law(Jurisdiction) Act, 1976 (unlawful seizure of vehicles)

Maritime security offences

"22A. —Any offence under *section 2* of the *Maritime Security Act 2004*.".

22A inserted by the Maritime Security Act 2004, s 12

Forgery etc. offences

16.
17.

23 and 24 deleted by Criminal Justice (Theft and Fraud Offences) Act 2001, s 64

Offences against the state

18. Any offence under the provisions of the Offences against the State Act, 1939 to 1998

25 substituted by the Offences Against the State (Amendment) Act 1998, s 16

19. Treason

Drugs offences

20. A drug trafficking offence within the meaning of section 3(1) of the Criminal Justice Act 1994.

27A. Any offence under section 2 of the *Illegal Immigrants (Trafficking) Act, 2000.*

27 A inserted by the Illegal Immigrants (Trafficking) Act 2000, s 8

Public order offences

21. Any offence under the following provisions of the Criminal Justice (Public Order) Act, 1994

(*a*) Section 14 (riot)
(*b*) Section 15 (violent disorder)
(*c*) section 16 (affray), and
(*d*) section 17 (blackmail, extortion and demanding money with menaces)

28 (c) substituted and 28 (d) inserted by the Criminal Justice (Miscellaneous Provisions) Act 2009, s 48

Offences under the Criminal Justice Act 2006.

"28A. Any offence under the following provisions of the Criminal Justice Act 2006 —

(*a*) section 71, 72 or 73 (organised crime);
(*b*) section 176 (reckless endangerment of children);
(*c*) section 183 (possession of article intended for use in connection with certain offences);
(*d*) section 183A (possession of monies intended for use in connection with certain offences).".

28A inserted by the Criminal Justice Act 2006, s 79 substituted by the Criminal Justice (Miscellaneous Provisions) Act 2009, s 48

Bail

Accomplices

22. References in this Schedule to an offence include references to participation as an accomplice of a person who commits the offence.

Attempts and conspiracy

23. An offence of attempting or conspiring to commit, or inciting the commission of, any offence mentioned in this Schedule

30 substituted by the Criminal Justice Act 2007, s 17

Torture

31. Any offence under the *Criminal Justice (United Nations Convention against Torture) Act, 2000.*

31 (Torture) Inserted By Criminal Justice (United Nations Convention Against Torture) Act 2000, s 10

Offences against United Nations workers

"32. Any offence under the *Criminal Justice (Safety of United Nations Workers) Act, 2000.*".

32 inserted by the Criminal Justice (Safety of United Nations Workers) Act 2000, s 9

Suppression of terrorism

33.—Any offence under the *Criminal Justice (Terrorist Offences) Act 2005.*

33 inserted by the Criminal Justice (Terrorist Offences) Act 2005, s 60

Offences under the Prisons Act 2007 .

"34. Any offence under section 36 of the Prisons Act 2007 .".

34 inserted by the Criminal Justice (Miscellaneous Provisions) Act 2009, s 48

The applicant

A person who is charged with a serious offence and applies for bail (in this section referred to as 'the applicant') shall, subject to subsections (4) and (5)(c), furnish to the prosecutor a written statement duly signed by the applicant and containing the following information relating to the applicant:

(*a*) his or her name and any other name or names previously used;
(*b*) his or her current occupation and any previous occupation or occupations within the immediately preceding 3 years;
(*c*) his or her source or sources of income within the immediately preceding 3 years;
(*d*) his or her property, whether wholly or partially owned by, or under the control of, the applicant and whether within or outside the State;
(*e*) any previous conviction or convictions of the applicant for a serious offence;
(*f*) any previous conviction or convictions of the applicant for an offence or offences committed while on bail;
(*g*) any previous application or applications by the person for bail, indicating whether or not it was granted and, if granted, the conditions to which the recognisance was subject.

Bail Act 1997, s 1A inserted by the Criminal Justice Act 2007, s 6

The person

Subject to subsection (2), where a person (in this section referred to as 'the person') who—

(*a*) is charged with a serious offence or is appealing against a sentence of imprisonment imposed by the District Court, and
(*b*) is admitted to bail on entering into a recognisance which is subject to any of the conditions mentioned in subparagraphs (i) and (iv) of section 6(1)(*b*),

the court may make the recognisance subject to the following further conditions:

(i) that the person's movements while on bail are monitored electronically so that his or her compliance or non-compliance with a condition mentioned in any of the said subparagraphs can be established;
(ii) that for that purpose the person has an electronic monitoring device attached to his or her person, either continuously or for such periods as may be specified; and
(iii) that an authorised person is responsible for monitoring the person's compliance or non-compliance with any condition mentioned in the said subparagraphs or in paragraph (ii) of this subsection.

Bail Act 1997, s 6B(1) inserted by the Criminal Justice Act 2007, s 11

This section applies where—

(*a*) an accused person or a person who is appealing against a sentence of imprisonment imposed by the District Court (in either case referred to in this section as 'the person') is admitted to bail on entering into a recognisance conditioned for his or her appearance before a specified court on a specified date at a specified time and place, and

(*b*) the person—

(i) fails to appear in accordance with the recognisance and the court issues a warrant for his or her arrest, or

(ii) is brought before the court in accordance with subsection (7) and the court is satisfied that the person has contravened a condition of the recognisance.

Bail Act, 1997, s 9(1) substituted by the Criminal Justice Act 2007, s 15

W

"WITNESS"

"witness" includes an expert witness and a person suspected of the offence which has given rise to the request concerned.

Criminal Justice (Mutual Assistance) Act 2008, s 61

This section applies, subject to *section 64*, in relation to a request for assistance in obtaining evidence in the State from a person (in this section referred to as a "witness") for the purpose of criminal proceedings, or a criminal investigation, in a designated state.

(2) On receipt of such a request the Minister, if of opinion that this section applies in relation to it, may, subject to *subsection (3)*—

(*a*) request the President of the District Court to nominate a judge of that Court to receive the evidence to which the request relates, and

(*b*) send the judge a copy of the request and of any accompanying or related documents.

Criminal Justice (Mutual Assistance) Act 2008, s 63(1)

"WITNESS ORDER"

In this section, 'witness order' means an order made under subsection (1).

Criminal Procedure Act 1967, s 4k(4) inserted by the Criminal Justice Act 1999, s 9

The trial court may, in relation to the trial of the accused, make an order requiring a person whose statement of evidence was served on the accused or whose deposition was taken to—

(*a*) attend before the trial court and give evidence at the trial of the accused, and
(*b*) produce to that court any document or thing specified in the order.

Criminal Procedure Act 1967, s 4k(1) inserted by Criminal Justice Act 1999, s 9

"WITNESS SUMMONS"

In this section, 'witness summons' means a summons issued under sub-section (1).

Criminal Procedure Act 1967, s 4L(4) inserted by Criminal Justice Act 1999, s 9

On application by the prosecutor or the accused, a summons may be issued out of the trial court requiring the person to whom the summons is directed to—

(*a*) attend before the trial court and give evidence at the trial of the accused, and
(*b*) produce to that court any document or thing specified in the summons,

unless the court is satisfied that the person proposed to be summoned cannot give any material evidence or, as the case may be, produce any document or thing likely to be material evidence.

Criminal Procedure Act 1967, s 4L(1) inserted by Criminal Justice Act 1999, s 9

"WORKING COPY"

"working copy" means any tape, that is not the master tape, used in the equipment.

SI 74/97 Art 2

"WRITTEN PUBLICATION"

"written publication" includes a film, a sound track and any other record in permanent form (including a record that is not in a legible form but which is capable of being reproduced in a legible form) but does not include an indictment or other document prepared for use in particular legal proceedings.

Bail Act 1997, s 4(5)

CHILDREN

A

"ACTION PLAN"

"action plan", where it occurs in *Part 4*, has the meaning assigned to it by section 39 and, where it occurs in *Part 8*, has the meaning assigned to it by section 80 *(1)* or *82(2)(a)*, as the case may be.

Children Act 2001, s 3

(1) The parents or guardian of a child, when present at a conference in respect of the child (or in their absence a member of the child's family or a relative of the

child), and the child may, with the assistance of the other persons present at the conference, formulate an action plan for the child.

(2) Any such action plan shall be agreed unanimously by those present at the conference, unless the disagreement of any person present is regarded by the facilitator as unreasonable, in which case that person's agreement to the plan shall not be necessary.

(3) An action plan may include provision for any one or more of the following matters:

(*a*) an apology, whether orally or in writing or both, by the child to any victim,
(*b*) financial or other reparation to any victim,
(*c*) participation by the child in an appropriate sporting or recreational activity,
(*d*) attendance of the child at a school or place of work,
(*e*) participation by the child in an appropriate training or educational course or a programme that does not interfere with any work or school schedule of the child,
(*f*) the child being at home at specified times,
(*g*) the child staying away from specified places or a specified person or both,
(*h*) taking initiatives within the child's family and community that might help to prevent the commission by the child of further offences, and
(*i*) any other matter that in the opinion of those present at the conference would be in the child's best interests or would make the child more aware of the consequences of his or her criminal behaviour.

(4) When the action plan and its duration have been agreed, the facilitator shall produce a written record of the plan in language that can be understood by the child.

(5) The action plan shall be signed by the child (where possible), the chairperson and one of the other persons present.

(6) The action plan shall come into operation on the date it is signed.

(7) A copy of the action plan shall be given or sent to the child by the chairperson.

(8) Those present at the conference may appoint one or more of their number to implement the action plan and monitor compliance with it.

(9) The chairperson shall, after consulting the other persons present, appoint a date, being a date after the period covered by the action plan has expired, for reconvening the conference to review compliance with the action plan.

(10) The reconvened conference shall be held not more than 6 months from the date on which the action plan was signed and may be held outside the period of the child's supervision by a juvenile liaison officer.

(11) The chairperson may reconvene the conference at an earlier date than that appointed under *subsection (9)* if it comes to his or her notice that the child is not complying with any of the terms of the action plan.

(12) The persons present at any conference reconvened pursuant to *subsection (11)* shall ascertain why the child is not complying with the action plan and shall encourage the child to comply with the plan or any amended version of it that they may agree upon.

(13) The provisions of *subsections (4)* to *(7)* shall apply to any action plan amended in accordance with *subsection (12)*.

(14) Subject to *subsection (10)*, a conference may be reconvened on any number of occasions to discuss any aspect of an action plan.

(15) Nothing in this section shall prevent any person or persons who implemented, and monitored compliance with, the action plan from continuing, with the agreement of the child, to implement and monitor compliance with the plan after the period covered by it has expired and it has been reviewed at a reconvened conference.

Children Act 2001, s 39

"ADULT"

"adult" means any person of or over the age of 18 years.

Children Act 2001, s 3

"ADULT RELATIVE"

In this section "adult relative" includes any adult reasonably named by the child pursuant to section 58 (2)(a).

Children Act 2001, s 63(5)

If the member in charge of the station—

(i) is unable to communicate with a parent or guardian of the child, or
(ii) the parent or guardian indicates that he or she cannot or will not attend at the station within a reasonable time,

the member shall inform the child or cause the child to be informed without delay of that fact and of the child's entitlement to have an adult relative or other adult reasonably named by him or her given the information specified in *subsection (1)(a)* and requested to attend at the station without delay.

Children Act 2001, s 58(2)(a)

"ANTI SOCIAL BEHAVIOUR" (CHILD)

For the purposes of this Part, a child behaves in an anti-social manner if the child causes or, in the circumstances, is likely to cause, to one or more persons who are not of the same household as the child—

(*a*) harassment,
(*b*) significant or persistent alarm, distress, fear or intimidation, or
(*c*) significant or persistent impairment of their use or enjoyment of their property.

Children Act 2001, s 257A(2) inserted by Criminal Justice Act 2006, s 159

"ATTENDANCE"

In this section "attendance", in relation to a day centre, includes participation under supervision in any occupation, activity or instruction outside the centre.

Children Act 2001, s 121(4)

"AUTHORISED PERSON"

"authorised person" means a person authorised by the Minister under section 185.

Children Act 2001, s 157 amended by Criminal Justice Act 2006, s 145(A)

B

"BEHAVIOUR ORDER"

(1) The Children Court may, on the application of a member of the Garda Síochána not below the rank of superintendent, make an order (in this Part referred to as a "behaviour order") prohibiting a child of or above the age of 12 years from doing anything specified in the order if the court is satisfied that—

(*a*) the child, notwithstanding his or her participation in the procedures provided for in section 257C, has continued and is likely to continue to behave in an anti-social manner,
(*b*) the order is necessary to prevent the child from continuing to behave in that manner,

(*c*) having regard to the effect or likely effect of that behaviour on other persons, the order is reasonable and proportionate in the circumstances.

(2) The application shall indicate the extent of the child's participation in the procedures under section 257C.

(3) The Court may impose terms or conditions in the behaviour order that it considers appropriate.

(4) An order under this section may, for the purpose of protecting a person or persons from further anti-social behaviour by a child—

(*a*) prohibit a child from behaving in a specified manner, and, where appropriate, from so behaving at or in the vicinity of a specified place,
(*b*) require the child to comply with specified requirements, including requirements relating to—
  (i) school attendance, and
  (ii) reporting to a member of the Garda Síochána, a teacher or other person in authority in a school,

And

(*c*) provide for the supervision of the child by a parent or guardian or any other specified person or authority with an interest in the child's welfare.

(5) The respondent child in an application under this section may not at any time be charged with, prosecuted or punished for an offence if the act or omission that constitutes the offence is the same behaviour that is the subject of the application and is to be determined by the court under subsection (1).

(6) Unless discharged under subsection (7), a behaviour order remains in force for no more than the lesser of the following:

(*a*) 2 years from the date of the order;
(*b*) the period specified in the order.

(7) The Court may vary or discharge a behaviour order on the application of the child concerned or his or her parents or guardian or of a member of the Garda Síochána not below the rank of superintendent.

(8) An applicant under subsection (1) or (7) shall give notice of the application—

(*a*) where the applicant under either subsection is a member of the Garda Síochána, to the child and his or her parents or guardian, or
(*b*) where the applicant under subsection (7) is the child, to the applicant under subsection (1) and the child's parents or guardian, and
(*c*) where the applicant under subsection (7) is the child's parent or guardian, to the child and the applicant under subsection (1).

(9) The standard of proof in proceedings under this section is that applicable to civil proceedings.

(10) The jurisdiction conferred on the Court by this section may be exercised as follows:

(*a*) in respect of subsections (1), (3) and (4), by a judge of the District Court for the time being assigned to the district court district in which the child resides at the time the application is made;
(*b*) in respect of subsection (7), by a judge of the District Court for the time being assigned to the district court district in which the child subject to the behaviour order resides at the time the application is made.".

Children Act 2001, s 257(D) inserted by Criminal Justice Act 2006, s 162

"BEHAVIOUR WARNING" (CHILD)

"Behaviour warning to child.

(1) Subject to subsection (5), a member of the Garda Síochána may issue a behaviour warning to a child who has behaved in an anti-social manner.

(2) The behaviour warning may be issued orally or in writing and, if it is issued orally, shall be recorded in writing as soon as reasonably practicable and a written record of the behaviour warning shall be served on the child and his or her parents or guardian personally or by post.

(3) The behaviour warning or, if it is given orally, the written record of it shall—

(*a*) include a statement that the child has behaved in an anti-social manner and indicate what that behaviour is and when and where it took place,
(*b*) demand that the child cease the behaviour or otherwise address the behaviour in the manner specified in the warning, and
(*c*) include notice that—
  (i) failure to comply with a demand under paragraph (*b*), or
  (ii) issuance of a subsequent behaviour warning,

may result in an application being made for a behaviour order.

(4) The member of the Garda Síochána referred to in subsection (1) may require the child to give his or her name and address to the member for the purposes of the behaviour warning or the written record of it.

(5) A behaviour warning may not be issued more than one month after the time that—

(*a*) the behaviour took place, or
(*b*) in the case of persistent behaviour, the most recent known instance of that behaviour took place.

(6) Subject to subsection (7), a behaviour warning remains in force against the child to whom it is issued for 3 months from the date that it is issued.

(7) If an application is made under section 257D in respect of the child, the behaviour warning remains in force against the child until the application is determined by the Children Court.".

Children Act 2001, s 257B inserted by Criminal Justice Act 2006, s 160

"BOARD"

(1) On the commencement of this section there shall stand established a body, to be known as the Special Residential Services Board, or in the Irish language An Bord Seirbhísí Cónaithe Spesialta, to perform the functions assigned to it by this Part.

(2) The Board shall be a body corporate with perpetual succession and an official seal and power to sue and be sued in its corporate name and, with the consent of the Ministers, to acquire, hold and dispose of land (including rights over or in respect of land) or any other property.

(3) The Board shall, subject to the provisions of this Part, be independent in the exercise of its functions.

Children Act 2001, ss 225(1) & 226

"BOARD OF MANAGEMENT"

"board of management" in relation to a certified industrial school, includes managers of the school within the meaning of the Act of 1908.

Children Act 2001, s 159B(1) inserted by Criminal Justice Act 2006, s 148

"BROADCAST"

"broadcast" means the transmission, relaying or distribution by wireless telegraphy of communications, sounds, signs, visual images or signals, intended for direct reception by the general public whether such communications, sounds, signs, visual images or signals are actually received or not.

Children Act 2001, s 51(6)

C

"CAUTION"

"caution" means either a formal caution or an informal caution, as appropriate.

Children Act 2001, s 17(1)

"CERTIFIED INDUSTRIAL SCHOOL"

"certified industrial school" means a certified industrial school under Part IV of the Act of 1908 which becomes transferred premises on the transfer day.

Children Act 2001, s 159B(1) inserted by Criminal Justice Act 2006, s 148

"CHILD"

"child" means a person under the age of 18 years.

Children Act 2001, s 3

"child" means a child found guilty or convicted of an offence by a court and in respect of whom a court has made a children detention order.

Children Act 2001, s 157

"child" means a child who is at least 12 years of age and under the age of 18 years.

Children Act 2001, s 257A(1) inserted by Criminal Justice Act 2006, s 159

In this section—

"child" means a child under 17 years of age.

Children Act 2001, s 249(4)

"CHILD DETENTION ORDER"

A court may, in accordance with this Part, by order (in this Part referred to as a "children detention order") impose on a child a period of detention in a children detention school or children detention centre specified in the order.

Children Act 2001, s 142

"CHILDREN COURT DISTRICT"

"children court district" has the same meaning as "district court district".

Children Act 2001, s 95

"CHILDREN DETENTION CENTRE"

Definition deleted by Criminal Justice Act 2006, sched 4, pt 7

"CHILDREN DETENTION SCHOOL"

"children detention school" means—

(*a*) any certified reformatory school or industrial school that becomes a children detention school by virtue of section 159, or
(*b*) any place, school, premises or building designated by the Minister [ ] pursuant to section 160 as a children detention school.

Children Act 2001, s 3 as amended by Criminal Justice Act 2006, s 122

"COMMUNITY SANCTION"

In this Part, "community sanction" means any of the orders referred to in *paragraphs (a)* to *(j)* which may be made by a court on being satisfied that a child is guilty of an offence—

(*a*) in the case of a child of 16 or 17 years of age, a community service order under section 3 of the Act of 1983,
(*b*) an order under section 118 (a day centre order),
(*c*) an order under section 2 of the Act of 1907 (a probation order),
(*d*) an order under section 124 (a probation (training or activities) order),
(*e*) an order under section 125 (a probation (intensive supervision) order),
(*f*) an order under section 126 (a probation (residential supervision) order),
(*g*) an order under section 129 (a suitable person (care and supervision) order),

(*h*) an order under section 131 (a mentor (family support) order),
(*i*) an order under section 133 (a restriction on movement order), or
(*j*) an order under section 137 (a dual order).

Children Act 2001, s 115

"COMPENSATION ORDER"

"compensation order" has the meaning assigned to it by section 6 of the Criminal Justice Act, 1993.

Children Act 2001, s 95

Subject to the provisions of this section, on conviction of any person of an offence, the court, instead of or in addition to dealing with him in any other way, may, unless it sees reason to the contrary, make (on application or otherwise) an order (in this Act referred to as a "compensation order") requiring him to pay compensation in respect of any personal injury or loss resulting from that offence (or any other offence that is taken into consideration by the court in determining sentence) to any person (in this Act referred to as the "injured party") who has suffered such injury or loss.

(2) The compensation payable under a compensation order (including a compensation order made against a parent or guardian of the convicted person and notwithstanding, in such a case, any other statutory limitation as to amount) shall be of such amount (not exceeding, in the case of such an order made by the District Court, such amount as may stand prescribed for the time being by law as the limit of that Court's jurisdiction in tort) as the court considers appropriate, having regard to any evidence and to any representations that are made by or on behalf of the convicted person, the injured party or the prosecutor, and shall not exceed the amount of the damages that, in the opinion of the court, the injured party would be entitled to recover in a civil action against the convicted person in respect of the injury or loss concerned.

(3) Where the commission of the offence by the convicted person involved the taking of property out of the possession of the injured party and the property has been recovered, any loss occurring to the injured party by reason of the property being damaged while out of his possession shall be treated for the purposes of *subsection (1)* as having resulted from the offence, irrespective of how the damage was caused or who caused it.

(4) A compensation order shall not be made in respect of an injury or loss that results from the use of a mechanically propelled vehicle (within the meaning of the Road Traffic Act, 1961) in a public place unless it appears to the court that—

(*a*) it is in respect of an injury or loss as respects which the use of the vehicle by the convicted person was in breach of section 56 (which provides for the compulsory insurance of mechanically propelled vehicles) of that Act, or
(*b*) it is in respect of a loss which is treated by *subsection (3)* as having resulted from the offence,

and, where a compensation order is made in respect of injury or loss resulting from such use, the amount of the compensation may include an amount representing the whole or part of any loss of or reduction in preferential rates of insurance resulting from such use.

(5) In determining whether to make a compensation order against a person, and in determining the amount of the compensation, the court shall have regard—

(*a*) to his means, or
(*b*) in a case to which section 99 of the Children Act, 1908 (which empowers a court to require a parent or guardian to pay any fine, damages or costs imposed on or awarded against a child or young person), applies, to the means of the parent or guardian,

so far as they appear or are known to the court and for that purpose the court may require the convicted person or his parent or guardian, as the case may be, to give evidence as to his means and financial commitments.

(6) A compensation order may provide for payment of the compensation by such instalments and at such times as the court shall in all the circumstances consider reasonable.

(7) Where the court considers—

(*a*) that it would be appropriate both to impose a fine and to make a compensation order, but
(*b*) that the convicted person has insufficient means to pay both an appropriate fine and appropriate compensation, the court may, if it is satisfied that the means are sufficient to justify its doing so, make a compensation order and, if it is satisfied that it is appropriate to do so having regard to the means that would remain after compliance with the order, impose a fine.

(8) At any time after a compensation order has ceased to be suspended by virtue of *section 8* and before it has been complied with or fully complied with, the District Court (or, where the amount payable under the order exceeds such amount as may stand prescribed for the time being by law as the limit of that Court's jurisdiction in tort, the court which made the order) may—

(*a*) on the application of the convicted person concerned and on being satisfied that the injured party concerned has been given an opportunity of making representations to the Court on the issue and having regard to any such representations that are made by him or on his behalf, reduce the amount remaining to be paid, vary any instalment payable, or direct that no payments or further payments be made, under the order if it appears to the Court that, because of a substantial reduction in the means of the convicted person, his means are insufficient to satisfy the order in full, or
(*b*) on the application of the injured party concerned and on being satisfied that the convicted person concerned has been given an opportunity of making

representations to the Court on the issue and having regard to any such representations that are made by him or on his behalf, increase the amount to be paid, the amount of any instalment or the number of instalments payable, under the order if it appears to the Court that—

(i) because of a substantial increase in the means of the convicted person, his means are sufficient for the relevant purposes aforesaid, and

(ii) any increased amount to be paid under the order would not exceed—

(I) the amount of the damages that the injured party concerned would be entitled to recover in a civil action against the convicted person in respect of the injury or loss concerned, or

(II) such amount as may stand prescribed for the time being by law as the limit of the Court's jurisdiction in tort,

whichever is the lesser.

(9) The references to damages in the aforesaid section 99 shall be construed as if they included references to compensation under a compensation order and subsections (5) and (6) of that section shall not apply in relation to a compensation order.

(10) This section is without prejudice to any other enactment which provides for the payment of compensation by a person convicted of an offence or otherwise proved to have committed an offence.

(11) The making of a compensation order against a parent or guardian of a convicted person shall not of itself give rise to any other liability on the part of the parent or guardian in respect of the injury or loss.

(12) In this section—

(*a*) in a case where death has resulted from an offence specified in *subsection (1)*—

"loss" means any matter (including mental distress resulting from the death and funeral expenses) for which damages could be awarded in respect of the death by virtue of Part V of the Civil Liability Act, 1961,

"injured party" includes a dependant (within the meaning of the said Part V) of the deceased person concerned,

(*b*) references to conviction of a person include references to dealing with a person under section 1 (1) of the Probation of Offenders Act, 1907, and

(*c*) the third reference in *subsection (1)*, the second reference in *subsection (2)* and the references in *subsections (7) (b)* and *(8)* (other than *paragraph (b) (ii)*) to a convicted person, however expressed, include, in a case to which the aforesaid section 99 applies, references to his parent or guardian.

(13) In assessing for the purposes of this section the means of a person, the court shall take into account his financial commitments.

Criminal Justice Act 1993, s 6

"CONFERENCE"

In this Part "conference", in relation to a child, means a meeting held pursuant to this Part of persons concerned with the child's welfare, and such a conference shall have the following functions:

(*a*) to bring together the child in respect of whom the conference is being held, his or her parents or guardian, such other family members, relatives and other persons as appropriate and the facilitator with a view to—
  (i) establishing why the child became involved in the behaviour that gave rise to his or her admission to the Programme,
  (ii) discussing how the parents or guardian, family members, relatives or any other person could help to prevent the child from becoming involved in further such behaviour, and
  (iii) where appropriate, reviewing the child's behaviour since his or her admission to the Programme;

(*b*) as appropriate and in accordance with this Part, to mediate between the child and the victim;

(*c*) to formulate an action plan for the child; and

(*d*) to uphold the concerns of the victim and have due regard to his or her interests.

Children Act 2001, s 29

"CONFIDENTIAL"

In this section "confidential" means that which is expressed to be confidential either as regards particular information or information of a particular class or description.

Children Act 2001, s 32(9)

In this section "confidential" means that which is expressed to be confidential either as regards particular information or information of a particular class or description.

Children Act 2001, s 44(12)

"COURT"

"Court", in *Parts 7* and *8*, means the Children Court.

Children Act 2001, s 3(1)

"CRIMINAL BEHAVIOUR"

"criminal behaviour", in relation to a child, means the act or omission constituting an offence alleged to have been committed by the child.

Children Act 2001, s 3(1)

D

"DAY CENTRE"

"day centre" means a place to which *subsection (2)* applies;

"day centre order" means an order under *subsection (5)*.

(2) For the purposes of this section the Minister shall provide or arrange for the provision of a sufficient number of places for use as day centres which shall be operated either by the probation and welfare service or by any body with the approval and assistance of that service.

(3) Before any place or part thereof may be used as a day centre, the principal probation and welfare officer shall inspect it and, if he or she considers that the place is suitable for such use, certify in writing accordingly.

(4) A certificate under subsection (3) shall remain in force for not more than one year from the date of its issue, unless it is cancelled by the principal probation and welfare officer before then on the ground that the place is no longer suitable for use as a day centre.

Children Act 2001, s 118(1)–(4)

"DAY CENTRE ORDER"

(*a*) A court may by order direct that a child shall attend at a specified day centre for the purpose of participating in an occupation or activity, or receiving instruction, which is suitable and beneficial for him or her.

(*b*) The child may participate in any such occupation or activity, or receive any such instruction, under supervision outside the day centre, and references in this section to attendance at a day centre include references to such participation or receiving outside it.

(6) The number of days a child shall be required to attend at a day centre pursuant to a day centre order shall be not more than 90, and attendance need not be on consecutive days.

(7) A child in respect of whom a day centre order has been made shall be under the supervision of a probation and welfare officer and while in attendance at a day centre shall be subject to the control, direction and supervision of the person in charge of the centre.

(8) A day centre order shall specify—

(*a*) the name and address of the day centre which the child shall be required to attend while the order is in force,
(*b*) the number of days that the child shall attend the centre,
(*c*) the period of time during which attendance at the centre is required, being a period not exceeding 6 months, and
(*d*) when and at what time the child is to report to the centre on the first occasion,

and it may specify—

(i) any programme of occupation, activity or instruction to be undertaken by the child,
(ii) such other matters with respect to the child's attendance at the centre as the court determines, or
(iii) such of the conditions provided for in section 117 as the court considers necessary for helping to improve the child's behaviour and to prevent him or her from committing further offences.

(9) When deciding on the number of days that the child shall attend at the day centre the court, in addition to and without prejudice to any other consideration, shall have regard to the child's age.

(10) A day centre order shall not be made unless the court is satisfied that the day centre to be specified in it is reasonably accessible to the child concerned or that arrangements can be made for the child's attendance at the centre, having regard to the child's age and sex, the means of access available to him or her and any other relevant circumstances.

(11) (*a*) The times at which a child is required to attend at a day centre shall, as far as practicable, be such as to avoid interference with any training the child is receiving, any attendance at a school or other educational establishment or any employment.

(*b*) The first of those times shall be a time at which the centre is available for the attendance of the child, and the subsequent days and times shall be fixed by the person in charge of the day centre, having regard to the child's circumstances and the terms of the day centre order, without prejudice to the power of the court to direct that, as far as practicable, some of those times shall coincide with a specific event which it considers the child, for whatever reason, should refrain from taking part in or being present at.

(12) The person in charge of a day centre may, for good reason, excuse a child from attendance at the centre on a particular occasion or occasions.

(13) A child shall not, subject to *subsection (14)*, be required to attend at a day centre on more than one occasion on any day or for more than 8 hours on any one day.

(14) Where the child participates in any occupation or activity, or receives any instruction, under supervision outside the day centre, *subsection (13)* shall not apply, and, where any such occupation, activity or instruction continues over more than one day, each such day shall count towards the number of days that the court has specified that the child shall attend at the centre.

(15) The person in charge of a day centre shall inform in writing the parent or guardian of the child of the days and times which the person in charge has fixed for the attendance of the child at the centre but in any case where a particular occupation, activity or instruction is arranged at short notice he or she may inform the parent or guardian orally.

Children Act 2001, s 118(5)–(15)

"DETENTION"

"detention" means detention in a children detention school [ ].

Children Act 2001, s 3 as amended by the Criminal Justice Act 2006, s 122(C)

"DETENTION AND SUPERVISION ORDER"

(1) Where a court is satisfied that detention is the only suitable way of dealing with a child who is between 16 and 18 years of age, it may, instead of making a children detention order, make a detention and supervision order.

(2) A detention and supervision order shall provide for detention in a children detention centre followed by supervision in the community.

(3) Subject to *subsection (4)*, half of the period for which a detention and supervision order is in force shall be spent by the child in detention in a children detention centre and half under supervision in the community.

(4) Where the child is released from detention on earning remission of sentence by industry or good conduct or on being given temporary release under section 2 or

3 of the Act of 1960, supervision of the child in the community under the order shall be deemed to commence on the child's release.

(5) The supervision provided for in this section shall be by a probation and welfare officer.

(6) A detention and supervision order, in so far as it relates to detention, shall be deemed for all purposes to be a children detention order.

(7) A detention and supervision order may specify such of the conditions provided for in section 117 as the court considers necessary for helping to ensure that the child concerned would be of good behaviour and for reducing the likelihood of the child's committing any further offences.

(8) Section 130 shall apply, with any necessary modifications, to non-compliance with a detention and supervision order, or with any condition to which it is subject, as if for the references to an order in that section there were substituted references to a detention and supervision order.

Children Act 2001, s 151

"DIRECTOR"

(1) The Programme shall be carried on and managed, under the general superintendence and control of the Commissioner of the Garda Síochána, by a member of the Garda Síochána not below the rank of superintendent who shall be assigned for that purpose by the Commissioner and is referred to in this Part as the Director.

(2) The Commissioner may assign duties other than those relating to the Programme to the Director during his or her period of assignment as Director.

Children Act 2001, s 20

"Director" means a person appointed under section 180 as Director of a children detention school or, as the case may be, of more than one such school.

Children Act 2001, s 157

"DISTRICT"

"district" means either a children court district or a district court district, as the context requires.

Children Act 2001, s 95

"DISTRICT OF RESIDENCE"

"district of residence" means—

(*a*) in relation to an order under this Part affecting a child, the circuit or, as the case may be, the district in which the child resides or will reside while the order is in force, and
(*b*) in relation to a parental supervision order, the circuit or, as the case may be, the district in which the parents concerned reside or will reside while the order is in force.

Children Act 2001, s 95

"DUAL ORDER"

(1) In this section "dual order" means an order which requires a child either—

(*a*) to be under the supervision of a probation and welfare officer for a specified period, or
(*b*) to attend at a day centre for a specified period not exceeding 90 days,

and which also restricts the child's movements for a specified period not exceeding 6 months.

(2) The court may make a dual order where it is of opinion that neither supervision by a probation and welfare officer nor attendance at a day centre, including any conditions to which such supervision or attendance would be made subject, would of itself adequately reduce the likelihood of the child committing further offences.

(3) A dual order shall be deemed for all purposes—

(*a*) in so far as it imposes a requirement mentioned in *subsection (1)(a)*, to be a probation order,
(*b*) in so far as it imposes a requirement mentioned in *subsection (1)(b)*, to be a day centre order, and
(*c*) in so far as it restricts a child's movements, to be an order under section 133.

Children Act 2001, s 137(1)

F

"FACILITATOR"

Where the Director decides that a conference should be held, he or she shall appoint a person (in this Part referred to as a "facilitator") to convene the conference and a person to be its chairperson.

(*b*) The facilitator shall be either the juvenile liaison officer supervising the child or another member of the Garda Síochána.
(*c*) The chairperson shall be the facilitator, another member of the Garda Síochána or another person, with that other person's agreement.

Children Act 2001, s 31(4)

"FAMILY CONFERENCE"

"family conference" means a conference convened by a probation and welfare officer pursuant to section 79.

Children Act 2001, s 3

"FAMILY WELFARE CONFERENCE"

"family welfare conference" means a conference convened by a health board pursuant to section 7.

Children Act 2001, s 3

"FORMAL CAUTION"

"formal caution" means a caution to be administered to a child where—

(*a*) no previous caution has been administered, or
(*b*) one or more than one informal or formal caution has been previously administered,

and the Director considers that the child's criminal or antisocial behaviour was of such a nature that it could not be adequately dealt with by way of informal caution.

Children Act 2001, s 25(4) as amended by Criminal Justice Act 2006, sched 4, pt 2

G

"GAELTACHT AREA"

"Gaeltacht area" means an area for the time being determined to be a Gaeltacht area by order under section 2 of the Ministers and Secretaries (Amendment) Act, 1956.

Children Act 2001, s 3

"GOOD BEHAVIOUR CONTRACT"

"good behaviour contract" has the meaning given to it in section 257C.

Children Act 2001, s 257A inserted by the Criminal Justice Act 2006, s 159

(7) Subject to subsection (8), at the meeting—

(*a*) the superintendent shall explain in simple language to the child and the parents or guardian what the offending behaviour is and the effect it is having on any other person or persons,
(*b*) the child shall be asked to acknowledge that the behaviour has occurred and to undertake to stop it,
(*c*) the parents or guardian shall be asked to acknowledge the child's behaviour and to undertake to take steps to prevent a recurrence,
(*d*) if the child and the parents or guardian agree to give those undertakings, a document (in this section referred to as a "good behaviour contract") incorporating the undertakings shall be prepared and, where practicable, be signed by the child and the parents or guardian.

Children Act 2001, s 257C(7) inserted by Criminal Justice Act 2006, s 161(7)

"GUARDIAN"

"guardian" means—

(*a*) any legal guardian of a child,
(*b*) any person who, in the opinion of the court having cognisance of any case in relation to a child or in which the child is concerned, has for the time being the charge of or control over the child, or
(*c*) any person who has custody or care of a child by order of a court,

but does not include a health board.

Children Act 2001, s 3

H

"HOSTEL RESIDENCE"

(1) A court may order that a child shall reside in a hostel residence in accordance with the provisions of this section.

(2) An order under this section shall for all purposes be a probation order, with the addition of such requirements as are imposed by this section.

(3) The order shall require the child concerned, as a condition of his or her recognisance, to reside in any hostel residence provided by the probation and welfare service or recommended to the court by a probation and welfare officer on days to be determined by the probation and welfare officer supervising the child.

(4) A residence shall not be used as a hostel residence unless the principal probation and welfare officer has inspected it and a certificate by him or her that it is suitable for such use is in force.

(5) A certificate under *subsection (4)* shall remain in force for not more than one year from the date of its issue, unless it is cancelled by the principal probation and welfare officer before then on the ground that the residence is no longer suitable for use as a hostel residence.

(6) Where a hostel residence is not provided by the probation and welfare service, the agreement of the person or body providing it shall be required before an order is made under this section.

(7) An order under this section shall specify—

(*a*) the period, not exceeding one year, during which the order is in force,
(*b*) the name and address of the hostel residence concerned, and
(*c*) any other conditions that the child may be required to observe while the order is in force, as provided for in section 2 of the Act of 1907 and section 117.

(8) The child shall, while in the hostel residence, be subject to the control, direction and supervision of the person in charge of the residence.

(9) Subject to *subsection (10)*, an order shall not be made under this section unless the court is satisfied that the hostel residence specified in it is reasonably close to the child's usual place of residence or to any place where the child is receiving education or training or is employed, and the court, in making such an order, shall have regard to the child's age, sex, means of access to his or her usual residence or any such place and any other relevant circumstances.

(10) Where the court is of opinion that it would be in the interests of a child to specify in the order a hostel residence that is not reasonably close to the child's usual place of residence and a suitable such hostel residence is available, it may specify that hostel in the order.

(11) The person in charge of the hostel residence, in consultation with the probation and welfare officer supervising a child, shall decide the times at which the child shall be required to be in the hostel, having regard to the child's education, training or employment commitments and any other relevant circumstances, and any non-compliance with those times by the child, without good reason, shall be regarded as a breach of the order under this section.

(12) The court shall cause certified copies of its order to be sent to—

(*a*) the person in charge of the hostel residence concerned,
(*b*) the probation and welfare officer who is supervising the child, and
(*c*) the parents or guardian of the child or, as appropriate, another adult with whom the child has been residing.

(13) The person in charge of the hostel residence shall give a copy of the order to the child.

Children Act 2001, s 126

"HOUSE"

"house" includes any building occupied for residential or business purposes and any part of a building so occupied.

Children Act 2001, s 247(4)

I

"ILL TREATMENT OF A CHILD"

For the purposes of this section ill-treatment of a child includes any frightening, bullying or threatening of the child, and "ill-treat" shall be construed accordingly.

Children Act 2001, s 246(7)

"INFORMAL CAUTION"

"informal caution" means a caution to be administered to a child where—

(*a*) no previous caution has been administered, or
(*b*) one or more than one informal caution has been previously administered,

and the Director considers that the child's criminal **[or antisocial]** behaviour was not sufficiently serious to warrant a formal caution.

Children Act 2001, s 25(4) amended by Criminal Justice Act 2006, sched 4, pt 2

"INSPECTOR"

"Inspector" and "recognised school" have the meanings given to them in section 2 of the Education Act 1998.

Children Act 2001, s 159(A) inserted by Criminal Justice Act 2006, s 147

"Inspector" means a member of the Inspectorate;

"Inspectorate" means the Inspectorate appointed under *section 13*.

Education Act 1998, s 2

"INSPECTORATE"

The Minister shall appoint a Chief Inspector and such and so many Inspectors as the Minister considers appropriate and the Chief Inspector and Inspectors collectively shall be known and are referred to in this Act as the "Inspectorate".

Education Act 1998, s 13(1)

K

"KEEPER OF A BROTHEL"

A person who—

(*a*) keeps or manages or acts or assists in the management of a brothel,
(*b*) being the tenant, lessee, occupier or person in charge of a premises, knowingly permits such premises or any part thereof to be used as a brothel or for the purposes of habitual prostitution, or
(*c*) being the lessor or landlord of any premises or the agent of such lessor or landlord, lets such premises or any part thereof with the knowledge that such premises or some part thereof are or is to be used as a brothel, or is wilfully a party to the continued use of such premises or any part thereof as a brothel,

shall be guilty of an offence.

Children Act 2001, s 249(4)

L

"LAND"

"land" includes any rights, liabilities, powers or privileges relating to or connected with the land.

Children Act 2001, s 159B(1) inserted by Criminal Justice Act 2006, s 148

"LEGAL GUARDIAN"

"legal guardian", in relation to a child, means any person who is the guardian of a child pursuant to the Guardianship of Infants Act, 1964, or who is appointed to be his or her guardian by deed or will or by order of a court.

Children Act 2001, s 3

M

"MENTOR"

(1) A court may by order assign a child to a person, including a relative of the child concerned (a "mentor"), to help, advise and support the child and the child's family in its efforts to prevent the child from committing further offences and to monitor the child's behaviour generally.

(2) An order under this section shall specify the period, not exceeding 2 years, during which the order shall remain in force and also specify that the child shall live with his or her parents or guardian at their normal place of residence during that period.

(3) A child in respect of whom an order under this section has been made shall, while the order is in force, be under the supervision of a probation and welfare officer who, in addition to his or her duty to supervise the child, shall help and advise the mentor in supporting the child and the child's family in its efforts to prevent the child from committing further offences.

(4) The court shall not make an order under this section unless—

(*a*) a probation and welfare officer has informed the court that a mentor is available, and

(*b*) the child and the child's parents or guardian consent to the making of the order and agree to cooperate with the mentor in accordance with its terms.

(5) The order may specify such of the conditions provided for in as the court section 117 considers necessary for helping to ensure that while the order is in force the child will be of good behaviour and will not commit any further offences.

(6) The court shall cause certified copies of its order to be sent to—

(*a*) the parents or guardian of the child, and
(*b*) the probation and welfare officer who is supervising the child.

(7) The probation and welfare officer who is supervising the child shall give a copy of the order to the mentor and to the child.

(8) Where—

(*a*) on application by a probation and welfare officer to the court which made the order, the court is satisfied that its continuance in force—
  (i) would not be in the interests of the mentor or the child, or
  (ii) is no longer necessary because of the progress made by the child;
(*b*) the parents or guardian of the child notify the court in writing that they are withdrawing their consent to the making of the order; or
(*c*) the mentor applies to the court to have the order revoked,

the court may, having regard to the period for which the order was in force and any other relevant circumstances—

(i) revoke the order,
(ii) revoke it and substitute another community sanction, or
(iii) revoke it and deal with the case in any other way in which it could have been dealt with before the order was made.

Children Act 2001, s 131

"MOBILITY TRIPS"

In this section "mobility trips" means authorised absences from a children detention school of children detained therein for the purpose of—

(*a*) assisting their reintegration into society by promoting their personal and social development, their awareness and appreciation in matters of culture, education and recreation, and
(*b*) where appropriate, the implementation of any necessary treatment or counselling directions.

(2) Each mobility trip shall be authorised by the Director of the children detention school concerned and shall be granted for a specified period.

(3) During a mobility trip the child shall be accompanied at all times by at least one member of the staff of the school.

(4) Before authorising any mobility trip, the Director shall be satisfied, on the basis of an assessment of the child's suitability for such trips, that the purpose of the mobility trip is appropriate for the child.

(5) The Minister may suspend, for a specified period, mobility trips for a particular child or for any children detention school where he or she is satisfied that they would not be in the best interests of the child or school or of society generally during that period.

(6) Any period specified in *subsection (5)* may be renewed on as many occasions as the Minister considers necessary until the circumstances that gave rise to the suspension of the mobility trips no longer apply.

(7) Any breach by a child of the rules governing the grant of mobility trips shall render that child ineligible for such trips for such period as the Director may determine.

(8) Absconding while on a mobility trip shall be treated as a breach of discipline of the school.

(9) The Director of each children detention school shall keep the board of management of the school informed of the implementation of the board's rules in relation to the grant of mobility trips.

Children Act 2001, s 204

O

"OFFICER"

In this section "officer" means an officer of the Minister who is an established civil servant for the purposes of the Civil Service Regulation Act, 1956.

Children Act 2001, s 220(5)

established civil servant" means a civil servant who is rendering established service.

Civil Service Regulation Act 1956, s 1(1)

P

"PARENTAL SUPERVISION ORDER"

In any proceedings in which a child is found guilty of an offence, the court may make an order for the supervision of the child's parents (a "parental supervision order") where it is satisfied that a wilful failure of the child's parents to take care of or control the child contributed to the child's criminal behaviour.

(2) Subject to *subsection (3)*, the court may make a parental supervision order in addition to any other order it may make in relation to either the child or the child's parents.

(3) The court may not make an order under section 114 at the same time as a parental supervision order.

(4) Before making a parental supervision order, the court shall obtain and consider information about the parents' family and social circumstances and the likely effect of the order on those circumstances.

(5) A parental supervision order shall not be made without the parents of the child being given an opportunity to be heard.

(6) A parental supervision order may order the parents of the child to do any or all of the following:

(*a*) to undergo treatment for alcohol or other substance abuse, where facilities for such treatment are reasonably available,
(*b*) to participate in any course that is reasonably available for the improvement of parenting skills,
(*c*) adequately and properly to control or supervise the child to the best of their ability, except where the terms of any community sanction imposed on the child make such control or supervision impracticable,
(*d*) to comply with any other instructions of the court that would in its opinion assist in preventing the child from committing further offences.

(7) A parental supervision order shall be made for a period not exceeding 6 months.

(8) The court shall appoint a probation and welfare officer to supervise the parents, to assist them in complying with the order and to monitor compliance with it.

(9) When making a parental supervision order, the court shall have regard to any order it has made or is making in respect of the child concerned and, where any such order involves the supervision of the child by a probation and welfare officer, that officer shall also be appointed to supervise the child's parents.

(10) A parental supervision order shall specify—

(*a*) where appropriate, the address of any place where the parents may undergo treatment or participate in any course for the improvement of parenting skills,
(*b*) any particular requirements of the court in relation to the control or supervision of the child,
(*c*) any other instructions of the court, and
(*d*) the period during which the order is to be in force,

and the court shall explain to the parents in ordinary language the effects of the order and any requirements or instructions specified in it.

(11) Where for any reason the court considers that a parental supervision order should be made in respect of one parent only, the order may provide accordingly, notwithstanding that both parents have the custody, charge or care of the child.

(12) A parent who is the subject of a parental supervision order may appeal against the order.

Children Act 2001, s 111

"PERIOD OF DETENTION"

"Period of detention in children detention school.

Where a child is found guilty of an offence in the Children Court, any term of detention in a children detention school imposed for the offence shall not be for a period longer than the term of detention or imprisonment which the court could impose on an adult who commits such an offence.".

Children Act 2001, s 149 substituted by Criminal Justice Act 2006, s 141

"PLACE"

In this section, "place" includes part of a building.".

Children Act 2001, s 161(7) inserted by Criminal Justice Act 2006, s 149

"PLACE OF DETENTION"

In this section, "place of detention" means a place of detention provided under section 2 of the Act of 1970.".

Children Act 2001, s 156A(5) inserted by Criminal Justice Act 2006, s 143

"PRESCRIBED"

"prescribed" means prescribed by regulations made by the Minister, [ ] for Health and Children, as appropriate.

Children Act 2001, s 3 amended by Criminal Justice Act 2006, s 122(f)

"PRINCIPAL PROBATION AND WELFARE OFFICER"

"principal probation and welfare officer" means the principal probation and welfare officer of the probation and welfare service.

Children Act 2001, s 3

"PROBATION AND WELFARE OFFICER"

"probation and welfare officer" means a person appointed by the Minister to be a probation and welfare officer, or to be a welfare officer or probation officer.

Children Act 2001, s 3

"PROBATION AND WELFARE SERVICE"

"probation and welfare service" means the probation and welfare service of the Department of Justice, Equality and Law Reform.

Children Act 2001, s 3

"PROBATION OFFICERS REPORT"

Subject to *subsections (2)* and *(3)*, where a court is satisfied of the guilt of a child, it—

(*a*) may in any case, and
(*b*) shall, where it is of opinion that the appropriate decision would be to impose a community sanction, detention (whether or not deferred under section 144) or detention and supervision,

adjourn the proceedings, remand the child and request a probation and welfare officer to prepare a report in writing (a "probation officer's report") which—

(i) would assist the court in determining a suitable community sanction (if any) or another way of dealing with the child, and
(ii) would contain information on such matters as may be prescribed, including any information specifically requested by the court.

(2) The probation officer's report shall, at the request of the court, indicate whether, and if so how, in his or her opinion any lack of care or control by the parents or guardian of the child concerned contributed to the behaviour which resulted in the child being found guilty of an offence.

(3) The court may, in addition, request that a victim impact report be furnished to it in respect of any victim of the child where it considers that such a report would assist it in dealing with the case.

(4) The court may decide not to request a probation officer's report where—

(*a*) the penalty for the offence of which the child is guilty is fixed by law, or
(*b*) (i) the child was the subject of a probation officer's report prepared not more than 2 years previously,
(ii) the attitude of the child to, and the circumstances of, the offence or offences to which that report relates are similar to his or her attitude to, and the circumstances of, the offence of which the child has been found guilty, and
(iii) the previous report is available to the court and the court is satisfied that the material in it is sufficient to enable it to deal with the case.

(5) Where a court requests a report under this section, it may at any time summon as a witness any person whose evidence in its opinion would assist it in dealing with the case.

Children Act 2001, s 99

"PROBATION ORDER"

"probation order" has the meaning assigned to it by section 2 of the Act of 1907.

Children Act 2001, s 95

(1) A recognizance ordered to be entered into under this Act shall, if the court so order, contain a condition that the offender be under the supervision of such person as may be named in the order during the period specified in the order and such other conditions for securing such supervision as may be specified in the order, and an order requiring the insertion of such conditions as aforesaid in the recognizance is in this Act referred to as a probation order.

Probation of Offenders Act 1907, s 2(1)

"PROGRAMME"

Unless the interests of society otherwise require and subject to this Part, any child who—

(*a*) has committed an offence, or
(*b*) has behaved anti-socially,

and who accepts responsibility for his or her criminal or anti-social behaviour shall be considered for admission to a diversion programme (in this Part referred to as the Programme) having the objective set out in section 19.".

Children Act 2001, s 18 substituted by Criminal Justice Act 2006, s 123

"PROGRAMME OBJECTIVE"

The objective of the Programme is to divert any child who accepts responsibility for his or her criminal or anti-social behaviour from committing further offences or engaging in further anti-social behaviour.".

Children Act 2001, s 19 substituted by Criminal Justice Act 2006, s 124

"PROPERTY"

"property" includes any rights or liabilities relating to or connected with the property.

Children Act 2001, s 159B inserted by Criminal Justice Act 2006, s 148

"PUBLIC PLACE"

"public place" means any place to which the public have or are permitted to have access whether as of right or by permission and whether on payment or without payment.

Children Act 2001, s 247(4)

"PUBLISH"

"publish" means publish to the public or a section of the public, and cognate words shall be construed accordingly.

Children Act 2001, s 51(6)

R

"RECOGNISED SCHOOL"

"recognised school" have the meanings given to them in section 2 of the Education Act 1998.

Children Act 2001, s 159A(1) inserted by the Criminal Justice Act 2006, s 147

"recognised school" means a school which is recognised by the Minister in accordance with *section 10.*

Education Act 1998, s 2

On a request being made for that purpose, the Minister may from time to time designate a school or a proposed school to be a school recognised for the purposes of this Act.

(2) The Minister may designate a school or a proposed school to be a school recognised for the purposes of this Act where the Minister, on a request being made for that purpose by the patron of a school or a proposed school, is satisfied that—

(*a*) the number of students who are attending or are likely to attend the school is such or is likely to be such as to make the school viable,
(*b*) in the case of a proposed school, and having regard to the desirability of diversity in the classes of school operating in the area likely to be served by the school, the needs of students attending or likely to attend the school cannot reasonably be met by existing schools,
(*c*) the patron undertakes that the school shall provide the curriculum as determined in accordance with *section 30*,
(*d*) the patron agrees to permit and co-operate with regular inspection and evaluation by the Inspectorate,
(*e*) the school complies, or in the case of a proposed school shall comply, with health, safety and building standards as are determined by law and any further such standards as are determined from time to time by the Minister, and
(*f*) the patron agrees that the school shall operate in accordance with such regulations as may be made by the Minister from time to time under *section 33* and with this Act and with any other terms and conditions as may reasonably be attached to recognition by the Minister.

(3) A school that, on the commencement of this section, is in receipt of funds provided by the Oireachtas in respect of—

(*a*) the education activities for students of that school, or
(*b*) the remuneration of teachers in that school,

shall be deemed to be a school recognised in accordance with this section.

(4) The Minister may from time to time designate a place to be a centre for education.

Education Act 1998, s 10

"REGISTERED MEDICAL PRACTITIONER"

In this Part "registered medical practitioner" means a person registered in the General Register of Medical Practitioners established under the Medical Practitioners Acts, 1978 to 2000.

Children Act 2001, s 245

"RELATIVE"

"relative", in relation to a child, means a brother, sister, uncle or aunt, or a spouse of the brother, sister, uncle or aunt, or a grandparent or step-parent, of the child.

Children Act 2001, s 3

"REMAND CENTRE"

"remand centre" means a centre designated as such under section 88.

Child Act 2001, s 3

Where the Court remands in custody a child—

(*a*) who is charged with or found guilty of one or more offences,
(*b*) who is being sent forward for trial, or
(*c*) in respect of whom the Court has postponed a decision,

the following provisions of this section shall apply.

(2) Where the child is under the age of 16 years, he or she shall be remanded to a place designated by order of the Minister under this section as a junior remand centre.

(3) Where the child is of or over the age of 16 years, he or she shall be remanded to a place designated by order of the Minister under this section as a remand centre.

(4) Where the Court remands a child in custody it shall explain the reasons for its decision in open court in language that is appropriate to the age and level of understanding of the child.

(5) The Minister may, with the agreement of the Minister for Education and Science, by order designate as a junior remand centre any place, including part of any children detention school, which in his or her opinion is suitable for the custody of children who are remanded in custody pursuant to *subsection (2)*.

(6) The Minister may, with the agreement of the Minister for Education and Science, by order amend an order under *subsection (5)*, including an order under this subsection.

(7) The Minister may by order designate as a remand centre any place (including part of a children detention centre) which in his or her opinion is suitable for the custody of children who are remanded in custody pursuant to *subsection (3)*.

(8) The Minister may by order amend an order made under *subsection (7)*, including an order under this subsection.

(9) The Minister shall cause a copy of any order under *subsections (5)* to *(8)* to be sent to the President of the High Court, the President of the Circuit Court and the President of the District Court.

(10) A place may be designated as a junior remand centre only with the consent of its owners or, as the case may be, its managers.

(11) Where a junior remand centre is part of a children detention school, children remanded in custody to the centre shall, as far as practicable and where it is in the interests of the child, be kept separate from and not be allowed to associate with children in respect of whom a period of detention has been imposed.

(12) Where a remand centre is part of a children detention centre, a child remanded to the remand centre shall, as far as practicable and where it is in the interests of the child, be kept separate from and not be allowed to associate with children in respect of whom a period of detention has been imposed.

(13) The Court shall not remand a child in custody under this section if the only reason for doing so is that the child is in need of care or protection.

(14) Such matters as may be necessary or expedient for enabling junior remand centres to operate and be administered in accordance with this Act may be prescribed by the Minister for Education and Science.

Children Act 2001, s 88

"RESPONSIBLE PERSON"

"responsible person", in relation to a child, means a relative of the child or a person in whose care the child is placed under this Act.

Children Act 2001, s 157

S

"SAINT PATRICK'S INSTITUTION"

"Saint Patrick's Institution" means the institution called and known as "Saint Patrick's" and situate at North Circular Road, Dublin.

Children Act 2001, s 3

Criminal Justice Act 1960, s 1

"Saint Patrick's Institution" has the same meaning as in the Criminal Justice Act, 1960.

"SCHOOL"

"school" means a children detention school.

Children Act 2001, s 3

"SPECIAL CARE UNIT"

"special care unit" has the meaning assigned to it by section 23K (inserted by section 16) of the Act of 1991.

Child Care Act 1991, s 23a inserted by Children Act 2001, s 16

A health board may, with the approval of the Minister, for the purposes of section 23B and 23C—

(*a*) provide and maintain a special care unit, or
(*b*) make arrangements with a voluntary body or any other person for the provision and operation of such a unit by that body or person on behalf of the board.

(2) The Minister shall not approve of the provision of a special care unit unless—

(*a*) having caused the unit to be inspected by a person authorised in that behalf by the Minister, and
(*b*) having considered a report in writing of the inspection,

he or she is satisfied that the requirements of regulations under this section will be complied with by the health board, voluntary body or other person, as the case may be, in relation to the unit.

(3) The duration of an approval of a special care unit by the Minister shall be 3 years from the date of approval, and thereafter the Minister may renew the approval for a further period, or further periods, of the like duration.

(4) The Minister, on approving of a special care unit, shall cause a certificate to that effect to be issued to the health board concerned and the certificate shall without further proof, unless the contrary is shown, be admissible in any proceedings as evidence that the unit has been approved of by the Minister for the purposes of sections 23B and 23C.

(5) The Minister may cancel such a certificate if he or she is of opinion that the special care unit concerned is no longer suitable for use as such a unit or is no longer required for that purpose.

(6) The Minister shall make regulations with respect to the operation of special care units provided by or on behalf of health boards under this section and for securing the welfare of children detained therein.

Child Care Act 1991, s 23k inserted by Children Act 2001, s 16

"STAFF"

"staff" does not include teaching staff.".

Children Act 2001, s 157 amended by Criminal Justice Act 2006, s 145(a)

"STREET"

"street" includes any road, bridge, lane, footway, subway, square, alley or passage, whether a thoroughfare or not, which is for the time being open to the public, and any ground or carpark adjoining and open to a street shall be treated as forming part of a street.

Children Act 2001, s 247(4)

"SUMMONS"

Proceedings in the District Court in respect of an offence may be commenced by the issuing, as a matter of administrative procedure, of a document (in this section referred to as a 'summons') to the prosecutor by the appropriate office.

Courts (No. 3) Act 1986, s 1(1) substituted by the Civil Liability and Courts Act 2004, s 49

"SUPERVISION IN THE COMMUNITY"

Where a child is detained in a children detention school, the Director of the school may at any time, after consultation with the principal probation and welfare officer, authorise the placing out of the child under supervision in the community to reside with his or her parents or guardian or a responsible person who is willing to receive and take charge of the child.

(2) Before authorising a placing out under *subsection (1)*, the Director shall be satisfied that the child will continue to receive appropriate education or training while he or she is placed out and that the placing out conforms to the rules of the school's board of management in that regard.

(3) A child placed out under *subsection (1)* shall be under the supervision in the community of a probation and welfare officer.

(4) (*a*) An authorisation under *subsection (1)* shall be in writing and be signed by the Director and shall specify—

(i) the name of the person who is willing to receive and take charge of the child, and

(ii) any conditions imposed by the Director which he or she considers appropriate and which are consistent with any rules made by the board of management of the school under section 179.

(*b*) The child shall comply with any conditions so specified.

(5) Where a child is placed out under this section, the Director shall ensure that at the time of the placing out—

(*a*) the conditions of the child's placing out are communicated in writing to the child, to the person receiving and taking charge of the child and to the probation and welfare officer supervising the child in the community, and
(*b*) the placing out and those conditions are notified to the member in charge of the Garda Síochána station for the area in which the child will be residing.

(6) A placing out under this section shall be in force until revoked or until the period of detention imposed by the court has expired, whichever is the sooner, and while it is in force the child shall be deemed to be under the care of the Director.

(7) The Director may at any time, after consultation with the principal probation and welfare officer, revoke a placing out where—

(*a*) he or she has reason to believe that it is necessary to do so for the protection or welfare of the child,
(*b*) the child, without reasonable excuse, fails to comply with a condition imposed under *subsection (4) (a) (ii)*, or
(*c*) the child is not receiving appropriate education or training,

and order the child to return to the school.

(8) Any child escaping from the person with whom he or she is placed out shall be liable to the same penalty as if he or she had escaped from the school itself.

(9) The period during which a child who is placed out is absent from a school shall be deemed to be part of the child's period of detention in the school but, if a child fails to return to the school when the placing out is revoked, the time that elapses thereafter shall be excluded in calculating the period during which he or she is to be detained.

(10) Where a member of the Garda Síochána has been notified that a child whose placing out has been revoked refuses or fails, without reasonable cause, to return to the school, the member may arrest the child without warrant and forthwith return the child to the school.

(11) Where a placing out of a child has been revoked and the child has returned or has been returned to the school, the Director of the school shall inform the member in charge of the Garda Síochána station for the area where the child resided accordingly.

(12) Where a child is found guilty of an offence committed while placed out, the placing out shall be deemed to be revoked.

Children Act 2001, s 207

T

"TRANSFER DAY"

"transfer day" means the day on which a certified industrial school becomes, by virtue of section 159(2), premises provided and maintained by the Health Service Executive under section 38(2) of the Act of 1991 for the provision of residential care for children in care.

Children Act 2001, s 159B(1) inserted by Criminal Justice Act 2006, s 148

"TRANSFERRED PREMISES"

1. "transferred premises" means a certified reformatory or an industrial school under Part IV of the Act of 1908 which, on the commencement of section 159 in relation to it, becomes a children detention school or premises provided and maintained by the Health Service Executive under section 38(2) of the Act of 1991.

Children Act 2001, s 159A(1) inserted by Criminal Justice Act 2006, s 147

2. "transferred premises" means premises which on the transfer day become premises so provided and maintained.

Children Act 2001, s 159B(1) inserted by Criminal Justice Act 2006, s 148

V

"VICTIM"

"victim" means a person who through or by means of an offence committed by a child, suffers physical or emotional harm, or loss of or damage to property [**"and, in relation to anti-social behaviour by a child, means a person who suffers physical or emotional harm as a consequence of that behaviour".**].

Children Act 2001, s 3(1) amended by Criminal Justice Act 2006, s 122

"VOCATIONAL EDUCATIONAL COMMITTEE"

"vocational education committee" means a committee established by section 7 of the Vocational Education Act 1930.

Children Act 2001, s 159A (1) inserted by Criminal Justice Act 2006, s 147

(1) There shall be a committee (in this Act referred to as a vocational education committee) in and for every vocational education area to fulfil in respect of such area the duties assigned to vocational education committees by this Act.

(2) Every vocational education committee shall be styled and known by such style or name as the Minister shall appoint, but unless and until the Minister appoints the style and name of any particular committee, such committee shall be styled and known—

(*a*) in the case of the committee for a borough vocational education area, by the style or name "The City of (*name of the county borough*) Vocational Education Committee"; and
(*b*) in the case of the committee for an urban district vocational education area, by the style or name "The Town of (*name of the urban district*) Vocational Education Committee"; and
(*c*) in the case of the committee for a county vocational education area, by the style or name "The County (*name of the county*) Vocational Education Committee."

(3) Every vocational education committee shall be a body corporate by its said style or name, and shall have perpetual succession and an official seal (which shall be judicially noticed), with power to acquire and hold land for the purpose of its powers and duties.

Vocational Education Act 1930, s 7

CRIMINAL ASSETS

A

"APPLICANT"

"'the applicant' means a person, being a member, an authorised officer or the Criminal Assets Bureau, who has applied to the Court for the making of an interim order or an interlocutory order and, in relation to such an order that is in force, means, as appropriate, any member, any authorised officer or the Criminal Assets Bureau.

Proceeds of Crime Act, 1996 s 1(1) Inserted by the Proceeds of Crime (Amendment) Act 2005, s 3

"AUTHORISED OFFICER"

"authorised officer" means an officer of the Revenue Commissioners authorised in writing by the Revenue Commissioners to perform the functions conferred by this Act on authorised officers.

Proceeds of Crime Act 1996, s 1(1)

B

"BUREAU OFFICER"

"bureau officer" means a person appointed as a bureau officer under *section 8*.

Criminal Assets Bureau Act 1996, s 1(1)

(1) (*a*) The Minister may appoint, with the consent of the Minister for Finance, such and so many—

(i) members of the Garda Síochána nominated for the purposes of this Act by the Commissioner,
(ii) officers of the Revenue Commissioners nominated for the purposes of this Act by the Revenue Commissioners, and
(iii) officers of the Minister for Social Welfare nominated for the purposes of this Act by that Minister,

to be bureau officers for the purposes of this Act.

(*b*) An appointment under this subsection shall be confirmed in writing, at the time of the appointment or as soon as may be thereafter, specifying the date of the appointment.

(2) The powers and duties vested in a bureau officer for the purposes of this Act, shall, subject to *subsections (5)*, *(6)* and *(7)*, be the powers and duties vested in the bureau officer, as the case may be, by virtue of—

(*a*) being a member of the Garda Síochána,
(*b*) the Revenue Acts or, any provision of any other enactment, whether passed before or after the passing of this Act, which relates to revenue, including any authorisation or nomination made thereunder, or
(*c*) the Social Welfare Acts, including any appointment made thereunder,

and such exercise or performance of any power or duty for the purposes of this Act shall be exercised or performed in the name of the Bureau.

(3) A bureau officer, when exercising or performing any powers or duties for the purposes of this Act, shall be under the direction and control of the Chief Bureau Officer.

(4) Where in any case a bureau officer (other than the Chief Bureau Officer) who, prior to being appointed a bureau officer, was required to exercise or perform any power or duty on the direction of any other person, it shall be lawful for the bureau officer to exercise or perform such power or duty for the purposes of this Act on the direction of the Chief Bureau Officer.

(5) A bureau officer may exercise or perform his or her powers or duties on foot of any information received by him or her from another bureau officer or on foot of any action taken by that other bureau officer in the exercise or performance of that other bureau officer's powers or duties for the purposes of this Act, and any information, documents or other material obtained by bureau officers under this subsection shall be admitted in evidence in any subsequent proceedings.

(6) (*a*) A bureau officer may be accompanied or assisted in the exercise or performance of that bureau officer's powers or duties by such other persons (including bureau officers) as the first-mentioned bureau officer considers necessary.

(*b*) A bureau officer may take with him or her, to assist him or her in the exercise or performance of his or her powers or duties, any equipment or materials as that bureau officer considers necessary.

(*c*) A bureau officer who assists another bureau officer under *paragraph (a)* shall have and be conferred with the powers and duties of the first-mentioned bureau officer for the purposes of that assistance only.

(*d*) Information, documents or other material obtained by any bureau officer under *paragraph (a)* or *(c)* may be admitted in evidence in any subsequent proceedings.

(7) Any information or material obtained by a bureau officer for the purposes of this Act may only be disclosed by the bureau officer to—

(*a*) another bureau officer or a member of the staff of the Bureau,

(*b*) any member of the Garda Síochána for the purposes of Garda functions,

(*c*) any officer of the Revenue Commissioners for the purposes of the Revenue Acts or any provision of any other enactment, whether passed before or after the passing of this Act, which relates to revenue,

(*d*) any officer of the Minister for Social Welfare for the purposes of the Social Welfare Acts, or

(*e*) with the consent of the Chief Bureau Officer, any other officer of another Minister of the Government or of a local authority (within the meaning of the Local Government Act, 1941) for the purposes of that other officer exercising or performing his or her powers or duties,

and information, documents or other material obtained by a bureau officer or any other person under the provisions of this subsection shall be admitted in evidence in any subsequent proceedings.

(8) A member of the Garda Síochána, an officer of the Revenue Commissioners or an officer of the Minister for Social Welfare, who is a bureau officer, notwithstanding his or her appointment as such, shall continue to be vested with and may exercise or perform the powers or duties of a member of the Garda Síochána, an officer of the Revenue Commissioners or an officer of the Minister for Social Welfare, as the case may be, for purposes other than the purposes of this Act, as well as for the purposes of this Act.

(9) The Chief Bureau Officer may, at his or her absolute discretion, at any time, with the consent of the Commissioner, remove any bureau officer from the Bureau whereupon his or her appointment as a bureau officer shall cease.

(10) Nothing in this section shall affect the powers and duties of a member of the Garda Síochána, an officer of the Revenue Commissioners or an officer of the Minister for Social Welfare, who is not a bureau officer.

Criminal Assets Bureau Act, 1996, s 8

"BUSINESS"

In this section—

'business' includes—

(*a*) an undertaking not carried on for profit, and
(*b*) a public authority.

Proceeds of Crime Act 1996, s 16(a)(4) inserted by Proceeds of Crime (Amendment) Act 2005, s 12

C

"CHIEF BUREAU OFFICER" SEE THE:

"COMMISSIONER" SEE THE:

"COMPENSATION"

Where—

(*a*) an interim order is discharged or lapses and an interlocutory order in relation to the matter is not made or, if made, is discharged (otherwise than pursuant to *section 3(7)*), (*b*) an interlocutory order is discharged (otherwise than pursuant to *section 3(7)*) or lapses and a disposal order in relation to the matter is not made or, if made, is discharged,

(*c*) an interim order or an interlocutory order is varied (otherwise than pursuant to *section 3(7)*) or a disposal order is varied on appeal,

the Court may, on application to it in that behalf by a person who shows to the satisfaction of the Court that—

(i) he or she is the owner of any property to which—

(I) an order referred to in *paragraph (a)* or (*b*) related, or

(II) an order referred to in *paragraph (c)* had related but, by reason of its being varied by a court, has ceased to relate,

and

(ii) the property does not constitute, directly or indirectly, proceeds of crime or was not acquired, in whole or in part, with or in connection with property that, directly or indirectly, constitutes proceeds of crime, award to the person such (if any) compensation payable by the Minister as it considers just in the circumstances in respect of any loss incurred by the person by reason of the order concerned.

(2) The Minister shall be given notice of, and be entitled to be heard in, any proceedings under this section.

Proceeds of Crime Act 1996, s 16

"COMPUTER AT THE PLACE"

'computer at the place which is being searched' includes any other computer, whether at that place or at any other place, which is lawfully accessible by means of that computer.

Criminal Assets Bureau Act 1996, s 14(9) inserted by the Proceeds of Crime (Amendment) Act 2005, s 16

"CONSENT DISPOSAL ORDER"

" 'consent disposal order' means an order under section 3(1a) or 4A(1).

Proceeds of Crime Act 1996, s 1(1) inserted by the Proceeds of Crime (Amendment) Act 2005, s 3(a)(ii)

"(1A) On such an application the Court, with the consent of all the parties concerned, may make a consent disposal order, and section 4A shall apply and have effect accordingly.".

Proceeds of Crime Act, 1996, s 3(1a) Inserted by the Proceeds of Crime Amendment) Act 2005, s 5(B)

(1) Where in relation to any property—

(*a*) an interlocutory order has been in force for a period of less than 7 years, and

(*b*) an application is made to the Court with the consent of all the parties concerned,

the Court may make an order (a 'consent disposal order') directing that the whole or a specified part of the property be transferred to the Minister or to such other person as the Court may determine, subject to such terms and conditions as it may specify.

Proceeds of Crime Act 1996, s 1(1) inserted by the Proceeds of Crime (Amendment) Act 2005, s 7

"CORRUPT CONDUCT"

'corrupt conduct' is any conduct which at the time it occurred was an offence under the Prevention of Corruption Acts 1889 to 2001, the Official Secrets Act 1963 or the Ethics in Public Office Act 1995.

Proceeds of Crime Act 1996, s 16b(1)(b) inserted by the Proceeds of Crime (Amendment) Act 2005, s 12

"CORRUPT ENRICHMENT"

a person is corruptly enriched if he or she derives a pecuniary or other advantage or benefit as a result of or in connection with corrupt conduct, wherever the conduct occurred.

Proceeds of Crime Act 1996, s 16b(1)(a) inserted by the Proceeds of Crime (Amendment) Act 2005, s 12

"CORRUPT ENRICHMENT ORDER"

For the purposes of this section—

(*a*) a person is corruptly enriched if he or she derives a pecuniary or other advantage or benefit as a result of or in connection with corrupt conduct, wherever the conduct occurred;
(*b*) 'corrupt conduct' is any conduct which at the time it occurred was an offence under the Prevention of Corruption Acts 1889 to 2001, the Official Secrets Act 1963 or the Ethics in Public Office Act 1995;
(*c*) 'property' includes—
  (i) money and all other property, real or personal, heritable or moveable,
  (ii) choses in action and other intangible or incorporeal property, and
  (iii) property situated outside the State,

and references to property shall be construed as including references to any interest in property. (2) Where, on application to it in that behalf by the applicant, it appears to the Court, on evidence tendered by the applicant, consisting of or including evidence admissible by virtue of subsection (5), that a person (a 'defendant') has been corruptly enriched, the Court may make an order (a 'corrupt enrichment order') directing the defendant to pay to the Minister or such other person as the Court may specify an amount equivalent to the amount by which it determines that the defendant has been so enriched.

(3) Where—

(*a*) the defendant is in a position to benefit others in the exercise of his or her official functions,
(*b*) another person has benefited from the exercise, and
(*c*) the defendant does not account satisfactorily for his or her property or for the resources, income or source of income from which it was acquired,

it shall be presumed, until the contrary is shown, that the defendant has engaged in corrupt conduct.

(4) In any proceedings under this section the Court may, on application to it *ex parte* in that behalf by the applicant, make an order prohibiting the defendant or any other person having notice of the order from disposing of or otherwise dealing with specified property of the defendant or diminishing its value during a period specified by the Court.

(5) Where in any such proceedings a member or an authorised officer states on affidavit or, where the respondent requires the deponent to be produced for cross-examination or the Court so directs, in oral evidence that he or she believes that the defendant—

(*a*) has derived a specified pecuniary or other advantage or benefit as a result of or in connection with corrupt conduct,
(*b*) is in possession or control of specified property and that the property or a part of it was acquired, directly or indirectly, as a result of or in connection with corrupt conduct, or

(*c*) is in possession or control of specified property and that the property or a part of it was acquired, directly or indirectly, with or in connection with the property referred to in paragraph (*b*),

then, if the Court is satisfied that there are reasonable grounds for the belief aforesaid, the statement shall be evidence of the matters referred to in any or all of paragraphs (*a*) to (*c*), as may be appropriate.

(6) (*a*) In any such proceedings, on an application to it in that behalf by the applicant, the Court may make an order directing the defendant to file an affidavit specifying—

(i) the property owned by the defendant, or

(ii) the income and sources of income of the defendant, or

(iii) both such property and such income or sources.

(*b*) Such an affidavit is not admissible in evidence in any criminal proceedings against the defendant or his or her spouse, except any such proceedings for perjury arising from statements in the affidavit.

(7) Sections 14 to 14C shall apply, with the necessary modifications, in relation to assets or proceeds deriving from unjust enrichment as they apply to assets or proceeds deriving from criminal conduct.

(8) The standard of proof required to determine any question arising in proceedings under this section as to whether a person has been corruptly enriched and, if so, as to the amount of such enrichment shall be that applicable in civil proceedings.

(9) The rules of court applicable in civil proceedings shall apply in relation to proceedings under this section.".

Proceeds of Crime Act 1996, s 16b inserted by the Proceeds of Crime (Amendment) Act 2005, s 12

"COURT" SEE THE

"CRIMINAL CONDUCT"

" 'criminal conduct' means any conduct which—

(*a*) constitutes an offence or more than one offence, or

(*b*) where the conduct occurs outside the State, constitutes an offence under the law of the state or territory concerned and would constitute an offence or more than one offence if it occurred within the State.

Criminal Assets Bureau Act 1996, s 1(1), inserted by the Proceeds of Crime (Amendment) Act 2005, s 13

"CRIMINAL CONDUCT"

'criminal conduct' means any conduct—

(*a*) which constitutes an offence or more than one offence, or
(*b*) which occurs outside the State and which would constitute an offence or more than one offence—
  (i) if it occurred within the State,
  (ii) if it constituted an offence under the law of the state or territory concerned, and
  (iii) if, at the time when an application is being made for an interim order or interlocutory order, any property obtained or received at any time (whether before or after the passing of this Act) by or as a result of or in connection with the conduct is situated within the State.".

Proceeds of Crime Act 1996, s1(1), inserted by the Proceeds of Crime (Amendment) Act 2005, s 3(A)(ii)

D

"DEALING"

"dealing", in relation to property in the possession or control of a person, includes—

(*a*) where a debt is owed to that person, making a payment to any person in reduction of the amount of the debt,
(*b*) removing the property from the State, and
(c) in the case of money or other property held for the person by another person, paying or releasing or transferring it to the person or to any other person.

Proceeds of Crime Act 1996, s 1(1)

"DEED"

'deed' means any document by which an estate or interest in land is created, transferred, charged or otherwise affected and includes a contract for the sale of land.

Proceeds of Crime Act 1996, s 16a(4) inserted by the Proceeds of Crime (Amendment) Act 2005, s 12

"DISPOSAL ORDER"

(1) Subject to *subsection (2)*, where an interlocutory order has been in force for not less than 7 years in relation to specified property, the Court, on application to it

in that behalf by the applicant, may make an order ("a disposal order") directing that the whole or, if appropriate, a specified part of the property be transferred, subject to such terms and conditions as the Court may specify, to the Minister or to such other person as the Court may determine.

(2) Subject to *subsections (6)* and *(8)*, the Court shall make a disposal order in relation to any property the subject of an application under *subsection (1)* unless it is shown to its satisfaction that that particular property does not constitute, directly or indirectly, proceeds of crime and was not acquired, in whole or in part, with or in connection with property that, directly or indirectly, constitutes proceeds of crime.

(3) The applicant shall give notice to the respondent (unless the Court is satisfied that it is not reasonably possible to ascertain his or her whereabouts), and to such other (if any) persons as the Court may direct of an application under this section.

(4) A disposal order shall operate to deprive the respondent of his or her rights (if any) in or to the property to which it relates and, upon the making of the order, the property shall stand transferred to the Minister or other person to whom it relates.

(5) The Minister may sell or otherwise dispose of any property transferred to him or her under this section, and any proceeds of such a disposition and any moneys transferred to him or her under this section shall be paid into or disposed of for the benefit of the Exchequer by the Minister.

(6) In proceedings under *subsection (1)*, before deciding whether to make a disposal order, the Court shall give an opportunity to be heard by the Court and to show cause why the order should not be made to any person claiming ownership of any of the property concerned.

(7) The Court, if it considers it appropriate to do so in the interests of justice, on the application of the respondent or, if the whereabouts of the respondent cannot be ascertained, on its own initiative, may adjourn the hearing of an application under *subsection (1)* for such period not exceeding 2 years as it considers reasonable.

(8) The Court shall not make a disposal order if it is satisfied that there would be a serious risk of injustice.

Proceeds of Crime Act 1996, s 4

"DOCUMENT"

'document' includes a reproduction in legible form of a record in non-legible form.

Proceeds of Crime Act 1996, s 16a(4) inserted by the Proceeds of Crime (Amendment) Act 2005, s 12

E

"ESTABLISHMENT DAY" SEE THE

F

"FUNCTIONS"

In this section "functions" includes powers and duties.

Criminal Assets Bureau Act, 1996, s 6(4)

G

"GARDA FUNCTION"

"Garda functions" means any power or duty conferred on any member of the Garda Síochána by or under any enactment (including an enactment passed after the passing of this Act) or the common law.

Criminal Assets Bureau Act 1996, s 1(1)

I & J

"INFORMATION"

(7) In this section 'information' includes—

(*a*) a document or record, and
(*b*) information in non-legible form.".

Criminal Assets Bureau Act 1996, s 14c (7) inserted by the Proceeds of Crime (Amendment) Act 2005, s 18

"INTEREST"

"interest", in relation to property, includes right.

Proceeds of Crime Act 1996, s 1(1)

"INTERIM ORDER"

Where it is shown to the satisfaction of the Court on application to it *ex parte* in that behalf by a member or an authorised officer—

(*a*) that a person is in possession or control of—
  (i) specified property and that the property constitutes, directly or indirectly, proceeds of crime, or
  (ii) specified property that was acquired, in whole or in part, with or in connection with property that, directly or indirectly, constitutes proceeds of crime,

and

(*b*) that the value of the property or, as the case may be, the total value of the property referred to in both *subparagraphs (i)* and *(ii)*, of *paragraph (a)* is not less than £10,000, the Court may make an order ("an interim order") prohibiting the person or any other specified person or any other person having notice of the order from disposing of or otherwise dealing with the whole or, if appropriate, a specified part of the property or diminishing its value during the period of 21 days from the date of the making of the order.

(2) An interim order—

(*a*) may contain such provisions, conditions and restrictions as the Court considers necessary or expedient, and
(*b*) shall provide for notice of it to be given to the respondent and any other person who appears to be or is affected by it unless the Court is satisfied that it is not reasonably possible to ascertain his, her or their whereabouts.

(3) Where an interim order is in force, the Court, on application to it in that behalf by the respondent or any other person claiming ownership of any of the property concerned may, if it is shown to the satisfaction of the Court that—

(*a*) the property concerned or a part of it is not property to which *subparagraph (i)* or *(ii)* of *subsection (1) (a)* applies, or
(b) the value of the property to which those subparagraphs apply is less than £10,000,

discharge or, as may be appropriate, vary the order.

(4) The Court shall, on application to it in that behalf at any time by the applicant, discharge an interim order.

(5) Subject to *subsections (3)* and *(4)*, an interim order shall continue in force until the expiration of the period of 21 days from the date of its making and shall then lapse unless an application for the making of an interlocutory order in respect of any of the

property concerned is brought during that period and. if such in application is brought, the interim order shall lapse upon—

(*a*) the determination of the application,
(*b*) the expiration of the ordinary time for bringing an appeal from the determination,
(*c*) if such an appeal is brought, the determination or abandonment of it or of any further appeal or the expiration of the ordinary time for bringing any further appeal,

whichever is the latest.

(6) Notice of an application under this section shall he given—

(*a*) in case the application is under *subsection (3)* by the respondent or other person, making the application to the applicant,
(*b*) in case the application is under *subsection (4)*, by the applicant to the respondent unless the Court is satisfied that it is not reasonably possible to ascertain his or her whereabouts, and, in either case, to any other person in relation to whom the Court directs that notice of the application be given to him or her.

Proceeds of Crime Act 1996, s 2

"INTERLOCUTORY ORDER"

Where, on application to it in that behalf by the applicant, it appears to the Court, on evidence tendered by the applicant, consisting of or including evidence admissible by virtue of *section 8*—

(*a*) that a person is in possession or control of—
  (i) specified property and that the property constitutes, directly or indirectly, proceeds of crime, or
  (ii) specified property that was acquired, in whole or in part, with or in connection with property that, directly or indirectly, constitutes proceeds of crime,

and

(*b*) that the value of the property or, as the case may be, the total value of the property referred to in both *subparagraphs (i)* and *(ii)* of *paragraph (a)* is not less than £10,000,

the Court shall make an order ("an interlocutory order") prohibiting the respondent or any other specified person or any other person having notice of the order from disposing of or otherwise dealing with the whole or, if appropriate, a specified part of the property or diminishing its value, unless, it is shown to the satisfaction of the Court, on evidence tendered by the respondent or any other person—

(I) that that particular property does not constitute, directly or indirectly, proceeds of crime and was not acquired, in whole or in part, with or in connection with property that, directly or indirectly, constitutes proceeds of crime, or

(II) that the value of all the property to which the order would relate is less than £10,000:

Provided, however, that the Court shall not make the order if it is satisfied that there would be a serious risk of injustice.

(2) An interlocutory order—

(*a*) may contain such provisions, conditions and restrictions as the Court considers necessary or expedient, and

(*b*) shall provide for notice of it to be given to the respondent and any other person who appears to be or is affected by it unless the Court is satisfied that it is not reasonably possible to ascertain his, her or their whereabouts.

(3) Where an interlocutory order is in force, the Court, on application to it in that behalf at any time by the respondent or any other person claiming ownership of any of the property concerned, may, if it is shown to the satisfaction of the Court that the property or a specified part of it is property to which *paragraph (I)* of *subsection (1)* applies, or that the order causes any other injustice, discharge or, as may be appropriate, vary the order.

(4) The Court shall, on application to it in that behalf at any time by the applicant, discharge an interlocutory order.

(5) Subject to *subsections (3)* and *(4)*, an interlocutory order shall continue in force until—

(*a*) the determination of an application for a disposal order in relation to the property concerned,

(*b*) the expiration of the ordinary time for bringing an appeal from that determination,

(*c*) if such an appeal is brought, it or any further appeal is determined or abandoned or the ordinary time for bringing any further appeal has expired,

whichever is the latest, and shall then lapse.

(6) Notice of an application under this section shall be given—

(*a*) in case the application is under *subsection (1)* or *(4)*, by the applicant to the respondent, unless the Court is satisfied that it is not reasonably possible to ascertain his or her whereabouts,

(*b*) in case the application is under *subsection (3)*, by the respondent or other person making the application to the applicant, and, in either case, to any other person in relation to whom the Court directs that notice of the application he given to him or her.

(7) Where a forfeiture order, or a confiscation order, under the Criminal Justice Act, 1994, or a forfeiture, order under the Misuse of Drugs Act, 1977, relates to any property that is the subject of an interim order, or an interlocutory order, that is in force, ("the specified property"), the interim order or, as the case may be, the interlocutory order shall—

(*a*) if it relates only to the specified property, stand discharged, and
(*b*) if it relates also to other property, stand varied by the exclusion from it of the specified property.

Proceeds of Crime Act 1996, s 3

"JURY SUMMONS"

Each county registrar shall cause a written summons, in such form as the Minister may by regulations prescribe, to be served on every person whom he has selected as a juror requiring him to attend as a juror at the court in question on the day and at the time specified in the summons and thereafter at the times directed by the court.

(2) A jury summons served on a person under this section shall be accompanied by a notice informing him—

(*a*) of the effect of sections 6, 7, 8, 9 (1), 35 and 36, and
(*b*) that he may make representations to the county registrar with a view to obtaining a withdrawal of the summons, if for any reason he is not qualified for jury service or wishes or is entitled to be excused.

Juries Act 1976, s 12

M

"MATERIAL"

'material' includes a copy of the material and a document or record.".

Criminal Assets Bureau Act 1996, s 14(9) substituted by Proceeds of Crime (Amendment) Act 2005, s 16

"MEMBER"

"member" means a member of the Garda Síochána not below the rank of Chief Superintendent.

Proceeds of Crime Act 1996, s 1(1)

"MEMBER OF THE FAMILY"

"member of the family", in relation to an individual who is a bureau officer or a member of the staff of the Bureau, means the spouse, parent, grandparent, step-parent, child (including a step-child or an adopted child), grandchild, brother, sister, half-brother, half-sister, uncle, aunt, nephew or niece of the individual or of the individual's spouse, or any person who is cohabiting or residing with the individual.

Criminal Assets Bureau Act 1996, s 1(1)

P

"PLACE"

'place' includes a dwelling.".

Criminal Assets Bureau Act 1996, s 1(1) inserted by the Proceeds of Crime (Amendment) Act 2005, s 13

"PROCEEDINGS"

"proceedings" includes any hearing before the Appeal Commissioners (within the meaning of the Revenue Acts) or before an appeals officer or the Social Welfare Tribunal under the Social Welfare Acts or a hearing before any committee of the Houses of the Oireachtas.

Criminal Assets Bureau Act 1996, s 1(1)

"PROCEEDS OF CRIME"

'proceeds of crime' means any property obtained or received at any time (whether before or after the passing of this Act) by or as a result of or in connection with criminal conduct.

Proceeds of Crime Act 1996, s 1(1) substituted by the Proceeds of Crime (Amendment) Act 2005, s 3

"PROPERTY"

'property', in relation to proceeds of crime, includes—

(*a*) money and all other property, real or personal, heritable or moveable,
(*b*) choses in action and other intangible or incorporeal property, and
(*c*) property situated outside the State where—
 (i) the respondent is domiciled, resident or present in the State, and
 (ii) all or any part of the criminal conduct concerned occurs therein,

and references to property shall be construed as including references to any interest in property.

Proceeds of Crime Act 1996, s 1(1) substituted by the Proceeds of Crime (Amendment) Act 2005, s 3

"PUBLIC AUTHORITY"

'public authority' has the meaning given to it by section 2(1) of the Local Government Act 2001 and includes a local authority within the meaning of that section.

Proceeds of Crime Act 1996, s 16a(4) inserted by the Proceeds of Crime (Amendment) Act 2005, s 12

"public authority" means—

(*a*) a Minister of the Government,
(*b*) the Commissioners of Public Works in Ireland,
(*c*) a harbour authority within the meaning of the Harbours Act, 1946,
(*d*) (i) a health board,
 (ii) the Eastern Regional Health Authority, or
 (iii) an Area Health Board established under the Health (Eastern Regional Health Authority) Act, 1999;
(e) a board or other body (but not including a company under the Companies Acts, 1963 to 1999) established by or under statute,
(*f*) a company under the Companies Acts, 1963 to 1999, in which all the shares are held—
 (i) by or on behalf of a Minister of the Government,
 (ii) by directors appointed by a Minister of the Government, or
 (iii) by a board, company or other body referred to in *paragraph (e)* or *subparagraph (i)* or *(ii)*,
(*g*) such other body as may be prescribed by regulations made by the Minister for the purposes of any provision of this Act.

Local Government Act 2001, s 2

R

"RECEIVER"

Where an interim order or an interlocutory order is in force, the Court may at any time appoint a receiver—

(*a*) to take possession of any property to which the order relates,
(*b*) in accordance with the Court's directions, to manage, keep possession or dispose of or otherwise deal with any property in respect of which he or she is appointed,

subject to such exceptions and conditions (if any) as may be specified by the Court, and may require any person having possession or control of property in respect of which the receiver is appointed to give possession of it to the receiver.

(2) Where a receiver takes any action under this section—

(*a*) in relation to property which is not property the subject of an interim order or an interlocutory order, being action which he or she would be entitled to take if it were such property, and
(*b*) believing, and having reasonable grounds for believing, that he or she is entitled to take that action in relation to that property,.

he or she shall not be liable to any person in respect of any loss or damage resulting from such action except in so far as the loss or damage is caused by his or her negligence.

Proceeds of Crime Act 1996, s 7(1)

"RECORDS"

'records' includes records in non-legible form and any reproduction thereof in legible form.

Proceeds of Crime Act 1996, s 16a (4) inserted by the Proceeds of Crime (Amendment) Act 2005, s 12

"RESPONDENT" SEE UNDER THE

"REVENUE ACTS"

"Revenue Acts" means—

(*a*) the Customs Acts,
(*b*) the statutes relating to the duties of excise and to the management of those duties,

(*c*) the Tax Acts,
(*d*) the Capital Gains Tax Acts,
(e) the Value-Added Tax Act, 1972,
(*f*) the Capital Acquisitions Tax Act, 1976,
(*g*) the statutes relating to stamp duty and to the management of that duty,
(*h*) Part VI of the Finance Act, 1983,
(*i*) Chapter IV of Part 11 of the Finance Act, 1992,

and any instruments made thereunder and any instruments made under any other enactment and relating to tax.

Criminal Assets Bureau Act 1996, s 1(1)

T

"TAX"

"tax" means any tax, duty, levy or charge under the care and management of the Revenue Commissioners.

Criminal Assets Bureau Act 1996, s 1(1)

"THE BUREAU"

"the Bureau" means the Criminal Assets Bureau established by *section 3*.

Criminal Assets Bureau Act 1996, s 1(1)

On the establishment day there shall stand established a body to be known as the Criminal Assets Bureau, and in this Act referred to as "the Bureau", to perform the functions conferred on it by or under this Act.

(2) The Bureau shall be a body corporate with perpetual succession and an official seal and power to sue and be sued in its corporate name and to acquire, hold and dispose of land or an interest in land and to acquire, hold and dispose of any other property.

Criminal Assets Bureau Act 1996, s 3

"THE BUREAU LEGAL OFFICER"

"the bureau legal officer" means the legal officer of the Bureau.

Criminal Assets Bureau Act 1996, s 1(1)

"THE CHIEF BUREAU OFFICER"

"the Chief Bureau Officer" means the chief officer of the Bureau.

Criminal Assets Bureau Act 1996, s 1(1)

There shall be a chief officer of the Bureau who shall be known, and is referred to in this Act, as the Chief Bureau Officer.

(2) The Commissioner shall, from time to time, appoint to the Bureau the Chief Bureau Officer and may, at any time, remove the Chief Bureau Officer from his or her appointment with the Bureau.

(3) The Chief Bureau Officer shall carry on and manage and control generally the administration and business of the Bureau.

(4) The Chief Bureau Officer shall be responsible to the Commissioner for the performance of the functions of the Bureau.

Criminal Assets Bureau Act 1996, s 7(1)(2)(3)(4)

"THE COMMISSIONER"

"the Commissioner" means the Commissioner of the Garda Síochána.

Criminal Assets Bureau Act 1996, s 1(1)

"THE COURT"

"the Court" means the High Court.

Proceeds of Crime Act 1996, s 1(1)

"THE ESTABLISHMENT DAY"

"the establishment day" means the day appointed by the Minister under *section 2*.

Criminal Assets Bureau Act 1996, s 1(1)

The Minister may, after consultation with the Minister for Finance, by order appoint a day to be the establishment day for the purposes of this Act.

Criminal Assets Bureau Act 1996, s 2

"THE RESPONDENT"

'the respondent' means a person, wherever domiciled, resident or present, in respect of whom an interim order or interlocutory order, or an application for such an order, has been made and includes any person who, but for this Act, would become entitled, on the death of the first-mentioned person, to any property to which such an order relates (being an order that is in force and is in respect of that person).".

Proceeds of Crime Act 1996, s 1(1) substituted by Proceeds of Crime (Amendment) Act 2005, s 3(i)

DRUGS, MONEY LAUNDERING AND CUSTOMS

F

G

H

I & J

L

M

N

O

S

T

A

"A PRISONER"

The Minister may, if he thinks fit, issue a warrant providing for any person (referred to in this section as "a prisoner") serving a sentence in a prison or any other place for which rules or regulations may be made under the Prisons Acts, 1826 to 1980, or section 13 of the Criminal Justice Act, 1960, to be transferred to a country or territory outside the State for the purpose—

(*a*) of giving evidence in criminal proceedings there, or
(*b*) of being identified in, or otherwise by his presence assisting, such proceedings or the investigation of an offence.

Criminal Justice Act 1994, s 53(1)

"ACTS RELATING TO MERCHANT SHIPPING" SEE UNDER THE

"AGREEMENT"

"Agreement" means the Council of Europe Agreement on Illicit Traffic by Sea implementing Article 17 of the United Nations Convention against Illicit Traffic in Narcotic Drugs and Psychotropic Substances, done at Strasbourg on 31 January 1995.

Criminal Justice (Illicit Traffic by Sea) Act 2003, s 1(1)

"AGREEMENT" (SEE THE AGREEMENT)

"AIRCRAFT"

In this section "aircraft" includes a glider, balloon and model aircraft.

Customs and Excise (Miscellaneous Provisions) Act 1988, s 2(8)

"AN AUTHORISED MEMBER OF THE STAFF"

In this section—

'an authorised member of the staff'—

(*a*) in relation to a children detention school, means a member of the staff of the school who is authorised in writing for the purposes of this section by the Director (within the meaning of section 157 of the Children Act 2001) of the school, and
(*b*) in relation to a remand centre, means a member of the staff of the centre who is authorised in writing for the purposes of this section by the owners or, as the case may be, the managers of the centre.

Misuse of Drugs Act 1977, s 15C(8) inserted by Criminal Justice Act 2006, s 83

"AN ENFORCEMENT OFFICER"

"an enforcement officer" means—

(*a*) a member of the Garda Síochána,
(*b*) an officer of customs and excise,
(*c*) a member of the Naval Service of the Defence Forces not below the rank of petty officer, and
(*d*) any other person of a description specified in an order made for the purposes of this Schedule by the Minister.

Criminal Justice Act 1994, Sched 1, s 1(1)

"AN OFFICER OF CUSTOMS AND EXCISE"

'an officer of customs and excise' has the same meaning as in section 6 of the Criminal Justice (Drug Trafficking) Act, 1996.".

Misuse of Drugs Act, 1977, s 15A(5) inserted by Criminal Justice Act 1999, s 4

(4) In this section "an officer of customs and excise" means a person appointed by the Revenue Commissioners under the Customs Acts and under the statutes which relate to the duties of excise or any instrument relating to duties of excise made under statute.

Criminal Justice (Drug Trafficking) Act 1996, s 6(4)

"AN POST"

"An Post" means the company referred to in section 10 (1) (*a*) of the Postal and Telecommunications Services Act, 1983 (No. 24 of 1983).

SI No 328/88, s 3(1)

(1) The names of the companies shall be, respectively—

(*a*) An Post or, in the English language, The Post Office, and.

Postal and Telecommunications Services Act 1983, s 10(1)(a)

"ANIMAL REMEDY"

"animal remedy" has the same meaning as in the Animal Remedies Act, 1956 (No. 41 of 1956).

SI No 326/88, s 3

"animal remedy" means any substance, preparation, mixture or compound, other than a feeding stuff commonly known and used as such, which is intended for administration or application whether internally or externally to an animal by any means for the purpose of preventing, diagnosing or treating any injury, disease, ailment or defect or improving its health or condition.

Animal Remedies Act 1956, s 2

"APPEAL"

In *subsection (3)* of this section "appeal" includes—

(*a*) any proceedings by way of discharging or setting aside a judgment, and
(*b*) an application for a new trial or a stay of execution.

Criminal Justice Act 1994, s 46(4)

"APPEAL PROCEEDINGS"

In this section, "appeal proceedings" means proceedings relating to—

(*a*) a complaint under Article 40.4.2° of the Constitution (including proceedings on appeal from a decision on that complaint), or

(*b*) an appeal on a point of law to the Supreme Court.

Criminal Justice (Illicit Traffic by Sea) Act 2003, s 19(2)

"APPLICANT AUTHORITY"

'applicant authority': the competent authority of the Member State which makes a request for assistance.

Customs and Excise (Mutual Assistance) Act 2001, sched 4, art 4(5)

"APPROVED"

Approved.

"approved", except in relation to an approved route, means approved by the Revenue Commissioners.

SI No 117/68, Art 4

"ARRESTED PERSON"

The Criminal Justice (Drug Trafficking) Act 1996 is amended—

(*a*) in section 2—

(i) in subsection (1), by the substitution of the following paragraph for paragraph (*a*):

"(*a*) Where a member of the Garda Síochána arrests without warrant, whether in a Garda Síochána station or elsewhere, a person (an 'arrested person') whom he or she, with reasonable cause, suspects of having committed a drug trafficking offence, the arrested person—

(i) if not already in a Garda Síochána station, may be taken to and detained in a Garda Síochána station, or

(ii) if he or she is arrested in a Garda Síochána station, may be detained in the station, for a period or periods authorised by subsection (2) if the member of the Garda Síochána in charge of the station to which the arrested person is taken on arrest or in which he or she is arrested has at the time of the arrested person's arrival at the station or his or her arrest in the station, as may be appropriate, reasonable grounds for believing that his or her detention is necessary for the proper investigation of the offence.",

(ii) by the insertion of the following subsection after subsection (7):

"(7A) Notwithstanding subsections (2) and (7), if—

(*a*) an application is made under subsection (2) for a warrant authorising the detention for a further period of a person detained under that subsection, and

(*b*) the period of detention under that subsection has not expired at the commencement of the hearing of the application but would, but for this subsection, expire during that hearing,

it shall be deemed not to expire until the determination of the application.",

and

(*b*) in section 4(3), by the insertion of the following paragraph as paragraph (*a*) and the re-lettering of paragraphs (*a*) and (*b*) as paragraphs (*b*) and (*c*):

"(*a*) the substitution for paragraph (*a*) in subsection (1) of the following paragraph:

'(*a*) Where a member of the Garda Síochána arrests a person (an "arrested person") under a warrant issued pursuant to section 4(1), the arrested person may be taken to and detained in a Garda Síochána station for a period or periods authorised by subsection (2) if the member of the Garda Síochána in charge of the station to which the arrested person is taken on arrest has at the time of the arrested person's arrival at the station reasonable grounds for believing that his or her detention is necessary for the proper investigation of the offence.'".

Criminal Justice (Drugs Trafficking Act) 1996, s 2(1)(a) substituted by Criminal Justice Act 2006, s 10

"ASSESSED VALUE"

8A.—(1) Where a person has been sentenced or otherwise dealt with by a court in respect of one or more offences of financing terrorism of which that person has been convicted, the Director of Public Prosecutions may make, or cause to be made, an application to the court to determine whether the convicted person holds funds subject to confiscation.

(2) For the purposes of this Act, funds subject to confiscation are—

(*a*) funds used or allocated for use in connection with an offence of financing terrorism, or
(b) funds that are the proceeds of such an offence.

(3) An application under subsection (1) of this section may be made at the conclusion of the proceedings at which the person is sentenced or otherwise dealt with or at a later stage in the proceedings.

(4) An application under subsection (1) of this section shall not be made unless it appears to the Director of Public Prosecutions that the person in question holds funds subject to confiscation.

(5) If the court determines that the person in question holds funds subject to confiscation, the court shall—

(*a*) determine in accordance with section 8C of this Act the amount to be recovered in that person's case by virtue of this section, and
(*b*) make a confiscation order under this section requiring the person to pay that amount.

(6) The standard of proof applicable in civil proceedings is the standard required to determine a question arising under this Act as to—

(*a*) whether a person holds funds subject to confiscation, and
(*b*) the amount to be recovered in that person's case by virtue of this section.

Assessing the value of funds subject to confiscation.

8B.—(1) For the purposes of this Act, the value of the funds that are subject to confiscation is the aggregate of the values of those funds held by the defendant.

(2) For the purpose of assessing the value of funds subject to confiscation, the court shall, subject to subsection (3) of this section, make the following assumptions:

(*a*) that any funds appearing to the court—
  (i) to have been held by the defendant at any time since the conviction, or
  (ii) to have been transferred to the defendant at any time since the beginning of the period of six years ending when the proceedings were instituted against the defendant,

  were received or collected by the defendant, at the earliest time at which the defendant appears to the court to have held them, for use (whether or not used) in connection with the offence of financing terrorism or as the proceeds of such offence;

(*b*) that any expenditure of the defendant since the beginning of that period was met out of funds subject to confiscation;

(*c*) that the funds subject to confiscation are held by the defendant free of any other interests in them.

(3) The court shall not make an assumption set out in subsection (2) of this section if—

(*a*) that assumption is shown to be incorrect in the case of the defendant, or

(*b*) the court is satisfied that there would be a serious risk of injustice in that case were the assumption made.

(4) Where the court does not apply one or more of the assumptions set out in subsection (2) of this section, it shall state its reasons.

(5) For the purpose of assessing the value of funds subject to confiscation in a case where a confiscation order has previously been made against the defendant, the court shall not take into account any of that defendant's funds subject to confiscation that are shown to the court to have been taken into account in determining the amount to be recovered under the confiscation order.

Amount to be recovered under a confiscation order made under section 8A.

8C.—(1) Subject to subsection (2) of this s, where a confiscation order has been made under s 8A of this Act, the amount to be recovered under the order shall be equal to the amount assessed by the court to be the value of the defendant's funds subject to confiscation.

(2) If the court is satisfied that the amount that might be realised at the time the confiscation order is made is less than the amount the court assesses to be the value of the funds subject to confiscation, the amount to be recovered in the defendant's case under the confiscation order shall be the amount appearing to the court to be the amount that might be so realised.

Re-assessment of whether defendant holds funds subject to confiscation.

8D.—(1) This section applies where an application has previously been made to the court under section 8A of this Act and the court has determined that the defendant did not hold funds subject to confiscation.

(2) The Director of Public Prosecutions may make, or cause to be made, an application to the court for it to consider evidence—

(*a*) which was not considered by the court in making the determination referred to in subsection (1) of this section, and

(*b*) which, had it been considered, the Director of Public Prosecutions believes would have led the court to determine that the defendant held funds subject to confiscation.

(3) If, having considered the evidence, the court is satisfied that, had that evidence been available to it, it would have determined that the defendant held funds subject to confiscation, the court—

(*a*) shall—

(i) make a fresh determination of whether the defendant holds funds subject to confiscation, and

(ii) make a determination under section 8A(5) of this Act of the amount to be recovered by virtue of that section,

and

(*b*) may make a confiscation order under section 8A(5) of this Act.

(4) In considering an application under this section, the court may take into account any funds held by the defendant on or after the date of the determination referred to in subsection (1) of this section, but only if the Director of Public Prosecutions shows that the funds relate to an offence of financing terrorism committed on or before that date by the defendant or another person.

(5) In considering any evidence under this section relating to any funds to which subsection (4) applies, the court shall not make the assumptions which would otherwise be required under section 8B of this Act.

(6) No application shall be entertained by the court under this section if it is made after the end of the period of six years beginning with the date on which the defendant was convicted.

Revised assessment of funds subject to confiscation.

8E.—(1) This section applies where a court has made a determination (referred to in this section as 'the current determination') under section 8A(5) of this Act of the amount to be recovered in a particular case by virtue of that section.

(2) Where the Director of Public Prosecutions is of the opinion that the real value of the defendant's funds subject to confiscation was greater than their assessed value, the Director of Public Prosecutions may make, or cause to be made, an application to the court for the evidence on which that opinion was formed to be considered by the court.

(3) In subsections (2) and (4) of this section.—

'assessed value' means the value of the defendant's funds subject to confiscation as assessed by the court under s 8C(1) of this Act;

'real value' means the value of the defendant's funds subject to confiscation which relate to an offence of financing terrorism committed either in the period by reference to which the current determination was made or in any earlier period.

(4) If, having considered the evidence, the court is satisfied that the real value of the defendant's funds subject to confiscation is greater than their assessed value (whether because their real value was higher at the time of the current determination than was thought or because the value of the funds subject to confiscation has subsequently increased), the court shall make a fresh determination under section 8A(5) of this Act of the amount to be recovered by virtue of that section.

(5) Any determination under section 8A(5) of this Act by virtue of this section shall be by reference to the amount that might be realised at the time the determination is made.

(6) For any determination under section 8A(5) of this Act by virtue of this section, section 8B(5) of this Act shall not apply in relation to any of the defendant's funds subject to confiscation that were taken into account in respect of the current determination.

(7) In relation to a determination under section 8A(5) of this Act by virtue of this section—

(*a*) section 3(2) of this Act shall have effect as if for 'a confiscation order is made against the defendant' there were substituted 'of the determination',
(*b*) sections 3(8), 10(5)(*a*) and 12(4) of this Act shall have effect as if for 'confiscation order' there were substituted 'determination', and
(*c*) section 8C(2) of this Act shall have effect as if for 'confiscation order is made' there were substituted 'determination is made'.

(8) The court may take into account any funds held by the defendant on or after the date of the current determination, but only if the Director of Public Prosecutions shows that the funds relate to an offence of financing terrorism committed before that date by the defendant or another person.

(9) In considering any evidence relating to any funds to which subsection (8) applies, the court shall not make the assumptions which would otherwise be required by section 8B of this Act.

(10) If, as a result of making the fresh determination required by subsection (4) of this section, the amount to be recovered exceeds the amount set by the current determination, the court may substitute for the amount to be recovered under the confiscation order which was made by reference to the current determination such greater amount as it thinks just in all the circumstances of the case.

(11) No application shall be entertained by the court under this section if it is made after the end of the period of six years beginning with the date on which the defendant was convicted.".

Criminal Justice Act 1994, ss 8A to 8E inserted by the Criminal Justice (Terrorist Offences) Act 2005, s 22

"ATTORNEY GENERAL"

'Attorney Generals' shall include Solicitor General, Attorney General in the Isle of Man, Procureur, or other chief law officer of the Crown in any of Her Majesty's possessions abroad where there is no Attorney General.

Customs Consolidation Act 1876, s 284

"AUTHORISED AS A MEMBER OF A GROUP"

"authorised as a member of a group" means authorised by virtue of being a member of a class in respect of which the Minister has granted an authority which is in force under and for the purposes of article 8(2) and "his group authority" in relation to a person who is a member of such a class means the authority so granted to that class.

SI No 328/88, art 3(1)

"AUTHORISED MEDICAL PRACTITONER"

"authorised medical practitioner" means a registered medical practitioner authorised for the purposes of this section by the Minister in writing or a registered medical practitioner of a class specified by the Minister as being authorised for the said purposes.

Misuse of Drugs Act 1977, s 28(11)

"AUTHORISED MOTOR VEHICLE"

"authorised motor vehicle" means a motor vehicle in respect of which a temporary importation permit or a motor vehicle pass is in force and which is travelling on its own wheels or tracks.

SI No 117/68, s 4

B

"BENEFITED FROM DRUG TRAFFICKING"

For the purposes of this Act, a person who has at any time (whether before or after the commencement of this section) received any payment or other reward in connection with drug trafficking carried on by him or another has benefited from drug trafficking.

Criminal Justice Act 1994, s 3 defined in s 4(5)

"BENEFITED FROM OFFENCES OTHER THAN DRUG TRAFFICKING"

For the purposes of this Act, a person benefits from an offence other than a drug trafficking offence if he obtains property as a result of or in connection with the commission of that offence and his benefit is the value of the property so obtained.

Criminal Justice Act 1994, s 3 defined in s (9)(4)

"BRITISH POSSESSIONS"

'British possession' shall mean and include colony, plantation, island, territory, or settlement belonging to Her Majesty.

Customs Consolidation Act 1876, s 284

"BUSINESS"

" 'business' includes a profession.".

Misuse of Drugs Act 1977, s 1(1) inserted by the Irish Medicines Board (Miscellaneous Provisions) Act 2006, s 3(a)

C

"CANNABINOL DERIVATIVES"

"cannabinol derivatives" means the following substances, except where contained in cannabis or cannabis resin, namely, tetrahydro derivatives of cannabinol and 3-alkyl homologues of cannabinol or of its tetrahydro derivatives.

Misuse of Drugs Act 1977, sched, s 6

"CANNABIS"

(*a*) the substitution of the following definition for the definition of "cannabis":

" 'cannabis' (except in 'cannabis resin') means any plant of the genus *Cannabis* or any part of any such plant (by whatever name designated) but includes neither cannabis resin nor any of the following products after separation from the rest of any such plant, namely—

(*a*) mature stalk of any such plant,
(*b*) fibre produced from such mature stalk, or
(*c*) seed of any such plant.".

Misuse of Drugs Act 1977, s 1(1) as amended by the Misuse of Drugs Act 1984, s 2

"CASH"

"cash" includes coins and notes in any currency.

Criminal Justice Act 1994, s 43(1)

"CENTRAL TREATMENT LIST"

(2) The Eastern Health Board shall maintain a record to be known and in these Regulations referred to as the "Central Treatment List" which shall contain the information notified to it under paragraph (1) and the list may be maintained in electronic form.

SI No 225/98, art 3(2)

"CHANNEL ISLANDS"

'Channel Islands' shall mean the islands of Guernsey, Jersey, Alderney, and Sark, and their respective dependencies.

Customs Consolidtion Act 1876, s 284

"CIS CONVENTION" SEE THE

"COCA LEAF"

"coca leaf" means the leaf of any plant of the genus *Erythroxylon* from whose leaves cocaine can be extracted either directly or by chemical transformation.

Misuse of Drugs Act 1977, sched, s 6

"COMMISSIONERS OF THE TREASURY"

'Commissioners of the Treasury' shall mean the Lords Commissioners of Her Majesty's Treasury.

Customs Consolidation Act 1876, s 284

"COMMUNITY CUSTOMS PROVISIONS"

'Community customs provisions':

- the body of Community provisions and associated implementing provisions governing the import, export, transit and presence of goods traded between Member States and third countries, and between Member States in the case of goods that do not have Community status within the meaning of Article 9(2) of the Treaty establishing the European Community or goods subject to additional controls or investigations for the purposes of establishing their Community status;
- the body of provisions adopted at Community level under the common agricultural policy and the specific provisions adopted with regard to goods resulting from the processing of agricultural products;
- the body of provisions adopted at Community level for harmonised excise duties and for value-added tax on importation together with the national provisions implementing them.

Customs and Excise (Mutual Assistance Act) 2001, sched 4, art 4(2)

"COMPANY"

"company" means any company which may be wound up under the Companies Acts, 1963 to 1990.

Criminal Justice Act 1994, s 30(3)

"CONCENTRATE OF POPPY STRAW"

"concentrate of poppy straw" means the material produced when poppy straw has entered into a process for the concentration of its alkaloids.

Misuse of Drugs Act 1977, sched, s 6

"CONFISCATION ORDER"

" 'confiscation order' means an order made under section 4(4), 8A(5) or 9(1) of this Act;";

(4) If the court determines that the person in question has benefited from drug trafficking, the court shall determine in accordance with *section 6* of this Act the amount to be recovered in his case by virtue of this section and shall make a confiscation order under this section requiring the person concerned to pay that amount.

Criminal Justice Act 1994, s 4(4)

(1) Where a person has been sentenced or otherwise dealt with by a court in respect of one or more offences of financing terrorism of which that person has been convicted, the Director of Public Prosecutions may make, or cause to be made, an application to the court to determine whether the convicted person holds funds subject to confiscation.

(2) For the purposes of this Act, funds subject to confiscation are—

(*a*) funds used or allocated for use in connection with an offence of financing terrorism, or
(*b*) funds that are the proceeds of such an offence.

(3) An application under subsection (1) of this section may be made at the conclusion of the proceedings at which the person is sentenced or otherwise dealt with or at a later stage in the proceedings.

(4) An application under subsection (1) of this section shall not be made unless it appears to the Director of Public Prosecutions that the person in question holds funds subject to confiscation.

(5) If the court determines that the person in question holds funds subject to confiscation, the court shall—

(*a*) determine in accordance with section 8C of this Act the amount to be recovered in that person's case by virtue of this section, and
(*b*) make a confiscation order under this section requiring the person to pay that amount.

(6) The standard of proof applicable in civil proceedings is the standard required to determine a question arising under this Act as to—

(*a*) whether a person holds funds subject to confiscation, and
(*b*) the amount to be recovered in that person's case by virtue of this section.

Criminal Justice Act 1994, s 8a inserted by Criminal Justice (Terrorist Offences) Act 2005, s 22

(1) Where a person has been sentenced or otherwise dealt with in respect of an offence, other than a drug trafficking offence, of which he has been convicted on indictment, then, if an application is made, or caused to be made, to the court by the Director of Public Prosecutions the court may, subject to the provisions of this section, make a confiscation order under this section requiring the person concerned to pay such sum as the court thinks fit.

Criminal Justice Act 1994, s 9(1)

"CONTROLLED DRUG"

1. (1) In this Act "controlled drug" means any substance, product or preparation (other than a substance, product or preparation specified in an order under subsection (3) of this section which is for the time being in force) which is either specified in the Schedule to this Act or is for the time being declared pursuant to subsection (2) of this section to be a controlled drug for the purposes of this Act.

(2) The Government may by order declare any substance, product or preparation (not being a substance, product or preparation specified in the Schedule to this Act) to be a controlled drug for the purposes of this Act and so long as an order under this subsection is in force, this Act shall have effect as regards any substance, product or preparation specified in the order as if the substance, product or preparation were specified in the said Schedule.

Misuse of Drugs Act 1977, s 2(1)

2. Each of the substances, products and preparations specified in the Schedule to this Order is hereby declared to be a controlled drug for the purposes of the Misuse of Drugs Act, 1977 (No. 12 of 1977).

SCHEDULE

1. The following substances and products, namely:
N-Hydroxy-tenamphetamine
Khat (being the leaves of Catha edulis (Celastraceae))
4-Methyl-aminorex

2. Any ester or ether of a substance specified in paragraph 1 of this Schedule.

3. Midazolam.

4. Any stereoisomeric form of a substance specified in paragraph 1, 2 or 3 of this Schedule.

5. The following substances, namely:
   Acetic anhydride
   Acetone
   N-Acetylanthranilic acid
   Anthranilic acid
   Ephedrine
   Ergometrine
   Ergotamine
   Ethyl ether
   4-Hydroxybutanoic acid
   Isosafrole (cis isomer)
   Isosafrole (trans isomer)
   Lysergic acid
   3, 4-Methylenedioxyphenylpropan-2-one
   Methylethylketone
   Phenylacetic acid
   Piperidine
   Piperonal
   Potassium permanganate
   Pseudoephedrine
   Safrole
   Toluene.

6. Any salt of a substance specified in any of paragraphs 1 to 5 of this Schedule.

7. The following substances, namely:
   Hydrochloric acid
   Sulphuric acid

8. Any preparation or other product containing any proportion of a substance or product specified in any of paragraphs 1 to 7 of this Schedule.

SI No 328/93, art 2 and sched

"CONVENTION"

'Convention' means the Convention drawn up on the basis of Article K.3 of the Treaty on European Union on the use of information technology for customs purposes.

Customs and Excise (Mutual Assistance Act) 2001, sched 2, art 1

"CONVENTION STATE"

"Convention state" means a state other than the State that is a party to the United Nations Convention against Illicit Traffic in Narcotic Drugs and Psychotropic Substances done at Vienna on the 20th day of December, 1988.

Criminal Justice Act 1994, s 3(1)

"CORRESPONDING LAW"

"corresponding law" has the same meaning as in section 20 (2) of the Misuse of Drugs Act, 1977.

Criminal Justice Act 1994, s 3(1)

In this section "a corresponding law" means a law stated in a certificate purporting to be issued by or on behalf of the government of a country outside the State to be a law providing for the control or regulation in that country of the manufacture, production, supply, use, exportation or importation of dangerous or otherwise harmful drugs in pursuance of any treaty, convention, protocol or other agreement between states and prepared or implemented by, or under the auspices of the League of Nations or the United Nations Organisation and which for the time being is in force.

Misuse of Drugs Act 1977, s 20(2)

"COUNTY"

'County' shall mean and include any city, county of a city, county of a town, borough, or other magisterial jurisdiction where such construction is not inconsistent with the context.

Customs Consolidation Act 1876, s 284

"CRIMINAL CONDUCT"

(7) (*a*) In this section—

(i) 'criminal conduct' means conduct which—
(I) constitutes an indictable offence, or

(II) where the conduct occurs outside the State, would constitute such an offence if it occurred within the State and also constitutes an offence under the law of the country or territorial unit in which it occurs,

and includes participation in such conduct.

Criminal Justice Act 1994, s 31(7)(a)(i) as substituted by the Criminal Justice (Theft and Fraud Offences) Act 2001, s 21

"CROSS BORDER COOPERATION"

'cross-border cooperation': cooperation between customs administrations across the borders of each Member State.

Customs and Excise (Mutual Assistance) Act 2001, sched 4, art 4(9)

"CUSTOMS ACTS"

'Customs Acts' shall mean and include this and all or any other Acts or Act relating to the Customs.

Customs Consolidation Act 1876, s 284

"CUSTOMS ADMINISTRATIONS"

'customs administrations': Member States' customs authorities as well as other authorities with jurisdiction for implementing the provisions of this Convention.

Customs and Excise (Mutual Assistance Act) 2001, sched 4, art 4(7)

"CUSTOMS COOPERATION CONVENTION" SEE THE

"CUSTOMS INFORMATION SYSTEM"

Establishment of a Customs Information System

Article 2

1. The customs administrations of the Member States shall set up and maintain a joint automated information system for customs purposes, hereinafter referred to as the 'Customs Information System'.

2. The aim of the Customs Information System, in accordance with the provisions of this Convention, shall be to assist in preventing, investigating and prosecuting serious contraventions of national laws by increasing, through the rapid dissemination of information, the effectiveness of the co-operation and control procedures of the customs administrations of the Member States.

Customs and Excise (Mutual Assistance Act) 2001, sched 1, art 2

"CUSTOMS STATION"

Customs Station.

"Customs Station", in relation to an approved route, means the office maintained by the Revenue Commissioners for the transaction of Customs business in regard to goods being imported or exported by that route at a place mentioned in any of the columns headed "Location of Customs Station" in the First Schedule to these Regulations opposite any mention of that route in any of the columns headed "Route" in that Schedule.

SI No 117/1968, art 4

D

"DEALING WITH PROPERTY"

For the purposes of this Act, dealing with property held by any person includes (without prejudice to the generality of the expression)—

(*a*) where a debt is owed to that person, making a payment to any person in reduction of the amount of the debt, and

(*b*) removing the property from the State.

Criminal Justice Act 1994, s 24(8)

"DEFENDANT"

"'defendant' means, for the purposes of any provision of this Act relating to confiscation, and subject to section 23(2)(*a*) of this Act, a person against whom proceedings for the relevant drug trafficking offence, offence of financing terrorism or other offence have been instituted.".

Criminal Justice Act 1994, s 3(1) substituted by Criminal Justice (Terrorist Offences) Act 2005, s 21

"DENTAL BOARD" SEE THE

"DESIGNATED BODIES"

(1) This section shall apply to the following persons or bodies (referred to in this section as "designated bodies") namely—

(*a*) a body licensed to carry on banking business under the Central Bank Act, 1971 or authorised to carry on such business under regulations made under the European Communities Act, 1972,
(*b*) a building society incorporated or deemed to be incorporated under section 10 of the Building Societies Act, 1989,
(*c*) a person authorised to carry on a money broking business under section 110 of the Central Bank Act, 1989,
(*d*) a society licensed to carry on the business of a trustee savings bank under section 10 of the Trustee Savings Banks Act, 1989,
(*e*) a life assurance undertaking which is the holder of an authorisation under the Insurance Acts, 1909 to 1990, or under regulations made under the European Communities Act, 1972,
(*f*) a person providing a service in financial futures and options exchanges within the meaning of section 97 of the Central Bank Act, 1989,
(*g*) An Post,
(*h*) ACC Bank p.l.c.,
(*i*) ICC Bank p.l.c.,
(*j*) a society which is registered as a credit union under the Industrial and Provident Societies Acts, 1893 to 1978, by virtue of the Credit Union Act, 1966,
(*k*) a person providing a service in relation to buying and selling stocks, shares and other securities,
(*l*) a person providing foreign currency exchange services, and
(*m*) any other person or body prescribed in regulations made under subsection (10) (a) of this section.

Criminal Justice Act 1994, s 32(1)

"DESIGNATED COUNTRY"

If an application is made to the High Court by or on behalf of the government of a country designated under *subsection (1)* of this section (referred to in this section as a "designated country") and with the consent of the Minister for the making of a confiscation co-operation order pursuant to an external confiscation order made by a court in that country, and the High Court is satisfied that the conditions specified in *subsection (3)* of this section are satisfied, the court may make a confiscation co-operation order.

Criminal Justice Act 1994, s 46(2)

Subject to *subsection (3)* of this section, if an application is made to the High Court by or on behalf of the government of a country designated under *subsection (1)* of this section (referred to in this section as a "designated country") and with the consent of the Minister for the making of a forfeiture co-operation order pursuant to an external forfeiture order made by a court in that country, and the High Court is satisfied that the conditions corresponding to those specified in *subsections (3)* and *(4)* of *section 46* of this Act are satisfied, the court may make a forfeiture co-operation order.

Criminal Justice Act 1994, s 47(2)

"DRUG TRAFFICKING"

(1) "drug trafficking" means doing or being concerned in any of the following, whether in the State or elsewhere, that is to say—

(*a*) producing or supplying a controlled drug where the production or supply contravenes any regulations made under section 5 of the Misuse of Drugs Act, 1977, and in force at the material time (whether before or after the commencement of the relevant provision of this Act) or a corresponding law,

(*b*) transporting or storing a controlled drug where possession of the drug contravenes section 3 of that Act or a corresponding law,

(*c*) importing or exporting a controlled drug where the importation or exportation contravenes any such regulations as mentioned in *paragraph (a)* of this definition or a corresponding law,

(*d*) doing any act, whether in the State or elsewhere and whether before or after the commencement of the relevant provision of this Act, in relation to property obtained, whether directly or indirectly, from anything done in relation to a controlled drug, that amounts to an offence under *section 31* of this Act or would have amounted to such an offence if that section had been in operation at the time when the act was done or, in the case of an act done in a country or territory outside the State, would amount or have amounted to such an offence if done in corresponding circumstances in the State (and for the purpose of this definition the references in *subsections (1)* and *(2)* of the said *section 31* to removing property from the State shall include references to removing it from the country or territory in question), or

(e) using any ship for illicit traffic in controlled drugs in contravention of *section 33* or *34* of this Act.

Criminal Justice Act 1994, s 3(1)

(2) "drug trafficking offence" means any of the following—

(*a*) an offence under any regulations made under section 5 of the Misuse of Drugs Act, 1977, involving the manufacture, production, preparation, importation, exportation, supply, offering to supply, distribution or transportation of a controlled drug,

(*b*) an offence under section 15 of that Act of possession of a controlled drug for unlawful sale or supply,

(*c*) an offence under section 20 of that Act (assisting in or inducing the commission outside the State of an offence punishable under a corresponding law),

(*d*) an offence under the Customs Acts in relation to the importation or exportation of a controlled drug or in relation to the fraudulent evasion of any prohibition, restriction or obligation in relation to such importation or exportation,

(e) an offence under *section 31* of this Act in relation to the proceeds of drug trafficking,

(*f*) an offence under *section 33* or *34* of this Act, or

(*g*) an offence of aiding, abetting, counselling or procuring the commission of any of the offences mentioned in *paragraphs (a)* to (*f*)of this definition or of attempting or conspiring to commit any such offence or inciting another person to do so.

Criminal Justice Act 1994, s 3(1)

"DRUG TRAFFICKING OFFENCE (SHIPS)"

(1) A person is guilty of a drug trafficking offence if the person does, on an Irish ship, a ship registered in a Convention state or a ship not registered in any country or territory, any act which, if done in the State, would constitute such an offence.

(2) This section is without prejudice to section 34 of this Act.".

Criminal Justice Act 1994, s 33(1) as inserted by the Criminal Justice (Illicit Traffic by Sea) Act 2003, s 28(b)

"DRUG TREATMENT CARD"

(1) A health board shall issue a drug treatment card in respect of a person participating in a programme of treatment involving the use of a specified controlled drug and in respect of whom the information referred to in Regulation 3(1) has been notified to the Eastern Health Board.

(2) A drug treatment card shall be valid for such period as may be specified on the card but in any case shall not be valid for more than one year from the date of issue.

SI No 225/98, art 4

"DULY ISSUED PRESCRIPTION"

A person shall not with intent to deceive either alter or use a prescription which has been duly issued by a practitioner (which document is in this Act referred to as a duly issued prescription).

Misuse of Drugs Act 1977, s 18(2)

"DURING OFFICIAL HOURS"

During official hours.

"during official hours" means on a day and during the hours prescribed or allowed by the Revenue Commissioners under Article 8 of these Regulations.

SI No 117/68, art 4

"DUTIES OF A CARRIER EXPORTING"

Duties of carrier of ordinary merchandise exported.

10. Every person conveying any ordinary merchandise out of the State shall:

(*a*) produce such merchandise for examination by an Officer at the Customs Station during official hours;

(*b*) present to such Officer during official hours a manifest in duplicate in an approved form and containing the particulars indicated therein or required thereby;

(*c*) after one copy of the manifest has been returned to him by the Officer duly signed, forthwith convey the merchandise by the approved route to the Frontier Post;

(*d*) produce the merchandise and copy of the manifest during official hours for examination by an Officer at the Frontier Post, together with copies of the entry of such merchandise required by Article 11 of these Regulations where the Officer at the Customs Station so directs;

(*e*) after production of the merchandise at the Frontier Post, forthwith convey the merchandise over the Land Frontier by the approved route.

SI No 117/68, art 10

"DUTIES OF A CARRIER (IMPORTING)"

Duties of carrier of ordinary merchandise imported.

9. Every person conveying ordinary merchandise into the State shall:

(*a*) present to the Officer at the Frontier Post during official hours a report in duplicate in an approved form and containing the particulars indicated therein or required thereby and shall not proceed on his journey until he has so presented such report;

(*b*) after one copy of such report has been returned to him by such Officer duly signed, forthwith convey such merchandise by the approved route to the Customs Station in the vehicle in which it is imported, without alteration of such merchandise or of the packages containing it;

(*c*) produce such merchandise and copy of the report during official hours for examination by an Officer at the Customs Station;

(*d*) not convey such merchandise away from the Customs Station until the delivery of the merchandise has been authorised by the Officer and any permit necessary for its removal has been granted by him; and

(*e*) where such merchandise is entered for warehousing convey, after examination by the Officer at the Customs Station, such merchandise with all reasonable despatch to the appropriate warehouse and deposit it therein.

SI No 117/68, art 9

E

"ENACTMENT"

"enactment" means any enactment being—

(*a*) a British statute,

(*b*) a Saorstát Éireann statute, or

(*c*) an Act of the Oireachtas (whether passed before or after this Act).

Customs Act 1956, s 1

"ENFORCEMENT OFFICER"

"an enforcement officer" means—

(*a*) a member of the Garda Síochána,

(*b*) an officer of customs and excise,

(*c*) a member of the Naval Service of the Defence Forces not below the rank of petty officer, and
(*d*) any other person of a description specified in an order made for the purposes of this Schedule by the Minister.

Criminal Justice Act 1994, sched 1, pt 1

"EVIDENCE"

In this section "evidence" includes documents and other articles.

Criminal Justice Act 1994, s 51(4)

In this section "evidence" includes documents and other articles.

Criminal Justice Act 1994, s 52(5)

In this section "evidence" includes documents and other articles.

Criminal Justice Act 1994, s 55(11)

"EXEMPT FARM PRODUCE"

Exempt farm produce.

"exempt farm produce" means farm produce being moved by a farmer or his servant in the course of the farmer's business as a farmer and not subject to any duty or prohibition or restriction on (in the case of goods being imported) importation or on (in the case of goods being exported) exportation, but does not include live pigs, sheep or cattle being moved to Northern Ireland.

SI No 117/1968, s 4

"EXEMPT VEHICLE"

Exempt vehicle.

"exempt vehicle" means a vehicle (not being a motor vehicle) which is either owned in the State or not chargeable with any duty or subject to any prohibition or restriction on importation, and which is travelling on its own wheels.

SI No 117/1968, art 4

"EXPORTED"

"exported" in relation to any cash, includes its being brought to any place in the State for the purpose of being exported.

Criminal Justice Act 1994, s 43(1)

"EXPORTER"

"importer" and "exporter" mean respectively the owner or other person for the time being possessed of or beneficially interested in goods to which these Regulations apply at the time of the importation or exportation thereof, and include any person acting in relation thereto as agent for the owner or other person.

SI No 117/1968, art 4

"EXTERNAL CONFISCATION ORDER"

The Government may by order designate countries as countries in whose case orders (referred to in this section as "confiscation co-operation orders") may be made for the confiscation, in accordance with the law of the State, of property which is liable to confiscation in accordance with orders (referred to in this section as "external confiscation orders") made by a court in the country in question for the purpose—

(*a*) of recovering payments or other rewards received as a result of or in connection with drug trafficking or their value, or

(*b*) of recovering—

(i) property obtained as a result of or in connection with conduct corresponding to an offence in respect of which a confiscation order could be made under *section 9* of this Act, or

(ii) the value of property so obtained,

or

(*c*) of depriving a person of a pecuniary advantage obtained as mentioned in *paragraph (b)* of this subsection.

(2) If an application is made to the High Court by or on behalf of the government of a country designated under *subsection (1)* of this section (referred to in this section as a "designated country") and with the consent of the Minister for the making of a confiscation co-operation order pursuant to an external confiscation order made by a court in that country, and the High Court is satisfied that the conditions specified in *subsection (3)* of this section are satisfied, the court may make a confiscation co-operation order.

(3) The conditions referred to in *subsection (2)* of this section are that the High Court should—

(*a*) be satisfied that at the time of the making of the order the external confiscation order is in force and not subject to appeal,
(*b*) be satisfied, where the person against whom that order was made did not appear in the proceedings, that he received notice of the proceedings in sufficient time to enable him to defend them, and
(*c*) be of the opinion that the making of a confiscation co-operation order corresponding to the external confiscation order would not be contrary to the interests of justice.

(4) In *subsection (3)* of this section "appeal" includes—

(*a*) any proceedings by way of discharging or setting aside a judgment, and
(*b*) an application for a new trial or a stay of execution.

(5) A confiscation co-operation order shall have the like effect as a confiscation order made under *section 4* or *9* of this Act save that—

(*a*) if the external confiscation order was for the confiscation of specified property (other than money), the confiscation co-operation order shall be an order for the recovery of that property (or of so much of the property as is specified in the application), and
(*b*) if the external confiscation order was for the recovery of a sum of money, the confiscation co-operation order shall be for the recovery of that sum (or, if a lesser sum is specified in the application, then for the recovery of the lesser sum).

(6) The Government may by regulations make such modifications of this Act as appear to it to be necessary or expedient for the purpose of adapting to confiscation co-operation orders any of the provisions of this Act relating to confiscation orders, in particular in relation to enforcement and the taking of provisional measures to prevent any dealing in, or transfer or disposal of, property that may be liable to confiscation in accordance with any confiscation co-operation order that may be made.

(7) The High Court shall revoke the confiscation co-operation order if it appears to the court that the external confiscation order has been satisfied in accordance with the law of the country in which it was made.

Criminal Justice Act 1994, s 46(1)–(7)

"EXTERNAL FORFEITURE ORDER"

The Government may by order designate countries in whose case orders (referred to in this section as "forfeiture co-operation orders") may be made for the forfeiture, in accordance with the law of the State, of anything—

(*a*) in respect of which an offence to which this section applies has been committed or which was used or intended to be used in connection with the commission of such an offence, and

(*b*) in respect of which an order (referred to in this section as an "external forfeiture order") has been made by a court in the country in question.

(2) Subject to *subsection (3)* of this section, if an application is made to the High Court by or on behalf of the government of a country designated under *subsection (1)* of this section (referred to in this section as a "designated country") and with the consent of the Minister for the making of a forfeiture co-operation order pursuant to an external forfeiture order made by a court in that country, and the High Court is satisfied that the conditions corresponding to those specified in *subsections (3)* and *(4)* of *section 46* of this Act are satisfied, the court may make a forfeiture co-operation order.

(3) The court shall not make an order under *subsection (2)* of this section if a person claiming to be the owner of the thing in question or otherwise interested in it applies to be heard by the court unless an opportunity has been given to him to show cause why the order should not be made.

(4) A forfeiture co-operation order shall have the like effect as a forfeiture order made under *section 61* of this Act as specified in *subsection (4)* of that section, and *subsections (7)* and *(8)* of that section shall apply accordingly.

(5) This section applies to any offence which corresponds to—

(a) an offence under the Misuse of Drugs Act, 1977,

(*b*) a drug trafficking offence, or

(*c*) an offence in respect of which a confiscation order could be made under *section 9* of this Act.

Criminal Justice Act 1994, s 47 (1)–(5)

F

"FARM PRODUCE"

"farm produce" means farm produce of any description whether intended for sale or not, and includes peat, turf, firewood, livestock, poultry and eggs and all agricultural, horticultural and dairy produce.

SI No 117/1968, art 4

"FORFEITURE ORDER"

Subject to the following provisions of this section, where a person is convicted of an offence, and—

(*a*) the court by or before which he is convicted is satisfied that any property which has been lawfully seized from him or which was in his possession or under his control at the time when he was apprehended for the offence or when a summons in respect of it was issued—
  (i) has been used for the purpose of committing, or facilitating the commission of, any offence, or
  (ii) was intended by him to be used for that purpose,

or

(*b*) the offence, or an offence which the court has taken into consideration in determining his sentence, consists of unlawful possession of property which—
  (i) has been lawfully seized from him, or
  (ii) was in his possession or under his control at the time when he was apprehended for the offence of which he has been convicted or when a summons in respect of that offence was issued,

the court may make an order under this section (referred to in this Act as a "forfeiture order") in respect of that property, and may do so whether or not it also deals with the offender in respect of the offence in any other way.

(2) In considering whether to make a forfeiture order in respect of any property a court shall have regard—

(*a*) to the value of the property, and
(*b*) to the likely financial and other effects on the offender of the making of the order (taken together with any other order that the court contemplates making).

(3) Facilitating the commission of an offence shall be taken for the purposes of this section to include the taking of any steps after it has been committed for the purpose of disposing of any property to which the offence relates or of avoiding, or enabling any other person to avoid, apprehension or detection.

(4) An order under this section shall operate to deprive the offender of his rights, if any, in the property to which it relates, and the property shall (if not already in their possession) be taken into the possession of the Garda Síochána.

(5) A court shall not order property to be forfeited under this section if a person claiming to be the owner of it or otherwise interested in it applies to be heard by the court, unless an opportunity has been given to him to show cause why the order should not be made.

(6) An order under this section shall not take effect until the ordinary time for instituting an appeal against the conviction or order concerned has expired or, where such an appeal is instituted, until it or any further appeal is finally decided or abandoned or the ordinary time for instituting any further appeal has expired.

(7) The Police Property Act, 1897, shall apply, with the following modifications, to property which is in the possession of the Garda Síochána by virtue of this section, that is to say:

(*a*) no application shall be made under section 1 (1) of that Act by any claimant of the property after the expiration of 6 months from the date on which the order in respect of the property was made under this section, and

(*b*) no such application shall succeed unless the claimant satisfies the court either that he had not consented to the offender having possession of the property or that he did not know, and had no reason to suspect, that the property was likely to be used for a purpose mentioned in *subsection (1)* of this section.

(8) In relation to property which is in the possession of the Garda Síochána by virtue of this section, the power to make regulations under section 2 (1) of the Police Property Act, 1897 (disposal of property in cases where the owner of the property has not been ascertained etc.), shall include power to make regulations for disposal in cases where no application by a claimant of the property has been made within the period specified in *subsection (7) (a)* of this section or no such application has succeeded.

(9) Nothing in this section shall affect the provisions of any enactment whereby property is, or may be ordered to be, forfeited as a result of a conviction for an offence.

Criminal Justice Act 1994, s 61

"FORGED PRESCRIPTION"

(1) A person shall not forge a document purporting to be a prescription issued by a practitioner (which document is in this Act referred to as a forged prescription).

(2) A person shall not with intent to deceive either alter or use a prescription which has been duly issued by a practitioner (which document is in this Act referred to as a duly issued prescription).

(3) A person shall not have in his possession either a forged prescription or a duly issued prescription which has been altered with intent to deceive.

Misuse of Drugs Act 1977, s 18

"FRONTIER POST"

Frontier Post.

"Frontier Post", in relation to an approved route, means the office maintained by the Revenue Commissioners for the transaction of Customs business in regard to goods being imported or exported by that route at a place mentioned in any of the columns headed "Location of Frontier Post" in the First Schedule to these Regulations opposite any mention of that route in any of the columns headed "Route", in that Schedule.

SI No 117/1968, art 4

"FUNDS"

" 'funds' has the meaning given by *section 12* of the *Act of 2005*.".

Criminal Justice Act 1994, s 3(1) inserted by Criminal Justice (Terrorist Offences) Act 2005, s 21

"funds" means—

(*a*) assets of every kind, whether tangible or intangible, movable or immovable, however acquired, and

(*b*) any legal document or instrument in any form, including electronic or digital, evidencing title to, or any interest in, any asset, including, but not limited to, a bank credit, traveller's cheque, bank cheque, money order, share, security, bond, draft and letter of credit.

Criminal Justice (Terrorist Offences) Act 2005, s 12

"FUNDS SUBJECT TO CONFISCATION"

" 'funds subject to confiscation' has the meaning given by section 8A(2) of this Act."

Criminal Justice Act 1994, s 3(1) inserted by Criminal Justice (Terrorist Offences) Act 2005, s 21

(2) For the purposes of this Act, funds subject to confiscation are—

(*a*) funds used or allocated for use in connection with an offence of financing terrorism, or

(*b*) funds that are the proceeds of such an offence.

Criminal Justice Act 1994, s 8A(2) inserted by Criminal Justice (Terrorist Offences) Act 2005, s 21

G

"GOODS"

Goods.

"goods" means goods of any description, whether intended for sale or not, and includes baggage, vehicles and farm produce.

SI No 117/1968, art 4

H

"HEALTH BOARD"

"health board" means a board established under section 4 of the Health Act, 1970 (No. 1 of 1970).

SI No 328/1988, s 3(1) AM TO HSE [Health Act, 2004 s 59 and Sch 3]

"HEALTH PRESCRIPTION"

"health prescription" and "health service requisition" means a prescription or a requisition issued in connection with arrangements made under section 59 of the Health Act, 1970 upon a form supplied by or on behalf of a health board.

SI No 328/1988, s 3

"HEALTH SERVICE PROVIDER"

'health service provider' means the Health Service Executive, a hospital, a nursing home, a clinic or other person whose sole or principal activity or business is the provision of health services, or a class of health services, to the public or a class of the public.

SI No 328/1988, s 3A(4) inserted by SI No 200/07, art 4

"HIGH CONTRACTING PARTIES"

THE HIGH CONTRACTING PARTIES to this Convention, Member States of the European Union.

Criminal Justice (Theft and Fraud Offences) Act 2001, sched 2, convention

I & J

"IMPORTER"

Importer.
Exporter.

"importer" and "exporter" mean respectively the owner or other person for the time being possessed of or beneficially interested in goods to which these Regulations apply at the time of the importation or exportation thereof, and include any person acting in relation thereto as agent for the owner or other person.

SI No 117/1968, art 4

"INDUSTRIAL MEDICAL ADVISER (OFFSORE INSTALLATIONS)"

"installation manager" "offshore installation" and "Industrial Medical Adviser (Offshore Installations)" have the same meaning as in the Safety, Health and Welfare (Offshore Installations) Act, 1987 (No. 18 of 1987).

SI No 328/1988, art 3(1)

The Minister may assign to any registered medical practitioner who stands designated under section 50 of the Act of 1980 as an industrial medical adviser the function of advising the Minister professionally in relation to his functions under this Act.

(2) A person to whom there is assigned under this section the functions described in *subsection (1)* of this section is in this Act referred to as an Industrial Medical Adviser (Offshore Installations)".

(3) Without prejudice to the generality of *section 40 (1)* of this Act, the Minister may authorise an Industrial Medical Adviser (Offshore Installations) to be an inspector for the purposes of this Act.

Safety Health and Welfare (Off Shore Installations) Act 1987, s 33

"INFRINGEMENTS"

'infringements': acts in conflict with national or Community customs provisions, including, inter alia:

— participation in, or attempts to commit, such infringements,
— participation in a criminal organization committing such infringements,
— the laundering of money deriving from the infringements referred to in this paragraph.

Customs and Excise (Mutual Assistance) Act 2001, sched 4, art 4(3)

"INSTALLATION MANAGER"

"installation manager" "offshore installation" and "Industrial Medical Adviser (Offshore Installations)" have the same meaning as in the Safety, Health and Welfare (Offshore Installations) Act, 1987 (No. 18 of 1987).

SI No 328/1988, art 3(1)

Every offshore installation which is an offshore installation to which the Act applies shall be under the charge of a person (in this Act referred to as an "installation manager") who shall be appointed in writing by the owner of the installation and in accordance with such regulations (if any) under this section as are for the time being in force.

(*b*) Regulations under this section may include requirements as to qualifications, experience, health or age.

(*c*) In making an appointment pursuant to the requirements of this subsection the person making the appointment shall appoint to be an installation manager a person who, to the best of his knowledge and belief, has the skills and competence suitable for the appointment.

(*d*) Where an installation manager is appointed, the person by whom the appointment is made shall, as soon as may be after the making of the appointment, inform the Minister in writing of the appointment.

(2) (*a*) The Minister, after consultation with the Minister for Energy, may make regulations relating to the duties of an installation manager concerning the safety, health and welfare of persons employed on, in or in the neighbourhood of an offshore installation.

(*b*) The proviso to *section 5 (1)* of this Act shall, with the necessary modifications, apply to regulations under this subsection.

(3) If at any time the owner of an offshore installation is satisfied that an installation manager appointed in pursuance of *subsection (1)* of this section does not have the requisite skills and competence, he shall terminate the appointment as soon as practicable, and shall, as soon as may be, give the Minister notice, in the form approved of for the time being for the purposes of this subsection by the Minister, of the action taken by him.

(4) It shall be the duty of the owner of an offshore installation, in order to ensure that an installation manager appointed under *subsection (1)* of this section is on the installation when it is manned, from time to time to place a person so appointed on the installation, and to ensure that he remains there until relieved, or for so long as it is manned.

Safety, Health and Welfare (Off Shore Installations) Act 1987, s 11

"INTEREST"

"interest", in relation to property, includes right.

Criminal Justice Act, 1994 s 3(1)

"INTERVENING STATE"

"Intervening State" means a State Party which has requested or proposes to request authorisation from another Party to take action under this Agreement in relation to a vessel flying the flag or displaying the marks of registry of that other State Party.

Criminal Justice (Illicit Traffic by Sea) Act 2003, sched, chp 1(A)

"IRISH MEDICINES BOARD"

"'Irish Medicines Board' means the Irish Medicines Board established under section 3 of the Irish Medicines Board Act 1995.".

Misuse of Drugs Act 1977 (as amended by s 2 of the Misuse of Drugs Act 1984) as amended by Irish Medicines Board (Miscellaneous Provisions) Act 2006, s 3

On the establishment day there shall stand established a board to be known as the Irish Medicines Board (in this Act referred to as "the Board") to perform the functions conferred on it by or under this Act.

(2) The Board shall be a body corporate with perpetual succession and an official seal and power to sue and be sued in its corporate name and, with the consent of the Minister, to acquire, hold and dispose of land or an interest in land and to acquire, hold and dispose of any other property.

(3) The Board shall, subject to the provisions of this Act, be independent in the exercise of its functions.

Irish Medicines Board Act 1995, s 3

L

"LAND"

"land" includes land covered wholly or partly with water.

Misuse of Drugs Act 1977, s 1(1)

(6) In this section

"land" includes any structure on land;

"structure" means building, structure or any other thing constructed, erected, placed or made on, in or under any land.

Customs and Excise (Miscellaneous Provisions) Act 1988, s 3(6)

"LAND FRONTIER"

"Land Frontier" means the frontier between the State and Northern Ireland.

SI No 117/1968, art 4

Land Frontier.

"Land Frontier" means the frontier between the State and Northern Ireland.

Customs and Excise (Miscellaneous Provisions) Act 1988, s 1(1)

"LETTER OF REQUEST"

Where on an application made in accordance with *subsection (2)* of this section it appears to a judge of any court—

(*a*) that an offence has been committed or that there are reasonable grounds for suspecting that an offence has been committed, and
(*b*) that proceedings in respect of the offence have been instituted or that the offence is being investigated,

he may issue a letter ("a letter of request") requesting assistance in obtaining outside the State such evidence as is specified in the letter for use in the proceedings or investigation.

Criminal Justice Act 1994, s 52(1)

M

"MARKET VALUE"

'market value', in relation to a controlled drug, means the price that drug could be expected to fetch on the market for the unlawful sale or supply of controlled drugs.

Misuse of Drugs Act 1977, s 15a(5) inserted by Criminal Justice Act 1999, s 4

"MASTER"

"master" has the same meaning as in the Acts relating to merchant shipping.

SI No 328/1988, s 3(1)

"MATERIAL TIME" SEE THE

"MATRON OR ACTING MATRON"

"matron or acting matron" includes any male nurse occupying a similar position.

SI No 328/1988, s 3(1)

"MEDICAL PREPARATION"

"medical preparation" has the same meaning as in section 65 of the Health Act, 1947 (No. 28 of 1947) as amended by section 39 of the Health Act, 1953 (No. 26 of 1953).

SI No 328/1988, s 3(1)

the expression "medical preparation" means—

(*a*) a substance which is sold under a proprietary designation and which may be used for the prevention or treatment of any human ailment, infirmity, injury or defect, or

(*b*) any other prophylactic, diagnostic or therapeutic substance which may be used for the prevention or treatment of any human ailment, infirmity, injury or defect.

HEALTH ACT 1947, s 65 as amended by Mental Health Act 1953, s 39

"MEDICAL REGISTRATION COUNCIL" SEE THE

"MEDICINAL OPIUM"

"medicinal opium" means raw opium which has undergone the process necessary to adapt it for medicinal use in accordance with the requirements of the Irish Pharmacopoeia, whether it is in the form of powder or is granulated or is in any other form, and whether it is or is not mixed with neutral substances.

Misuse of Drugs Act 1977, sched, s 6

"MUTUAL ASSISTANCE"

'mutual assistance': the granting of assistance between customs administrations as provided for in this Convention.

Customs and Excise (Mutual Assistance) Act 2001, sched 4, art 4(4)

N

"NATIONAL CUSTOM PROVISIONS"

'National customs provisions': all laws, regulations and administrative provisions of a Member State the application of which comes wholly or partly within the jurisdiction of the customs administration of that Member State concerning:

— cross-border traffic in goods subject to bans, restrictions or controls, in particular under Articles 36 and 223 of the Treaty establishing the European Community.

Customs and Excise (Mutual Assistance) Act 2001, sched 4, art 4(1)

"NATIONAL LAWS"

The term 'national laws' means laws or regulations of a Member State, in the application of which the customs administration of that Member State has total or partial competence, concerning:

— the movement of goods subject to measures of prohibition, restriction or control, in particular those measures covered by Articles 36 and 223 of the Treaty establishing the European Community;
— the transfer, conversion, concealment, or disguise of property or proceeds derived from, obtained directly or indirectly through or used in, illicit international drug trafficking.

Customs and Excise (Mutual Assistance) Act 2001, sched, art 1(1)

O

"OFFENCE OF FINANCING TERRORISM"

" 'offence of financing terrorism' means an offence under *section 13* of the *Act of 2005*.".

Criminal Justice Act 1994, s 3(1) inserted by Criminal Justice (Terrorist Offences) Act 2005, s 21

Subject to *subsections (6)* and *(7)*, a person is guilty of an offence if, in or outside the State, the person by any means, directly or indirectly, unlawfully and wilfully provides, collects or receives funds intending that they be used or knowing that they will be used, in whole or in part in order to carry out—

(*a*) an act that constitutes an offence under the law of the State and within the scope of, and as defined in, any treaty that is listed in the annex to the Terrorist Financing Convention, or
(*b*) an act (other than one referred to in *paragraph (a)*)—
  (i) that is intended to cause death or serious bodily injury to a civilian or to any other person not taking an active part in the hostilities in a situation of armed conflict, and
  (ii) the purpose of which is, by its nature or context, to intimidate a population or to compel a government or an international organisation to do or abstain from doing any act.

(2) Subject to *subsections (6)* and *(7)*, a person who attempts to commit an offence under *subsection (1)* is guilty of an offence.

(3) A person is guilty of an offence if the person by any means, directly or indirectly, unlawfully and wilfully provides, collects or receives funds intending that they be used or knowing that they will be used, in whole or in part—

(*a*) for the benefit or purposes of a terrorist group as defined in section 4, or
(*b*) in order to carry out an act (other than one referred to in *paragraph (a)* or *(b)* of *subsection (1)*) that is an offence under section 6.

(4) A person who attempts to commit an offence under *subsection (3)* is guilty of an offence.

(5) An offence may be committed under *subsection (1)* or *(3)* whether or not the funds are used to carry out an act referred to in *subsection (1)* or *(3)(b)*, as the case may be.

(6) *Subsections (1)* and *(2)* apply to an act committed outside the State if the act—

(*a*) is committed on board an Irish ship,
(*b*) is committed on an aircraft registered in or operated by the State,
(*c*) is committed by a citizen of Ireland or by a stateless person habitually resident in the State,
(*d*) is directed towards or results in the carrying out of an act referred to in *subsection (1)* in the State or against a citizen of Ireland,
(*e*) is directed towards or results in the carrying out of an act referred to in *subsection (1)* against a State or Government facility of the State abroad, including an embassy or other diplomatic or consular premises of the State, or
(*f*) is directed towards or results in the carrying out of an act referred to in *subsection (1)* in an attempt to compel the State to do or abstain from doing any act.

(7) *Subsections (1)* and *(2)* apply also to an act committed outside the State in circumstances other than those referred to in *subsection (6)*, but in that case the Director of Public Prosecutions may not take, or consent to the taking of, proceedings referred to in *section 43 (2)* for an offence in respect of that act except as authorised by *section 43 (3)*.

Criminal Justice (Terrorist Offences) Act 2005, s 13

"OFFICER"

Officer.

"Officer" means an officer of Customs and Excise or any person acting under the orders of such officer, or any member of the Garda Síochána or Defence Forces assisting such officer.

SI No 117/1968, art 4

"OFFICER OF THE STATE LABORATORY"

In this section "officer of the State Laboratory" means the State Chemist or a person acting under his direction.

Customs and Excise (Miscellaneous Provisions) Act 1988, s 4(2)

"OFFICERS OF CUSTOMS AND EXCISE"

"officer of Customs and Excise" includes a member of the Garda Síochána and any person in the public service who is for the time being employed in the prevention of the illegal importation or exportation of goods.

Customs and Excise (Miscellaneous Provisions) Act 1988, s 1(1)

the expression "officer of customs and excise" includes a member of the Gárda Síochána and any person in the public service who is for the time being employed in the prevention of the illegal importation or exportation of goods.

Customs (Amendment) Act 1942, s 1

"officer of Customs and Excise" includes a member of the Garda Síochána and any person in the public service who is for the time being employed in the prevention of the illegal importation or exportation of goods.

Customs Act 1956, s 1

"OFFICIAL HOURS"

Official hours.

8. The days on and the hours during which Customs Stations and Frontier Posts shall be open for the transaction of Customs business shall be as prescribed or allowed by the Revenue Commissioners, either generally or in regard to a particular Customs Station or Frontier Post.

SI No 117/1968, art 8

"OFFSHORE INSTALLATION"

"offshore installation" and "Industrial Medical Adviser (Offshore Installations)" have the same meaning as in the Safety, Health and Welfare (Offshore Installations) Act, 1987 (No. 18 of 1987).

SI No 328/1988, art 3(1)

"offshore installation" means any installation which is or has been maintained, or is intended to be established, for the exploration for or exploitation of minerals and includes any installation providing accommodation for persons who work on or from any such offshore installation so engaged in exploration or exploitation of minerals.

Safety Health and Welfare (Offshore Installation) Act 1987, s 2(1)

"OPIUM POPPY"

"'opium poppy' means a plant of the species Papaver *somniferum L* or *Papaver bracteatum Lindl.*".

Misuse of Drugs Act 1977, s 1(1) amended by Misuse of Drugs Act 1984, s 2(b)

"ORDINARY MERCHANDISE"

Ordinary merchandise.

"ordinary merchandise" means goods other than exempt farm produce, baggage, authorised motor vehicles and exempt vehicles.

SI No 117/1968, art 4

"OUTER LIMIT OF THE TERRITORIAL SEAS"

"outer limit of the territorial seas" has the meaning given to that expression by the Maritime Jurisdiction Acts 1959 to 1988.

Criminal Justice (Illicit Traffic by Sea) Act 2003, s 1(1)

Section 3 (which specifies the outer limit of the territorial seas) of the Principal act is hereby amended by the substitution of "12 nautical miles" for "three nautical miles" and the said section 3, as so amended, is set out in *Part I* of the Table to this section.

(2) Section 4 (which specifies the baseline) of the Principal act is hereby amended by the substitution in paragraph (*b*) of subsection (1) of "12 nautical miles" for "three nautical miles" and the said paragraph (*b*), as so amended, is set out in *Part II* of the Table to this section.

(3) Section 14 (which provides for the adaptation of enactments) of the Principal act is hereby amended by the insertion in subsection (1) after "three miles" of "three nautical miles" and the said subsection (1), as so amended, is set out in *Part III* of the Table to this section.

TABLE

PART I

3. For the purposes of this Act, the outer limit of the territorial seas is the line every point of which is at a distance of 12 nautical miles from the nearest point of the baseline.

PART II

(*b*) on any low-tide elevation situated wholly or partly at a distance not exceeding 12 nautical miles from the mainland or an island.

PART III

(1) References in any enactment to sea areas and waters within three miles, three nautical miles or one league of the coast or shore and cognate expressions shall be construed as references to sea areas and waters lying within the outer limit of the territorial seas.

Maritime Jurisdiction (Amendment) Act 1988, s 2(1)

P

"PARTIES"

'Parties' means the Member States of the European Union, parties to this Agreement.

Customs and Excise (Mutual Assistance) Act 2001, sched 2, art 1

"PERMISSION TO USE UNAPPROVED ROADS"

Permission to use unapproved routes.

(1) The Revenue Commissioners may permit the importation or exportation of any goods by a route other than an approved route and may attach to such permission such conditions as they see fit and a person availing himself of such permission shall be deemed not to contravene Article 6 of these Regulations so long as he shall comply with such conditions.

(2) An exempt vehicle may be moved into or out of the State by any route at any time.

SI 117/1968, art 7

"PERSON KEEPING OPEN SHOP"

"person keeping open shop for the dispensing or compounding of medical prescriptions or for the sale of poisons" has the same meaning as in Regulation 3 of the Regulations of 1988.

SI No 225/1998, art 2(1)

person keeping open shop for the dispensing or compounding of medical prescriptions or for the sale of poisons" means a person lawfully keeping open shop for the dispensing or compounding of medical prescriptions or for the sale of poisons under the Pharmacy Acts 1875-1977 as amended by the European Communities (Recognition of Qualifications in Pharmacy) Regulations, 1987 (S.I. No. 239 of 1987).

SI No 328/1988, art 3(1)

"PERSONAL DATA"

The term 'personal data' means any information relating to an identified or identifiable individual.

Customs and Excise (Mutual Assistance) Act 2001, sched 1, art 1(2)

'personal data': all information relating to an identified or identifiable natural person; a person is considered to be identifiable if he or she can be directly or indirectly identified, inter alia by means of an identification number or of one or more specific elements which are characteristic of his or her physical, physiological, psychological, economic, cultural or social identity.

Customs and Excise (Mutual Assistance) Act 2001, sched 4, art 4(8)

"PHARMACIST"

"pharmacist" means a registered pharmaceutical chemist, a registered dispensing chemist and druggist and a registered druggist.

Misuse of Drugs Act 1977, s 1(1)

"PIPELINE"

In this section "pipeline" means a pipe together with any apparatus and works associated therewith, or system of pipes together with any apparatus or works associated therewith, used for the conveyance of goods into or out of the State.

Customs and Excise (Miscellaneous Provisions) Act 1988, s 13(3)

"PLACE OF DETENTION"

The Minister may make regulations prescribing specified places as places where a person may be detained pursuant to *subsection (1) (b)*, and a place for the time being standing so specified is referred to in this Act as a "place of detention".

Criminal Justice (Drug Trafficking) Act 1996, s 2(9)(a)

"POPPY STRAW"

"poppy straw" means all parts, except the seeds, of the opium poppy, after mowing.

Misuse of Drugs Act 1977, Sched, art 6

"PRACTITIONER"

"practitioner" means a registered medical practitioner, a registered dentist and a registered veterinary surgeon.

Misuse of Drugs Act 1977, s 1(1)

"'practitioner' means —

(a) a registered medical practitioner, a registered dentist or a registered veterinary surgeon, or
(b) subject to *article 3A*, a registered nurse.

SI No 328/1988, art 3(1) substituted by SI No 200/2007, art 3

"PREFERENTIAL JURISDICTION"

"Preferential jurisdiction" means, in relation to a flag State having concurrent jurisdiction over a relevant offence with another State, the right to exercise its jurisdiction on a priority basis, to the exclusion of the exercise of the other State's jurisdiction over the offence.

Criminal Justice (Illicit Traffic by Sea) Act 2003, sched, chap 1(b)

"PREMISES"

"premises" includes any building or any part of a building and any vehicle, vessel or structure.

Criminal Justice Act 1994, s 3(1)

"PREPARED OPIUM"

"prepared opium" means opium prepared for smoking and includes dross and any other residues remaining after opium has been smoked.

Misuse of Drugs Act 1977, s 1(1)

"PRESCRIBED"

"prescribed" means prescribed by regulations made by the Minister under this Act.

Misuse of Drugs Act 1977, s 1(1)

"PRESCRIBED SUM" SEE THE

"PRESCRIPTION"

'prescription' means a prescription issued by—

(*a*) a registered medical practitioner for the medical treatment of an individual,
(*b*) a registered dentist for the dental treatment of an individual,
(*c*) a registered veterinary surgeon for the purposes of animal treatment, or
(*d*) subject to *article 3A*, a registered nurse for the medical treatment of an individual.".

SI No 328/1988, art 3(1) substituted by SI No 200/2007, art 3

"PRISON"

'prison' means a place of custody administered by the Minister for Justice, Equality and Law Reform and includes Saint Patrick's Institution and a place of detention provided under section 2 of the Prisons Act 1970, and 'prison officer', in relation to a prison, shall be construed accordingly.".

Misuse of Drugs Act 1977, s 15C(8) inserted by Criminal Justice Act 2006, s 83

"PROCEEDS OF DRUG TRAFFICKING"

"proceeds of drug trafficking" has the meaning assigned to it by *section 5 (1) (a)* of this Act.

Criminal Justice Act 1994, s 3(1)

For the purposes of this Act—

(*a*) any payments or other rewards received by a person at any time (whether before or after the commencement of *section 4* of this Act) in connection with drug trafficking carried on by him or another are his proceeds of drug trafficking, and

(*b*) the value of his proceeds of drug trafficking is the aggregate of the values of the payments or other rewards.

Criminal Justice Act 1994, s 5(1)(a) and (b)

"PRODUCE"

"produce", where the reference is to producing a controlled drug, means producing it by cultivation, manufacture, synthesis or by any other method.

SI No 328/1988, art 3(1)

"PROHIBITED GOODS"

that the expression "prohibited goods" where it occurs in sections 172, 182, 202, 204 and 205, respectively, of the Customs Consolidation Act, 1876, includes and always included goods the export of which is prohibited as well as goods the import of which is prohibited and that section 19 (amending the said section

205) of the Finance Act, 1936 (No. 31 of 1936), has and always had effect accordingly, and

(*b*) that every act which is declared by section 12 of the Customs and Inland Revenue Act, 1881, to be an offence is and always was an offence under that section whether done in relation to the illegal exportation or attempted exportation of goods or the illegal importation or attempted importation of goods.

Customs (Amendment) Act 1942, s 2

"PROPERTY"

" 'property' includes money and all other property, real or personal, heritable or moveable, including choses-in-action and other intangible or incorporeal property and, in relation to an offence of financing terrorism, includes funds.".

Criminal Justice Act 1994, s 3(1) substituted by the Criminal Justice (Terrorist Offences) Act 2005, s 21(e)

"1996 PROTOCOL" SEE THE

"1999 PROTOCOL:" SEE THE

R

"RAW OPIUM"

"raw opium" includes powdered or granulated opium but does not include medicinal opium.

Misuse of Drugs Act 1977, sched, art 6

"REAL VALUE"

'real value' means the value of the defendant's funds subject to confiscation which relate to an offence of financing terrorism committed either in the period by reference to which the current determination was made or in any earlier period.

Criminal Justice Act 1994, s 8E(3) inserted by Criminal Justice (Terrorist Offences) Act 2005, s 22

"REALISABLE PROPERTY"

"realisable property" means—

(*a*) any property held by the defendant, and
(*b*) any property held by a person to whom the defendant has directly or indirectly made a gift caught by this Act,

but does not include property which is the subject of—

(*a*) an order under section 30 of the Misuse of Drugs Act, 1977 (forfeiture orders), or
(*b*) an order under *section 61* of this Act.

Criminal Justice Act 1994, s 3(1)

"RECEIVER"

"receiver" means a person appointed as a receiver under *section 20 (2)* or *24 (7)* of this Act.

Criminal Justice Act 1994, s 3(1)

"RECIPIENT" SEE THE

"RECKLESS"

'reckless' shall be construed in accordance with section 16 *(2)* of the *Criminal Justice (Theft and Fraud Offences) Act, 2001*.

Criminal Justice Act 1994, s 31(7)(a)(ii) substituted by Criminal Justice (Theft and Fraud Offences) Act 2001, s 21

For the purposes of this Part, a person is reckless if he or she disregards a substantial risk that the property handled is stolen, and for those purposes "substantial risk" means a risk of such a nature and degree that, having regard to the circumstances in which the person acquired the property and the extent of the information then available to him or her, its disregard involves culpability of a high degree.

Criminal Justice (Theft and Fraud Offences) Act 2001, s 16(2)

"REGISTER"

"register" means a bound book and does not include any form of loose leaf register or card index.

SI No 328/1988, rt 3(1)

"REGISTRATION AUTHORITY"

"registration authority" means such one of the following as the context requires namely, the Dental Board, the Medical Registration Council and the Veterinary Council.

Misuse of Drugs Act 1977, s 1(1)

"REGISTERED DENTIST"

"registered dentist" means a person registered in the register established under the Dentists Act, 1928.

Misuse of Drugs Act 1977, s 1(1)

"REGISTERED DISPENSING CHEMIST"

"registered dispensing chemist and druggist" means a person registered in the register of dispensing chemists and druggists established under the Pharmacy Act, 1951.

Misuse of Drugs Act 1977, s 1(1)

"REGISTERED DRUGGIST"

"registered druggist" means a person registered in the register of registered druggists in Ireland established under the Pharmacy Act (Ireland) 1875, Amendment Act 1890.

Misuse of Drugs Act 1977, s 1(1)

"REGISTERED MEDICAL PRACTITIONER"

"registered medical practitioner" means a person registered in the register established under the Medical Practitioners Act, 1927.

Misuse of Drugs Act 1977, s 1(1)

"REGISTERED NURSE"

"'registered nurse' means a person whose name is entered in the register of nurses maintained by An Bord Altranais under section 27 of the Nurses Act 1985.".

Misuse of Drugs Act 1977, s 1(1) inserted by Irish Medicines Board (Miscellaneous Provisions) Act 2006, s 3

"REGISTERED PHARMACEUTICAL CHEMIST"

"registered pharmaceutical chemist" means a person registered in the register of pharmaceutical chemists for Ireland established under the Pharmacy Act (Ireland), 1875.

Misuse of Drugs Act 1977, s 1(1)

"REGISTERED VETERINARY SURGEON"

"registered veterinary surgeon" means a person registered in the register established under the Veterinary Surgeons Act, 1931.

Misuse of Drugs Act 1977, s 1(1)

"RELEVANT INVESTIGATION"

'relevant investigation' means an investigation of a kind referred to in subsection (1) of section 63 of this Act.

Criminal Justice Act 1994, s 63A(1) inserted by Disclosure of Certain Information for Taxation and Other Purposes Act 1996, s 1

A member of the Garda Síochána may, for the purpose of an investigation into drug trafficking or an offence under *section 31* of this Act or an investigation into whether a person has benefited from drug trafficking or an offence in respect of which a confiscation order might be made under *section 9* of this Act, apply to a judge of the District Court for an order under *subsection (2)* of this section in relation to any particular material or material of a particular description.

Criminal Justice Act 1994, s 63(1)

"RELEVANT OFFENCE"

"Relevant offence" means any offence of the kind described in Article 3, paragraph 1, of the Vienna Convention.

Criminal Justice (Illicit Traffic by Sea) Act 2003, sched, chap 1(c)

"RELEVANT PERSON"

'relevant person' means—

(*a*) a member of the Garda Síochána not below the rank of Chief Superintendent, or

(*b*) the head of any body, or any member of that body nominated by the head of the body, being a body established by or under statute or by the Government, the purpose. or one of the principal purposes of which is—

(i) the identification of the assets of persons which derive or are suspected to derive, directly or indirectly, from criminal activity,

(ii) the taking of appropriate action under the law to deprive or to deny those persons of the assets or the benefit of such assets, in whole or in part, as may be appropriate, and

(III) the pursuit of any investigation or the doing of any other preparatory work in relation to any proceedings arising from the objectives mentioned in *subparagraphs (i)* and *(ii)*.

Criminal Justice Act 1994, s 63A(1) inserted by Disclosure of Certain Information for Taxation and Other Purposes Act 1996, s 1

"RELEVANT TIME"

"relevant time" means—

(*a*) where no order for the winding up of the company has been made, the time of the passing of the resolution for voluntary winding up,

(*b*) where such an order has been made and, before the presentation of the petition for the winding up of the company by the court, such a resolution had been passed by the company, the time of the passing of the resolution, and

(*c*) in any other case where such an order has been made, the time of the making of the order.

Criminal Justice Act 1994, s 30(3)

"REQUESTED AUTHORITY"

'requested authority': the competent authority of the Member State to which a request for assistance is made.

Customs and Excise (Mutual Assistance) Act 2001, sched 4, art 4(6)

"RESPONDENT" SEE THE

"RESTRAINT ORDER" (FREEZING ORDER)

The High Court may by order (in this Act referred to as a "restraint order") prohibit any person from dealing with any realisable property, subject to such conditions and exceptions as may be specified in that order.

(2) Without prejudice to the generality of *subsection (1)* of this section, a restraint order may make such provision as the court thinks fit for living expenses and legal expenses.

(3) A restraint order may apply—

(*a*) to all realisable property held by a specified person, whether the property is described in the order or not, and
(*b*) to realisable property held by a specified person, being property transferred to him after the making of the order.

(4) A restraint order—

(*a*) may be made only on an application by the Director of Public Prosecutions, which may be made *ex parte* and otherwise than in public, and
(*b*) shall provide for notice to be given to persons affected by the order.

(5) A restraint order—

(*a*) may be discharged or varied in relation to any property, and
(*b*) shall be discharged on the conclusion of the proceedings or of the application in question.

(6) An application for the discharge or variation of a restraint order may be made by any person affected by it.

(7) Where the High Court has made a restraint order, the court may at any time appoint a receiver—

(*a*) to take possession of any realisable property, and
(*b*) in accordance with the court's directions, to manage or otherwise deal with any property in respect of which he is appointed,

subject to such exceptions and conditions as may be specified by the court, and may require any person having possession or control of property in respect of which a receiver is appointed under this section to give possession of it to the receiver.

(8) For the purposes of this Act, dealing with property held by any person includes (without prejudice to the generality of the expression)—

(*a*) where a debt is owed to that person, making a payment to any person in reduction of the amount of the debt, and
(*b*) removing the property from the State.

(9) Where the High Court has made a restraint order, a member of the Garda Síochána or an officer of customs and excise may, for the purpose of preventing any realisable property being removed from the State, seize the property.

(10) Property seized under *subsection (9)* of this section shall be dealt with in accordance with the court's directions.

Criminal Justice Act 1994, s 24

NOTE: NOW KNOWN AS A FREEZING ORDER PURSUANT TO CRIMINAL JUSTICE (MUTUAL ASSISTANCE) ACT 2008, s 105

"RESTRICTION ON MOVEMENTS"

Restrictions on movement.

6. Save as otherwise provided in these Regulations, no person shall import or export, or attempt to import or export, or be concerned in the importation or exportation of, or in an attempt to import or export, any goods by a route other than an approved route.

SI No 117/1968, art 6

"REVENUE OFFENCE"

In this section 'revenue offences' means an offence in connection with taxes, duties or exchange control.".

Criminal Justice Act 1994, s 56A(2) inserted by Criminal Justice (Miscellaneous Provisions) Act 1997, s 15(b) amended by Criminal Justice (Theft and Fraud Offences) Act 2001, s 22

"ROUTE"

Each route mentioned in any of the columns headed "Route" in the First Schedule to these Regulations shall be an approved route only for the purpose or purposes mentioned in the heading or headings to the Part or Parts of that Schedule in which that route is mentioned.

SI No 117/1968, art 5

FIRST SCHEDULE

PART I.

ROUTES APPROVED—

(*a*) for the importation of goods of every description, and
(*b*) for the exportation of goods of every description except live pigs, sheep or attested cattle.

Route	Location of Frontier Post	Location of Customs Station
(1)	(2)	(3)
Road from Newry to Greenore.	Ferryhill.	Greenore.
Road from Newry to Dundalk via Killeen.	Carrickcarnan.	Dundalk.
Road from Armagh to Dundalk via Newtown-hamilton.	Drumbilla.	Dundalk.
Railway line from Belfast to Dundalk.	Dundalk Railway Station except for trains running non-stop in either direction between Belfast and Dublin and carrying only passengers and their baggage, newspapers and mails.	Dundalk Railway Station.
Road from Armagh to Castleblaney.	Tullynagrow.	Castleblaney.
Road from Armagh to Monaghan.	Tyholland.	Monaghan.
Road from Aughnacloy to Monaghan.	Moybridge.	Monaghan.
Road from Enniskillen to Clones.	Clones.	Clones.

Road from Enniskillen to Swanlinbar.	Swanlinbar.	Swanlinbar.
Road from Enniskillen to Manorhamilton.	Blacklion.	Manorhamilton.
Road from Enniskillen to Ballyshannon via Belleek.	Cloghore.	Ballyshanon.
Road from Strabane to Lifford.	{Lifford Strabane} Bridge.	Lifford.
Road from Derry to St. Johnston.	Carrigans.	St. Johnson.
Road from Derry to Bridgend.	Bridgend.	Bridgend.
Road from Derry to Muff.	Muff.	Muff.

PART II.

ROUTES APPROVED—

(*a*) for the importation of goods not liable to any duty or to any prohibition or restriction on importation;
(*b*) for the exportation of goods (other than live pigs, sheep or attested cattle), not liable to any duty or prohibition or restriction on exportation; and
(*c*) for the importation and exportation of authorised motor vehicles and baggage.

Route (1)	Location of Frontier Post (2)
Road from Crossmaglen to Carrickmacross via Culloville Bridge.	Culloville Bridge.
Road from Rosslea to Monaghan via Inishammon.	Inishammon.
Road from Derrylin to Belturbet via Aghalane Bridge.	Aghalane Bridge.
Road from Kesh to Pettigo.	Pettigo.
Road from Castlederg to Castlefin via Kilclean.	Kilclean.
Road from Derry to Newtown Cunningham via Kildrum.	Kildrum.

PART III.

ROUTE APPROVED FOR RAILWAY TRAINS RUNNING NON-STOP IN EITHER DIRECTION BETWEEN BELFAST AND DUBLIN AND CARRYING ONLY PASSENGERS AND THEIR BAGGAGE, NEWSPAPERS AND MAILS.

Route	Location of Frontier Post
(1)	(2)
Railway line from Belfast to Dublin.	Connolly Railway Station, Dublin.

PART IV.

ROUTES APPROVED FOR THE EXPORTATION OF LIVE PIGS, SHEEP OR ATTESTED CATTLE.

Route	Location of Customs Station	Location of Frontier Post
(1)	(2)	(3)
Road from Dundalk to Newry.	Dundalk.	Carrickcarnan.
Railway line from Dundalk to Belfast.	Dundalk Railway Station.	Dundalk Railway Station.
Road from Castleblaney to Keady.	Castleblaney.	Tullynagrow.
Road from Monaghan to Armagh.	Monaghan.	Tyholland.
Road from Monaghan to Aughnacloy.	Monaghan.	Moybridge.
Road from Clones to Newtownbutler.	Clones.	Clones.
Road from Swanlinbar to Enniskillen.	Swanlinbar.	Swanlinbar.
Road from Manorhamilton to Enniskillen.	Manorhamilton.	Blacklion.
Road from Ballyshannon to Belleek.	Ballyshannon.	Cloghore.
Road from Pettigo to Kesh.	Ballyshannon.	Pettigo.
Road from Lifford to Strabane.	Lifford.	{Lifford Strabane} Bridge.

Road from Carrigans to Derry.	St. Johnston.	Carrigans.
Road from Muff to Derry.	Muff.	Muff.

SI 117/1968, 1st schedule

S

"SHIP"

"ship" includes any vessel used in navigation;

["'ship' includes a hovercraft or submersible craft, any vessel used in navigation and any other floating craft of any description.".]

Criminal Justice Act 1994, amended by the Criminal Justice (Illicit Traffic by Sea) Act 2003, s 28

"SHIP" SEE UNDER THE

"SISTER OR ACTING SISTER"

"sister or acting sister" includes any male nurse occupying a similar position.

SI No 328/1988, art 3(1)

"SPECIAL DIRECTION"

"special direction" has the meaning assigned to it by section 7 (2) of this Act.

Misuse of Drugs Act 1977, s 1

If the Minister believes that a practitioner is or has been, after the commencement of this section, prescribing, administering or supplying, or authorising the administration or supply of any controlled drug in an irresponsible manner, subject to the provisions of this Act, he may give a direction in respect of the practitioner prohibiting him prescribing, administering or supplying or authorising the administration or supply of such controlled drugs as may be specified in the direction.

(2) A direction given pursuant to this section (in this Act subsequently referred to as a special direction) shall come into force when a copy of it is given to the practitioner to whom it relates and, subject to subsection (3) of this section and section 11 (1) of this Act, the special direction shall remain in operation until it is cancelled.

(3) The Minister may, after consultation with the registration authority concerned, suspend the operation of a special direction.

(4) The Minister may, after consultation with the registration authority concerned, cancel a special direction.

(5) Where the Minister suspends the operation of or cancels a special direction, he shall cause notice to that effect to be given to the practitioner to whom the special direction applies and, as soon as may be, cause notice of the suspension or cancellation to be published in the *Iris Oifigiúil*.

(6) A person who contravenes a special direction shall be guilty of an offence.

Misuse of Drugs Act 1977, s 7

"SPECIFIED CONTROLLED DRUG"

"specified controlled drug" means a drug specified in the Schedule of these Regulations.

Regulation 2

1. Methadone.
2. Any steroisomeric form of a substance specified in paragraph (1).
3. Any salt of a substance specified in paragraph 1 or 2.
4. Any preparation or other product containing any proportion of a substance or product specified in paragraphs 1, 2 or 3.

SI No 225/1998, art 2(1) and sched

"STATE CHEMIST" SEE UNDER THE

"STATUTORY INSTRUMENT"

"statutory instrument" means an instrument for the time being in force being—

(*a*) an order made (whether before or after the passing of this Act) in exercise of powers conferred by any enactment, or

(*b*) an order made (whether before or after the passing of this Act) or a direction in writing given (whether before or after the passing of this Act) in exercise of powers conferred by an order made in exercise of powers conferred by any enactment.

Customs Act 1956, s 1

"STRUCTURE"

"structure" means building, structure or any other thing constructed, erected, placed or made on, in or under any land.

Customs and Excise (Miscellaneous Provisions) Act 1988, s 3(6)

"SUPPLIER" SEE UNDER THE

"SUPPLY"

"supply" includes giving without payment.

Misuse of Drugs Act 1977, s 1

"SUPPLYING MEMBER STATE"

The term 'supplying Member State' means a State which includes an item of data in the Customs Information System.

Customs and Excise (Mutual Assistance) Act 2001, sched 1, art 1(3)

T

"TEMPORARY DIRECTION"

"'temporary direction' means a direction under section 9 of this Act.".

Misuse of Drugs Act 1977, s 1(1) amended by Misuse of Drugs Act 1984, s 2

If the Minister considers that there are grounds for giving a special direction and that the circumstances of the case require such direction to be given as a matter of urgency, subject to subsections (3) to (7) of this section, he may give the special direction by virtue of this section.

(2) A special direction given by virtue of this section (subsequently in this Act referred to as a temporary direction) may specify such controlled drugs as the Minister thinks fit.

(3) Where the Minister proposes to give a temporary direction the following provisions shall apply:

(*a*) he shall refer the case to an advisory panel constituted for the purpose in accordance with any regulations made under section 12 of this Act which apply to it,
(*b*) it shall be the duty of the advisory panel, after affording the respondent an opportunity of appearing before and being heard by the panel, to consider the circumstances of the case, so far as known to it, and inform the Minister whether the information before the panel appears to it to afford reasonable grounds for considering that there has been such conduct by the respondent as is mentioned in section 7 (1) of this Act, and
(*c*) the Minister shall not give a temporary direction unless the advisory panel reports that the information before it appears to it to afford reasonable grounds for so considering.

(4) Where the Minister gives a temporary direction he shall, if he has not already done so, forthwith refer the matter for investigation to—

(*a*) in case the practitioner to whom the temporary direction relates is a registered dentist, the Dental Board,
(*b*) in case such practitioner is a registered medical practitioner, the Medical Registration Council,
(*c*) in case such practitioner is a registered veterinary surgeon, the Veterinary Council,

and the following provisions of section 8 of this Act, namely, the proviso to subsection (1), and subsections (2) to (11), shall apply in relation to the matter as if the matter were being referred under the said subsection (1).

(5) Subject to subsections (6) and (7) of this section, a temporary direction shall come into force when a copy thereof is given to the practitioner to whom it relates and shall remain in operation until—

(*a*) in case no notice relating to the direction is served pursuant to subsection (6) of this section, the expiration of the period of six weeks commencing on the day on which the direction is given, and
(*b*) in case such a notice is served, the expiration of the period of twenty-eight days to which the notice relates.

(6) Where a temporary direction has been given, at any time after the matter has been referred for investigation to a registration authority the Minister may, having consulted the authority, from time to time, by notice in writing served on the practitioner to

whom the temporary direction applies and while it is in operation, extend or further extend the period of operation of the temporary direction for a further twenty-eight days from the time at which that period would otherwise have ended.

(7) Without prejudice to subsection (5) of this section, a temporary direction shall (unless previously cancelled under this section) cease to have effect on the occurrence of any one of the following:

(*a*) the service of a notice required to be served by section 8 (3) of this Act, as applied by subsection (4) of this section, and relating to the case,
(*b*) the service of a notice required to be served by section 8 (5) of this Act, as so applied, relating to the case and stating that the Minister does not propose to give a special direction,
(*c*) the service pursuant to section 8 (11) of this Act of a copy of a direction relating to the case,
(*d*) the making by the Minister of a decision pursuant to section 8 (8) (*c*) of this Act and relating to the case.

(8) The Minister may, after consultation with the advisory panel concerned, suspend the operation of a temporary direction for such period as he considers appropriate in the particular case.

(9) The Minister may, after consultation with the registration authority concerned, cancel a temporary direction.

(10) Where the Minister suspends the operation of or cancels a temporary direction he shall cause to be served on the practitioner concerned a notice of the suspension or cancellation.

(11) Where—

(*a*) a temporary direction is given, cancelled, suspended, or ceases to have effect by virtue of subsection (7) of this section, or
(*b*) a notice is served pursuant to subsection (6) of this section,

the Minister shall, as soon as may be, cause to be published in the *Iris Oifigiúil* a notice of the temporary direction, cancellation, suspension or cesser, or of the service of the notice pursuant to the said subsection (6), as may be appropriate.

Misuse of Drugs Act 1977, s 9

"TEMPORARY IMPORTATION PERMIT"

Temporary importation permit.

"temporary importation permit" means a temporary importation permit issued under the Motor Vehicles (Temporary Importation) Regulations, 1967 (S.I. No. 220 of 1967).

SI No 117/1968, art 4

Temporary importation permit.

"Temporary Importation Permit" means a permit which authorises the importation without payment of customs duty of the motor vehicle to which it relates, bears such particulars as the Revenue Commissioners may deem necessary for the identification of the vehicle and is stamped by the officer with the date of issue, and includes a temporary importation permit issued under the Motor Vehicles (Temporary Importation) Regulations, 1965 (S.I. No. 87 of 1965).

SI No 220/1967, art 3

(1) Where a qualified person presents for importation a motor vehicle to which this Article applies, the vehicle shall be admitted under a Temporary Importation Permit and a Control Form each stamped by the officer with the date of issue and bearing such particulars as the Revenue Commissioners may deem necessary for the identification of the vehicle and the qualified person shall not be required to pay at the time of importation any customs duty that, but for these Regulations, would be chargeable on the vehicle.

(2) A motor vehicle to which this Article applies shall while in the State comply with the following conditions:

- (i) it may not be loaned, sold, hired, given away' exchanged or used for the carriage of persons for reward, and, if it is a commercial vehicle, it may be used only for private use;
- (ii) save as permitted by the Revenue Commissioners, it may not be driven by any person other than the importer.

(3) Notwithstanding paragraph 2 of this Article, a vehicle other than a commercial vehicle which at the time of importation is the subject of a temporary hiring contract entered into by the importer may, with the permission of the Revenue Commissioners, be re-hired once only to a qualified person; provided that the re-hiring is effected through a person whose business in the State is or includes the letting out of vehicles for hire and whose only or principal place of business and principal place of residence are within the State.

(4) Where a motor vehicle has been re-hired under paragraph (3) of this Article, the person to whom the vehicle is so re-hired shall be deemed, for the purposes of these Regulations, to be the importer of the vehicle.

(5) This Article applies to any motor vehicle designed and constructed solely or primarily for the carriage of persons and to a commercial vehicle when imported for private use, but does not apply to an omnibus, a hackney carriage, a hearse, a commercial trailer, any other commercial vehicle of an unladen weight exceeding 25 cwts., or to an unregistered motor vehicle being imported solely for a purpose not involving its being driven on a public road in the State.

SI No 87/1965, art 7

"THE ACTS RELATING TO MERCHANT SHIPPING"

"the Acts relating to merchant shipping" means the Merchant Shipping Acts, 1894 to 1983 and the Mercantile Marine Act, 1955 (No. 29 of 1955).

SI No 328/1988, art 3(1)

"THE AGREEMENT"

"the Agreement" means the Agreement on provisional application between certain Member States of the European Union of the Convention drawn up on the basis of Article K.3 of the Treaty on European Union on the use of information technology for customs purposes done at Brussels on the 26th day of July, 1995.

Customs and Excise (Mutual Assistance) Act 2001, s 1(1)

"THE CIS CONVENTION"

"the CIS Convention" means the Convention, drawn up on the basis of Article K.3 of the Treaty on European Union, on the use of information technology for customs purposes, done at Brussels on the 26th day of July, 1995, as amended by the 1999 Protocol.

Customs and Excise (Mutual Assistance) Act 2001, s 1(1)

"THE CURRENT DETERMINATION"

This section applies where a court has made a determination under *section 4 (4)* of this Act of the amount to be recovered in a particular case by virtue of that section referred to in this section as "the current determination".

Criminal Justice Act 1994, s 8(1)

"THE CUSTOMS CO-OPERATION CONVENTION"

"the Customs Co-operation Convention" means the Convention, drawn up on the basis of Article K.3 of the Treaty on European Union, on mutual assistance and co-operation between customs administrations, done at Brussels on the 18th day of December, 1997.

Customs and Excise (Mutual Assistance) Act 2001, s 1(1)

"THE DENTAL BOARD"

"the Dental Board" means the Dental Board established under the Dentists Act, 1928.

Misuse of Drugs Act 1977, s 1(1)

"THE MATERIAL TIME"

References in this Act to the value at any time (referred to in *subsection (5)* of this section as "the material time") of a person's proceeds of drug trafficking or, as the case may be, of any property obtained by a person as a result of or in connection with the commission of an offence other than a drug trafficking offence are references to—

(*a*) the value of the said proceeds or property to the recipient when he obtained them or it, adjusted to take account of subsequent changes in the value of money, or

(*b*) where *subsection (5)* of this section applies, the value there mentioned,

whichever is the greater.

Criminal Justice Act 1994, s 3(4)

"THE MEDICAL REGISTRATION COUNCIL"

"the Medical Registration Council" means the Medical Registration Council established under the Medical Practitioners Acts, 1927 to 1961.

Misuse of Drugs Act 1977, s 1(1)

"THE PRESCRIBED SUM"

In *section 38* of this Act "the prescribed sum" means such sum as may for the time being be prescribed for the purposes of that section by any regulations made under *section 44* of this Act.

Criminal Justice Act 1994, s 43(2)

"THE 1996 PROTOCOL"

"the 1996 Protocol" means the Protocol, drawn up on the basis of Article K.3 of the Treaty on European Union, on the interpretation, by way of preliminary rulings, by the Court of Justice of the European Communities of the CIS Convention, done at Brussels on the 29th day of November, 1996.

Customs and Excise (Mutual Assistance) Act 2001, s 1(1)

"THE 1999 PROTOCOL"

"the 1999 Protocol" means the Protocol, drawn up on the basis of Article K.3 of the Treaty on European Union, on the scope of the laundering of proceeds in the Convention on the use of information technology for customs purposes and the inclusion of the registration number of the means of transport in the Convention, done at Brussels on the 12th day of March, 1999.

Customs and Excise (Mutual Assistance) Act 2001, s 1(1)

"THE RECIPIENT"

Where a person (in this sub-article referred to as "the supplier") supplies a controlled drug, otherwise than on a prescription or by way of administration, to any of the persons specified in sub-article (4), the supplier shall not deliver the drug—

(*a*) until he has obtained a requisition in writing which—
- (i) is signed by the person to whom the drug is to be supplied (in this sub-article referred to as "the recipient"),
- (ii) states the name, address and occupation of the recipient,
- (iii) specifies the purpose for which the drug to be supplied is required and the total quantity to be supplied, and
- (iv) where appropriate, satisfies the requirements of sub-article (5); and

(*b*) unless he is reasonably satisfied that the signature on the requisition referred to at (*a*) is that of the recipient and that the recipient is engaged in the occupation specified in the requisition;

provided that where the recipient is a practitioner and he represents that he urgently requires a controlled drug for the purpose of his profession, the supplier may, if he is reasonably satisfied that the recipient so requires the drug and is unable by reason of urgency to furnish such requisition, deliver the drug to the recipient on an undertaking by the recipient to furnish such a requisition within twenty-four hours of such delivery.

SI No 328/1988, art 12(2)

"THE RESPONDENT"

"the respondent" in relation to a reference under section 8 or section 9 of this Act means the practitioner in respect of whom the reference is made.

Misuse of Drugs Act 1977, s 1(1); see also ss 8 and 9

"THE SHIP"

"the ship" means the ship in relation to which the powers conferred by this Schedule are exercised.

Criminal Justice Act 1994, sched 1, art 1(1)

"THE STATE CHEMIST"

"the State Chemist" means the head of the State Laboratory.

SI No 328/1988, art 3(1)

"THE SUPPLIER"

Documents to be obtained by a supplier.

(1) Where a person (in this sub-article referred to as "the supplier"), not being a practitioner, supplies a controlled drug otherwise than on a prescription, he shall not deliver the drug to a person who—

- (*a*) purports to be sent by or on behalf of the person to whom it is to be supplied (in this sub-article referred to as "the recipient"), and
- (*b*) is not authorised by any provision of these Regulations other than the provisions of article 11(1) (*g*) to have that drug in his possession,

unless the person produces to the supplier a statement in writing signed by the recipient to the effect that the person is empowered by the recipient to receive that drug on his behalf, and the supplier is reasonably satisfied that the document is a genuine document.

SI No 328/1968, art 12(1)

"THE VETERINARY COUNCIL"

"the Veterinary Council" means the Veterinary Council established under the Veterinary Surgeons Act, 1931.

Misuse of Drugs Act 1977, s 1(1)

A Council to be styled the Veterinary Council (in this Act referred to as the Council) shall be established in accordance with this Act to fulfil the functions assigned to it by this Act.

(2) The Council shall be a body corporate having perpetual succession and may provide itself with a seal and may sue and be sued under its said style and name.

(3) The Council shall consist of eight members who shall in the first instance be nominated and subsequently be elected by the persons and in the manner provided in this Act.

Veterinary Surgeons Act 1931, s 3

V

"VALUE OF FUNDS SUBJECT TO CONFISCATION"

" 'value of funds subject to confiscation' has the meaning given by section 8B(1) of this Act.".

Criminal Justice Act 1994, s 3(1) inserted by Criminal Justice (Terrorist Offences) Act 2005, s 21

For the purposes of this Act, the value of the funds that are subject to confiscation is the aggregate of the values of those funds held by the defendant.

(2) For the purpose of assessing the value of funds subject to confiscation the court shall, subject to subsection (3) of this section, make the following assumptions:

(*a*) that any funds appearing to the court—
  (i) to have been held by the defendant at any time since the conviction, or
  (ii) to have been transferred to the defendant at any time since the beginning of the period of six years ending when the proceedings were instituted against the defendant,

were received or collected by the defendant, at the earliest time at which the defendant appears to the court to have held them, for use (whether or not used) in connection with the offence of financing terrorism or as the proceeds of such offence;

(*b*) that any expenditure of the defendant since the beginning of that period was met out of funds subject to confiscation;
(*c*) that the funds subject to confiscation are held by the defendant free of any other interests in them.

(3) The court shall not make an assumption set out in subsection (2) of this section if—

(*a*) that assumption is shown to be incorrect in the case of the defendant, or
(*b*) the court is satisfied that there would be a serious risk of injustice in that case were the assumption made.

(4) Where the court does not apply one or more of the assumptions set out in subsection (2) of this section, it shall state its reasons.

(5) For the purpose of assessing the value of funds subject to confiscation in a case where a confiscation order has previously been made against the defendant, the court shall not take into account any of that defendant's funds subject to confiscation that are shown to the court to have been taken into account in determining the amount to be recovered under the confiscation order.

Criminal Justice Act 1994, s 8b inserted by Criminal Justice (Terrorist Offences) Act 2005, s 22

"VALUE OF PROCEEDS OF DRUG TRAFFICKING"

For the purposes of this Act—

(*a*) any payments or other rewards received by a person at any time (whether before or after the commencement of *section 4* of this Act) in connection with drug trafficking carried on by him or another are his proceeds of drug trafficking, and (*b*) the value of his proceeds of drug trafficking is the aggregate of the values of the payments or other rewards.

(2) The court shall, for the purpose of determining whether the defendant has benefited from drug trafficking and, if he has, of assessing the value of his proceeds of drug trafficking, make the assumptions set out in *subsection (4)* of this section except that the court shall not make any of the said assumptions if—

(*a*) the assumption is shown to be incorrect in the case of the defendant, or
(*b*) it is satisfied that there would be a serious risk of injustice in his case if the assumption were to be made.

Criminal Justice Act 1994, s 5(1)(B)

"VEHICLE"

"(9) In this section 'vehicle' means a mechanically propelled vehicle or any other conveyance, and includes any container, trailer, tank or any other thing, which—

(*a*) is or may be used for the storage of goods in the course of carriage, and
(*b*) is designed or constructed to be placed on, in or attached to any such vehicle or other conveyance.".

Customs and Excise (Miscellaneous Provisions) Act 1988, s 2(9) inserted by Finance Act 2005, s 96

"VESSEL"

In this section "vessel" includes a hovercraft.

Customs and Excise (Miscellaneous Provisions) Act 1988, s 2(7)

"vessel" means a ship or other floating craft of any description and includes a hovercraft or submersible craft.

Criminal Justice (Illicit Traffic by Sea) Act 2003, s 1(1)

"Vessel" means a ship or any other floating craft of any description, including hovercrafts or submersible crafts.

Criminal Justice (Illicit Traffic by Sea) Act 2003, sched, chap 1(d)

W

"WHOLESALER"

"wholesaler" means a person who carries on the business of selling drugs to persons for the purpose of resale.

SI No 328/1988, art 3(1)

EVIDENCE

A

"APPROPRIATE CONSENT"

In this Act "appropriate consent" means—

(*a*) in the case of a person who has attained the age of 17 years, the consent of that person,
(*b*) in the case of a person who has not attained the age of 17 years but has attained the age of 14 years, the consent of that person and of a parent or guardian of that person, and
(*c*) in the case of a person who has not attained the age of 14 years, the consent of a parent or guardian of that person.

Criminal Justice (Forensic Evidence) Act 1990, s 2(10)

C

"COURT"

"court" includes court-martial.

Criminal Evidence Act 1992, s 2(1)

"CRIMINAL PROCEEDINGS"

"criminal proceedings" includes proceedings before a court-martial and proceedings on appeal.

Criminal Evidence Act 1992, s 2(1)

"CUSTODY RECORD"

"custody record" means a record kept under Regulation 6 of the Criminal Justice Act, 1984 (Treatment of Persons in Custody in Garda Síochána Stations) Regulations, 1987 (S.I. No. 119 of 1987).

SI No 130/92, art 2(1)

Custody record.

6. (1) A record (in these Regulations referred to as the custody record) shall be kept in respect of each person in custody.

(2) The member in charge shall record or cause to be recorded in the custody record as soon as practicable such information as is required to be recorded by these Regulations. Each entry in the record shall be signed or initialled by the member making it.

(3) Where a person in custody is transferred to another station, the member in charge of the station from which he is transferred shall send with him the custody record relating to him, or a copy of it, to the member in charge of that other station.

(4) Without prejudice to the responsibility of any other member for the accuracy and completeness of any entry which he has made in a custody record, the member in charge shall be responsible for the accuracy and completeness of all entries made in the custody record while he is the member in charge.

(5) Paragraph (2) does not apply to a record referred to in Regulation 10(5) or paragraph (10) or (11) of Regulation 12.

SI No 119/1987, reg 6

D

"DECREE OF DIVORCE"

"'decree of divorce' means a decree under *section 5* of the *Family Law (Divorce) Act, 1996* or any decree that was granted under the law of a country or jurisdiction other than the State and is recognised in the State.".

Criminal Evidence Act 1992, s 20 substituted by Family Law (Divorce) Act 1996, s 49

"DOCUMENT"

"document" includes—

(i) a map, plan, graph, drawing or photograph, or
(ii) a reproduction in permanent legible form, by a computer or other means (including enlarging), of information in non-legible form.

Criminal Evidence Act 1992, s 2(1)

(3) In *subsection (1)* "document" includes a film, sound recording or videorecording.

Criminal Evidence Act 1992, s 30(3)

F

"FORMER SPOUSE"

'former spouse' includes a person who, in respect of his or her marriage to an accused—

(*a*) has been granted a decree of judicial separation, or
(*b*) has entered into a separation agreement, or
(*c*) has been granted a decree of divorce.".

Criminal Evidence Act 1992, s 20 as inserted by Family Law (Divorce) Act 1996, s 49

I & J

"INFORMATION"

"information" includes any representation of fact, whether in words or otherwise.

Criminal Evidence Act 1992, s 2(1)

"INFORMATION IN NON LEGIBLE FORM"

"information in non-legible form" includes information on microfilm, microfiche, magnetic tape or disk.

Criminal Evidence Act 1992, s 2(1)

M

"MEMBER"

"member" means a member of the Garda Síochána.

SI No 130/92, art 2(1)

"MEMBER IN CHARGE" (SEE ALSO UNDER PRACTICE AND PROCEDURE)

"member in charge" has the same meaning as in Regulation 4 (1) of the Criminal Justice Act, 1984 (Treatment of Persons in Custody in Garda Síochána Stations) Regulations, 1987.

SI No 130/1992, art 2(1)

P

"PRESCRIBED"

"prescribed" means prescribed by regulations made by the Minister under *section 5* of this Act.

Criminal Justice (Forensic Evidence) Act 1990, s 1

"PRISON"

"prison" means any place for which rules or regulations may be made under the Prisons Acts, 1826 to 1980, or *section 13* of the Criminal Justice Act, 1960.

Criminal Justice (Forensic Evidence) Act 1990, s 1

"PRISON RECORD"

"prison record" means a record kept in a prison in respect of a person in custody in that prison.

SI No 130/1992, art 2(1)

R

"REGISTERED DENTIST"

"registered dentist" means a person whose name is entered for the time being on the Register of Dentists maintained under the Dentists Act, 1985.

Criminal Justice (Forensic Evidence) Act 1990, s 1

"REGISTERED MEDICAL PRACTITIONER"

"registered medical practitioner" has the meaning assigned to it by section 2 of the Medical Practitioners Act, 1978.

Criminal Justice (Forensic Evidence) Act 1990, s 1

"registered medical practitioner" means a person whose name is entered in the register.

Medical Practitioners Act 1978, s 2

S

"SAMPLES"

Subject to the provisions of *subsections (4)* to *(8)* of this section, where a person is in custody under the provisions of section 30 of the Offences against the State Act, 1939, or section 4 of the Criminal Justice Act, 1984, a member of the Garda Síochána may take, or cause to be taken, from that person for the purpose of forensic testing all or any of the following samples, namely—

(*a*) a sample of—
 (i) blood,
 (ii) pubic hair,
 (iii) urine,
 (iv) saliva,
 (v) hair other than pubic hair,
 (vi) a nail,
 (vii) any material found under a nail,
(*b*) a swab from any part of the body other than a body orifice or a genital region,
(*c*) a swab from a body orifice or a genital region,
(*d*) a dental impression,
(*e*) a footprint or similar impression of any part of the person's body other than a part of his hand or mouth.

Criminal Justice (Forensic Evidence) Act 1990, s 2(1)(a)–(e)

"SEPARATION AGREEMENT"

"separation agreement" means an agreement in writing which provides for the spouses concerned living separately and apart from each other.

Criminal Evidence Act 1992, s 20

"SEXUAL OFFENCE"

"sexual offence" means rape, buggery, sexual assault (within the meaning of section 2 of the Criminal Law (Rape) (Amendment) Act, 1990), aggravated sexual assault (within the meaning of section 3 of that Act), rape under section 4 of that Act or an offence under—

(i) section 3 (as amended by section 8 of the Act of 1935), 6 (as amended by section 9 of that Act) or 11 of the Criminal Law Amendment Act, 1885,
(ii) section 1 or 2 (as amended by section 12 of the Act of 1935) of the Punishment of Incest Act, 1908,
(iii) section 17 (as amended by section 11 of the Act of 1935) of the Children Act, 1908, or
[(iv) "(iv) the *Criminal Law (Sexual offences) Act 2006* or section 5 of the Criminal Law (Sexual offences) Act 1993;".]

["(aa) section 6 (inserted by *section* 2 of the *Criminal Law (Sexual Offences) (Amendment) Act 2007*) of the Criminal Law (Sexual Offences) Act 1993;".

(2) The Schedule to the Sexual Offences (Jurisdiction) Act 1996 is amended by the insertion of the following paragraph:

"2. Section 6 (inserted by *section* 2 of the *Criminal Law (Sexual Offences) (Amendment) Act 2007*) of the Criminal Law (Sexual Offences) Act 1993."]

excluding an attempt to commit any such offence.

Criminal Evidence Act 1992, s 2(1) amended by the Criminal Law (Sexual Offences) Act 2006, s 4(1) and sub paragraph (aa) inserted by Criminal Law (Sexual Offences) (Amendment) Act 2007, s 16

"STATEMENT"

In this section "statement" includes any representation of fact, whether in words or otherwise.

Criminal Evidence Act 1992, s 16(4)

"STATION"

"station" means a Garda Síochána station.

SI No 130/92, art 2(1)

V

"VIDEO RECORDING"

"video recording" means any recording, on any medium, from which a moving image may by any means be produced and includes the accompanying soundtrack (if any), and cognate words shall be construed accordingly.

Criminal Evidence Act 1992, s 2(1)

FIREARMS AND EXPLOSIVES

I & J

L

M

P

R

S

T

A

"A PERSON OFFICIALLY AUTHORISED"

(*a*) the expression "a person officially authorised" means a person authorised by the Minister for Defence to effect the transaction in question for the purposes of the Defence Forces of Saorstát Eireann or authorised by the Minister to effect the transaction in question for the purposes of any lawful police force in Saorstát Eireann, and.

Firearms Act 1925, s 10(6)(a)

"ACT OF 1997"

"Act of 1997" means the Taxes Consolidation Act, 1997.

Firearms Act 1925, s 9A(1) inserted by the Criminal Justice (Miscellaneous Provisions) Act 2009, s 30

"AMMUNITION"

"(1) In this Act—

"ammunition" (except where used in relation to a prohibited weapon) means ammunition for a firearm and includes—

(*a*) grenades, bombs and other similar missiles, whether or not capable of being used with a firearm,
(*b*) any ingredient or component part of any such ammunition or missile, and
(*c*) restricted ammunition, unless the context otherwise requires.

Firearms Act 1925, s 1(1) substituted by Criminal Justice Act 2006, s 26

NOTE: for the purposes of ammunition contained in the Firearms Act 1964, s 21, the definition of ammunition the following applies:

"(3) In this section, "ammunition" does not include—

(*a*) component parts of ammunition, or
(*b*) grenades, bombs and other similar missiles or their component parts.".

Firearms Act 1964, s 21 amended by Criminal Justice Act 2006, s 56

B

"BOAT"

The expression 'boat' means every vessel not a ship as above defined which is used in navigation in any inland water or any harbour, whether propelled by oars or otherwise.

Explosives Act 1875, s 108

C

"CANAL COMPANY"

The expression 'canal company' means any person or body of persons, corporate or unincorporate, being owner or lessee or owners or lessees of, or working, or entitled to charge tolls for the use of any canal in the United Kingdom, constructed or carried on under the powers of any Act of Parliament, or intrusted with the duty of conserving, maintaining, or improving the navigation of any inland water, and every such canal and inland water under the control of a canal company as above defined, and any wharf, dock, pier, jetty, and work in or at which barges do or can ship or unship goods or passengers, and other area, whether land or water, which belong to or are under the control of such canal company, are in the other portions of this Act included in the expression 'canal'.

Explosives Act 1875, s 108

"CARRIAGE"

The expression 'carriage' includes any carriage, waggon, cart, truck, vehicle, or other means of conveying goods or passengers by land, in whatever manner the same may be propelled.

Explosives Act 1875, s 108

"CARRIER"

The expression 'carrier' includes all persons carrying goods or passengers for hire by land or water.

Explosives Act 1875, s 108

"COLLECTOR GENERAL"

"collector general" means the collector general appointed under section 851 of the Act of 1997.

Firearms Act 1925, s 9(a)(1) inserted by the Criminal Justice (Miscellaneous Provisions) Act 2009, s 35

"COMMISSIONER"

"Commissioner" means the Commissioner of the Garda Síochána or a member of the Garda Síochána, or members of a particular rank in the Garda Síochána, not below the rank of superintendent appointed in writing by the Commissioner for the purpose of performing any of the Commissioner's functions under this Act.

Firearms Act 1925, s 1(1) amended and substituted by Criminal Justice Act 2006, s 26

"COMMISSIONER" SEE THE

D

"DEEMED MANUFACTURERS"

Any person who carries on any of the following processes, namely, the process of dividing into its component parts or otherwise breaking up or unmaking any explosive, or making fit for use any damaged explosive, or the process of remaking, altering, or repairing any explosive, shall be subject to the provisions of this Act as if he manufactured an explosive, and the expression 'manufacture' shall in this Act be construed accordingly.

Explosives Act 1875, s 105

E

"EXPLOSIVE"

The term 'explosive' in this Act—

(1) Means gunpowder, nitro-glycerine, dynamite, guncotton, blasting powders, fulminate of mercury or of other metals, coloured fires, and every other substance, whether similar to those above mentioned or not, used or manufactured with a view to produce a practical effect by explosion or a pyrotechnic effect; and

(2) Includes fog-signals, fireworks, fuzes, rockets, percussion caps, detonators, cartridges, ammunition of all descriptions, and every adaptation or preparation of an explosive as above defined.

Explosives Act 1875, s 3

"EXPLOSIVE SUBSTANCES"

The expression 'explosive substance' shall be deemed to include any materials for making any explosive substance; also any apparatus, machine, implement, or materials used, or intended to be used, or adapted for causing, or aiding in causing, any explosion in or with any explosive substance; also any part of any such apparatus, machine, or implement.

Explosive Substances Act 1883, s 9

"EXPORT"

In this Act the word "port" means any authorised place of entry into Saorstát Eireann, and the words "export" and "import" include respectively export and import over a land frontier as well as export and import over a sea frontier, and all cognate words shall be construed accordingly.

Firearms Act 1925, s 1(2)

F

"FACTORY MAGAZINE"

The expression 'factory magazine' means a building for keeping the finished explosive made in the factory, and includes, if such explosive is not gunpowder, any building for keeping the partly manufactured explosive or the ingredients of such explosive which is mentioned in that behalf in the license.

Explosives Act 1875, s 108

"FIREARM"

"firearm" means—

(*a*) a lethal firearm or other lethal weapon of any description from which any shot, bullet or other missile can be discharged,
(*b*) an air gun (including an air rifle and air pistol) with a muzzle energy greater than one joule or any other weapon incorporating a barrel from which any projectile can be discharged with such a muzzle energy,
(*c*) a crossbow,
(*d*) any type of stun gun or other weapon for causing any shock or other disablement to a person by means of electricity or any other kind of energy emission,
(e) a prohibited weapon,
(*f*) any article which would be a firearm under any of the foregoing paragraphs, [or paragraph (h)] but for the fact that, owing to the lack of a necessary component part or parts, or to any other defect or condition, it is incapable of discharging a shot, bullet or other missile or projectile or of causing a shock or other disablement, as the case may be,
(*g*) except where the context otherwise requires, any component part of any article referred to in any of the foregoing paragraphs and, without prejudice to the generality of the foregoing, the following articles shall be deemed to be such component parts:
 (i) telescope sights with a light beam, or telescope sights with an electronic light amplification device or an infra-red device, designed to be fitted to a firearm specified in paragraph (*a*), (*b*), (*c*) or (e),
 (ii) a silencer designed to be fitted to a firearm specified in paragraph (*a*), (*b*) or (e), and
 (iii) any object—
  (I) manufactured for use as a component in connection with the operation of a firearm, and
  (II) without which it could not function as originally designed,

and

(*h*) a device capable of discharging blank ammunition and to be used as a starting gun or blank firing gun,

and includes a restricted firearm, unless otherwise provided or the context otherwise requires.

Firearms Act 1925, s 1(1) substituted by Criminal Justice Act 2006, s 26 as amended by the Criminal Justice (Miscellaneous Provisions) Act 2009, s 25(9)

"FIREARM CERTIFICATE"

"firearm certificate" means a firearm certificate granted under this Act and, unless the context otherwise requires, includes a restricted firearm certificate, a firearms training certificate and a firearm certificate granted under the Firearms (Firearm Certificates for Non-Residents) Act 2000.

Firearms Act 1925, s 1(1) substituted by Criminal Justice Act 2006, s 26

"FIREARM CERTIFICATE"

(1) On application in that behalf in accordance with *subsection (2)* to the Minister or the appropriate Superintendent by a person not ordinarily resident in the State who is of or over the age of 16 years, the Minister or the Superintendent, as may be appropriate, shall, subject to the provisions of this section, grant to the person a firearm certificate authorising the person to—

(*a*) have in his or her possession, use and carry the particular firearm described in the certificate for the purpose specified in the certificate,
(*b*) purchase and use in such firearm during the currency of such certificate such quantity of ammunition for such firearm as shall be specified in the certificate, and
(*c*) have in his or her possession at any one time and carry so much ammunition as shall be specified in the certificate.

(2) An application referred to in *subsection (1)* shall be made—

(*a*) in case the firearm to which it relates is intended only for hunting or sporting purposes or for shooting species whose shooting is not proscribed by law—
  (i) if the application is made not later than 2 years after the commencement of this section, to the Minister, and
  (ii) if it is made later than 2 years after such commencement or if the Minister has made an order under *subsection (3)*, to the appropriate Superintendent,

and

(*b*) in any other case, to the Minister.

(3) The Minister may, following consultation with the Commissioner of the Garda Síochána, by order reduce the length of the period referred to in *subparagraph (i)* of *subsection (2)(a)* to such extent as he or she considers appropriate.

(4) An application to which *paragraph (a)* of *subsection (2)* relates for a firearm certificate under this section shall be in such form as may be prescribed or in a form to the like effect and shall be accompanied by the fee (if any) for the time being required by law.

(5) A person who applies to the Minister or a Superintendent of the Garda Síochána (referred to subsequently in this Act as "the issuing person") for a firearm certificate under this section shall furnish to that person the information requested in the application form together with such further information as the issuing person may request for the purposes of his or her functions under this section and, if the person fails to comply with this subsection, the issuing person may refuse to grant the firearm certificate to the person.

(6) A firearm certificate granted to a person under this section shall continue in force until the 31st day of July next after the grant thereof, but a firearm certificate granted before the 31st day of July in any year may be expressed to commence on the next following 1st day of August and shall in that case be in force on and from such 1st day of August until the next following 31st day of July or such earlier date as may be specified in the certificate.

(7) The issuing person, before granting a firearm certificate to a person under this section, shall be of the opinion that the application is *bona fide* and that there is no good reason to refuse to grant the certificate.

(8) The issuing person may, for the purpose of establishing that there is no good reason to refuse to grant a firearm certificate, treat any of the following as *prima facie* evidence of suitability to so grant—

(*a*) in the case of a person who is resident in a Member State of the European Community other than the State, any European Firearms Pass duly issued to such person to which paragraphs (4) and (5) of Regulation 7 of the European Communities (Acquisition and Possession of Weapons and Ammunition) Regulations, 1993 (S.I. No. 362 of 1993), relate, or

(*b*) in any other case, any other permit, licence, authorisation or other document duly issued by an appropriate authority or body outside the State which the issuing person considers acceptable.

(9) The issuing person may make such enquiries as he or she considers appropriate as to the suitability of any applicant for a firearm certificate under this section.

(10) The issuing person may attach such conditions, if any, as he or she considers necessary, to a firearm certificate granted to a person under this section.

(11) The issuing person shall not grant a firearm certificate to a person in respect of a firearm which is intended to be used for the purpose of hunting exempted wild mammals within the meaning of the Act of 1976 (other than hares) unless the issuing person is satisfied that the person is the holder of a current licence under section 29(1) of the Act of 1976.

(12) The Minister shall not grant a firearm certificate to a person in respect of a firearm which is intended to be used for the purpose of hunting protected wild

birds within the meaning of the Act of 1976 or hares unless the Minister is satisfied that the person is the holder of a current licence under section 29(5)(*b*) of the Act of 1976.

(13) The issuing person may at any time revoke a firearm certificate granted to a person under this section if he or she is of the opinion that the holder of such certificate—

(*a*) is a person who cannot, without danger to the public safety or to the peace, be permitted to have a firearm in his or her possession,
(*b*) is using, or has used, such firearm for purposes not authorised by the certificate, or
(*c*) is a person who has contravened a condition attaching to the firearm certificate granted to him or her.

(14) Where a firearm certificate is revoked under this section, the issuing person shall, as soon as may be, notify the holder of the certificate in writing of the revocation and the notice shall direct the holder of the certificate to deliver forthwith the firearm described in the certificate and ammunition (if any) to the Superintendent of the Garda Síochána of the district in which he or she is residing at the time of the receipt of the notice and the provisions of section 6 of the Principal Act shall apply to the disposal of a firearm and ammunition delivered under this section as they apply to the disposal of a firearm and ammunition delivered under that section with any necessary modifications.

(15) References to a firearm certificate in sections 2, 10, 16, 22 and 23 of the Principal Act shall include references to a firearm certificate granted under this Act.

(16) References to a firearm certificate in sections 11, 12, 21 and 24 of the Firearms Act, 1964 , shall include references to a firearm certificate granted under this Act.

(17) In this section, "the appropriate Superintendent", in relation to a firearm certificate, means the Superintendent of the Garda Síochána of the district in which the firearm will first be used by the person.

Firearms (Firearm Certificates for Non Residents) Act 2000, s 2

"FIREARM DEALER"

"firearm dealer" means a person who, by way of trade or business, manufactures, sells, lets on hire, repairs, tests, proves, purchases, or otherwise deals in firearms or ammunition.

Firearms Act 1925, s 1(1) substituted by Criminal Justice Act 2006, s 26

"FIREARM RANGE INSPECTOR"

"Firearms range inspectors.

(1) The Minister may by warrant appoint such and so many persons as he or she thinks necessary to be firearms range inspectors and may revoke any such appointment.

(2) It shall be the duty of a firearms range inspector—

(*a*) to examine applications for the authorisation of rifle and pistol shooting ranges, and

(*b*) to inspect rifle and pistol shooting ranges for the purpose of ensuring their compliance with the minimum standards provided for in regulations under section 4A(13) of this Act.

(3) After inspecting a rifle or pistol shooting range, an inspector may—

(*a*) if satisfied that the range complies with those minimum standards, issue a firearms range certificate in respect of it, and

(*b*) if not so satisfied, refuse to issue such a certificate or revoke any such certificate that is in force.

(4) An inspector who suspects, with reasonable cause, that any place is being used for rifle or pistol target shooting may enter and inspect it.

(5) The Minister shall issue to each inspector the warrant of appointment, or a copy of it, for production, on request, when an inspector is exercising any power conferred by this section.

(6) The terms and conditions of appointment of firearms range inspectors shall be determined by the Minister, with the consent of the Minister for Finance.".

Firearms Act 1925, s 4B inserted by Criminal Justice Act 2006, s 34

"FIREARM TRAINING CERTIFICATE"

"firearms training certificate" has the meaning given to it by section 2A of this Act.

Firearms Act 1925, s 1(1) substituted by Criminal Justice Act 2006, s 26

"Firearms training certificate.

(1) The Commissioner, on application and payment of the prescribed fee (if any), may issue to a person over 14 years of age a certificate (in this Act referred to as a "firearms training certificate") authorising the person to possess

a firearm and ammunition (except a restricted firearm and restricted ammunition) only while—

(*a*) carrying and using the firearm for hunting or target shooting—
  (i) under the supervision of a specified person over 18 years of age who holds a firearm certificate in respect of it, and
  (ii) where the firearm is used for target shooting, on the premises of an authorised rifle or pistol club or at an authorised shooting range or other place that stands authorised under section 2(5) of this Act,

and

(*b*) complying with such other conditions (if any) as the Commissioner may impose in the interests of public safety and security.

(2) Where the applicant is under 16 years of age, the application for a firearms training certificate shall be accompanied by the written consent of the applicant's parent or guardian.

(3) The firearms training certificate shall be in the prescribed form.

(4) Where such an application is refused, the Commissioner shall inform the applicant in writing and give the reasons for the refusal.

(5) A firearms training certificate shall continue in force for a period of 3 years from the date on which it was granted, unless revoked.

(6) The Commissioner may revoke a firearms training certificate if of opinion that the holder is not complying, or has not complied, with the conditions subject to which the certificate was granted.

Firearms Act 1925, s 1(1) substituted by Criminal Justice Act 2006, s 28

"FLICK KNIFE"

"flick-knife" has the meaning given to it in section 9(9) of the Firearms and Offensive Weapons Act 1990.

Firearms Act 1925, s 25A(7) inserted by Criminal Justice Act 2006, s 46

In this section "flick-knife" means a knife—

(*a*) which has a blade which opens when hand pressure is applied to a button, spring, lever or other device in or attached to the handle, or
(*b*) which has a blade which is released from the handle or sheath by the force of gravity or the application of centrifugal force and when released is locked in an open position by means of a button, spring, lever or other device.

Firearms and Offensive Weapons Act 1990, s 9(9)

G

"GUNPOWDER STORE"

20. Any magazine established without a license from a local authority in pursuance of the **Gunpowder** Act, 1860, or of any enactment repealed by that Act, for the use of any mine, quarry, colliery, or factory of safety-fuzes, and in use at the passing of this Act, is in this Act referred to as an existing **gunpowder store**.

An existing **gunpowder store** shall not require a continuing certificate as a magazine from the Secretary of State, but shall require a continuing certificate from the local authority, and if such certificate is not applied for and obtained in manner provided by this Act, shall not be deemed to be a lawfully existing **store**.

Explosives Act 1875, s 20

H

"HARBOUR AUTHORITY"

The expression "harbour authority" means any person or body of persons, corporate or un-incorporate, being or claiming to be proprietor or proprietors of or entrusted with the duty or invested with the power of improving managing, maintaining, or regulating any harbour properly so called, whether natural or artificial, and any port, haven, and estuary, or entrusted with the duty of conserving, maintaining, or improving the navigation of any tidal water, and any such harbour, port, haven, estuary, tidal water, and any wharf, dock, pier, jetty, and work, and other area, whether land or water, over which the harbour authority as above defined have control or exercise powers, axe in the other portions of this Act included in the expression "harbour".

Explosive Act 1875, s 108

"HEALTH PROFESSIONAL"

(6) In this section "health professional" means doctor or psychiatrist registered under any enactments governing the profession concerned or a clinical psychologist.".

Firearms Act 1925, s 4(6) substituted by Criminal Justice Act 2006, s 32

"HUNTING"

"hunting" means shooting with a firearm protected wild birds or protected wild animals within the meaning in each case of the Act of 1976.

Firearms (Firearms Certificates for Non Residents) Act 2000, s 1(1)

"hunt" means stalk, pursue, chase, drive, flush, capture, course, attract, follow, search for, lie in wait for, take, trap or shoot by any means whether with or without dogs, and, except in sections 28 and 29, includes killing in the course of hunting, but does not in this Act include stalking, attracting, searching for or lying in wait for any fauna by an unarmed person solely for the purpose of watching or of taking or making photographic or other pictures, and kindred words shall be construed accordingly.

Wildlife Act 1976, s 2

I & J

"IMITATION FIREARM"

In this section "imitation firearm" means anything which is not a firearm but has the appearance of being a firearm.

Firearms and Offensive Weapons Act 1990, s 9H(2) inserted by the Criminal Justice (Miscellneous Provisions) Act 2009, s 35

"IMPORT"

In this Act the word "port" means any authorised place of entry into Saorstát Eireann, and the words "export" and "import" include respectively export and import over a land frontier as well as export and import over a sea frontier, and all cognate words shall be construed accordingly.

Firearms Act 1925, s 1(2)

"INLAND WATER"

The expression 'inland water' means any canal, river, navigation, lake, or water which is not tidal water.

Explosives Act 1875, s 108

"INSTITUTE" SEE THE

"ISSUING PERSON"

"issuing person", in relation to the grant or renewal of a firearm certificate, authorisation or licence, means, as the case may be, the Minister, the Commissioner or the superintendent of the Garda Síochána of the district where an applicant for or holder of the firearm certificate, authorisation or licence is residing.

Firearms Act 1925, s 1(1) substituted by Criminal Justice Act 2006, s 26

"ISSUING PERSON"

On application in that behalf in accordance with *subsection (2)* to the Minister or the appropriate Superintendent by a person not ordinarily resident in the State who is of or over the age of 16 years, the Minister or the Superintendent, as may be appropriate, shall, subject to the provisions of this section, grant to the person a firearm certificate authorising the person to—

(*a*) have in his or her possession, use and carry the particular firearm described in the certificate for the purpose specified in the certificate,
(*b*) purchase and use in such firearm during the currency of such certificate such quantity of ammunition for such firearm as shall be specified in the certificate, and
(*c*) have in his or her possession at any one time and carry so much ammunition as shall be specified in the certificate.

(2) An application referred to in *subsection (1)* shall be made—

(*a*) in case the firearm to which it relates is intended only for hunting or sporting purposes or for shooting species whose shooting is not proscribed by law—
  (i) if the application is made not later than 2 years after the commencement of this section, to the Minister, and
  (ii) if it is made later than 2 years after such commencement or if the Minister has made an order under *subsection (3)*, to the appropriate Superintendent,

and

(*b*) in any other case, to the Minister.

(3) The Minister may, following consultation with the Commissioner of the Garda Síochána, by order reduce the length of the period referred to in *subparagraph (i)* of *subsection (2)(a)* to such extent as he or she considers appropriate.

(4) An application to which *paragraph (a)* of *subsection (2)* relates for a firearm certificate under this section shall be in such form as may be prescribed or in a form to the like effect and shall be accompanied by the fee (if any) for the time being required by law.

(5) A person who applies to the Minister or a Superintendent of the Garda Síochána (referred to subsequently in this Act **as "the issuing person"**) for a firearm certificate under this section shall furnish to that person the information requested in the application form together with such further information as the issuing person may request for the purposes of his or her functions under this section and, if the person fails to comply with this subsection, the issuing person may refuse to grant the firearm certificate to the person.

(6) A firearm certificate granted to a person under this section shall continue in force until the 31st day of July next after the grant thereof, but a firearm certificate granted before the 31st day of July in any year may be expressed to commence on the next following 1st day of August and shall in that case be in force on and from such 1st day of August until the next following 31st day of July or such earlier date as may be specified in the certificate.

(7) The issuing person, before granting a firearm certificate to a person under this section, shall be of the opinion that the application is *bona fide* and that there is no good reason to refuse to grant the certificate.

(8) The issuing person may, for the purpose of establishing that there is no good reason to refuse to grant a firearm certificate, treat any of the following as *prima facie* evidence of suitability to so grant—

(*a*) in the case of a person who is resident in a Member State of the European Community other than the State, any European Firearms Pass duly issued to such person to which paragraphs (4) and (5) of Regulation 7 of the European Communities (Acquisition and Possession of Weapons and Ammunition) Regulations, 1993 (S.I. No. 362 of 1993), relate, or

(*b*) in any other case, any other permit, licence, authorisation or other document duly issued by an appropriate authority or body outside the State which the issuing person considers acceptable.

(9) The issuing person may make such enquiries as he or she considers appropriate as to the suitability of any applicant for a firearm certificate under this section.

(10) The issuing person may attach such conditions, if any, as he or she considers necessary, to a firearm certificate granted to a person under this section.

(11) The issuing person shall not grant a firearm certificate to a person in respect of a firearm which is intended to be used for the purpose of hunting exempted wild mammals within the meaning of the Act of 1976 (other than hares) unless the issuing person is satisfied that the person is the holder of a current licence under section 29(1) of the Act of 1976.

(12) The Minister shall not grant a firearm certificate to a person in respect of a firearm which is intended to be used for the purpose of hunting protected wild birds within the meaning of the Act of 1976 or hares unless the Minister is satisfied

that the person is the holder of a current licence under section 29(5)(*b*) of the Act of 1976.

(13) The issuing person may at any time revoke a firearm certificate granted to a person under this section if he or she is of the opinion that the holder of such certificate—

(*a*) is a person who cannot, without danger to the public safety or to the peace, be permitted to have a firearm in his or her possession,

(*b*) is using, or has used, such firearm for purposes not authorised by the certificate, or

(*c*) is a person who has contravened a condition attaching to the firearm certificate granted to him or her.

(14) Where a firearm certificate is revoked under this section, the issuing person shall, as soon as may be, notify the holder of the certificate in writing of the revocation and the notice shall direct the holder of the certificate to deliver forthwith the firearm described in the certificate and ammunition (if any) to the Superintendent of the Garda Síochána of the district in which he or she is residing at the time of the receipt of the notice and the provisions of section 6 of the Principal Act shall apply to the disposal of a firearm and ammunition delivered under this section as they apply to the disposal of a firearm and ammunition delivered under that section with any necessary modifications.

(15) References to a firearm certificate in sections 2, 10, 16, 22 and 23 of the Principal Act shall include references to a firearm certificate granted under this Act.

(16) References to a firearm certificate in sections 11, 12, 21 and 24 of the Firearms Act, 1964 , shall include references to a firearm certificate granted under this Act.

(17) In this section, "the appropriate Superintendent", in relation to a firearm certificate, means the Superintendent of the Garda Síochána of the district in which the firearm will first be used by the person.

Firearms (Firearm Certificates for Non Residents) Act 2000, s 2

L

"LIMITED CERTIFICATE"

The following provisions have effect in relation to a certificate in the form referred to in subsection (6) of this section (in this subsection referred to as a "limited certificate"):

(*a*) a limited certificate relating to land occupied by a person other than the applicant for the certificate shall not be granted unless the occupier of the land has given the applicant a nomination in writing for holding the certificate;

(*b*) a limited certificate relating to any land shall not be granted in respect of any period if there is a limited certificate relating to the land already in force in respect of that period;

(*c*) a limited certificate shall not be granted unless the whole of the land to which it would relate is occupied by the same person;

(*d*) where a nomination referred to in paragraph(a) of this subsection is revoked, the limited certificate to which it related, if then in force, shall not be capable of being renewed.

Criminal Justice Act 2006, s 30(11) substituted by the Criminal Justice (Miscellneous Provisions) Act 2009, s 24(11)

M

"MAGAZINE"

The expression 'magazine' includes any ship or other vessel used for the purpose of keeping any explosive.

Explosives Act 1875, s 108

"MASTER"

The expression 'master' includes every person (except a pilot) having command or charge of a ship, and in reference to any boat belonging to a ship, means the master of the ship; and when used in reference to any other boat, includes every person having command or charge of such boat.

Explosives Act 1875, s 108

"MUZZLE ENERGY"

"muzzle energy", in relation to a firearm, means the energy of a projectile discharged by it, measured at its muzzle in joules.

Firearms Act 1925, s 1(1) substituted by Criminal Justice Act 2006, s 26

P

"PLACE"

"place" includes a dwelling.

Firearms Act 1925, s 1(1) substituted by Criminal Justice Act 2006, s 26

"PORT"

In this Act the word "port" means any authorised place of entry into Saorstát Eireann, and the words "export" and "import" include respectively export and import over a land frontier as well as export and import over a sea frontier, and all cognate words shall be construed accordingly.

Firearms Act 1925, s 1(2)

"PRACTICAL AND DYNAMIC SHOOTING"

In this section "practical or dynamic shooting" means any form of activity in which firearms are used to simulate combat or combat training.".

Firearms Act 1925, s 4c(4) inserted by the Criminal Justice (Miscellaneous Provisions) Act 2009, s 33(4)

"PREMISES"

"premises" means any building, any part of a building and any land ancillary to a building.

Firearms and Offensive Weapons Act 1990, s 10(1)(2)

"PRESCRIBED"

"prescribed" means prescribed by regulations made under this Act.

Firearms Act 1925, s 1(1) substituted by Criminal Justice Act 2006, s 26

"PROHIBITED AMMUNITION"

"prohibited ammunition" means ammunition that is declared by order under section 2C of this Act to be prohibited ammunition.

Firearms Act 1925, s 1(1) substituted by Criminal Justice Act 2006, s 26 as amended by the Criminal Justice (Miscellaneous Provisions) Act 2009, s 25(b)

"PROHIBITED FIREARM"

"prohibited firearm" means a firearm that is declared by order under section 2C of this Act to be a prohibited firearm.

Firearms Act 1925, s 1(1) substituted by Criminal Justice Act 2006, s 26 as amended by the Criminal Justice (Miscellaneous Provisions) Act 2009, s 25(b)

"PROHIBITED WEAPON"

"prohibited weapon" means and includes any weapon of whatever description designed for the discharge of any noxious liquid, noxious gas or other noxious thing, and also any ammunition (whether for any such weapon or any other weapon) which contains or is designed or adapted to contain any noxious liquid, noxious gas or other noxious thing.

Firearms Act 1925, s 1(1) substituted by Criminal Justice Act 2006, s 26

"PUBLIC PLACE"

In this section "public place" includes any highway and any other premises or place to which at the material time the public have or are permitted to have access, whether on payment or otherwise, and includes any club premises and any train, vessel or vehicle used for the carriage of persons for reward.

Firearms and Offensive Weapons Act 1990, s 9A(3) inserted by the Criminal Justice (Miscellneous Provision) Act 2009, s 40(3)

R

"RAILWAY COMPANY"

The expression 'railway company' means any person or body of persons, corporate or unincorporate, being the owner or lessee or owners or lessees of or working any railway worked by steam or otherwise than by animal power in the United Kingdom, constructed or carried on under the powers of any Act of Parliament and used for public traffic, and every building, station, wharf, dock, and place which belong to or are under the control of a railway company, are in the other portions of this Act included in the expression 'railway'.

Explosives Act 1875, s 108

"REALISTIC IMITATION FIREARM"

In this section and in sections 9B to 9G "realistic imitation firearm" means a device that appears to the ordinary observer so realistic as to make it indistinguishable from a firearm.

Firearms and Offensive Weapons Act 1990, s 9A(4) inserted by the Criminal Justice (Miscellneous Provisions) Act 2009, s 40(4)

"REGISTERED FIREARMS DEALER"

"registered firearms dealer" means a firearms dealer who is for the time being registered in the register of firearms dealers established in pursuance of this Act.

Firearms Act 1925, s 1(1) substituted by Criminal Justice Act 2006, s 26

"RESTRICTED AMMUNITION"

"restricted ammunition" means ammunition which is declared under section 2B(*b*) of this Act to be restricted ammunition.

Firearms Act 1925, s 1(1) substituted by Criminal Justice Act 2006, s 26

"Restricted firearms and ammunition.

2B.—The Minister may, in the interests of public safety and security, by order—

(*a*) declare specified firearms to be restricted firearms for the purposes of this Act by reference to one or more than one of the following criteria:
- (i) category;
- (ii) calibre;
- (iii) working mechanism;
- (iv) muzzle energy;
- (v) description;

and

(*b*) declare specified ammunition to be restricted ammunition for the purposes of this Act by reference to one or more than one of the following criteria:
(i) category;
(ii) calibre;
(iii) weight;
(iv) kinetic energy;
(v) ballistic co-efficient;
(vi) design;
(vii) composition;
(viii) description.".

Firearms Act 1925, s 2B(a) inserted by Criminal Justice Act 2006, s 29

"RESTRICTED FIREARM"

"'restricted firearm' means a firearm which is declared under section 2B(*a*) of the Principal Act to be a restricted firearm.".

Firearms (Firearm Certificates for Non-Residents) Act 2000, s 1(1) inserted by Criminal Justice Act 2006, s 66

"Restricted firearms and ammunition.

2B.—The Minister may, in the interests of public safety and security, by order—

(*a*) declare specified firearms to be restricted firearms for the purposes of this Act by reference to one or more than one of the following criteria:
(i) category;
(ii) calibre;
(iii) working mechanism;
(iv) muzzle energy;
(v) description;

and

(*b*) declare specified ammunition to be restricted ammunition for the purposes of this Act by reference to one or more than one of the following criteria:
(i) category;
(ii) calibre;
(iii) weight;
(iv) kinetic energy;
(v) ballistic co-efficient;

(vi) design;
(vii) composition;
(viii) description.".

Firearms Act 1925, s 2B(a) inserted by Criminal Justice Act 2006, s 29

"RIFLE OR PISTOL CLUB"

"rifle or pistol club" means a club established for the purpose of promoting skill in the use of rifles and pistols for target shooting.

Firearms Act 1925, s 4A(21) inserted by Criminal Justice Act 2006, s 33

S

"SAFETY CARTRIDGES"

The expression 'safety cartridges' means cartridges for small arms of which the case can be extracted from the small arm after firing, and which are so closed as to prevent any explosion in one cartridge being communicated to other cartridges.

Explosives Act 1875, s 108

"SECOND PROTOCOL"

"Second Protocol" means the Protocol drawn up on the basis of Article K.3 of the Treaty on European Union, to the Convention on the protection of the European Communities' financial interests done at Brussels on 19 June 1997.

Criminal Justice (Theft and Fraud Offences) Act 2001, s 40(1)

"SELL"

the word "sell" includes letting on hire [GIVING] and lending and the word "purchase" includes hiring [RECEIVING] and borrowing, and cognate words shall be construed accordingly.

Firearms Act 1925, s 10(6)(b) amended by Firearms Act 1964, s 19

"SHIP"

The expression 'ship' includes every description of vessel used in sea navigation, whether propelled by oars or otherwise.

Explosives Act 1875, s 108

"SHOOTING RANGE"

"shooting range" does not include a range or shooting gallery referred to in section 2(4)(e) of this Act.".

Firearms Act 1925, s 4A(21) inserted by Criminal Justice Act 2006, s 33

"SHORT FIREARM"

For the purposes of this section "short firearm" means a firearm either with a barrel not longer than 30 centimetres or whose overall length (excluding the length of any detachable component) does not exceed 60 centimetres.

Firearms Act 1925, s 30(3) inserted by the Criminal Justice (Miscellaneous Provisions) Act 2009, s 30

"SPORTING PURPOSES"

"sporting purposes" means the purposes of target shooting or clay pigeon shooting or shooting in a competition or event.

Firearms (Firearm Certificates for Non-Residents) Act 2000, s 1(1)

"STORE"

The expression 'store' means an existing gunpowder store as defined by this Act, or a place for keeping an explosive licensed by a license granted by a local authority under this Act.

Explosives Act 1975, s 108

T

"TAX CLEARANCE CERTIFICATE"

(1) "tax clearance certificate" means a certificate under section 1095 (as substituted by section 127(b) of the Finance Act, 2002) of the Act of 1997.

Firearms Act 1925, s 9(A)(1) inserted by the Criminal Justice (Miscellaneous Provisions) Act 2009, s 35

(2) Subject to this section, where a person who is in compliance with the obligations imposed on the person by the Acts in relation to—

(*a*) the payment or remittance of any taxes, interest or penalties required to be paid or remitted under the Acts, and
(*b*) the delivery of any returns to be made under the Acts,

applies to the Collector-General in that behalf the Collector-General shall issue to the person a certificate (in this section referred to as a 'tax clearance certificate') stating that the person is in compliance with those obligations.

Taxes Consolidation Act 1997, s 1095(3) substituted by Finance Act 2002, s 127(b)

"THE COMMISSIONER"

"'the Commissioner'" means the Commissioner of the Garda Síochána or a member of the Garda Síochána, or members of a particular rank in the Garda Síochána, not below the rank of superintendent appointed in writing by the Commissioner for the purpose of performing any of the Commissioner's functions under this Act.

Firearms Act 1964, s 1(1) substituted by Criminal Justice Act 2006, s 52

"THE INSTITUTE"

"the Institute" means the Institute for Industrial Research and Standards.

Firearms (Proofing) Act 1968, s 1

"TIDAL WATER"

The expression 'tidal water' means any part of the sea or of a river within the ebb and flow of the tides at ordinary spring tides.

Explosives Act 1875, s 108

W

"WAREHOUSEMAN"

The expression 'warehouseman' includes all persons owning or managing any warehouse, store, wharf, or other premises in which goods are deposited.

Explosives Act 1875, s 108

"WEAPON OF OFFENCE"

"weapon of offence" has the meaning given to it in section 10(2) of the said Act of 1990.".

Firearms Act 1925, s 25a(7) inserted by Criminal Justice Act 2006, s 46

"weapon of offence" means any article made or adapted for use for causing injury to or incapacitating a person, or intended by the person having it with him for such use.

Firearms and Offensive Weapons Act 1990, s 10(2)

"WHARF"

The expression 'wharf' includes any quay, landing-place, siding, or other place at which goods are landed, loaded, or unloaded.

Explosives Act 1875, s 108

"WORKING MECHANISM"

"working mechanism", in relation to a firearm, includes the mechanism for loading, cocking and discharging it and ejecting spent ammunition.".

Firearms Act 1925, s 1(1) substituted by Criminal Justice Act 2006, s 26

HUMAN RIGHTS

A

"AGREEMENT" SEE THE

"AN ENQUIRY"

The Commission may—

(*a*) of its own volition, if it considers it necessary or expedient to do so for the purpose of the performance of any of its functions under *paragraph (a), (c), (d)* or *(e)* of section **8**, or

(*b*) subject to *subsections (2)* to *(5)*, at the request of any person who considers the conducting of such an enquiry to be necessary or expedient for the performance of any of those functions,

conduct an enquiry under this section into any relevant matter (and such an enquiry is referred to in this section as "an enquiry").

Human Rights Commission Act 2000, s 9(1)

"APPLICANT" SEE THE

"AWARD REDRESS OR GRANT RELIEF"

"award redress or grant relief", in relation to the powers of a tribunal or other person, includes making a finding that a person has done, or omitted to do, an act specified in the enactment vesting the said powers in the tribunal or other person or, as the case may be, specified in the resolution of either House of the Oireachtas with respect to the establishment of the tribunal or the appointment of the other person.

Human Rights Commission Act 2000, s 1(1)

C

"COMMISSION" SEE THE

"CONVENTION PROVISIONS"

"Convention provisions" means, subject to any derogation which the State may make pursuant to Article 15 of the Convention, Articles 2 to 14 of the Convention and the following protocols thereto as construed in accordance with Articles 16 to 18 of the Convention:

(*a*) the Protocol to the Convention done at Paris on the 20th day of March, 1952;
(*b*) Protocol No. 4 to the Convention securing certain rights and freedoms other than those already included in the Convention and in the First Protocol thereto done at Strasbourg on the 16th day of September, 1963;
(*c*) Protocol No. 6 to the Convention concerning the abolition of the death penalty done at Strasbourg on the 28th day of April, 1983;
(*d*) Protocol No. 7 to the Convention done at Strasbourg on the 22nd day of November, 1984;

(the texts of which protocols, in the English language, are, for convenience of reference, set out in *Schedules 2, 3, 4* and *5* respectively, to this Act);

"declaration of incompatibility" means a declaration under section 5;

"European Court of Human Rights" shall be construed in accordance with section 4;

"functions" includes powers and duties and references to the performance of functions includes, as respects powers and duties, references to the exercise of the powers and the performance of the duties;

"Minister" means the Minister for Justice, Equality and Law Reform;

"organ of the State" includes a tribunal or any other body (other than the President or the Oireachtas or either House of the Oireachtas or a Committee of either such House or a Joint Committee of both such Houses or a court) which is established by law or through which any of the legislative, executive or judicial powers of the State are exercised;

"rule of law" includes common law;

"statutory provision" means any provision of an Act of the Oireachtas or of any order, regulation, rule, licence, bye-law or other like document made, issued or otherwise created thereunder or any statute, order, regulation, rule, licence, bye-law or other like document made, issued or otherwise created under a statute which continued in force by virtue of Article 50 of the Constitution.

European Convention on Human Rights Act 2003, s 1(1)

"CONVENTION" SEE THE

D

"DECLARATION OF INCOMPATABILITY"

(1) In any proceedings, the High Court, or the Supreme Court when exercising its appellate jurisdiction, may, having regard to the provisions of section 2, on application to it in that behalf by a party, or of its own motion, and where no other legal remedy is adequate and available, make a declaration (referred to in this Act as "a declaration of incompatibility") that a statutory provision or rule of law is incompatible with the State's obligations under the Convention provisions.

(2) A declaration of incompatibility—

(*a*) shall not affect the validity, continuing operation or enforcement of the statutory provision or rule of law in respect of which it is made, and
(*b*) shall not prevent a party to the proceedings concerned from making submissions or representations in relation to matters to which the declaration relates in any proceedings before the European Court of Human Rights.

European Convention on Human Rights Act 2003, s 5

E

"EUROPEAN COURT OF HUMAN RIGHTS"

(1) "European Court of Human Rights" shall be construed in accordance with section 4; s 1(1)

(2) Judicial notice shall be taken of the Convention provisions and of—

(*a*) any declaration, decision, advisory opinion or judgment of the European Court of Human Rights established under the Convention on any question in respect of which that Court has jurisdiction,
(*b*) any decision or opinion of the European Commission of Human Rights so established on any question in respect of which it had jurisdiction,
(*c*) any decision of the Committee of Ministers established under the Statute of the Council of Europe on any question in respect of which it has jurisdiction,

and a court shall, when interpreting and applying the Convention provisions, take due account of the principles laid down by those declarations, decisions, advisory opinions, opinions and judgments.

European Convention on Human Rights Act 2003, s 1(1) & 4

F

"FUNCTIONS"

"functions" includes powers and duties and references to the performance of functions includes, as respects powers and duties, references to the exercise of the powers and the performance of the duties.

European Convention on Human Rights Act 2003, s 1(1)

"functions" includes powers and duties and references to the performance of functions includes, as respects powers and duties, references to the exercise of the powers and the carrying out of the duties.

Human Rights Commission Act 2000, s 1(1)

H

"HUMAN RIGHTS"

In this Act (other than section 11) "human rights" means—

(*a*) the rights, liberties and freedoms conferred on, or guaranteed to, persons by the Constitution, and
(*b*) the rights, liberties or freedoms conferred on, or guaranteed to, persons by any agreement, treaty or convention to which the State is a party.

Human Rights Commission Act 2000, s 2

(3) In this section—

"human rights" means—

(*a*) the rights, liberties and freedoms conferred on, or guaranteed to, persons by the Constitution, and
(*b*) the rights, liberties or freedoms conferred on, or guaranteed to, persons by any agreement, treaty or convention to which the State is a party and which has been given the force of law in the State or by a provision of any such agreement, treaty or convention which has been given ["such force

and

(c) the rights, liberties and freedoms conferred on, or guaranteed to, persons by the Convention provisions within the meaning of the *European Convention on Human Rights Act 2003*.".]

Human Rights Commission Act 2000, s 11(3)(b) amended by European Convention on Human Rights Act 2003, s 7

I & J

"JUDICIAL OFFICE IN THE SUPERIOR COURTS"

"judicial office in the Superior Courts" means the office of judge of the High Court or the office of judge of the Supreme Court.

Human Rights Commission Act 2000, s 1(1)

O

"ORGAN OF THE STATE"

"organ of the State" includes a tribunal or any other body (other than the President or the Oireachtas or either House of the Oireachtas or a Committee of either such House or a Joint Committee of both such Houses or a court) which is established by law or through which any of the legislative, executive or judicial powers of the State are exercised.

European Convention on Human Rights Act 2003, s 1(1)

R

"RULE OF LAW"

"rule of law" includes common law.

European Convention on Human Rights Act 2003, s 1(1)

S

"STATUTE"

"statute" has the same meaning as it has in the Interpretation Act, 1937.

Human Rights Commission Act 2000, s 11(3)

"STATUTORY PROVISIONS"

"statutory provision" means any provision of an Act of the Oireachtas or of any order, regulation, rule, licence, bye-law or other like document made, issued or otherwise created thereunder or any statute, order, regulation, rule, licence, bye-law or other like document made, issued or otherwise created under a statute which continued in force by virtue of Article 50 of the Constitution.

European Convention on Human Rights Act 2003, s 1(1)

T

"THE AGREEMENT REACHED IN THE MULTI PARTY TALKS"

"the Agreement Reached in the Multi-Party Talks" means the agreement set out in Annex 1 to the Agreement between the Government of Ireland and the Government of the United Kingdom of Great Britain and Northern Ireland done at Belfast on the 10th day of April, 1998.

Human Rights Commission Act 2000, s 1(1)

"THE APPLICANT"

A person (in this section referred to as "the applicant") may apply under *subsection (3)* to the Commission for assistance of the kind referred to in *subsection (5)* in relation to legal proceedings to which this section applies.

Human Rights Commission Act 2000, s 10(2)

"THE COMMISSION"

"the Commission" has the meaning assigned to it by section 4.

Human Rights Commission Act 2000, s 1(1)

There shall stand established, on the establishment day, a body which shall be known as An Coimisiún um Chearta an Duine or, in the English language, the Human Rights Commission (in this Act referred to as "the Commission") to perform the functions conferred on it by this Act.

Human Rights Commission Act 2000, s 4

"THE CONVENTION"

"the Convention" means the Convention for the Protection of Human Rights and Fundamental Freedoms done at Rome on the 4th day of November, 1950 (the text of which, in the English language, is, for convenience of reference, set out in *Schedule 1* to this Act), as amended by Protocol No. 11 done at Strasbourg on the 11th day of May, 1994.

European Convention on Human Rights Act 2003, s 1(1)

HUMAN TRAFFICKING

E

"EXPLOITATION"

"exploitation" means—

(*a*) labour exploitation,
(*b*) sexual exploitation, or
(*c*) exploitation consisting of the removal of one or more of the organs of a person.

Criminal Law (Human Trafficking) Act 2008, s 1

L

"LABOUR EXPLOITATION"

"labour exploitation" means, in relation to a person (including a child)—

(*a*) subjecting the person to forced labour,
(*b*) forcing him or her to render services to another, or
(*c*) enslavement of the person or subjecting him or her to servitude or a similar condition or state.

Criminal Law (Human Trafficking) Act 2008, s 1

M

"MENTALLY IMPAIRED"

In this section "mentally impaired" has the same meaning as it has in the Criminal Law (Sexual Offences) Act 1993.

Criminal Law (Human Trafficking) Act 2008, s 4(8)

In this section "mentally impaired" means suffering from a disorder of the mind, whether through mental handicap or mental illness, which is of such a nature or degree as to render a person incapable of living an independent life or of guarding against serious exploitation.

Criminal Law (Sexual Offences) Act 1993, s 5(5)

P

"PUBLISHES"

"publishes" means publishes to any person, and includes publishes on the internet.

Criminal Law (Human Trafficking) Act 2008, s 11(5)

S

"SEXUAL EXPLOITATION"

"sexual exploitation" means, in relation to a person—

(*a*) the production of pornography depicting the person either alone or with others,
(*b*) causing the person to engage in sexual activity for the purpose of the production of pornography,

(*c*) the prostitution of the person,
(*d*) the commission of an offence specified in the Schedule to the Act of 2001 against the person; causing another person to commit such an offence against the person; or causing the person to commit such an offence against another person, or
(*e*) otherwise causing the person to engage or participate in any sexual, indecent or obscene act.

Criminal Law (Human Trafficking) Act 2008, s 1

"SOLICITS OR IMPORTUNES"

"Act of 1993" means the Criminal Law (Sexual Offences) Act 1993;

"solicits or importunes" has the same meaning as it has in the Act of 1993.

Criminal Law (Human Trafficking) Act 2008, s 5(6)

"solicits or importunes" includes soliciting or importuning from or in a motor vehicle, and cognate words shall be construed accordingly.

Criminal Law (Sexual Offences) act 1993, s 1

T

"TRAFFICKS"

"trafficks" means, in relation to a person (including a child)—

(*a*) procures, recruits, transports or harbours the person, or
  (i) transfers the person to,
  (ii) places the person in the custody, care or charge, or under the control, of, or
  (iii) otherwise delivers the person to,

another person,

(*b*) causes a person to enter or leave the State or to travel within the State,
(*c*) takes custody of a person or takes a person—
  (i) into one's care or charge, or
  (ii) under one's control,

or

(*d*) provides the person with accommodation or employment.

Criminal Law (Human Trafficking) Act 2008, s 1

"TRAFFICKS" (CHILD)

'trafficks' means, in relation to a child—

(*a*) procures, recruits, transports or harbours the child, or—
 (i) transfers the child to,
 (ii) places the child in the custody, care or charge, or under the control, of, or
 (iii) otherwise delivers the child to,

another person,

(*b*) causes the child to enter or leave the State or to travel within the State,
(*c*) takes custody of the child or takes the child—
 (i) into one's care or charge, or
 (ii) under one's control,

or

(*d*) provides the child with accommodation or employment.".

Child Trafficking and Pornography Act 1998, s 3 (amended by s 6 of the Criminal Law (Sexual Offences) (Amendment) Act 2007) substituted by Criminal Law (Human Trafficking) Act 2008, s 3

LEGAL AID

A

"ACCUSED" SEE THE

L

"LEGAL AID (APPEAL CERTIFICATE)"

Where—

(*a*) a person is convicted of an offence, and

(*b*) a certificate for free legal aid (in this Act referred to as a legal aid (appeal) certificate) is granted in respect of him by the District Court or by the judge of the court before which he was tried or under subsection (3) of this section,

the person shall be entitled to free legal aid in the preparation and conduct of an appeal from the conviction or the penalty (if any) imposed on conviction and to have a solicitor and (where the appeal lies to the Court of Criminal Appeal) counsel assigned to him for that purpose in such manner as may be prescribed by regulations under section 10 of this Act.

Criminal Justice (Legal Aid) Act 1962, s 4(1)

"LEGAL AID (CASE STATED) CERTIFICATE"

(1) Where—

(*a*) a person is charged with an offence before the District Court or the Circuit Court or appeals to the Circuit Court against a conviction of an offence by the District Court and the justice or judge (as the case may be) of the court before which the charge or appeal (as the case may be) is heard refers a question of law arising in the proceedings to the High Court or Supreme Court (as the case may be) by way of case stated or the justice states a case in relation to the proceedings for the opinion of the High Court, and

(*b*) a certificate for free legal aid (in this Act referred to as a legal aid (case stated) certificate) is granted in respect of the person by the court before which the charge or appeal (as the case may be) is heard or under subsection (3) of this section,

the person shall be entitled to free legal aid in the preparation and conduct of his case in relation to the case stated and to have a solicitor and counsel assigned to him for that purpose in such manner as may be prescribed by regulations under section 10 of this Act.

Criminal Justice (Legal Aid) Act 1962, s 5(1)

"LEGAL AID (CIVIL ORDER) CERTIFICATE"

Subject to *subsection (2)*, a person who is the subject of an application for a civil order may be granted a certificate for free legal aid (in this Part referred to as a "legal aid (civil order) certificate") in preparation for and representation at the hearing of—

(*a*) the application,
(*b*) an application by the person to vary or discharge a civil order,
(*c*) any appeal by the person against the making of the civil order, and
(*d*) any proceedings in the High Court or Supreme Court arising out of the making of the application, the appeal or any subsequent proceedings.

(2) A legal aid (civil order) certificate may not be granted under *subsection (1)* unless it appears to the court hearing the application for the certificate that—

(*a*) the means of the person concerned are insufficient to enable that person to obtain legal aid, and
(*b*) by reason of the gravity of the behaviour alleged to be anti-social or of exceptional circumstances, it is essential in the interests of justice that the person should have legal aid in preparation for and representation at the hearing concerned.

(3) A person who is granted a legal aid (civil order) certificate is entitled—

(*a*) to free legal aid in preparation for and representation at the hearing of the application for a civil order and any proceedings referred to in *subsection (1) (b)*, *(c)* and *(d)*, and
(*b*) to have, in such manner as may be prescribed,
   (i) a solicitor assigned to the person in relation to the application for the civil order or any application to vary or discharge it,
   (ii) a solicitor assigned to the person in relation to any other such proceedings, and
   (iii) if the court granting the certificate considers it appropriate, a counsel assigned to the person in relation to proceedings referred to in *subparagraph (ii)*.

(4) If a legal aid (civil order) certificate is granted, any fees, costs or other expenses properly incurred in preparation for and representation at the proceedings concerned shall, subject to regulations under *section* 119, be paid out of moneys provided by the Oireachtas.

(5) A person applying for a legal aid (civil order) certificate may be required by the court granting the certificate to furnish a written statement of the person's means.

(6) A person who, for the purpose of obtaining free legal aid under this section, whether for himself or herself or for some other person, knowingly makes a false or misleading statement or representation either orally or in writing, or knowingly conceals any material fact, commits an offence and is liable on summary conviction to a fine not exceeding €2,500 or imprisonment for a term not exceeding 6 months or both.

(7) On conviction of a person for an offence under this section, the court by which the person is convicted may, if in the circumstances of the case it thinks fit, order the person to pay to the Minister the whole or part of any sum paid under *subsection (4)*

in respect of the free legal aid in relation to which the offence was committed, and any sum so paid to the Minister shall be paid into and disposed of for the benefit of the Exchequer in accordance with the directions of the Minister for Finance.

Criminal Justice Act 2006, s 118(1)

"LEGAL AID (DISTRICT COURT) CERTIFICATE"

(6) Section 2 of the Criminal Justice (Legal Aid) Act, 1962, is hereby amended by the substitution of the following subsection for subsection (1):

"(1) If it appears to the District Court before which a person is charged with an offence or an alternative court within the meaning of *section 5* of the Criminal Justice (Miscellaneous Provisions) Act, 1997 before which a person is appearing—

(*a*) that the means of the person before it are insufficient to enable him to obtain legal aid, and

(*b*) that by reason of the gravity of the offence with which he is charged or of exceptional circumstances it is essential in the interests of justice that he should have legal aid in the preparation and conduct of his defence before it,

the said District Court or the alternative court, as may be appropriate, shall, on application being made to it in that behalf, grant a certificate, in respect of him, for free legal aid (in this Act referred to as a legal aid (District Court) certificate) and thereupon he shall be entitled to such aid and to have a solicitor and (where he is charged with murder and the said District Court or the alternative court, as the case may be, thinks fit) counsel assigned to him for that purpose in such manner as may be prescribed by regulations under section 10 of this Act.".

Criminal Justice (Legal Aid) Act 1962, s 2 substituted by Criminal Justice (Miscellaneous Provisions) Act 1997, s 5(6)

"LEGAL AID (MONITORING ORDER) CERTIFICATE"

(*a*) by the insertion of the following sections after section 6:

"Legal aid (monitoring order) certificate.

6A.—(1) Where—

(*a*) a monitoring order has been made in relation to a person, and

(*b*) a certificate for free legal aid (in this Act referred to as a 'legal aid (monitoring order) certificate') is granted in respect of him or her by the court to which an application is made to vary or revoke the order, the person shall be entitled to free legal aid in the preparation and conduct of an application under *section 26 (8)* of the *Criminal Justice Act 2007* to vary or revoke the order and to have a solicitor and, if the court considers it appropriate, counsel assigned to him or her for that purpose in such manner as may be prescribed by regulations under section 10 of this Act.

(2) A legal aid (monitoring order) certificate shall be granted in relation to a person in respect of whom a monitoring order has been made if (but only if)—

(*a*) application is made therefor,
(*b*) it appears to the court to which the application is made to vary or revoke the order that—
   (i) the means of the person are insufficient to enable him or her to obtain legal aid, and
   (ii) by reason of the conditions specified in the order or of exceptional circumstances, it is essential in the interests of justice that the person should have legal aid in the preparation and conduct of the application to vary or revoke the order.

(3) In this section 'monitoring order' has the meaning it has in *section* 26 of the *Criminal Justice Act 2007*.

Criminal Justice (Legal Aid) Act 1962, s 6A(1)(b) inserted by Criminal Justice Act 2007, s 27(a)

"LEGAL AID (PROTECTION OF PERSONS ORDER) CERTIFICATE"

Where—

(*a*) a protection of persons order has been made in relation to a person, and
(*b*) a certificate for free legal aid (in this Act referred to as a 'legal aid (protection of persons order) certificate') is granted in respect of him or her by the court to which an application is made to vary or revoke the order,

the person shall be entitled to free legal aid in the preparation and conduct of an application under *section* 26 *(8)* of the *Criminal Justice Act 2007* to vary or revoke the order and to have a solicitor and, if the court considers it appropriate, counsel assigned to him or her for that purpose in such manner as may be prescribed by regulations under section 10 of this Act.

(2) A legal aid (protection of persons order) certificate shall be granted in respect of a person in relation to whom a protection of persons order has been made if (but only if)—

(*a*) application is made therefor,
(*b*) it appears to the court to which the application is made to vary or revoke the order that—

(i) the means of the person are insufficient to enable him or her to obtain legal aid, and

(ii) by reason of the conditions specified in the order or of exceptional circumstances, it is essential in the interests of justice that the person should have legal aid in the preparation and conduct of the application to vary or revoke the order.

(3) In this section 'protection of persons order' has the meaning it has in *section* 26 of the *Criminal Justice Act 2007*.".

Criminal Justice (Legal Aid) Act 1962, s 6B(1)(b) inserted by Criminal Justice Act 2007, s 27(A)

"LEGAL AID (SUPREME COURT) CERTIFICATE"

Where—

(*a*) a person is charged with an offence,

(*b*) an appeal is brought to the Supreme Court from a determination of the Court of Criminal Appeal in relation to the offence or the penalty (if any) imposed in respect thereof or from a determination of the High Court on a case stated by a justice in relation to the proceedings in the District Court in regard to the offence or in relation to a question of law arising in those proceedings, and

(*c*) a certificate for free legal aid (in this Act referred to as a legal aid (Supreme Court) certificate) is granted in respect of the person charged with the offence to which the appeal relates by the Court of Criminal Appeal or the High Court (as the case may be) or under subsection (3) of this section,

the person shall be entitled to free legal aid in the preparation and conduct of his case in relation to the appeal and to have a solicitor and counsel assigned to him for that purpose in such manner as may be prescribed by regulations under section 10 of this Act.

Criminal Justice (Legal Aid) Act 1962, s 6(1)

"LEGAL AID (TRIAL ON INDICTMENT) CERTIFICATE"

Where—

(*a*) a person is **[sent forward for trial]** for an indictable offence, and

(*b*) a certificate for free legal aid (in this Act referred to as a legal aid (trial on indictment) certificate) is granted in respect of him by the District Court, upon his being [sent forward for trial], or by the judge of the court before which he is to be or is being tried,

the person shall be entitled to free legal aid in the preparation and conduct of his defence at the trial and to have a solicitor and counsel assigned to him for that purpose in such manner as may be prescribed by regulations under section 10 of this Act.

(2) A legal aid (trial on indictment) certificate shall be granted in respect of a person returned for trial for an indictable offence if (but only if)—

(*a*) application is made therefor,

(*b*) it appears to the District Court or the judge of the court before which the person is to be or is being tried that the means of the person are insufficient to enable him to obtain legal aid, and

(*c*) either—

(i) the person is charged with murder, or

(ii) it appears to the District Court or the judge of the court before which the person is to be or is being tried (as the case may be) that, having regard to all the circumstances of the case (including the nature of such defence (if any) as may have been set up), it is essential in the interests of justice that the person should have legal aid in the preparation and conduct of his defence at the trial.

Criminal Justice (Legal Aid) Act 1962, s 3(1)(b) as amended by the Criminal Justice Act 1999, s 12

M

"MONITORING ORDER"

(1) Where a person (other than a person under the age of 18 years) (in this section referred to as "the offender") is convicted on indictment of an offence specified in Schedule 2, the court shall consider whether it is appropriate to make an order or orders under this section in relation to the offender for the purpose of monitoring the offender after release from prison or for the purpose of protecting any person.

(2) The court may make an order (in this section referred to as a "monitoring order") in relation to the offender requiring the offender, as soon as practicable after the order comes into force, to notify in writing an inspector of the Garda Síochána of the district in which his or her home is located of the address of it and to notify in writing such an inspector of any change of address of his or her home or any proposed absence for a period of more than 7 days from his or her home before any such change of address or any such absence, as the case may be, occurs.

Criminal Justice Act 2007, s 26

P

"PRESCRIBED AUTHORITY" SEE THE

"PROTECTION OF PERSONS ORDER"

Where—

(*a*) a protection of persons order has been made in relation to a person, and
(*b*) a certificate for free legal aid (in this Act referred to as a 'legal aid (protection of persons order) certificate') is granted in respect of him or her by the court to which an application is made to vary or revoke the order,

the person shall be entitled to free legal aid in the preparation and conduct of an application under *section* 26 *(8)* of the *Criminal Justice Act 2007* to vary or revoke the order and to have a solicitor and, if the court considers it appropriate, counsel assigned to him or her for that purpose in such manner as may be prescribed by regulations under section 10 of this Act.

Criminal Justice (Legal Aid) Act 1962, s 6B(1) inserted by Criminal Justice Act 2007, s 27

T

"THE ACCUSED" (COURTS MARTIAL)

Where—

(*a*) an order is made for the trial by court-martial of a person (in this section referred to as "the accused"), and
(*b*) a certificate for free legal aid (in this Part of this Act referred to as "a legal aid (court-martial) certificate") is granted in respect of the accused by the prescribed authority,

the accused shall be entitled to free legal aid in the preparation and conduct of his defence at the trial and to have a solicitor and (where the prescribed authority thinks fit) counsel assigned to him for that purpose in such manner as may be prescribed by regulations under *section 33* of this Act.

Courts-Martial Appeals Act 1983, s 27(1)

"THE COUNCIL"

In this Regulation "the Council" means the General Council of the Bar of Ireland.

SI No 12/1965, art 5(5)

"THE COUNCIL" (COURTS MARTIAL)

In this Regulation "the Council" means the General Council of the Bar of Ireland.

SI No 425/1986, art 6(5)

"THE PRESCRIBED AUTHORITY" (COURTS MARTIAL)

"the prescribed authority" means the person prescribed by regulations under *section 33* of this Act to be the prescribed authority for the purposes of this Part of this Act.

Courts-Martial Appeals Act 1983, s 25

MUTUAL ASSISTANCE AND JOINT INVESTIGATION

A

"1959 CONVENTION"

"1959 Convention" means the European Convention on Mutual Assistance in Criminal Matters, done at Strasbourg on 20 April 1959, and includes the Additional Protocol of 17 March 1978 thereto.

Criminal Justice (Mutual Assistance) Act 2008, s 2(1)

"2000 CONVENTION"

"2000 Convention" means the Convention on Mutual Assistance in Criminal Matters between the Member States of the European Union, done at Brussels on 29 May 2000.

Criminal Justice (Mutual Assistance) Act 2008, s 2(1)

"2005 CONVENTION"

"2005 Convention" means the Council of Europe Convention on Laundering, Search, Seizure and Confiscation of the Proceeds from Crime and on the Financing of Terrorism, done at Warsaw on 16 May 2005.

Criminal Justice (Mutual Assistance) Act 2008, s 2(1)

"2005 COUNCIL DECISION"

"2005 Council Decision" means Council Decision 2005/671/JHA of 20 September 2005 on the exchange of information and co-operation concerning terrorist offences.

Criminal Justice (Mutual Assistance) Act 2008, s 2(1)

"ACCOUNT"

"account" means an account, of whatever nature, in a financial institution, whether in the State or a designated state, which is held or controlled by a person and includes—

(*a*) an account held by the person under a different name or different version of the person's name,

(*b*) an account held by the person jointly with another person,

(*c*) an account held by another person on which the person is authorised to operate, whether by way of a power of attorney or otherwise,

(*d*) an account held by another person (in this Part referred to as a "sending or recipient account") to or from which payments have been or are being made from or to an account in the name of a person specified in an account information order, and

(e) any other account held by another person, where information in relation to it would be relevant to the investigation referred to in the request.

Criminal Justice (Mutual Assistance) Act 2008, s 12(1)

"ACCOUNT INFORMATION ORDER"

"account information order" means an order under *section* 13 or 17 that a specified financial institution shall, within a time to be specified by the applicant for the order by notice in writing or any extension of that time under *subsection (2)*—

(*a*) state—
  (i) whether an account or accounts in the name or names of a specified person or persons or in a specified different version or versions of that name or those names is or are held in the financial institution, and
  (ii) whether it has become aware, in the ordinary course of business, of any other account or accounts in the institution on which the specified person or persons is or are authorised to operate, whether by way of a power of attorney or otherwise,

and

(*b*) if so, provide to the applicant or his or her nominee, in a manner and form specified in the notice, any information that it has in relation to any such account or accounts and any sending or recipient accounts, including details of any operations thereon specified in the notice during any period so specified.

Criminal Justice (Mutual Assistance) Act 2008, s 12(1)

"ACCOUNT MONITORING ORDER"

"account monitoring order" means an order under *section* 13 or 17 that a specified financial institution shall enable the applicant for the order to monitor, during a period, and in a manner and form, specified by the applicant by notice in writing, any operations so specified that are being carried out on an account or accounts in a specified name or names or in a specified different version or versions of that name or those names in the financial institution.

Criminal Justice (Mutual Assistance) Act 2008, s 12(1)

"ANOTHER MEMBER STATE"

"another Member State" means a Member State other than the State.

Criminal Justice (Joint Investigation) Team Act 2004, s 1(1)

"APPEAL"

"appeal" includes any proceedings for the discharge or setting aside of a judgment and any application for a new trial or stay of execution.

Criminal Justice (Mutual Assistance) Act 2008, s 31(1)

"APPROPRIATE AUTHORITY"

In this section, "appropriate authority", in relation to the place where the evidence is to be obtained, means—

(*a*) a court or tribunal specified in the letter of request and exercising jurisdiction in that place, or
(*b*) any other authority recognised by the government of the state concerned as the appropriate authority for receiving the letter.

Criminal Justice (Mutual Assistance) Act 2008, s 62(11)

(9) In this section, "appropriate authority" means—

(*a*) a court or tribunal exercising criminal jurisdiction in the place in a designated state where the evidence referred to in the letter of request is to be obtained, or
(*b*) any other body or authority recognised by the government of that state as the appropriate authority for receiving the letter.

Criminal Justice (Mutual Assistance) Act 2008, s 73(9)

In this section, "appropriate authority" means the authority in the designated state concerned appearing to the Director of Public Prosecutions to possess the identification evidence requested or to have the function of obtaining or arranging to obtain it.

Criminal Justice (Mutual Assistance) Act 2008, s 77(9)

"ARRESTABLE OFFENCE"

"arrestable offence" means an offence for which a person of full capacity and not previously convicted may, under or by virtue of any enactment, [**or the common law**] be punished by imprisonment for a term of five years or by a more severe penalty and includes an attempt to commit any such offence.

Criminal Law Act 1997, s 2 amended by the Criminal Justice Act 2006, s 8

"arrestable offence" means an offence for which a person of full capacity and not previously convicted may, under or by virtue of any enactment or of the common law, be punished by imprisonment for a term of 5 years or by a more severe penalty, and includes an attempt to commit any such offence.

Criminal Justice (Mutual Assistance) Act 2008, s 79(12)

"ARTICLE"

"Article" means an Article of the Ireland-US Treaty.

Criminal Justice (Mutual Assistance) Act 2008, s 93

"ARTICLES 49 AND 51"

"Articles 49 and 51", in relation to the Schengen Convention, means those Articles of the Convention, as applied to the State by Council Decision (2002/192/EEC) of 28 February 2002 concerning Ireland's request to take part in some of the provisions of the Schengen *acquis*, but does not include paragraph (a) (repealed by Article 2.2 of the 2000 Convention) of Article 49.

Criminal Justice (Mutual Assistance) Act 2008, s 2(1)

"AUTHORITY"

"authority" includes a person.

Criminal Justice (Mutual Assistance) Act 2008, s 2(1)

B

"BODILY SAMPLE"

"bodily sample" means any of the following:

(*a*) a sample of blood, hair, urine or saliva;
(*b*) a nail or any material found under a nail;
(*c*) a swab from any part of the body;
(*d*) a footprint or a similar impression of any part of the body, including a dental impression.

Criminal Justice (Mutual Assistance) Act 2008, s 76

"CENTRAL AUTHORITY"

(1) The Minister is the Central Authority for the purposes of this Act.

(2) The Central Authority has the function of receiving, transmitting and otherwise dealing with requests, except those made under Part 3, and of co-operating, in accordance with the relevant international instrument, with corresponding persons or bodies in designated states in relation to requests received from them.

(3) The Minister may, if he or she considers it appropriate, designate persons to perform specified functions of the Central Authority, and different persons may be so designated to perform different such functions.

(4) While such a designation is in force, a reference in this Act to the Central Authority, in so far as it relates to the performance of a function specified in the designation, is to be construed as a reference to the person so designated to perform that function.

(5) The Minister may amend or revoke a designation.

(6) The Minister shall, by notice in writing, inform the General Secretariat of the Council of the European Union of the names of any persons designated for the time being under this section.

Criminal Justice (Mutual Assistance) Act 2008, s 8

"COMPETENT AUTHORITY"

(1) Subject to *subsection (2)*, the competent authority of the State for the purposes of the Council Framework Decision and this Act (in this Act referred to as "the Competent Authority") is the Commissioner.

(2) Where the competent authority of another Member State requires a request to it under section 3 *(1)* to be made, or a request from it under section 4 *(1)* to be received, by a judicial authority, the Minister shall be the Competent Authority in relation to the request.

(3) In this Act "competent authority", in relation to another Member State, means the authority designated by that Member State to be the competent authority of that Member State for the purposes of the Council Framework Decision.

Criminal Justice (Joint Investigation Teams) Act 2004, s 2

"competent authority" means the person or body in a member state who or which in the opinion of the Minister is the competent authority for the purposes of Title III of the 2000 Convention.

Criminal Justice (Mutual Assistance) Act 2008, s 22

"COMPETENT AUTHORITY IN A DESIGNATED STATE"

"competent authority in a designated state", in relation to a request for a controlled delivery to or from a designated state, means a person or body in that state appearing to the Competent Authority in the State to have the function of receiving or making the request.

Criminal Justice (Mutual Assistance) Act 2008, s 88(1)

"COMPETENT AUTHORITY IN THE STATE"

"Competent Authority in the State", in relation to a request for a controlled delivery to or from a designated state, means—

(*a*) the Commissioner of the Garda Síochána or a member of the Garda Síochána authorised by him or her for the time being to exercise his or her functions under this Chapter, or

(*b*) if the controlled delivery is concerned with a revenue offence, the Revenue Commissioners or a person authorised by them for the time being to exercise their functions under this Chapter.

Criminal Justice (Mutual Assistance) Act 2008, s 88(1)

"CONFISCATION CO-OPERATION ORDER"

(1) The Central Authority, on receipt of an external confiscation order and accompanying documents, may cause an application to be made to the High Court for an order (a "confiscation co-operation order") for the confiscation of the property in the State to which the external confiscation order relates.

(2) The application shall be accompanied by the request, the accompanying documents and any other related documents or by copies thereof.

(3) On the application the Court may, subject to *subsection (4)*, make a confiscation co-operation order.

(4) The Court may not make a confiscation co-operation order unless—

(*a*) it is satisfied—

(i) that the application is made with the consent of the Minister,

(ii) as to the matters mentioned in *section* 50 *(2) (b),*

(iii) that the conduct which resulted in the making of the external confiscation order constitutes criminal conduct, and

(iv) that the making of the order is otherwise in accordance with the relevant international instrument,

and

(*b*) an opportunity has been given to any person claiming to own, or have an interest in, the property subject to the external confiscation order to show cause why the order should not be made.

(5) The Court—

(*a*) may vary or discharge a confiscation co-operation order on the application of any person claiming to have an interest in the property concerned or to be otherwise affected by the order and may in that connection consult the court which made the external confiscation order, and

(*b*) shall—

(i) vary a confiscation co-operation order in accordance with any variation made in the external confiscation order, and

(ii) if satisfied that the external confiscation order has been revoked or has been satisfied in accordance with the law of the designated state concerned, discharge it.

Criminal Justice (Mutual Assistance) Act 2008, s 51

"CONFISCATION ORDER"

"confiscation order" means a confiscation order within the meaning of the Act of 1994.

Criminal Justice (Mutual Assistance) Act 2008, s 31(1)

" 'confiscation order' means an order made under section 4(4), 8A(5) or 9(1) of this Act;";

(4) If the court determines that the person in question has benefited from drug trafficking, the court shall determine in accordance with *section 6* of this Act the amount to be recovered in his case by virtue of this section and shall make a confiscation order under this section requiring the person concerned to pay that amount.

Criminal Justice Act 1994, s 4(4)

(1) Where a person has been sentenced or otherwise dealt with by a court in respect of one or more offences of financing terrorism of which that person has

been convicted, the Director of Public Prosecutions may make, or cause to be made, an application to the court to determine whether the convicted person holds funds subject to confiscation.

(2) For the purposes of this Act, funds subject to confiscation are—

(*a*) funds used or allocated for use in connection with an offence of financing terrorism, or
(*b*) funds that are the proceeds of such an offence.

(3) An application under subsection (1) of this section may be made at the conclusion of the proceedings at which the person is sentenced or otherwise dealt with or at a later stage in the proceedings.

(4) An application under subsection (1) of this section shall not be made unless it appears to the Director of Public Prosecutions that the person in question holds funds subject to confiscation.

(5) If the court determines that the person in question holds funds subject to confiscation, the court shall—

(*a*) determine in accordance with section 8C of this Act the amount to be recovered in that person's case by virtue of this section, and
(*b*) make a confiscation order under this section requiring the person to pay that amount.

(6) The standard of proof applicable in civil proceedings is the standard required to determine a question arising under this Act as to—

(*a*) whether a person holds funds subject to confiscation, and
(*b*) the amount to be recovered in that person's case by virtue of this section.

Criminal Justice Act 1994, s 8a inserted by Criminal Justice (Terrorist Offences) Act 2005, s 22

(1) Where a person has been sentenced or otherwise dealt with in respect of an offence, other than a drug trafficking offence, of which he has been convicted on indictment, then, if an application is made, or caused to be made, to the court by the Director of Public Prosecutions the court may, subject to the provisions of this section, make a confiscation order under this section requiring the person concerned to pay such sum as the court thinks fit.

Criminal Justice Act 1994, s 9(1)

"CONSENT"

"consent" means consent in writing and a reference to the consent of a person is a reference to—

(*a*) in the case of a person who has attained the age of 18 years, the consent of that person,

(*b*) in the case of a person who has not attained the age of 18 years but has attained the age of 12 years, the consent of that person and of his or her parent or guardian, and

(*c*) in the case of a child aged 10 or 11 years who is detained on suspicion of having committed an offence mentioned in subsection (2) of section 52 (restriction on criminal proceedings against children) of the Children Act 2001, as substituted by section 129 of the Criminal Justice Act 2006, the consent of his or her parent or guardian.

Criminal Justice (Mutual Assistance) Act 2008, s 79(12)

"CONTROLLED DELIVERY"

"controlled delivery" means a delivery permitted in the State in accordance with this Chapter or in a designated state in accordance with the relevant international instrument for the purposes of an investigation into an offence.

Criminal Justice (Mutual Assistance) Act 2008, s 88(1)

"CONTROLLED DRUG"

"controlled drug" has the meaning given to it by section 2 of the Misuse of Drugs Act 1977.

Criminal Justice (Mutual Assistance) Act 2008, s 88(1)

(1) In this Act "controlled drug" means any substance, product or preparation (other than a substance, product or preparation specified in an order under subsection (3) of this section which is for the time being in force) which is either specified in the Schedule to this Act or is for the time being declared pursuant to subsection (2) of this section to be a controlled drug for the purposes of this Act.

(2) The Government may by order declare any substance, product or preparation (not being a substance, product or preparation specified in the Schedule to this Act) to be a controlled drug for the purposes of this Act and so long as an order under this subsection is in force, this Act shall have effect as regards any substance, product or preparation specified in the order as if the substance, product or preparation were specified in the said Schedule.

Misuse of Drugs Act 1977, s 2(1)

"CRIMINAL CONDUCT"

"criminal conduct" means any conduct—

(*a*) which constitutes an offence, or
(*b*) which occurs in a designated state and would, if it occurred in the State, constitute an offence.

Criminal Justice (Mutual Assistance) Act 2008, s 2(1)

In this section—

"criminal conduct" means—

(*a*) drug trafficking,
(*b*) the commission of an indictable offence or more than one such offence,
(*c*) holding funds subject to confiscation,
(*d*) benefiting from—
  (i) drug trafficking,
  (ii) an indictable offence or more than one such offence,
  (iii) assets or proceeds deriving from criminal conduct or the receipt or control of such assets or proceeds, including conduct which occurs outside the State and which would constitute an indictable offence or more than one such offence—
    (I) if it occurred in the State, and
    (II) if it constituted an offence or more than one such offence under the law of the state or territory concerned.".

Criminal Justice Act 1994, s 63 substituted by Criminal Justice (Mutual Assistance) Act 2008, s 105(f)

"CRIMINAL INVESTIGATION"

"criminal investigation"—

(*a*) means an investigation into whether a person has committed an offence (within the meaning of the relevant Part) under the law of the State or a designated state in respect of which, where appropriate, a request for assistance may be made under the relevant international instrument, and
(*b*) includes an investigation into whether a person has benefited from assets or proceeds deriving from criminal conduct or is in receipt of or controls such assets or proceeds.

Criminal Justice (Mutual Assistance) Act 2008, s 2(1)

"CRIMINAL PROCEEDINGS"

"criminal proceedings" means proceedings, whether in the State or a designated state, against a person for an offence and includes—

(*a*) proceedings to determine whether a person has benefited from assets or proceeds deriving from criminal conduct or is in receipt of or controls such assets or proceeds,

(*b*) proceedings concerning measures relating to—

- (i) the deferral of delivery or suspension of enforcement of a sentence or preventive measure,
- (ii) conditional release, or
- (iii) a stay or interruption of enforcement of a sentence or preventive measure.

Criminal Justice (Mutual Assistance) Act 2008, s 2(1)

D

"DEFENDANT"

"defendant" means the person to whose property an external freezing order or external confiscation order relates.

Criminal Justice (Mutual Assistance) Act 2008, s 31(1)

"DENTIST"

"dentist" means a person whose name is entered for the time being in the Register of Dentists maintained under the Dentists Act 1985.

Criminal Justice (Mutual Assistance) Act 2008, s 76

"DESIGNATED STATE"

The Minister for Foreign Affairs, after consultation with the Minister, may by order designate a state (other than a member state) for the purposes of mutual assistance between the State and that state under this Act or specified Parts or provisions of it in accordance with the relevant international instrument.

Criminal Justice (Mutual Assistance) Act 2008, s 4

"DOCTOR"

"doctor" means a person whose name is entered for the time being in the General Register of Medical Practitioners established under section 26 of the Medical Practitioners Act 1978.

Criminal Justice (Mutual Assistance) Act 2008, s 76

E

"EC/SWISS CONFEDERATION AGREEMENT"

"EC/Swiss Confederation Agreement" means the Co-operation Agreement between the European Community and its member states, of the one part, and the Swiss Confederation, of the other part, to combat fraud and any other illegal activity to the detriment of their financial interests, done at Luxembourg on 26 October 2004.

Criminal Justice (Mutual Assistance) Act 2008, s 2(1)

"EU–US AGREEMENT"

"EU–US Agreement" means the Agreement on Mutual Legal Assistance between the European Union and the United States of America, done at Washington D.C. on 25 June 2003.

Criminal Justice (Mutual Assistance) Act 2008, s 93

"EVIDENCE"

In this section "evidence" includes documents and other articles.

Criminal Justice (Joint Investigation Teams) Act 2004, s 7(12)

"evidence" includes evidence of or relating to assets or proceeds deriving from criminal conduct in the designated state concerned or their identity or whereabouts.

Criminal Justice (Mutual Assistance) Act 2008, s 74(16)

"evidence" does not include information provided under *Part 2* in relation to financial transactions.

Criminal Justice (Mutual Assistance) Act 2008, s 61

"EVIDENTIAL MATERIAL"

"evidential material" includes any such material relating to assets or proceeds deriving from criminal conduct in the designated state concerned or their identity or whereabouts.

Criminal Justice (Mutual Assistance) Act 2008, s 75(19)

"EXPLANATORY NOTE"

"Explanatory Note" means the Explanatory Note which—

(*a*) is annexed to the Council Decision of 6 June 2003 concerning the signature of the Agreements between the European Union and the United States of America on extradition and mutual assistance in criminal matters, and

(*b*) records an understanding between the European Union and the United States of America on the EU–US Agreement.

Criminal Justice (Mutual Assistance) Act 2008, s 93

"EXTERNAL CONFISCATION ORDER"

"external confiscation order" means an order made by a court in a designated state for the purpose of—

(*a*) recovering property in the State which was received or obtained as a result of or in connection with conduct which would, if it occurred in the State, constitute an indictable offence,

(*b*) recovering the value of such property, or

(*c*) depriving a person of a pecuniary advantage so received or obtained.

Criminal Justice (Mutual Assistance) Act 2008, s 31(1)

"EXTERNAL FORFEITURE ORDER"

"external forfeiture order" means an order for the forfeiture of property in the State which is made by a court in a designated state in or in connection with proceedings resulting from conduct which would, if it occurred in the State, constitute an indictable offence.

Criminal Justice (Mutual Assistance) Act 2008, s 31(1)

"EXTERNAL FREEZING ORDER"

"external freezing order" means any measure—

(*a*) taken provisionally by a competent judicial authority of a designated state in criminal proceedings to prevent the destruction, transformation, moving, transfer, disposal or use of specified property in the State that could be subject to confiscation or be evidence in those proceedings, and

(*b*) made for the purpose of—

 (i) subsequent confiscation of the property, or

 (ii) protection of evidence.

Criminal Justice (Mutual Assistance) Act 2008, s 31(1)

F

"FORM"

"form", where it occurs in the definition of account information order and account monitoring order, means a form which—

(*a*) is permanent and legible, whether or not it has been converted into such a form from an electronic or other non-legible form, or

(*b*) if so specified by the applicant for such an order, is an electronic or other non-legible form which is capable of being converted into a permanent and legible form.

Criminal Justice (Mutual Assistance) Act 2008, s 12(1)

"FORFEITURE CO-OPERATION ORDER"

(1) The Central Authority, on receipt of an external forfeiture order and accompanying documents, may cause an application to be made to the High Court for an order (a "forfeiture co-operation order") for the forfeiture of realisable property in the State to which the external forfeiture order relates.

(2) The application shall be accompanied by the request, the accompanying documents and any other related documents or by copies thereof.

(3) On the application the Court may, subject to *subsection (4)*, make a forfeiture co-operation order.

(4) The Court may not make a forfeiture co-operation order unless—

(*a*) it is satisfied—
- (i) that the application is made with the consent of the Minister,
- (ii) as to the matters mentioned in *section* 59 *(2) (b)*,
- (iii) that the conduct which resulted in the making of the external forfeiture order constitutes criminal conduct, and
- (iv) that the making of the order is otherwise in accordance with the relevant international instrument,

and

(*b*) an opportunity has been given to any person claiming to own, or have an interest in, the property subject to the external forfeiture order to show cause why the order should not be made.

(5) A forfeiture co-operation order operates to deprive the defendant in the proceedings in which the external forfeiture order was made of any right or interest in the property and to vest the property in the Commissioner of the Garda Síochána.

(6) The forfeited property or the proceeds of any sale of the property shall be disposed of for the benefit of the Exchequer in accordance with the directions of the Minister for Finance, unless, on request by or on behalf of the designated state concerned and in accordance with the relevant international instrument, the Court provides otherwise.

(7) The Court—

(*a*) may vary or discharge a forfeiture co-operation order on the application of any person claiming to own or have an interest in the property concerned or to be otherwise affected by the order and may in that connection consult the court which made the external forfeiture order, and

(*b*) shall—
- (i) vary a forfeiture co-operation order in accordance with any variation in the external forfeiture order, and
- (ii) if satisfied that the external forfeiture order has been revoked, discharge it.

(8) The Police (Property) Act 1897 does not apply to property which vests in the Commissioner of the Garda Síochána by virtue of this section.

(9) This section applies to any property which is in the possession of the Garda Síochána under section 61(4) of the Act of 1994.

(10) Nothing in this section affects any enactment whereby property is, or may be ordered to be, forfeited as a result of a conviction for an offence.

Criminal Justice (Mutual Assistance) Act 2008, s 60

"FRAMEWORK DECISION"

"Framework Decision" means Council Framework Decision (2003/577/JHA) of 22 July 2003 on the execution in the European Union of orders freezing property or evidence.

Criminal Justice (Mutual Assistance) Act 2008, s 2(1)

"FREEZING CO-OPERATION ORDER"

(1) The Central Authority shall, on receipt of an external freezing order, certificate (where appropriate), any other supporting or related documents and any translation, forthwith cause an application to be made to the High Court for an order (in this Part referred to as a " freezing co-operation order") recognising the external freezing order and prohibiting any person from dealing with the property specified in the external freezing order.

(2) The application may be made *ex parte* and otherwise than in public and shall be accompanied by the documents mentioned in *subsection (1)* or copies thereof and, in the case of a designated state (other than a member state), shall be made with the consent of the Minister.

(3) An application from a member state for the enforcement of an external freezing order shall be dealt with as soon as possible and, whenever practicable, within 24 hours of receipt of the order and a duly completed certificate.

(4) On an application under this section the Court may, subject to *subsection (5)*, make a freezing co-operation order, subject to any conditions that may be specified in the order.

(5) The Court may—

(*a*) refuse to make a freezing co-operation order on a ground mentioned in *section* 3 or 46, or
(*b*) postpone its making on a ground mentioned in *section* 47.

(6) Where a request from a member state concerns an offence referred to in Article 3(2) of the Framework Decision which is punishable in that state by a maximum term of imprisonment of not less than 3 years, the Court may not refuse to make a freezing co-operation order solely on the ground that the conduct constituting the offence concerned does not constitute an offence under the law of the State.

(7) Where—

(*a*) an external freezing order is for the protection of evidence,
(*b*) it is necessary to ensure that the evidence is admissible in the proceedings concerned, and

(*c*) for that purpose certain formalities and procedures in the enforcement of the external freezing order are expressly indicated by the issuing judicial authority,

the freezing co-operation order shall make provision for observing those formalities and procedures, unless their observance would be contrary to the fundamental principles of the law of the State.

(8) The Court shall cause notice of the freezing co-operation order to be given to any person who appears to be or is affected by it, unless the Court is satisfied that it is not reasonably possible to ascertain the person's whereabouts.

Criminal Justice (Mutual Assistance) Act 2008, s 35

"FREEZING ORDER"

"freezing order" means—

(*a*) an order under section 24 (as amended by *section* 105 *(a)* of this Act) of the Act of 1994,
(*b*) an order under section 14 or 15 of the Criminal Justice (Terrorist Offences) Act 2005, or
(*c*) an order under *section* 32,

which relates to property in a designated state or in so far as it does so.

Criminal Justice (Mutual Assistance) Act 2008, s 31(1)

I & J

"IDENTIFICATION EVIDENCE"

"identification evidence" means a fingerprint, palm print or photograph of, or bodily sample from, a person and includes any related records.

Criminal Justice (Mutual Assistance) Act 2008, s 76

"IMPRISONMENT"

"imprisonment" includes detention and, in relation to a designated state, any other form of deprivation of liberty.

Criminal Justice (Mutual Assistance) Act 2008, s 2(1)

"INSTRUMENT"

"Instrument" means the Instrument contemplated by Article 3(2) of the EU–US Agreement as to the application of the US–Ireland Treaty and done at Dublin on 14 July 2005.

Criminal Justice (Mutual Assistance) Act 2008, s 93

"INTERCEPTION"

"interception" means the interception of telecommunication messages to or from a person specified in the authorisation of the interception at a telecommunications address so specified.

Criminal Justice (Mutual Assistance) Act 2008, s 22

"INTERNATIONAL INSTRUMENT"

"international instrument" means any of the following agreements, or provisions of agreements, between the State and other states or another state in relation to mutual assistance in criminal matters:

(*a*) the 2000 Convention;
(*b*) the 2001 Protocol;
(*c*) the Agreement with Iceland and Norway;
(*d*) Articles 49 and 51 of the Schengen Convention;
(*e*) the Framework Decision;
(*f*) Title III of the EC/Swiss Confederation Agreement;
(*g*) the 2005 Council Decision;
(*h*) the 1959 Convention;
(*i*) the Second Additional Protocol;
(*j*) Chapter IV of the 2005 Convention;
(*k*) Articles 13, 14, 18, 19 and 20 of the United Nations Convention against Transnational Organised Crime, done at New York on 15 November 2000;
(*l*) Articles 46, 49, 50 and 54 to 57 of the United Nations Convention against Corruption, done at New York on 31 October 2003;
(*m*) a bilateral agreement between the State and a designated state for the provision of such assistance; and
(*n*) any reservation or declaration made in accordance with such an instrument.

Criminal Justice (Mutual Assistance) Act 2008, s 2(1)

"IRELAND–US TREATY"

"Ireland–US Treaty" means the Treaty between the Government of Ireland and the Government of the United States of America on Mutual Assistance in Criminal Matters, done at Washington D.C. on 18 January 2001, as applied by the Instrument.

Criminal Justice (Mutual Assistance) Act 2008, s 93

"ISSUING JUDICIAL AUTHORITY"

"issuing judicial authority" means a judicial authority in a designated state, as defined in the law of that state, which makes, validates or in any way confirms an external freezing order.

Criminal Justice (Mutual Assistance) Act 2008, s 31(1)

"ISSUING STATE"

"issuing state" means the designated state in which an issuing judicial authority exercises jurisdiction.

Criminal Justice (Mutual Assistance) Act 2008, s 31(1)

"JOINT INVESTIGATION TEAM"

Where the Competent Authority receives a request specifying the matters mentioned in section 3 *(2)* from one or more competent authorities of other Member States to establish a joint investigation team, the Competent Authority shall consider the request.

(2) The Competent Authority may seek from the competent authority or authorities concerned such other information (if any) as is specified to that authority or those authorities and is reasonably required by the Competent Authority to decide whether or not to agree to establish a joint investigation team.

(3) The Competent Authority may, subject to this Act, agree with the competent authority or authorities concerned to establish a joint investigation team to investigate certain conduct if the Competent Authority is satisfied that—

(*a*) either—

(i) the conduct which would constitute an offence if it occurred in the State has occurred, or there are reasonable grounds for suspecting that such conduct has occurred, partly in the State and partly in another Member State or States, or

(ii) the conduct which would constitute an offence if it occurred in the State has occurred, or there are reasonable grounds for suspecting that such conduct has occurred, in another Member State or States and the investigation of it has links with the State,

And

(*b*) there are reasonable grounds for believing that it is in the public interest, having regard to the benefit likely to accrue to the investigation into the conduct concerned, to agree to the establishment of a joint investigation team with the other Member State or States concerned because—

(i) part of the investigation is being, or it is anticipated that it will be, conducted in the State, or

(ii) the investigation requires coordinated and concerted action by the Member States (including the State) concerned.

(4) The Competent Authority and the competent authority or authorities concerned may, pursuant to an agreement under *subsection (3),* establish a joint investigation team.

Criminal Justice (Joint Investigation Teams) Act 2004, s 4

L

"LETTER OF REQUEST"

Where this section applies, an application may be made by or on behalf of the Director of Public Prosecutions or the accused to a judge of the court of trial at a sitting of the court to issue a letter (a "letter of request") requesting the provision of facilities in the designated state concerned to enable the witness to give evidence in the proceedings through a live television link.

Criminal Justice (Mutual Assistance) Act 2008, s 67(2)

Where it appears to a judge of any court that—

(*a*) criminal proceedings have been instituted or a criminal investigation is taking place, and

(*b*) identification evidence for the purposes of the proceedings or investigation may be obtained from an authority in a designated state,

the judge may issue a letter (a "letter of request") requesting assistance in obtaining the evidence.

Criminal Justice (Mutual Assistance) Act 2008, s 77(1)

M

"MEMBER"

"member", in relation to a joint investigation team or a part of such a team, means a person who is assigned or appointed under section 6 to be a member of the team.

Criminal Justice (Joint Investigation Teams) Act 2004, s 1

"MEMBER STATE"

"Member State" means Member State of the European Communities.

Criminal Justice (Joint Investigation Teams) Act 2004, s 1(1)

"member state" means—

(*a*) a member state of the European Union (other than the State), for the purposes of mutual assistance under the provisions of the 2000 Convention, 2001 Protocol, Articles 49 and 51 of the Schengen Convention, Framework Decision or 2005 Council Decision, and
(*b*) Iceland and Norway or any other designated state, for the purposes of mutual assistance under any of those provisions.

Criminal Justice (Mutual Assistance) Act 2008, s 2(1)

"member state" includes the Swiss Confederation.

Criminal Justice (Mutual Assistance) Act 2008, s 74(16)

"member state" includes the Swiss Confederation.

Criminal Justice (Mutual Assistance) Act 2008, s 75(19)

N

"NURSE"

"nurse" means a person whose name is entered for the time being in the register of nurses established under section 27 of the Nurses Act 1985.

Criminal Justice (Mutual Assistance) Act 2008, s 76

O

"OFFENCE"

"offence"—

(*a*) means an offence in respect of which a request for mutual assistance may be made under the relevant international instrument,
(*b*) includes a revenue offence, if or to the extent that the relevant international instrument or the law of the designated state concerned provides for mutual assistance in respect of such an offence, but
(*c*) does not include a political offence.

Criminal Justice (Mutual Assistance) Act 2008, s 2(1)

"offence" includes an offence which is suspected, with reasonable cause, to have been or to be about to be committed.

Criminal Justice (Mutual Assistance) Act 2008, s 88(1)

P

"2001 PROTOCOL"

"2001 Protocol" means the Protocol to the 2000 Convention, done at Luxembourg on 16 October 2001.

Criminal Justice (Mutual Assistance) Act 2008, s 12(1)

"PARTICIPANTS"

The Competent Authority may agree with the other competent authority or authorities concerned to permit any of the following persons (in this Act referred to as "participants") to participate, on such terms and conditions as may be agreed with the body or authority designating those persons, in the activities of a joint investigation team:

(*a*) one or more officers designated by Europol,
(*b*) one or more officers designated by a body, such as Eurojust, established under Title VI of the Treaty on European Union,
(*c*) one or more officers designated by the European Commission or other institution of the European Communities, or

(*d*) one or more officers designated by an authority of a country or territory other than a Member State or a part of such a State, and the Minister may designate such a country or territory by order.

(2) Participants in a joint investigation team shall provide support or advice or both to the team.

Criminal Justice (Joint Investigation Teams) Act 2004, s 9

"PLACE"

"'place' means a physical location and includes—

(*a*) a dwelling, residence, building or abode,
(*b*) a vehicle, whether mechanically propelled or not,
(*c*) a vessel, whether sea-going or not,
(*d*) an aircraft, whether capable of operation or not, and
(*e*) a hovercraft.".

Criminal Justice (Mutual Assistance) Act 2008, s 2(1)

"Place" includes premises.

Criminal Justice (Mutual Assistance) Act 2008, s 61

"POLITICAL OFFENCE"

"political offence", except in Part 2—

(*a*) includes an offence connected with a political offence,
(*b*) does not include any offence in respect of which a person may be surrendered to another state under the European Arrest Warrant Act 2003 or the Extradition Acts 1965 to 2001.

Criminal Justice (Mutual Assistance) Act 2008, s 2(1)

"political offence"—

(*a*) includes an offence connected with a political offence,
(*b*) does not include—
  (i) an offence to which section 3 of the Extradition (European Convention on the Suppression of Terrorism) Act 1987 (the "Act of 1987") applies, or
  (ii) an offence, as defined in *subsection (3)*, of conspiracy or association to commit such an offence.

Criminal Justice (Mutual Assistance) Act 2008, s 12(1)

"PRISON"

"prison" means a place of custody administered by or on behalf of the Minister (other than a Garda Síochána station) and includes—

(*a*) St. Patrick's Institution,
(*b*) a place provided under section 2 of the Prisons Act 1970, and
(*c*) a place specified under section 3 of the Prisons Act 1972.

Criminal Justice (Mutual Assistance) Act 2008, s 2(1)

"PRISONER"

In this section, "prisoner" means a person who is detained in custody in a designated state—

(*a*) under a sentence or order of a court exercising criminal jurisdiction in that state, or
(*b*) having been transferred there from the State under section 5 (issue of warrants for the transfer of sentenced prisoners outside State) of the Transfer of Sentenced Prisoners Act 1995.

Criminal Justice (Mutual Assistance) Act 2008, s 65(1)

"PROPERTY"

"property", except in Part 4, includes—

(*a*) money and all other property, real or personal, movable or immovable,
(*b*) a chose in action and any other intangible or incorporeal property,
(*c*) proceeds of the disposal of property, and
(*d*) evidence.

Criminal Justice (Mutual Assistance) Act 2008, s 2(1)

"property" includes property of any description, corporeal or incorporeal, movable or immovable and wherever situated, which the competent judicial authority in the designated state considers—

(*a*) to be the proceeds of an offence,
(*b*) to be equivalent to either the full value or a part of the value of such proceeds, or
(*c*) to be the instrumentalities or objects of an offence,

and includes documents evidencing title to or an interest in the property.

Criminal Justice (Mutual Assistance) Act 2008, s 31(1)

R

"REALISABLE PROPERTY"

"realisable property" means—

(*a*) in relation to a freezing co-operation order or confiscation co-operation order made in respect of specified property, the property specified in the order, and

(*b*) in any other case—

(i) any property held by the defendant, and

(ii) any property held by a person to whom the defendant has directly or indirectly made a gift,

but does not include property which is the subject of an order made by a court in other proceedings in the State unless or until that order is discharged.

Criminal Justice (Mutual Assistance) Act 2008, s 31(1)

"REGISTER OF COMPANIES"

"Register of Companies" means the Register of Companies maintained under the Companies Acts 1963 to 2006.

Criminal Justice (Mutual Assistance) Act 2008, s 37(6)

"REGISTERED COMPANY"

"registered company" means—

(*a*) a company formed and registered under those Acts,

(*b*) an existing company within the meaning of those Acts, or

(*c*) a company registered under Part XI of the Companies Act 1963 or the European Communities (Branch Disclosure) Regulations 1993 (S.I. No. 395 of 1993).

Criminal Justice (Mutual Assistance) Act 2008, s 37(6)

"RELEVANT INTERNATIONAL INSTRUMENT"

"relevant international instrument" means the international instrument in accordance with which a request for assistance is made.

Criminal Justice (Mutual Assistance) Act 2008, s 2(1)

"RELEVANT TIME"

"relevant time" means—

(*a*) where no order for the winding up of the company has been made, the time of the passing of the resolution for its voluntary winding up,
(*b*) where such an order has been made and, before presentation of the petition for the winding up of the company by the court, such a resolution had been passed by the company, the time of the passing of the resolution, and
(*c*) in any other case where such an order has been made, the time of the making of the order.

Criminal Justice (Mutual Assistance) Act 2008, s 43(3)

"REQUEST"

"request" means a request for assistance which is made by a requesting authority under and in accordance with a relevant international instrument.

Criminal Justice (Mutual Assistance) Act 2008, s 2(1)

"REQUESTING AUTHORITY"

"requesting authority" means—

(*a*) a court or tribunal exercising jurisdiction in criminal proceedings in a designated state and making a request, or
(*b*) any other authority in that state appearing to the Minister to have the function of making the request.

Criminal Justice (Mutual Assistance) Act 2008, s 2(1)

"REVENUE OFFENCE"

"revenue offence"—

(*a*) means an offence under the law of the State or a designated state in connection with taxes, duties, customs or exchange regulation,
(*b*) includes such an offence under the law of a designated state irrespective of whether the law of the State provides for taxes, duties, customs or exchange regulation of the same kind as that state provides, but

(*c*) does not include—
  (i) an offence involving the use or threat of force or perjury or the forging of a document issued under statutory authority, or
  (ii) an offence alleged to have been committed by an officer of the Revenue of that state in his or her capacity as such officer.

Criminal Justice (Mutual Assistance) Act 2008, s 2(1)

S

"SCHENGEN CONVENTION"

"Schengen Convention" means the Convention, signed in Schengen on 19 June 1990, implementing the Schengen Agreement of 14 June 1985.

Criminal Justice (Mutual Assistance) Act 2008, s 2(1)

Criminal Justice (Miscellaneous Provisions) Act 2009, s 4

"SECOND ADDITIONAL PROTOCOL"

"Second Additional Protocol" means the Second Additional Protocol of 8 November 2001 to the 1959 Convention.

Criminal Justice (Mutual Assistance) Act 2008, s 2(1)

"SECONDED MEMBER"

"seconded member", in relation to a joint investigation team or a part of such a team, means—

(*a*) if and when the team or the part is operating in the State, a member of the team or the part aforesaid appointed by the competent authority of another Member State that established the team, and
(*b*) if and when the team or the part is operating in another Member State, a member of the team or the part aforesaid assigned or appointed under section 6.

Criminal Justice (Joint Investigation Teams) Act 2004, s 1(1)

"SENDING OR RECIPIENT ACCOUNT"

"sending or recipient account" has the meaning given to it by *paragraph (d)* of the definition of "account".

Criminal Justice (Mutual Assistance) Act 2008, s 12(1)

(*d*) an account held by another person (in this Part referred to as a "sending or recipient account") to or from which payments have been or are being made from or to an account in the name of a person specified in an account information order, and.

Criminal Justice (Mutual Assistance) Act 2008, s 12 (1)(d)

"SERIOUS OFFENCE"

The list of offences which constitute **serious offences** is set out in the schedule to the Bail Act 1997. However this schedule has been heavily amended and where there is an amendment to one of numbered offences in the schedule this is set out directly under that number.

Common law offences

1. Murder.

2. Manslaughter.

3.

4.

5.

6. Rape.

Definitions 3, 4 and 5 deleted by **Non-Fatal Offences Against the Person Act, 1997, s 30(a)(b)(c)**

Offences against the person

7. Any offence under the following provisions of the *Non-Fatal Offences against the Person Act, 1997*—

(*a*) *section 3* (assault causing harm);
(*b*) *section 4* (causing harm);
(*c*) *section 5* (threats to kill or cause serious harm);
(*d*) *section 6* (syringe, etc. attacks);
(e) *section 7* (1) (offence of possession of syringe, etc. in certain circumstances);
(*f*) *section 8* (placing or abandoning syringe);
(*g*) *section 9* (coercion);
(*h*) *section 10* (harassment);
(*i*) *section 13* (endangerment);
(*j*) *section 14* (endangering traffic);
(*k*) *section 15* (false imprisonment);

(*l*) *section 16* (abduction of child by parent, etc.);
(*m*) *section 17* (abduction of child by other persons).".

7 substituted by the Non-Fatal Offences Against the Person Act 1997, s 30(d)

7A. Any offence under section 3 of the Criminal Justice Act 1990 (certain murders and attempts)

7A inserted by the Criminal Justice (Miscellaneous Provisions) Act 2009, s 48

1. Any offence under the provisions of the Criminal Justice (Public Order) Act 1994:—

(*a*) Section 18 (assault to cause bodily harm or commit indictable offence);
(*b*) Section 19 (assault or obstruction of peace officer)

Sexual offences

2. Any offence under section 1 (incest by males) and section 2 (incest by female of or over 17 years) of the Punishment of Incest Act 1908.

3. Any offence under section 1 (defilement of girl under fifteen years of age) and section 2 (defilement of girl between fifteen and seventeen years of age) of the Criminal Law Amendment Act, 1935

4. Any offence under the following provisions of the Criminal Law (Rape) (Amendment) Act 1990;

(*a*) Section 2 (sexual assault);
(*b*) Section 3 (aggravated sexual assault);
(*c*) Section 4 (rape under section 4);

5. Any offence under the following provisions of the Criminal Law (Sexual Offences) Act, 1993—

(*a*) Section 3 (buggery of persons under 17 years of age);
(*b*) Section 5 (protection of mentally impaired persons);
(*c*) Sections 9 and 11 (organisation etc. of prostitution).

"12A. Any offence under the following provisions of the *Child Trafficking and Pornography Act, 1998* —

(*a*) *section 3* (child trafficking and taking, etc., child for sexual exploitation);
(*b*) *section 5* (producing, distributing, etc., child pornography).".

12 A inserted by the Child Trafficking and Pornography Act 1998, s 12

Explosives

6. Any offence under the following provisions of the Explosives Substances Act, 1883—

(*a*) Section 2 (causing explosions likely to endanger life or damage tom property)
(*b*) Section 3 (possession etc. of explosive substances);
(*c*) Section 4 (making or possessing explosives in suspicious circumstances)

Firearms

7.
Any offence under the following provisions of the Firearms Act 1925:

(*a*) section 2 (restrictions on possession, use, and carriage of firearms);
(*b*) section 3 (applications for, and form and effect of, firearm certificates);
(*c*) section 4A(18) (authorisation of rifle or pistol clubs or shooting ranges);
(*d*) section 10A (reloading of ammunition);
(*e*) section 15 (possession of firearms with intent to endanger life);
(*f*) section 25 (punishments).".

14 substituted by the Criminal Justice Act 2007, s 17

8. Any offence under the following provisions of the Firearms Act, 1964—
(*a*) Section 26 (possession of firearm while taking vehicle without authority);
(*b*) Section 27 (use of firearm to resist arrest or aid escape);
(*c*) Section 27A (possession of firearm or ammunition in suspicious circumstances);
(*d*) Section 27B (carrying firearm with criminal intent).

9. I
Any offence under the following provisions of the Firearms and Offensive Weapons Act 1990:

(*a*) section 7 (possession, sale, etc., of silencers);
(*b*) section 8 (reckless discharge of firearm);
(*c*) section 9 (possession of knives and other articles);
(*d*) section 10 (trespassing with a knife, weapon of offence or other article);
(*e*) section 11 (production of article capable of inflicting serious injury);
(*f*) section 12 (power to prohibit manufacture, importation, sale, hire or loan of offensive weapons);
(g) section 12A (shortening barrel of shotgun or rifle).",
(*c*) by the insertion of the following paragraph after paragraph 16:

"16A. Any offence under section 3 of the Firearms (Firearm Certificates for Non-Residents) Act 2000 (prohibition of false information and alteration of firearm certificates).".

16 substituted and 16A inserted by the Criminal Justice Act 2007, s 17

Robbery and burglary

10. Any offence under the *Criminal Justice (Theft and Fraud Offences) Act, 2001*

17 amended by the Criminal Justice (Theft and Fraud Offences) Act, 2001 section 64

11. Any offence under the following provisions of the Criminal Damage Act, 1991—:

(*a*) Section 2 (damaging property);
(*b*) Section 3 (threat to damaging property);
(*c*) Section 4 (possessing any thing with intent to damage property)

Road traffic offences

12. Any offence under the following provisions of the Road Traffic Act, 1961:—

(*a*) Section 53 (dangerous driving causing death or serious bodily harm);
(*b*) Section 112 (taking vehicle without authority)

Offences in relation to aircraft and vehicles

13. Any offence under section 11 of the Air Navigation and Transport Act, 1973 (unlawful seizure of aircraft).

14. Any offence under section 3 of the Air Navigation and Transport Act 1975 (unlawful acts against the safety of aviation)

15. Any offence under section 10 of the Criminal Law(Jurisdiction) Act, 1976 (unlawful seizure of vehicles)

Maritime security offences

"22A. —Any offence under *section* 2 of the *Maritime Security Act 2004*.".

22A inserted by the Maritime Security Act 2004, s 12

Forgery etc. offences

16.
17.

23 and 24 deleted by Criminal Justice (Theft and Fraud Offences) Act 2001, s 64

Offences against the state

18. Any offence under the provisions of the Offences against the State Act, 1939 to 1998

25 substituted by the Offences Against the State (Amendment) Act 1998, s 16

19. Treason

Drugs offences

20. A drug trafficking offence within the meaning of section 3(1) of the Criminal Justice Act 1994.

27A. Any offence under section 2 of the *Illegal Immigrants (Trafficking) Act, 2000.*

27 A inserted by the Illegal Immigrants (Trafficking) Act 2000, s 8

Public order offences

21. Any offence under the following provisions of the Criminal Justice (Public Order) Act, 1994

(*a*) Section 14 (riot)
(*b*) Section 15 (violent disorder)
(*c*) section 16 (affray), and
(*d*) section 17 (blackmail, extortion and demanding money with menaces)

28 (c) substituted and 28 (d) inserted by the Criminal Justice (Miscellaneous Provisions) Act 2009, s 48

Offences under the Criminal Justice Act 2006.

"28A. Any offence under the following provisions of the Criminal Justice Act 2006 —

(*a*) section 71, 72 or 73 (organised crime);
(*b*) section 176 (reckless endangerment of children);
(*c*) section 183 (possession of article intended for use in connection with certain offences);
(*d*) section 183A (possession of monies intended for use in connection with certain offences).".

28A inserted by the Criminal Justice Act 2006, s 79 substituted by the Criminal Justice (Miscellaneous Provisions) Act 2009, s 48

Accomplices

22. References in this Schedule to an offence include references to participation as an accomplice of a person who commits the offence.

Attempts and conspiracy

23. An offence of attempting or conspiring to commit, or inciting the commission of, any offence mentioned in this Schedule

30 substituted by the Criminal Justice Act 2007, s 17

Torture

31. Any offence under the *Criminal Justice (United Nations Convention against Torture) Act, 2000.*

31 (Torture) Inserted By Criminal Justice (United Nations Convention Against Torture) Act 2000, s 10

Offences against United Nations workers

"32. Any offence under the *Criminal Justice (Safety of United Nations Workers) Act, 2000.*".

32 inserted by the Criminal Justice (Safety of United Nations Workers) Act 2000, s 9

Suppression of terrorism

33. Any offence under the *Criminal Justice (Terrorist Offences) Act 2005.*

33 inserted by the Criminal Justice (Terrorist Offences) Act 2005, s 60

Offences under the Prisons Act 2007 .

"34. Any offence under section 36 of the Prisons Act 2007 .".

34 inserted by the Criminal Justice (Miscellaneous Provisions) Act 2009, s 48

The applicant

A person who is charged with a serious offence and applies for bail (in this section referred to as 'the applicant') shall, subject to subsections (4) and (5)(*c*), furnish to the prosecutor a written statement duly signed by the applicant and containing the following information relating to the applicant:

(*a*) his or her name and any other name or names previously used;
(*b*) his or her current occupation and any previous occupation or occupations within the immediately preceding 3 years;

(*c*) his or her source or sources of income within the immediately preceding 3 years;
(*d*) his or her property, whether wholly or partially owned by, or under the control of, the applicant and whether within or outside the State;
(*e*) any previous conviction or convictions of the applicant for a serious offence;
(*f*) any previous conviction or convictions of the applicant for an offence or offences committed while on bail;
(*g*) any previous application or applications by the person for bail, indicating whether or not it was granted and, if granted, the conditions to which the recognisance was subject.

Bail Act 1997, s 1A inserted by the Criminal Justice Act 2007, s 6

The person

Subject to subsection (2), where a person (in this section referred to as 'the person') who—

(*a*) is charged with a serious offence or is appealing against a sentence of imprisonment imposed by the District Court, and
(*b*) is admitted to bail on entering into a recognisance which is subject to any of the conditions mentioned in subparagraphs (i) and (iv) of section 6(1)(*b*),

the court may make the recognisance subject to the following further conditions:

(i) that the person's movements while on bail are monitored electronically so that his or her compliance or non-compliance with a condition mentioned in any of the said subparagraphs can be established;
(ii) that for that purpose the person has an electronic monitoring device attached to his or her person, either continuously or for such periods as may be specified; and
(iii) that an authorised person is responsible for monitoring the person's compliance or non-compliance with any condition mentioned in the said subparagraphs or in paragraph (ii) of this subsection.

Bail Act 1997, s 6B(1) inserted by the Criminal Justice Act 2007, s 11

This section applies where—

(*a*) an accused person or a person who is appealing against a sentence of imprisonment imposed by the District Court (in either case referred to in this section as 'the person') is admitted to bail on entering into a recognisance conditioned for his or her appearance before a specified court on a specified date at a specified time and place, and
(*b*) the person—
  (i) fails to appear in accordance with the recognisance and the court issues a warrant for his or her arrest, or

(ii) is brought before the court in accordance with subsection (7) and the court is satisfied that the person has contravened a condition of the recognisance.

Bail Act, 1997, s 9(1) substituted by the Criminal Justice Act 2007, s 15

"STATE"

"state", in relation to a state other than the State, includes a territory, whether in the state or outside it—

(*a*) for whose external relations the state or its government is wholly or partly responsible, and
(*b*) to which the relevant international instrument applies or whose law provides for mutual assistance in criminal matters,

and "designated state" and "member state" are to be construed accordingly.

Criminal Justice (Mutual Assistance) Act 2008, s 2(1)

T

"1977 TERRORISM CONVENTION"

"1977 Terrorism Convention" means the European Convention on the Suppression of Terrorism, done at Strasbourg on 27 January 1977.

Criminal Justice (Mutual Assistance) Act 2008, s 2(1)

"TEAM LEADER"

"team leader", in relation to a joint investigation team or a part of such a team, means—

(*a*) if and when the team or the part is operating in the State, the member of the team or the part aforesaid designated by the Commissioner under section 7 *(1)(d)* to be the team leader, and (*b*) if and when the team or the part is operating in another Member State, the member of the team or the part aforesaid designated by the competent authority of that Member State to be the team leader.

Criminal Justice (Joint Investigation Teams) Act 2004, s 1(1)

"TELECOMMUNICATIONS ADDRESS"

"telecommunications address" has the meaning that it has in the Act of 1993.

Criminal Justice (Mutual Assistance) Act 2008, s 22

"THE COMMISSIONER"

"the Commissioner" means the Commissioner of the Garda Síochána.

Criminal Justice (Joint Investigation Teams) Act 2004, s 2(1)

"THE COUNCIL FRAMEWORK DECISION"

"the Council Framework Decision" means the Framework Decision of 13 June 2002 of the Council of the European Union on joint investigation teams[1], the text of which is for convenience of reference set out—

(*a*) in *Part 1* of the *Schedule* to this Act, in the case of the Irish language text, and
(*b*) in *Part 2* of that *Schedule*, in the case of the English language text.

Criminal Justice (Joint Investigation Teams) Act 2004, s 1(1)

"THE REPRESENTATIVE"

The Minister may, at the instance of the designated state concerned, authorise a representative of the authority concerned in that state (in this section referred to as "the representative") to be present at the place where its request is being executed by a member or members of the Garda Síochána.

(2) Such an authorisation may be subject to such conditions as the Minister may determine.

(3) The presence of the representative at any such place does not require the consent of the person affected by the execution of the request.

(4) The representative, while so present—

(*a*) shall be subject to the direction of the member or members executing the request,
(*b*) shall have access to the same places and objects (including documents) as that member or those members, and
(*c*) may be authorised to put or propose questions and suggest measures of investigation.

(5) The representative shall not disclose, in breach of the rights of the person affected by the execution of the request, confidential information resulting from his or her presence, except to any other such representative or representatives and to his or her authorities.

Criminal Justice (Mutual Assistance) Act 2008, s 97(1)

"TORTURE"

In this section, "torture" has the meaning given to it by the Criminal Justice (United Nations Convention against Torture) Act 2000.

Criminal Justice (Mutual Assistance) Act 2008, s 3(2)

"torture" means an act or omission by which severe pain or suffering, whether physical or mental, is intentionally inflicted on a person—

(*a*) for such purposes as—
  (i) obtaining from that person, or from another person, information or a confession,
  (ii) punishing that person for an act which the person concerned or a third person has committed or is suspected of having committed, or
  (iii) intimidating or coercing that person or a third person,

or

(*b*) for any reason that is based on any form of discrimination,

but does not include any such act that arises solely from, or is inherent in or incidental to, lawful sanctions.

Criminal Justice (United Nations Convention against Torture) Act 2000, s 1(1)

V

"VIDEO RECORDING"

In this section "videorecording" means any recording, on any medium, from which a moving image may be produced and includes the accompanying soundtrack, and cognate words shall be construed accordingly.

Criminal Justice (Mutual Assistance) Act 2008, s 67(13)

W

"WITNESS"

"witness" includes an expert witness and a person suspected of the offence which has given rise to the request concerned.

Criminal Justice (Mutual Assistance) Act 2008, s 61

This section applies, subject to *section* 64, in relation to a request for assistance in obtaining evidence in the State from a person (in this section referred to as a "witness") for the purpose of criminal proceedings, or a criminal investigation, in a designated state.

(2) On receipt of such a request the Minister, if of opinion that this section applies in relation to it, may, subject to *subsection (3)*—

(*a*) request the President of the District Court to nominate a judge of that Court to receive the evidence to which the request relates, and
(*b*) send the judge a copy of the request and of any accompanying or related documents.

Criminal Justice (Mutual Assistance) Act 2008, s 63(1)

OFFENCES AGAINST PROPERTY AND CRIMINAL DAMAGE

G

I

L

M

N

O

P

R

S

A

"ACTIVE CORRUPTION"

"active corruption" has the meaning given to it by Article 3.1 of the First Protocol.

Article 3

Active corruption

1. For the purposes of this Protocol, the deliberate action of whosoever promises or gives, directly or through an intermediary, an advantage of any kind whatsoever to an official for himself or for a third party for him to act or refrain from acting in accordance with his duty or in the exercise of his functions in breach of his official duties in a way which damages or is likely to damage the European Communities' financial interests shall constitute active corruption.

Criminal Justice (Theft and Fraud Offences) Act 2001, sched 4, art 3

"AGGRAVATED BURGLARY"

(1) A person is guilty of aggravated burglary if he or she commits any burglary and at the time has with him or her any firearm or imitation firearm, any weapon of offence or any explosive.

(2) In *subsection (1)*—

"explosive" means any article manufactured for the purpose of producing a practical effect by explosion, or intended by the person having it with him or her for that purpose;

"firearm" means:

(*a*) a lethal firearm or other lethal weapon of any description from which any shot, bullet or other missile can be discharged,
(*b*) an air gun (which expression includes an air rifle and an air pistol) or any other weapon incorporating a barrel from which metal or other slugs can be discharged,
(*c*) a crossbow,
(*d*) any type of stun gun or other weapon for causing any shock or other disablement to a person by means of electricity or any other kind of energy emission;

"imitation firearm" means anything which is not a firearm but has the appearance of being one;

"weapon of offence" means:

(*a*) any article which has a blade or sharp point,
(*b*) any other article made or adapted for use for causing injury to or incapacitating a person, or intended by the person having it with him or her for such use or for threatening such use,
(*c*) any weapon of whatever description designed for the discharge of any noxious liquid, noxious gas or other noxious thing.

(3) A person guilty of aggravated burglary is liable on conviction on indictment to imprisonment for life.

Criminal Justice (Theft and Fraud Offences) Act 2001, s 13

"APPROPRIATES"

"appropriates", in relation to property, means usurps or adversely interferes with the proprietary rights of the owner of the property.

Criminal Justice (Theft and Fraud Offences) Act 2001, s 4(5)

"ARRESTABLE OFFENCE"

(4) In this section, "arrestable offence" means an offence for which a person of full age and not previously convicted may be punished by imprisonment for a term of five years or by a more severe penalty.

Criminal Justice (Theft and Fraud Offences) Act 2001, s 12(4)

B

"BURGLARY"

(1) A person is guilty of burglary if he or she—

(*a*) enters any building or part of a building as a trespasser and with intent to commit an arrestable offence, or

(*b*) having entered any building or part of a building as a trespasser, commits or attempts to commit any such offence therein.

(2) References in *subsection (1)* to a building shall apply also to an inhabited vehicle or vessel and to any other inhabited temporary or movable structure, and shall apply to any such vehicle, vessel or structure at times when the person having a habitation in it is not there as well as at times when the person is there.

(3) A person guilty of burglary is liable on conviction on indictment to a fine or imprisonment for a term not exceeding 14 years or both.

(4) In this section, "arrestable offence" means an offence for which a person of full age and not previously convicted may be punished by imprisonment for a term of five years or by a more severe penalty.

Criminal Justice (Theft and Fraud Offences) Act 2001, s 12

C

"COMMUNITY OFFICIAL"

"Community official" has the meaning given to it by Article 1.1(*b*) of the First Protocol.

Criminal Justice (Theft and Fraud Offences) Act 2001, s 40(1)

the term 'Community official' shall mean:

— any person who is an official or other contracted employee within the meaning of the Staff Regulations of officials of the European Communities or the Conditions of employment of other servants of the European Communities,
— any person seconded to the European Communities by the Member States or by any public or private body, who carries out functions equivalent to those performed by European Community officials or other servants.

Members of bodies set up in accordance with the Treaties establishing the European Communities and the staff of such bodies shall be treated as Community officials, inasmuch as the Staff Regulations of the European Communities or the Conditions of employment of other servants of the European Communities do not apply to them.

Criminal Justice (Theft and Fraud Offences) Act 2001, sched 4, art 1(1)(b)

"COMPENSATION ORDER"

(1) On conviction of any person of an offence under *section 2* of damaging property belonging to another, the court, instead of or in addition to dealing with him in any other way, may, on application or otherwise, make an order (in this Act referred to as a "compensation order") requiring him to pay compensation in respect of that damage to any person (in this section referred to as the "injured party") who, by reason thereof, has suffered loss (other than consequential loss).

(2) The compensation payable under a compensation order (including a compensation order made against a parent or guardian of the convicted person and notwithstanding, in such a case, any other statutory limitation as to amount) shall be of such amount (not exceeding £5,000 in the case of such an order made by the District Court or such other amount as may stand prescribed for the time being by law as the limit of that Court's jurisdiction in tort) as the court considers appropriate, having regard to any evidence and to any representations that are made by or on behalf of the convicted person or the prosecutor, and shall not exceed the amount of the damages that, in the opinion of the court, the injured party concerned would be entitled to recover in a civil action against the convicted person in respect of the damage concerned.

(3) A compensation order shall not be made unless both the injured party concerned and the approximate cost of making good the damage to it (or, where appropriate, of replacing it) are readily ascertainable at the time of the conviction concerned or within a reasonable period thereafter.

(4) In determining whether to make a compensation order against a person, and in determining the amount to be paid by a person under such an order, the court shall have regard—

(*a*) to his means, or
(*b*) in a case to which section 99 of the Children Act, 1908 (which empowers a court to require a parent or guardian to pay any fine, damages or costs imposed on a child or young person), applies, the means of the parent or guardian,

so far as they appear or are known to the court.

(5) A compensation order may provide for payment of the compensation by such instalments and at such times as the court shall in all the circumstances consider reasonable.

(6) Where the court considers—

(*a*) that it would be appropriate both to impose a fine and to make a compensation order, but
(*b*) that the convicted person has insufficient means to pay both an appropriate fine and appropriate compensation,

the court may, if it is satisfied that the means are sufficient to justify its doing so, make a compensation order and, if it is satisfied that it is appropriate to do so having regard to the means that would remain after compliance with the order, impose a fine.

(7) At any time after a compensation order has ceased to be suspended by virtue of *section 10 (1)* and before it has been complied with or fully complied with, the District Court may—

(*a*) on the application of the convicted person concerned—
   (i) reduce the amount to be paid, vary any instalment payable, or direct that no payments or further payments be made, under the order if it appears to the Court—
      (I) that the means of the convicted person are insufficient to satisfy the order in full, or
      (II) on being satisfied that the injured party concerned has been given an opportunity of making representations to the court on the issue and having regard to any such representations that are made by him or on his behalf, that the damage in respect of which the order was made is less than it was taken to be for the purposes of the order, and
   (ii) if any amount paid under the order exceeds the amount appearing to the Court to be reasonable compensation for the damage, order that the amount of the excess be repaid by the injured party to the convicted person, and, upon the making of such order, the compensation order shall cease to have effect,

or

(*b*) on the application of the injured party concerned, increase the amount to be paid, the amount of any instalment or the number of instalments payable, under the order if it appears to the Court—

(i) that the means of the convicted person are sufficient for the relevant purposes aforesaid, or

(ii) on being satisfied that the convicted person concerned has been given an opportunity of making representations to the court on the issue and having regard to any such representations that are made by him or on his behalf, that the damage in respect of which the order was made is more than it was taken to be for the purposes of the order.

(8) A compensation order and an order under *subsection* (7) (*b*) shall be treated for the purposes of enforcement as if they were orders made by the court concerned in civil proceedings and, without prejudice to the provisions of *subsection* (7), a compensation order shall be treated for those purposes as if it were an instalment order within the meaning of Part I of the Enforcement of Court Orders Act, 1940.

(9) The references to damages in the aforesaid section 99 shall he construed as if they included references to compensation under a compensation order and subsections (5) and (6) of that section shall not apply in relation to a compensation order.

(10) This section is without prejudice to any other enactment which provides for the payment of compensation by a person convicted of an offence of damaging property or otherwise proved to have committed such an offence.

(11) The making of a compensation order against a parent or guardian of a convicted person shall not of itself give rise to any other liability on the part of the parent or guardian in respect of the damage concerned.

(12) In this section—

(*a*) references to conviction of a person include references to dealing with a person under section 1 (1) of the Probation of Offenders Act, 1907, and

(*b*) the third reference in *subsection* (*1*), the first reference in *subsection* (2) and the references in *subsections* (6) (*b*) and (7) to a convicted person, however expressed, include, in cases to which the aforesaid section 99 applies, references to his parent or guardian.

Criminal Damage Act 1991, s 9

"CONVENTION"

'Convention' shall mean the Convention drawn up on the basis of Article K.3 of the Treaty on European Union, on the protection of the European Communities' financial interests, of 26 July 1995.

Criminal Justice (Theft and Fraud Offences) Act 2001, sched 4, art 1(2)

"COUNTERFEIT"

For the purposes of this Part, a thing is a counterfeit of a currency note or coin—

(*a*) if it is not a currency note or coin but resembles a currency note or coin (whether on one side only or on both) to such an extent that it is reasonably capable of passing for a currency note or coin of that description, or
(*b*) if it is a currency note or coin which has been so altered that it is reasonably capable of passing for a note or coin of some other description.

(3) For the purposes of this Part—

(*a*) a thing consisting of or containing a representation of one side only of a currency note, with or without the addition of other material, is capable of being a counterfeit of such a currency note, and
(*b*) a thing consisting—
 (i) of parts of two or more currency notes, or
 (ii) of parts of a currency note, or of parts of two or more currency notes, with the addition of other material,

is capable of being a counterfeit of a currency note.

Criminal Justice (Theft and Fraud Offences) Act 2001, s 32(2)

"CURRENCY NOTE"

"currency note" and "coin" mean, respectively, a currency note and coin lawfully issued or customarily used as money in the State or in any other state or a territorial unit within it and include a note denominated in euro and a coin denominated in euro or in cent and also any note or coin which has not been lawfully issued but which would, on being so issued, be a currency note or coin within the above meaning.

Criminal Justice (Theft and Fraud Offences) Act 2001, s 32(1)

D

"DAMAGE"

"damage", in relation to property, includes the total or partial destruction of the property and any injury thereto.

Malicious Injuries Act 1981, s 2

"DATA"

"data" means information in a form in which it can be accessed by means of a computer and includes a program.

Criminal Damage Act 1991, s 1(1)

"DECEPTION"

2) For the purposes of this Act a person deceives if he or she—

(*a*) creates or reinforces a false impression, including a false impression as to law, value or intention or other state of mind,
(*b*) prevents another person from acquiring information which would affect that person's judgement of a transaction, or
(*c*) fails to correct a false impression which the deceiver previously created or reinforced or which the deceiver knows to be influencing another to whom he or she stands in a fiduciary or confidential relationship.

Criminal Justice (Theft and Fraud Offences) Act 2001, s 2(2)

"DEPRIVING"

"depriving" means temporarily or permanently depriving.

Criminal Justice (Theft and Fraud Offences) Act 2001, s 4(5)

"DESIGNATED BODY"

"designated body" means:

(*a*) a body licensed to carry on banking business under the Central Bank Act, 1971, or authorised to carry on such business under the ACC Bank Acts, 1978 to 2001, or regulations under the European Communities Acts, 1972 to 1998,
(*b*) a building society within the meaning of the Building Societies Act, 1989,
(*c*) a trustee savings bank within the meaning of the Trustee Savings Banks Acts, 1989 and 2001,
(*d*) An Post,
(*e*) a credit union within the meaning of the Credit Union Act, 1997,
(*f*) a person or body authorised under the Central Bank Act, 1997, to provide *bureau de change* business,
(*g*) a person who in the course of business provides a service of sorting and redistributing currency notes or coins,

(*h*) any other person or body—
  (i) whose business consists of or includes the provision of services involving the acceptance, exchange, transfer or holding of money for or on behalf of other persons or bodies, and
  (ii) who is designated for the purposes of this section by regulations made by the Minister after consultation with the Minister for Finance.

Criminal Justice (Theft and Fraud Offences) Act 2001, s 39(1)

"DISHONESTY"

"dishonestly" means without a claim of right made in good faith.

Criminal Justice (Theft and Fraud Offences) Act 2001, s 2(1)

"DOCUMENT"

"document" includes—

(*a*) a map, plan, graph, drawing, photograph or record, or
(*b*) a reproduction in permanent legible form, by a computer or other means (including enlarging), of information in non-legible form.

Criminal Justice (Theft and Fraud Offences) Act 2001, s 2(1)

E

"EXPLOSIVE"

"explosive" means any article manufactured for the purpose of producing a practical effect by explosion, or intended by the person having it with him or her for that purpose.

Criminal Justice (Theft and Fraud Offences) Act 2001, s 13(2)
See also under "Firearms"

F

"FALSE"

An instrument is false for the purposes of this Part if it purports—

(*a*) to have been made in the form in which it is made by a person who did not in fact make it in that form,

(*b*) to have been made in the form in which it is made on the authority of a person who did not in fact authorise its making in that form,
(*c*) to have been made in the terms in which it is made by a person who did not in fact make it in those terms,
(*d*) to have been made in the terms in which it is made on the authority of a person who did not in fact authorise its making in those terms,
(*e*) to have been altered in any respect by a person who did not in fact alter it in that respect,
(*f*) to have been altered in any respect on the authority of a person who did not in fact authorise the alteration in that respect,
(*g*) to have been made or altered on a date on which, or at a place at which, or otherwise in circumstances in which, it was not in fact made or altered, or
(*h*) to have been made or altered by an existing person where that person did not in fact exist.

(2) A person shall be treated for the purposes of this Part as making a false instrument if he or she alters an instrument so as to make it false in any respect (whether or not it is false in some other respect apart from that alteration).

Criminal Justice (Theft and Fraud Offences) Act 2001, s 30

"FIREARM"

"firearm" means:

(*a*) a lethal firearm or other lethal weapon of any description from which any shot, bullet or other missile can be discharged,
(*b*) an air gun (which expression includes an air rifle and an air pistol) or any other weapon incorporating a barrel from which metal or other slugs can be discharged,
(*c*) a crossbow,
(*d*) any type of stun gun or other weapon for causing any shock or other disablement to a person by means of electricity or any other kind of energy emission.

Criminal Justice (Theft and Fraud Offences) Act 2001, s 13(2)

"FIRM"

"firm" means a partnership, a corporate or unincorporated body or a self-employed individual.

Criminal Justice (Theft and Fraud Offences) Act 2001, s 59(1)

"FIRST PROTOCOL"

"First Protocol" means the Protocol drawn up on the basis of Article K.3 of the Treaty on European Union to the Convention on the protection of the European Communities' financial interests done at Brussels on 27 September 1996.

Criminal Justice (Theft and Fraud Offences) Act 2001, s 40(1)

"FORGERY"

A person is guilty of forgery if he or she makes a false instrument with the intention that it shall be used to induce another person to accept it as genuine and, by reason of so accepting it, to do some act, or to make some omission, to the prejudice of that person or any other person.

Criminal Justice (Theft and Fraud Offences) Act 2001, s 25(1)

"FRAUD"

(*b*) 'fraud' shall mean the conduct referred to in Article 1 of the Convention.

Criminal Justice (Theft and Fraud Offences) Act 2001, sched 8, art 1(B)

"FRAUD AFFECTING THE EU"

"fraud affecting the European Communities' financial interests" has the meaning given to it by Article 1.1 of the Convention.

Criminal Justice (Theft and Fraud Offences) Act 2001, s 40(1)

G

"GAIN"

For the purposes of this Act—

(*a*) "gain" and "loss" are to be construed as extending only to gain or loss in money or other property, whether any such gain or loss is temporary or permanent,

(*b*) "gain" includes a gain by keeping what one has, as well as a gain by getting what one has not, and

(c) "loss" includes a loss by not getting what one might get, as well as a loss by parting with what one has.

Criminal Justice (Theft and Fraud Offences) Act 2001, s 2(3)

I

"IMITATION FIREARM"

"imitation firearm" means anything which is not a firearm but has the appearance of being one.

Criminal Justice (Theft and Fraud Offences) Act 2001, s 13(2)

"INDUCE"

Subject to *subsections (2)* and *(4)*, for the purposes of this Part, an act or omission intended to be induced shall be to a person's prejudice if, and only if, it is one which, if it occurs—

(*a*) will result, as respects that person—
  (i) in temporary or permanent loss of property,
  (ii) in deprivation of an opportunity to earn remuneration or greater remuneration, or
  (iii) in deprivation of an opportunity to gain a financial advantage otherwise than by way of remuneration,

or

(*b*) will result in another person being given an opportunity—
  (i) to earn remuneration or greater remuneration from him or her, or
  (ii) to gain a financial advantage from him or her otherwise than by way of remuneration,

or

(*c*) will be the result of his or her having accepted any false instrument as genuine, or any copy of it as a copy of a genuine instrument, in connection with his or her performance of any duty.

(2) An act which a person has an enforceable duty to do and an omission to do an act which a person is not entitled to do shall be disregarded for the purposes of this Part.

(3) In this Part references to inducing a person to accept a false instrument as genuine, or a copy of a false instrument as a copy of a genuine one, include references

to inducing a machine to respond to the instrument or copy as if it were a genuine instrument or copy of a genuine one.

(4) Where *subsection (3)* applies, the act or omission intended to be induced by the machine responding to the instrument or copy shall be treated as an act or omission to a person's prejudice.

Criminal Justice (Theft and Fraud Offences) Act 2001, s 31

"INFORMATION IN NON LEGIBLE FORM"

"information in non-legible form" means information which is kept (by electronic means or otherwise) on microfilm, microfiche, magnetic tape or disk or in any other non-legible form.

Criminal Justice (Theft and Fraud Offences) Act 2001, s 2(1)

"INSTRUMENT"

"instrument" means any document, whether of a formal or informal character (other than a currency note within the meaning of *Part 5*) and includes any—

(*a*) disk, tape, sound track or other device on or in which information is recorded or stored by mechanical, electronic or other means,
(*b*) money order,
(*c*) postal order,
(*d*) postage stamp issued or sold by An Post or any mark denoting payment of postage which is authorised by An Post to be used instead of an adhesive stamp,
(*e*) stamp of the Revenue Commissioners denoting any stamp duty or fee, whether it is an adhesive stamp or a stamp impressed by means of a die,
(*f*) licence or certificate issued by the Revenue Commissioners,
(*g*) cheque, including traveller's cheque, or bank draft,
(*h*) charge card, cheque card, credit card, debit card or any card combining two or more of the functions performed by such cards,
(*i*) share certificate,
(*j*) certified copy, issued by or on behalf of an tArd-Chláraitheoir, of an entry in any register of births, stillbirths, marriages or deaths or in the Adopted Children Register,
(*k*) certificate relating to such an entry,
(*l*) a certificate of insurance,
(*m*) passport or document which can be used instead of a passport,
(*n*) document issued by or on behalf of a Minister of the Government and permitting or authorising a person to enter or remain (whether temporarily or permanently) in the State or to enter employment therein,

(*o*) registration certificate issued under Article 11(1)(e)(i) of the Aliens Order, 1946 (S.I. No. 395 of 1946),
(*p*) public service card,
(*q*) ticket of admission to an event to which members of the public may be admitted on payment of a fee.

Criminal Justice (Theft and Fraud Offences) Act 2001, s 24

L

"LAND"

"land" does not include incorporeal hereditaments.

Criminal Justice (Theft and Fraud Offences) Act 2001, s 5(3)(a)

"LAWFULLY ISSUED"

"lawfully issued" means issued—

(*a*) by or under the authority of the European Central Bank,
(*b*) by the Central Bank of Ireland or the Minister for Finance, or
(*c*) by a body in a state (other than the State) or a territorial unit within it which is authorised under the law of that state or territorial unit to issue currency notes or coins.

Criminal Justice (Theft and Fraud Offences) Act 2001, s 32(1)

"LEGAL PERSON"

'legal person' shall mean any entity having such status under the applicable national law, except for States or other public bodies in the exercise of State authority and for public international organizations.

Criminal Justice (Theft and Fraud Offences) Act 2001, sched 8, art 1(D)

"LICENCE"

"licence" includes an agreement for a licence.

Criminal Justice (Theft and Fraud Offences) Act 2001, ss (3)(a)

"LOCAL AUTHORITY"

"local authority" means the council of a county or the corporation of a county borough.

Malicious Damage Act 1981, s 2

"LOSS"

"gain" and "loss" are to be construed as extending only to gain or loss in money or other property, whether any such gain or loss is temporary or permanent,

(*b*) "gain" includes a gain by keeping what one has, as well as a gain by getting what one has not, and

(*c*) "loss" includes a loss by not getting what one might get, as well as a loss by parting with what one has.

Criminal Justice (Theft and Fraud Offences) Act 2001, s 2(1)(3)

M

"MAKING"

An instrument is false for the purposes of this Part if it purports—

(*a*) to have been made in the form in which it is made by a person who did not in fact make it in that form,

(*b*) to have been made in the form in which it is made on the authority of a person who did not in fact authorise its making in that form,

(*c*) to have been made in the terms in which it is made by a person who did not in fact make it in those terms,

(*d*) to have been made in the terms in which it is made on the authority of a person who did not in fact authorise its making in those terms,

(*e*) to have been altered in any respect by a person who did not in fact alter it in that respect,

(*f*) to have been altered in any respect on the authority of a person who did not in fact authorise the alteration in that respect,

(*g*) to have been made or altered on a date on which, or at a place at which, or otherwise in circumstances in which, it was not in fact made or altered, or

(*h*) to have been made or altered by an existing person where that person did not in fact exist.

(2) A person shall be treated for the purposes of this Part as making a false instrument if he or she alters an instrument so as to make it false in any respect (whether or not it is false in some other respect apart from that alteration).

Criminal Justice (Theft and Fraud Offences) Act 2001, s 30

"MONEY LAUNDERING"

A person is guilty of money laundering if, knowing or believing that property is or represents the proceeds of criminal conduct or being reckless as to whether it is or represents such proceeds, the person, without lawful authority or excuse (the proof of which shall lie on him or her)—

(*a*) converts, transfers or handles the property, or removes it from the State, with the intention of—
 (i) concealing or disguising its true nature, source, location, disposition, movement or ownership or any rights with respect to it, or
 (ii) assisting another person to avoid prosecution for the criminal conduct concerned, or
 (iii) avoiding the making of a confiscation order or a confiscation co-operation order (within the meaning of section 46 of this Act) or frustrating its enforcement against that person or another person,

(*b*) conceals or disguises its true nature, source, location, disposition, movement or ownership or any rights with respect to it, or

(*c*) acquires, possesses or uses the property.

(2) A person guilty of money laundering is liable—

(*a*) on summary conviction, to a fine not exceeding £1,500 or to imprisonment for a term not exceeding 12 months or to both, or

(*b*) on conviction on indictment, to a fine or to imprisonment for a term not exceeding 14 years or to both.

(3) Where a person—

(*a*) converts, transfers, handles or removes from the State any property which is or represents the proceeds of criminal conduct,

(*b*) conceals or disguises its true nature, source, location, disposition, movement or ownership or any rights with respect to it, or

(*c*) acquires, possesses or uses it,

in such circumstances that it is reasonable to conclude that the person—
 (i) knew or believed that the property was or represented the proceeds of criminal conduct, or
 (ii) was reckless as to whether it was or represented such proceeds,

the person shall be taken to have so known or believed or to have been so reckless, unless the court or jury, as the case may be, is satisfied having regard to all the evidence that there is a reasonable doubt as to whether the person so knew or believed or was so reckless.

(4) Where a person first referred to in subsection (1) of this section does an act referred to in paragraph (*a*) of that subsection in such circumstances that it is reasonable to conclude that the act was done with an intention specified in that paragraph, the person shall be taken to have done the act with that intention unless the court or jury, as the case may be, is satisfied having regard to all the evidence that there is a reasonable doubt as to whether the person did it with that intention.

(5) This section does not apply to a person in respect of anything done by the person in connection with the enforcement of any law.

(6) This Part shall apply whether the criminal conduct in question occurred before or after the commencement of this section and whether it was or is attributable to the person first mentioned in subsection (1) or another.

(7) (*a*) In this section—

(i) 'criminal conduct' means conduct which—
  (I) constitutes an indictable offence, or
  (II) where the conduct occurs outside the State, would constitute such an offence if it occurred within the State and also constitutes an offence under the law of the country or territorial unit in which it occurs,

and includes participation in such conduct;

(ii) 'reckless' shall be construed in accordance with section 16 *(2)* of the *Criminal Justice (Theft and Fraud Offences) Act, 2001*;
(iii) references to converting, transferring, handling or removing any property include references to the provision of any advice or assistance in relation to converting, transferring, handling or removing it;
(iv) references to believing that any property is or represents the proceeds of criminal conduct include references to thinking that the property was probably, or probably represented, such proceeds;
(v) references to any property representing the proceeds of criminal conduct include references to the property representing those proceeds in whole or in part directly or indirectly, and cognate references shall be construed accordingly.

(*b*) For the purposes of this section a person handles property if he or she, without a claim of right made in good faith—
  (i) receives it, or
  (ii) undertakes or assists in its retention, removal, disposal or realisation by or for the benefit of another person, or
  (iii) arranges to do any of the things specified in subparagraph (i) or (ii).

(*c*) For the purposes of paragraph (*a*)(i)(II)—
   (i) a document purporting to be signed by a lawyer practising in the state or territorial unit in which the criminal conduct concerned is alleged to have occurred and stating that such conduct is an offence under the law of that state or territorial unit, and
   (ii) a document purporting to be a translation of a document mentioned in subparagraph (i) and to be certified as correct by a person appearing to be competent to so certify,

shall be admissible in any proceedings, without further proof, as evidence of the matters mentioned in those documents, unless the contrary is shown.

(8) Where—

(*a*) a report is made by a person or body to the Garda Síochána under section 57 of this Act in relation to property referred to in this section, or
(*b*) a person or body (other than a person or body suspected of committing an offence under this section) is informed by the Garda Síochána that property in the possession of the person or body is property referred to in this section,

the person or body shall not commit an offence under this section or section 58 of this Act if and for as long as the person or body complies with the directions of the Garda Síochána in relation to the property.".

Criminal Justice Act 1994, s 31 substituted by Criminal Justice (Theft and Fraud Offences) Act 2001, s 21

N

"NATIONAL OFFICIAL"

"national official", for the purposes of the application in the State of Article 1.1(*c*) of the First Protocol, means any one of the following persons:

(*a*) a Minister of the Government or Minister of State;
(*b*) an Attorney General who is not a member of Dáil Éireann or Seanad Éireann;
(*c*) the Comptroller and Auditor General;
(*d*) a member of Dáil Éireann or Seanad Éireann;
(*e*) a judge of a court in the State;
(*f*) the Director of Public Prosecutions;
(*g*) any other holder of an office who is remunerated wholly or partly out of moneys provided by the Oireachtas;
(*h*) any person employed by a person referred to in any of *paragraphs (d)* to *(g)* in the performance of that person's official functions; and

(i) a director of, or an occupier of a position of employment in, a public body as defined in the Ethics in Public Office Act, 1995,

and, for the purposes of the application in the State of Article 4.2 of the First Protocol, any one of the following persons shall be treated as a national official:

(i) a member of the Commission of the European Communities;
(ii) a member of the European Parliament;
(iii) a member of the Court of Justice of the European Communities;
(iv) a member of the Court of Auditors of the European Communities.

Criminal Justice (Theft and Fraud Offences) Act 2001, s 40(1)

the term 'national official' shall be understood by reference to the definition of 'official' or 'public officer' in the national law of the Member State in which the person in question performs that function for the purposes of application of the criminal law of that Member State.

Nevertheless, in the case of proceedings involving a Member State's official initiated by another Member State the latter shall not be bound to apply the definition of 'national official' except in so far as that definition is compatible with its national law.

Criminal Justice (Theft and Fraud Offences) Act 2001, sched 4, art (1)(C)

"NE BIS IN IDEM"

Member States shall apply in their national criminal laws the 'ne bis in idem' rule, under which a person whose trial has been finally disposed of in a Member State may not be prosecuted in another Member State in respect of the same facts, provided that if a penalty was imposed, it has been enforced, is actually in the process of being enforced or can no longer be enforced under the laws of the sentencing State.

2. A Member State may, when giving the notification referred to in Article 11 (2), declare that it shall not be bound by paragraph 1 of this Article in one or more of the following cases:

(*a*) if the facts which were the subject of the judgement rendered abroad took place on its own territory either in whole or in part; in the latter case this exception shall not apply if those facts took place partly on the territory of the Member State where the judgement was rendered;
(*b*) if the facts which were the subject of the judgment rendered abroad constitute an offence directed against the security or other equally essential interests of that Member State;

(*c*) if the facts which were the subject of the judgment rendered abroad were committed by an official of the Member State contrary to the duties of his office.

3. The exceptions which may be the subject of a declaration under paragraph 2 shall not apply if the Member State concerned in respect of the same facts requested the other Member State to bring the prosecution or granted extradition of the person concerned.

4. Relevant bilateral or multilateral agreements concluded between Member States and relevant declarations shall remain unaffected by this Article.

Criminal Justice (Theft and Fraud Offences) Act 2001, sched 2, art 7

O

"OFFICIAL"

'official' shall mean any 'Community' or 'national' official, including any national official of another Member State.

Criminal Justice (Theft and Fraud Offences) Act 2001, sched 4, art 1(1)(a)

"OWNER AND OWNERSHIP"

For the purposes of this Act—

(*a*) a person shall be regarded as owning property if he or she has possession or control of it, or has in it any proprietary right or interest (not being an equitable interest arising only from an agreement to transfer or grant an interest);
(*b*) where property is subject to a trust, the persons who own it shall be regarded as including any person having a right to enforce the trust, and an intention to defeat the trust shall be regarded accordingly as an intention to deprive of the property any person having that right;
(*c*) where a person receives property from or on behalf of another, and is under an obligation to that other person to retain and deal with that property or its proceeds in a particular way, that other person shall be regarded (as against the first-mentioned person) as the owner of the property;
(*d*) where a person gets property by another's mistake and is under an obligation to make restoration (in whole or in part) of the property or its proceeds or of the value thereof, then the person entitled to restoration shall to the extent of that obligation be regarded (as against the first-mentioned person) as the owner of the property or its proceeds or an amount equivalent to its value, and an intention not to make restoration shall be regarded accordingly as an intention to deprive that person of the property, proceeds or such amount;

(e) property of a corporation sole shall be regarded as belonging to the corporation notwithstanding a vacancy in the corporation,

and references to "owner" and "ownership" shall be construed accordingly.

Criminal Justice (Theft and Fraud Offences) Act 2001, s 2(4)

P

"PASSIVE CORRUPTION"

Passive corruption

1. For the purposes of this Protocol, the deliberate action of an official, who, directly or through an intermediary, requests or receives advantages of any kind whatsoever, for himself or for a third party, or accepts a promise of such an advantage, to act or refrain from acting in accordance with his duty or in the exercise of his functions in breach of his official duties in a way which damages or is likely to damage the European Communities' financial interests shall constitute passive corruption.

Criminal Justice (Theft and Fraud Offences) Act 2001, sched 4, art 2

"PREJUDICE"

(1) Subject to *subsections (2)* and *(4)*, for the purposes of this Part, an act or omission intended to be induced shall be to a person's prejudice if, and only if, it is one which, if it occurs—

(*a*) will result, as respects that person—
- (i) in temporary or permanent loss of property,
- (ii) in deprivation of an opportunity to earn remuneration or greater remuneration, or
- (iii) in deprivation of an opportunity to gain a financial advantage otherwise than by way of remuneration,

Or

(*b*) will result in another person being given an opportunity—
- (i) to earn remuneration or greater remuneration from him or her, or
- (ii) to gain a financial advantage from him or her otherwise than by way of remuneration,

Or

(*c*) will be the result of his or her having accepted any false instrument as genuine, or any copy of it as a copy of a genuine instrument, in connection with his or her performance of any duty.

(2) An act which a person has an enforceable duty to do and an omission to do an act which a person is not entitled to do shall be disregarded for the purposes of this Part.

(3) In this Part references to inducing a person to accept a false instrument as genuine, or a copy of a false instrument as a copy of a genuine one, include references to inducing a machine to respond to the instrument or copy as if it were a genuine instrument or copy of a genuine one.

(4) Where *subsection (3)* applies, the act or omission intended to be induced by the machine responding to the instrument or copy shall be treated as an act or omission to a person's prejudice.

Criminal Justice (Theft and Fraud Offences) Act 2001, s 31

"PREMISES"

"premises" includes a vehicle, vessel, aircraft or hovercraft or an installation in the territorial seas or in a designated area (within the meaning of the Continental Shelf Act, 1968) or a tent, caravan or other temporary or movable structure.

Criminal Justice (Theft and Fraud Offences) Act 2001, s 2(1)

"PRINCIPAL OFFENDER"

In this Part "principal offender", for the purposes of *sections 17* and *18*, means the person who has stolen or otherwise unlawfully obtained the property alleged to have been handled or possessed, and cognate words shall be construed accordingly.

Criminal Justice (Theft and Fraud Offences) Act 2001, s 16(1)

"PROPERTY"

"property" means—

(*a*) property of a tangible nature, whether real or personal, including money and animals that are capable of being stolen, and

(*b*) data.

Criminal Damage Act 1991, s (1)

"property" means money and all other property, real or personal, including things in action and other intangible property.

Criminal Justice (Theft and Fraud Offences) Act 2001, s 2(1)

"property" includes wild animals in captivity and incorporeal hereditaments (including easements, profits *a prendre* and other rights) but not a mere pleasure or amenity.

Malicious Injuries Act 1981

"property" means property of a tangible nature, whether real or personal, including money and animals that are capable of being stolen.

Non Fatal Offences Against the Person Act 1997, s 1

"PROTOCOL INTERPRETATION"

"Protocol on Interpretation" means the Protocol drawn up on the basis of Article K.3 of the Treaty on European Union, on the interpretation, by way of preliminary rulings, by the Court of Justice of the European Communities of the Convention on the protection of the European Communities' financial interests done at Brussels on 29 November 1996.

Criminal Justice (Theft and Fraud Offences) Act 2001, s 40(1)

"PUBLIC PLACE"

"public place" includes any street, seashore, park, land or field, highway and any other premises or place to which at the material time the public have or are permitted to have access, whether on payment or otherwise, and includes any train, vessel, aircraft or vehicle used for the carriage of persons for reward.

Non Fatal Offences Against the Person Act 1997, s 1

R

"RECOGNISED CODE OF PRACTICE"

"recognised code of practice" means a code of practice drawn up for the purposes of this section—

(*a*) by a designated body or class of designated bodies and approved by the Central Bank of Ireland, or

(*b*) by the Central Bank of Ireland for a designated body or class of such bodies.

Criminal Justice (Theft and Fraud Offences) Act 2001, s 39(1)

"RECORD"

"record" includes any information in non-legible form which is capable of being reproduced in permanent legible form.

Criminal Justice (Theft and Fraud Offences) Act 2001, s 2(1)

"RELEVANT PERSON"

"relevant person" means a person—

(*a*) who audits the accounts of a firm, or

(*b*) who otherwise with a view to reward assists or advises a firm in the preparation or delivery of any information, or of any declaration, return, account or other document, which the person knows will be, or is likely to be, used for the purpose of keeping or auditing the accounts of the firm,

but does not include an employee of a firm who—

(i) in that capacity so assists or advises the firm, and

(ii) whose income from so doing consists solely of emoluments chargeable to income tax under Schedule E, as defined in section 19 of the Taxes Consolidation Act, 1997.

Criminal Justice (Theft and Fraud Offences) Act 2001, s 59(1)

"ROBBERY"

A person is guilty of robbery if he or she steals, and immediately before or at the time of doing so, and in order to do so, uses force on any person or puts or seeks to put any person in fear of being then and there subjected to force.

Criminal Justice (Theft and Fraud Offences) Act 2001, s 14

S

"SHARE CERTIFICATE"

"share certificate" means a document entitling or evidencing the title of a person to a share or interest—

(*a*) in any public stock, annuity, fund or debt of the Government or the State or of any government or state, including a state which forms part of another state, or (*b*) in any stock, fund or debt of a body (whether corporate or unincorporated), wherever established.

Criminal Justice (Theft and Fraud Offences) Act 2001, s 24

"SHIP"

"ship" includes every description of vessel, boat and other craft, whether or not propelled by oars.

Malicious Injuries Act 1981, s 2

"STEALING"

"stealing" means committing an offence under section 4, and cognate words shall be construed accordingly.

Criminal Justice (Theft and Fraud Offences) Act 2001, s 2(1)

Subject to section 5, a person is guilty of theft if he or she dishonestly appropriates property without the consent of its owner and with the intention of depriving its owner of it.

(2) For the purposes of this section a person does not appropriate property without the consent of its owner if—

(*a*) the person believes that he or she has the owner's consent, or would have the owner's consent if the owner knew of the appropriation of the property and the circumstances in which it was appropriated, or
(*b*) (except where the property came to the person as trustee or personal representative) he or she appropriates the property in the belief that the owner cannot be discovered by taking reasonable steps,

but consent obtained by deception or intimidation is not consent for those purposes.

(3) (*a*) This subsection applies to a person who in the course of business holds property in trust for, or on behalf of, more than one owner.

(*b*) Where a person to whom this subsection applies appropriates some of the property so held to his or her own use or benefit, the person shall, for the purposes of *subsection (1)* but subject to *subsection (2)*, be deemed to have appropriated the property or, as the case may be, a sum representing it without the consent of its owner or owners.

(*c*) If in any proceedings against a person to whom this subsection applies for theft of some or all of the property so held by him or her it is proved that—

(i) there is a deficiency in the property or a sum representing it, and

(ii) the person has failed to provide a satisfactory explanation for the whole or any part of the deficiency,

it shall be presumed, until the contrary is proved, for the purposes of *subsection (1)* but subject to *subsection (2)*, that the person appropriated, without the consent of its owner or owners, the whole or that part of the deficiency.

(4) If at the trial of a person for theft the court or jury, as the case may be has to consider whether the person believed—

(*a*) that he or she had not acted dishonestly, or

(*b*) that the owner of the property concerned had consented or would have consented to its appropriation, or

(*c*) that the owner could not be discovered by taking reasonable steps,

the presence or absence of reasonable grounds for such a belief is a matter to which the court or jury shall have regard, in conjunction with any other relevant matters, in considering whether the person so believed.

(5) In this section—

"appropriates", in relation to property, means usurps or adversely interferes with the proprietary rights of the owner of the property;

"depriving" means temporarily or permanently depriving.

Criminal Justice (Theft and Fraud Offences) Act 2001, s 4

"STOLEN PROPERTY"

"stolen property" includes property which has been unlawfully obtained otherwise than by stealing, and cognate words shall be construed accordingly.

Criminal Justice (Theft and Fraud Offences) Act 2001, s 2(1)

"SUBSTANTIAL RISK"

For the purposes of this Part, a person is reckless if he or she disregards a substantial risk that the property handled is stolen, and for those purposes "substantial risk" means a risk of such a nature and degree that, having regard to the circumstances in which the person acquired the property and the extent of the information then available to him or her, its disregard involves culpability of a high degree.

Criminal Justice (Theft and Fraud Offences) Act 2001, 16(2)

T

"TENANCY"

"tenancy" means a tenancy for years or any less period and includes an agreement for such a tenancy.

Criminal Justice (Theft and Fraud Offences) Act 2001, s 5(3)(a)

"THEFT"

Subject to section 5, a person is guilty of theft if he or she dishonestly appropriates property without the consent of its owner and with the intention of depriving its owner of it.

(2) For the purposes of this section a person does not appropriate property without the consent of its owner if—

(*a*) the person believes that he or she has the owner's consent, or would have the owner's consent if the owner knew of the appropriation of the property and the circumstances in which it was appropriated, or

(*b*) (except where the property came to the person as trustee or personal representative) he or she appropriates the property in the belief that the owner cannot be discovered by taking reasonable steps,

but consent obtained by deception or intimidation is not consent for those purposes.

(3) (*a*) This subsection applies to a person who in the course of business holds property in trust for, or on behalf of, more than one owner.

(*b*) Where a person to whom this subsection applies appropriates some of the property so held to his or her own use or benefit, the person shall, for the purposes of *subsection (1)* but subject to *subsection (2)*, be deemed to have appropriated the property or, as the case may be, a sum representing it without the consent of its owner or owners.

(*c*) If in any proceedings against a person to whom this subsection applies for theft of some or all of the property so held by him or her it is proved that—

(i) there is a deficiency in the property or a sum representing it, and

(ii) the person has failed to provide a satisfactory explanation for the whole or any part of the deficiency, it shall be presumed, until the contrary is proved, for the purposes of *subsection (1)* but subject to *subsection (2)*, that the person appropriated, without the consent of its owner or owners, the whole or that part of the deficiency.

(4) If at the trial of a person for theft the court or jury, as the case may be has to consider whether the person believed—

(*a*) that he or she had not acted dishonestly, or
(*b*) that the owner of the property concerned had consented or would have consented to its appropriation, or
(*c*) that the owner could not be discovered by taking reasonable steps,

the presence or absence of reasonable grounds for such a belief is a matter to which the court or jury shall have regard, in conjunction with any other relevant matters, in considering whether the person so believed.

(5) In this section—

"appropriates", in relation to property, means usurps or adversely interferes with the proprietary rights of the owner of the property;

"depriving" means temporarily or permanently depriving.

Criminal Justice (Theft and Fraud Offences) Act 2001, s 4

"TO DAMAGE"

"to damage" includes.

(*a*) in relation to property other than data (but including a storage medium in which data are kept), to destroy, deface, dismantle or, whether temporarily or otherwise, render inoperable or unfit for use or prevent or impair the operation of,
(*b*) in relation to data—
   (i) to add to, alter, corrupt, erase or move to another storage medium or to a different location in the storage medium in which they are kept (whether or not property other than data is damaged thereby), or
   (ii) to do any act that contributes towards causing such addition, alteration, corruption, erasure or movement,
(*c*) to do any act within the State that damages property outside the State,
(*d*) to do any act outside the State that damages property within the State, and
(e) to make an omission causing damage,

and cognate words shall be construed accordingly.

Criminal Damage Act 1991, s 1(1)

U

"UNLAWFUL ORGANISATION"

"unlawful organisation" has the meaning assigned to it by section 18 of the Offences against the State Act, 1939.

Malicious Injuries (Amendment) Act 1986, s 1(1)

In order to regulate and control in the public interest the exercise of the constitutional right of citizens to form associations, it is hereby declared that any organisation which—

(*a*) engages in, promotes, encourages, or advocates the commission of treason or any activity of a treasonable nature, or
(*b*) advocates, encourages, or attempts the procuring by force, violence, or other unconstitutional means of an alteration of the Constitution, or
(*c*) raises or maintains or attempts to raise or maintain a military or armed force in contravention of the Constitution or without constitutional authority, or
(*d*) engages in, promotes, encourages, or advocates the commission of any criminal offence or the obstruction of or interference with the administration of justice or the enforcement of the law, or
(e) engages in, promotes, encourages, or advocates the attainment of any particular object, lawful or unlawful, by violent, criminal, or other unlawful means, or
(*f*) promotes, encourages, or advocates the non-payment of moneys payable to the Central Fund or any other public fund or the non-payment of local taxation,

shall be an unlawful organisation within the meaning and for the purposes of this Act, and this Act shall apply and have effect in relation to such organisation accordingly.

Offences Against the State Act 1939, s 18

"UNLAWFULLY OBTAINED"

"unlawfully obtained" means obtained in circumstances constituting an offence, and cognate words shall be construed accordingly.

(2) For the purposes of this Act a person deceives if he or she—

(*a*) creates or reinforces a false impression, including a false impression as to law, value or intention or other state of mind,
(*b*) prevents another person from acquiring information which would affect that person's judgement of a transaction, or

(*c*) fails to correct a false impression which the deceiver previously created or reinforced or which the deceiver knows to be influencing another to whom he or she stands in a fiduciary or confidential relationship,

and references to deception shall be construed accordingly.

Criminal Justice (Theft and Fraud Offences) Act 2001, s 2(1)

V

"VALUABLE SECURITY"

In this section, "valuable security" means any document—

(*a*) creating, transferring, surrendering or releasing any right to, in or over property,
(*b*) authorising the payment of money or delivery of any property, or
(*c*) evidencing the creation, transfer, surrender or release of any such right, the payment of money or delivery of any property or the satisfaction of any obligation.

Criminal Justice (Theft and Fraud Offences) Act 2001, s 11(3)

W

"WEAPON OF OFFENCE"

"weapon of offence" means:

(*a*) any article which has a blade or sharp point,
(*b*) any other article made or adapted for use for causing injury to or incapacitating a person, or intended by the person having it with him or her for such use or for threatening such use,
(*c*) any weapon of whatever description designed for the discharge of any noxious liquid, noxious gas or other noxious thing.

Criminal Justice (Theft and Fraud Offences) Act 2001, s 13(2)

"WITHOUT LAWFUL EXCUSE"

This section applies to—

(*a*) any offence under *section 2 (1) or 5*,
(*b*) any offence under *section 3* other than one involving a threat by the person charged to damage property in a way which he knows is likely to endanger the life of another, and
(*c*) any offence under *section 4* other than one involving an intent by the person charged to use, or cause or permit the use of, something in his custody or under his control to damage property in such a way as aforesaid.

(2) A person charged with an offence to which this section applies shall, whether or not he would be treated for the purposes of this Act as having a lawful excuse apart from this subsection, be treated for those purposes as having a lawful excuse—

(*a*) if at the time of the act or acts alleged to constitute the offence he believed that the person or persons whom he believed to be entitled to consent to or authorise the damage to (or, in the case of an offence under *section 5*, the accessing of) the property in question had consented, or would have consented to or authorised it if he or they had known of the damage or the accessing and its circumstances,
(*b*) in the case of an offence under section 5, if he is himself the person entitled to consent to or authorise accessing of the data concerned, or

["(*c*) if he damaged or threatened to damage the property in question or, in the case of an offence under s 4, intended to use or cause or permit the use of something to damage it, in order to protect himself or another or property belonging to himself or another or a right or interest in property which was or which he believed to be vested in himself or another and the act or acts alleged to constitute the offence were reasonable in the circumstances as he believed them to be.".]

Criminal Damage Act 1991, s 6(2)(c) substituted by Non-Fatal Offences Against the Person Act 1997, s 21

OFFENCES AGAINST THE PERSON AND PUBLIC ORDER

A

"ACT"

"act" includes omission and a reference to the doing of an act includes a reference to the making of an omission.

Criminal Justice (Safety of United Nations Workers) 2000, s 1(1)

"ADVERTISEMENT"

"advertisement" includes every form of advertising or promotion, whether in a publication or by the display of notices or posters or by the means of circulars, leaflets, pamphlets or cards or other documents or by way of radio, television, computer monitor, telephone, facsimile transmission, photography or cinematography or other like means of communication.

Criminal Justice (Public Order) Act 1994, s 23(5)

"AFFRAY"

(1) Where—

(*a*) two or more persons at any place (whether that place is a public place or a private place or both) use or threaten to use violence towards each other, and
(*b*) the violence so used or threatened by one of those persons is unlawful, and

(*c*) the conduct of those persons taken together is such as would cause a person of reasonable firmness present at that place to fear for his or another person's safety,

then, each such person who uses or threatens to use unlawful violence shall be guilty of the offence of affray.

(2) For the purposes of this section—

(*a*) a threat cannot be made by words alone;
(*b*) no person of reasonable firmness need actually be, or be likely to be, present at the place where the use or threat of violence occurred.

(3) A person shall not be convicted of the offence of affray unless the person intends to use or threaten to use violence or is aware that his conduct may be violent or threaten violence.

Criminal Justice (Public Order) Act 1994, s 16(1)–(3)

"ASSAULT"

(1) A person shall be guilty of the offence of assault who, without lawful excuse, intentionally or recklessly—

(*a*) directly or indirectly applies force to or causes an impact on the body of another, or
(*b*) causes another to believe on reasonable grounds that he or she is likely immediately to be subjected to any such force or impact,

without the consent of the other.

(2) In *subsection (1)(a)*, "force" includes—

(*a*) application of heat, light, electric current, noise or any other form of energy, and
(*b*) application of matter in solid liquid or gaseous form.

Non-Fatal Offences Against the Person Act 1997, s 2(1)

"ASSAULT WITH INTENT"

(1) Any person who assaults any person with intent to cause bodily harm or to commit an indictable offence shall be guilty of an offence.

Criminal Justice (Public Order) Act 1994, s 18(1)

"ASSOCIATED PERSONNEL"

"Associated personnel" means:

(i) Persons assigned by a Government or an intergovernmental organization with the agreement of the competent organ of the United Nations;
(ii) Persons engaged by the Secretary-General of the United Nations or by a specialized agency or by the International Atomic Energy Agency;
(iii) Persons deployed by a humanitarian non-governmental organization or agency under an agreement with the Secretary-General of the United Nations or with a specialized agency or with the International Atomic Energy Agency,

to carry out activities in support of the fulfilment of the mandate of a United Nations operation.

Criminal Justice (Safety of United Nations Workers) Act 2000, sched 1, art 1(B)

B

"BLOOD"

(6) In this section "blood" includes any fluid or substance resembling blood.

Non-Fatal Offences Against the Person Act 1997, s 7(6)

"BOTTLE OR CONTAINER"

" 'bottle or container' means a bottle or container irrespective of whether—

(*a*) the bottle or container is opened or unopened, and
(*b*) any or all of the contents of the bottle or container have been or are being consumed,

and includes the contents of the bottle or container, but does not include a bottle or container for a substance which is in the possession of the person concerned for a purpose other than the intoxication of that or any other person.".

Criminal Justice (Public Order) Act 1994, s 4(4) as amended by Intoxicating Liquor Act 2008, s 18

(9) In this section—

'bottle or container' means a bottle or container irrespective of whether—

(*a*) the bottle or container is opened or unopened, and
(*b*) any or all of the contents of the bottle or container have been or are being consumed,

and includes the contents of the bottle or container.

Criminal Justice (Public Order) Act 1994, s 8(A)(9) as inserted by Intoxicating Liquor Act 2008, s 19

C

"CATERING PREMISES"

"catering premises" means:

(*a*) licensed premises,
(*b*) food premises, or a food stall or food vehicle, within the meaning of the Food Hygiene Regulations 1950 to 1989.

Criminal Justice (Public Order) Act 2003, s 2(1)

"CLOSURE ORDER"

"closure order" means an order under section 5 for the closure of catering premises and includes such an order as affirmed, varied or extended under this Act.

Criminal Justice (Public Order) Act 2003, s 2(1)

(1) If on an application under section 4 the District Court is satisfied—

(*a*) that disorder or noise as referred to in *subsection (1)* of that section has occurred and is likely to recur, and
(*b*) that the making of a closure order is necessary to prevent a recurrence of the disorder or noise,

the Court shall make a closure order in respect of the catering premises concerned.

(2) A closure order shall order the closure of catering premises—

(*a*) at a specified time or between specified times on a specified day or days during a specified period, or

(*b*) for a period—

(i) not exceeding 7 days in the case of the first such order, or

(ii) not less than 7 and not exceeding 30 days in the case of a second or subsequent order.

(3) On making a closure order the Court may, having regard to the particular circumstances of the case, order that the licensee shall, within a specified period, comply with specified requirements in relation to the catering premises concerned, including, as appropriate, a requirement to install a closed circuit television system, restrict the type of substances to be sold or limit the number of persons to be admitted.

(4) A person who, without reasonable excuse, does not comply with an order under *subsection (3)* is guilty of an offence and liable on summary conviction to a fine not exceeding €650 or imprisonment for a term not exceeding 3 months or both.

(5) In determining whether to make a closure order the Court may take into account any conduct of the licensee or a manager or other person employed by the licensee in relation to the operation of the premises concerned.

(6) A closure order—

(*a*) may apply to the whole or part of catering premises,

(*b*) shall specify the ground or grounds for making it, and

(*c*) shall come into force when written notice of its making is given by a member of the Garda Síochána to the licensee or manager of the premises concerned.

(7) While a closure order is in force, a notice specifying the closure times or the period of closure under the order and the grounds for making it shall be affixed by the licensee to the exterior of the premises concerned in a conspicuous place.

(8) No employee who is working in the premises to which a closure order applies shall be disadvantaged in his or her employment by reason of the order or during the period of closure under it.

(9) The reference in *subsection (8)* to an employee is a reference to either a full-time employee or a part-time employee within the meaning of the Protection of Employees (Part-Time Work) Act 2001.

Criminal Justice (Public Order) Act 2003, s 5

"CLUB"

"club" means a club registered under the Registration of Clubs Acts 1904 to 2000.

Criminal Justice (Public Order) Act 2003, s 2(1)

"COERCION"

(1) A person who, with a view to compel another to abstain from doing or to do any act which that other has a lawful right to do or to abstain from doing, wrongfully and without lawful authority—

(*a*) uses violence to or intimidates that other person or a member of the family of the other, or
(*b*) injures or damages the property of that other, or
(*c*) persistently follows that other about from place to place, or
(*d*) watches or besets the premises or other place where that other resides, works or carries on business, or happens to be, or the approach to such premises or place, or
(e) follows that other with one or more other persons in a disorderly manner in or through any public place,

shall be guilty of an offence.

(2) For the purpose of this section attending at or near the premises or place where a person resides, works, carries on business or happens to be, or the approach to such premises or place, in order merely to obtain or communicate information, shall not be deemed a watching or besetting within the meaning of *subsection (1)(d)*.

Non Fatal Offences Against the Person Act 1997, s 9(1)

"CONTAINER"

"container" does not include a container for any medicinal product.

Criminal Justice (Public Order) Act 1994, s 20

"CONTAMINATED BLOOD"

"contaminated blood" means blood which is contaminated with any disease, virus, agent or organism which if passed into the blood stream of another could infect the other with a life threatening or potentially life threatening disease.

Non Fatal Offences Against the Person Act 1997, s 1

"CONTAMINATED FLUID"

"contaminated fluid" means fluid or substance which is contaminated with any disease, virus, agent or organism which if passed into the blood stream of another could infect the other with a life threatening or potentially life threatening disease.

Non Fatal Offences Against the Person Act 1997, s 1

"CONTAMINATED SYRINGE"

"contaminated syringe" means a syringe which has in it or on it contaminated blood or contaminated fluid.

Non Fatal Offences Against the Person Act 1997, s 1

"CONVENTION" SEE THE

"CONVEYANCE"

"conveyance" means any conveyance constructed or adapted for the carriage of a person or persons or of goods by land or water.

Non Fatal Offences Against the Person Act 1997, s 14(2)

D

"DISPOSABLE CONTAINER"

"disposable container" includes—

(*a*) any bottle, can or other portable container or any part thereof (including any crushed or broken portable container or part thereof) for holding any drink which, when empty, is of a kind normally discarded or returned to, or left to be recovered by, the supplier, and
(*b*) any crate or packaging designed to hold more than one such bottle, can or other portable container.

Criminal Justice (Public Order) Act 1994, s 20

"DISTRIBUTE"

"distribute" means distribute to the public or a section of the public and cognate words shall be construed accordingly.

Criminal Justice (Public Order) Act 1994, s 23(5)

"DWELLING"

"dwelling" includes a building, vehicle or vessel ordinarily used for habitation.

Criminal Justice (Public Order) Act 1994, s 3(1)

E

"ENDANGERING TRAFFIC"

A person shall be guilty of an offence who—

(*a*) intentionally places or throws any dangerous obstruction upon a railway, road, street, waterway or public place or interferes with any machinery, signal, equipment or other device for the direction, control or regulation of traffic thereon, or interferes with or throws anything at or on any conveyance used or to be used thereon, and

(*b*) is aware that injury to the person or damage to property may be caused thereby, or is reckless in that regard.

(2) In this section—

"conveyance" means any conveyance constructed or adapted for the carriage of a person or persons or of goods by land or water;

"railway" means a railway, a tramway, or a light railway or any part of a railway, tramway or light railway;

"waterway" means any route upon water used by any conveyance.

Non-Fatal Offences Against the Person Act 1997, s 14(1)

"ENDANGERMENT"

A person shall be guilty of an offence who intentionally or recklessly engages in conduct which creates a substantial risk of death or serious harm to another.

Non-Fatal Offences Against the Person Act 1997, s 13

"EVENT"

If it appears to a member of the Garda Síochána not below the rank of superintendent that it is necessary in the interests of safety or for the purpose of preserving order to restrict the access of persons to a place where an event is taking or is about to take place which attracts, or is likely to attract, a large assembly of persons (in this Part referred to as the "event"), he may authorise any member of the Garda Síochána to erect or cause to be erected a barrier or a series of barriers on any road, street, lane, alley or other means of access to such a place in a position not more than one mile therefrom for the purpose of regulating the access of persons or vehicles thereto.

Criminal Justice (Public Order) Act 1994, s 21(1)

"EXCLUSION ORDER"

The District Court, on conviction of a person for an offence under section 4, 5, 6, 7, 8 or 9 of the Criminal Justice (Public Order) Act 1994 , may by order prohibit the person from entering or being in the vicinity of specified catering premises between such times, and during such a period, as the Court may specify.

(2) Any period so specified shall not exceed 12 months and shall commence—

(*a*) in case the person has been sentenced to imprisonment or detention for the offence, on the date of his or her release therefrom, or
(*b*) in any other case, on the date of the order.

(3) The governor or other person in charge of the place where a person who is subject to an order under *subsection (1)* is serving a sentence shall inform the Commissioner of the Garda Síochána of the date on which the person is to be released.

(4) A person who, without reasonable excuse, does not comply with an order under *subsection (1)* is guilty of an offence and liable on summary conviction to a fine not exceeding €650 or imprisonment for a term not exceeding 3 months or both.

(5) An appeal lies to the Circuit Court from an order under *subsection (1)*.

(6) In *subsection (1)* "offence" means an offence committed after the commencement of this Act.

Criminal Justice (Public Order) Act 2003, s 3

F

"FALSE IMPRISONMENT"

A person shall be guilty of the offence of false imprisonment who intentionally or recklessly—

(*a*) takes or detains, or
(*b*) causes to be taken or detained, or
(*c*) otherwise restricts the personal liberty of,

another without that other's consent.

(2) For the purposes of this section, a person acts without the consent of another if the person obtains the other's consent by force or threat of force, or by deception causing the other to believe that he or she is under legal compulsion to consent.

Non-Fatal Offences Against the Person Act 1997, s 15(1)

"FORCE"

In *subsection (1)(a)*, "force" includes—

(*a*) application of heat, light, electric current, noise or any other form of energy, and
(*b*) application of matter in solid liquid or gaseous form.

Non-Fatal Offences Against the Person Act 1997, s 2(2)

H

"HARASSMENT"

Any person who, without lawful authority or reasonable excuse, by any means including by use of the telephone, harasses another by persistently following, watching, pestering, besetting or communicating with him or her, shall be guilty of an offence.

Non-Fatal Offences Against the Person Act 1997, s 10(1)

"HARM"

"harm" means harm to body or mind and includes pain and unconsciousness.

Non-Fatal Offences Against the Person Act 1997, s 1

"HOSPITAL"

"hospital" includes the lands, buildings and premises connected with and used wholly or mainly for the purposes of a hospital.

Criminal Justice (Public Order) Act 1994, s 19(6) substituted by Criminal Justice Act 2006, s 185(e)

I

"INTOXICATED"

"intoxicated" means under the intoxicating influence of any alcoholic drink, drug, solvent or other substance or a combination of substances and cognate words shall be construed accordingly.

Criminal Justice (Public Order) Act 1994, s 4(4)

"INTOXICATING LIQUOR"

"intoxicating liquor" includes any container containing intoxicating liquor, whether or not a disposable container.

Criminal Justice (Public Order) Act 1994, s 20

L

"LICENSED PREMISES"

"licensed premises" means:

(*a*) premises licensed for the sale of intoxicating liquor under the Licensing Acts 1833 to 2000,
(*b*) premises licensed under the Public Dance Halls Act 1935,
(*c*) premises licensed under the Gaming and Lotteries Acts 1956 to 1986,
(*d*) a club.

Criminal Justice (Public Order) Act 2003, s 2(1)

"LICENSEE"

"licensee" means:

(*a*) in relation to licensed premises (other than a club), the holder of the licence,
(*b*) in relation to a club, every person entered in the register of clubs as an official or member of its committee of management or governing body at the material time, and
(*c*) in relation to other catering premises, the registered proprietor (within the meaning of the Food Hygiene Regulations 1950 to 1989) of the premises.

Criminal Justice (Public Order) Act 2003, s 2(1)

M

"MANAGER"

"manager" means any person who works in catering premises in a capacity which gives him or her authority to close the premises.

Criminal Justice (Public Order) Act 2003, s 2(1)

"MEDICAL SERVICES"

"medical services" means services provided by—

(*a*) doctors, dentists, psychiatrists, nurses, midwives, pharmacists, health and social care professionals (within the meaning of the Health and Social Care Professionals Act 2005) or other persons in the provision of treatment and care for persons at or in a hospital, or

(*b*) persons acting under direction of those persons.".

Criminal Justice (Public Order) Act 1994, s 19(6) as substituted by Criminal Justice Act 2006, s 185(e)

"MEMBER OF THE FAMILY"

"member of the family" in relation to a person, means the spouse, a child (including step-child or adopted child), grandchild, parent, grandparent, step-parent, brother, sister, half-brother, half-sister, uncle, aunt, nephew or niece of the person or any person cohabiting or residing with him or her.

Non Fatal Offences Against the Person Act 1997, s 1

O

"OFFENCE OF TORTURE" SEE THE

"OFFENSIVE CONDUCT"

In this section "offensive conduct" means any unreasonable behaviour which, having regard to all the circumstances, is likely to cause serious offence or serious annoyance to any person who is, or might reasonably be expected to be, aware of such behaviour.

Criminal Justice (Public Order) Act 1994, s 5(3)

P

"PEACE OFFICER"

"peace officer" means a member of the Garda Síochána, a prison officer [a member of the fire brigade, ambulance personnel"] or a member of the Defence Forces.

Criminal Justice (Public Order) Act 1994, s 19(6) substituted by Criminal Justice Act 2006, s 185(e)

"PERSON"

'person' means a person of not less than 18 years of age.

Criminal Justice (Public Order) Act 1994, s 23A (10) inserted by Criminal Justice Act 2006, s 184

"POISONING"

A person shall be guilty of an offence if, knowing that the other does not consent to what is being done, he or she intentionally or recklessly administers to or causes to be taken by another a substance which he or she knows to be capable of interfering substantially with the other's bodily functions.

(2) For the purpose of this section a substance capable of inducing unconsciousness or sleep is capable of interfering substantially with bodily functions.

Non Fatal Offences Against the Person Act 1997, s 12(1)

"PREMISES"

"premises" means the official premises or private accommodation of a United Nations worker, and.

Criminal Justice (Safety of United Nations Workers) Act 2000, s 3(2)

"PRISON"

"prison" means any place for which rules or regulations may be made under the Prisons Acts, 1826 to 1980, section 7 of the Offences against the State (Amendment) Act, 1940, section 233 of the Defence Act, 1954, section 2 of the Prisoners of War and Enemy Aliens Act, 1956, or section 13 of the Criminal Justice Act, 1960.

Criminal Justice (Public Order) Act 1994, s 19(6)

"PRISON OFFICER"

"prison officer" includes any member of the staff of a prison and any person having the custody of, or having duties in relation to the custody of, a person detained in prison.

Criminal Justice (Public Order) Act 1994, s 19(6)

"PRIVATE PLACE"

"private place" means a place that is not a public place.

Criminal Justice (Public Order) Act 1994, s 3(1)

"PUBLIC PLACE"

"public place" includes—

(*a*) any highway,
(*b*) any outdoor area to which at the material time members of the public have or are permitted to have access, whether as of right or as a trespasser or otherwise, and which is used for public recreational purposes,
(*c*) any cemetery or churchyard,
(*d*) any premises or other place to which at the material time members of the public have or are permitted to have access, whether as of right or by express or implied permission, or whether on payment or otherwise, and
(*e*) any train, vessel or vehicle used for the carriage of persons for reward.

Criminal Justice (Public Order) Act 1994, s 3(1)

"PUBLISH"

"publish" means publish to the public or a section of the public and cognate words shall be construed accordingly.

Criminal Justice (Public Order) Act 1994, s 23(5)

R

"RAILWAY"

"railway" means a railway, a tramway, or a light railway or any part of a railway, tramway or light railway.

Non Fatal Offences Against the Person Act 1997, s 14(2)

"RELEVANT BELIEF"

'relevant belief', in relation to a member of the Garda Síochána, means the belief referred to in subsection (1) of the member.

Criminal Justice (Public Order) Act, 1994, s 8A(9) inserted by the Intoxicating Liquor Act 2008, s 19

"RELEVANT PERSON"

'relevant person' means the person first-mentioned in paragraph (*a*) of subsection (1).

Criminal Justice (Public Order) Act 1994, s 8a(9) inserted by the Intoxicating Liquor Act 2008, s 19

"RELEVANT PLACE"

"relevant place" means a place other than a place used as a private dwelling.

Criminal Justice (Public Order) Act 1994, s 8a(9) inserted by Intoxicating Liquor Act 2008, s 19

"RIOT"

Where—

(*a*) 12 or more persons who are present together at any place (whether that place is a public place or a private place or both) use or threaten to use unlawful violence for a common purpose, and (*b*) the conduct of those persons, taken together, is such as would cause a person of reasonable firmness present at that place to fear for his or another person's safety,

then, each of the persons using unlawful violence for the common purpose shall be guilty of the offence of riot.

Criminal Justice (Public Order) Act 1994, s 14(1)

S

"SERIOUS HARM"

"serious harm" means injury which creates a substantial risk of death or which causes serious disfigurement or substantial loss or impairment of the mobility of the body as a whole or of the function of any particular bodily member or organ.

Non-Fatal Offences Against the Person Act 1997, s 1

"SPECIALISED AGENCY"

"specialised agency" has the meaning assigned to it by Article 57 of the Charter of the United Nations.

Criminal Justice (Safety of United Nations Workers) Act 2000, s 1(1)

"STREET"

"street" includes any road, bridge, lane, footway, subway, square, court, alley or passage, whether a thoroughfare or not, which is for the time being open to the public; and the doorways, entrances and gardens abutting on a street and any ground or car-park adjoining and open to a street, shall be treated as forming part of a street.

Non-Fatal Offences Against the Person Act 1997, s 1

"SUICIDE"

(1) Suicide shall cease to be a crime.

(2) A person who aids, abets, counsels or procures the suicide of another, or an attempt by another to commit suicide, shall be guilty of an offence and shall be liable on conviction on indictment to imprisonment for a term not exceeding fourteen years.

(3) If, on the trial of an indictment for murder, murder to which section 3 of the Criminal Justice Act, 1990 applies or manslaughter, it is proved that the person charged aided, abetted, counselled or procured the suicide of the person alleged to have been killed, he may be found guilty of an offence under this section.

(4) No proceedings shall be instituted for an offence under this section except by or with the consent of the Director of Public Prosecutions.

Criminal Law (Suicide) Act 1993, s 2

"SYRINGE"

"syringe" includes any part of a syringe or a needle or any sharp instrument capable of piercing skin and passing onto or into a person blood or any fluid or substance resembling blood.

Non-Fatal Offences Against the Person Act 1997, s 1

T

"THE CONVENTION"

"the Convention" means the Convention on the Safety of United Nations and Associated Personnel done at New York on the 9th day of December, 1994, the text of which, in the English language, is, for convenience of reference, set out in the *First Schedule* to the Act.

Criminal Justice (Safety of United Nations Workers) Act, 2000 s 1(1)

"the Convention" means the Convention against Torture and Other Cruel, Inhuman or Degrading Treatment or Punishment adopted by resolution 39/46 of the General Assembly of the United Nations on 10 December 1984, the text of which, in the English language, is, for convenience of reference, set out in the *Schedule* to this Act.

Criminal Justice (United Nations Convention Against Torture) Act 2000, s 1(1)

"THE OFFENCE OF TORTURE"

"the offence of torture" shall be construed in accordance with *section* 2 of this Act.

Criminal Justice (United Nations Convention Against Torture) Act 2000, s 1(1)

A public official, whatever his or her nationality, who carries out an act of torture on a person, whether within or outside the State, shall be guilty of the offence of torture.

(2) A person, whatever his or her nationality, other than a public official, who carries out an act of torture on another person, whether within or outside the State, at the instigation of, or with the consent or acquiesence of, a public official shall be guilty of the offence of torture.

Criminal Justice (United Nations Convention Against Torture) Act 2000, s 2

"TORTURE"

"torture" means an act or omission by which severe pain or suffering, whether physical or mental, is intentionally inflicted on a person—

(*a*) for such purposes as—
   (i) obtaining from that person, or from another person, information or a confession,
   (ii) punishing that person for an act which the person concerned or a third person has committed or is suspected of having committed, or
   (iii) intimidating or coercing that person or a third person,

or

(*b*) for any reason that is based on any form of discrimination,

but does not include any such act that arises solely from, or is inherent in or incidental to, lawful sanctions.

Criminal Justice (United Nations Convention Against Torture) Act 2000, s 1(1)

For the purposes of this Convention, the term "torture" means any act by which severe pain or suffering, whether physical or mental, is intentionally inflicted on a person for such purposes as obtaining from him or a third person information or a confession, punishing him for an act he or a third person has committed or is suspected of having committed, or intimidating or coercing him or a third person, or for any reason based on discrimination of any kind, when such pain or suffering is inflicted by or at the instigation of or with the consent or acquiescence of a public official or other person acting in an official capacity. It does not include pain or suffering arising only from, inherent in or incidental to lawful sanctions.

Criminal Justice (United Nations Convention Against Torture) Act 2000, sched, art 1(1)

"TRANSIT STATE"

"Transit State" means a State, other than the host State, in whose territory United Nations and associated personnel or their equipment are in transit or temporarily present in connection with a United Nations operation.

Criminal Justice (Safety of United Nations Workers) Act 2000, sched 1, art 1(e)

U

"UNITED NATIONS OPERATIONS"

"United Nations operation" means an operation established by the competent organ of the United Nations in accordance with the Charter of the United Nations and conducted under United Nations authority and control where—

(*a*) the operation is for the purpose of maintaining or restoring international peace and security, or

(*b*) the Security Council or the General Assembly has declared, for the purposes of the Convention, that there exists an exceptional risk to the safety of the personnel participating in the operation,but does not include a United Nations operation authorised by the Security Council as an enforcement action under Chapter VII of the Charter of the United Nations in which any of the personnel are engaged as combatants against organised armed forces and to which the law of international armed conflict applies.

Criminal Justice (Safety of United Nations Workers) Act 2000, s 1(1)

"United Nations operation" means an operation established by the competent organ of the United Nations in accordance with the Charter of the United Nations and conducted under United Nations authority and control:

(i) Where the operation is for the purpose of maintaining or restoring international peace and security; or

(ii) Where the Security Council or the General Assembly has declared, for the purposes of this Convention, that there exists an exceptional risk to the safety of the personnel participating in the operation.

Criminal Justice (Safety of United Nations Workers) Act 2000, sched 1, art 1(c)

"UNITED NATIONS PERSONNEL"

"United Nations personnel" means:

(i) Persons engaged or deployed by the Secretary-General of the United Nations as members of the military, police or civilian components of a United Nations operation;

(ii) Other officials and experts on mission of the United Nations or its specialized agencies or the International Atomic Energy Agency who are present in an official capacity in the area where a United Nations operation is being conducted.

Criminal Justice (Safety of United Nations Workers) Act 2000, sched 1, art 1(a)

"UNITED NATIONS WORKER"

"United Nations worker" means a person who, in relation to an alleged offence, at the time of the alleged offence—

(*a*) is engaged or deployed by the Secretary-General of the United Nations as a member of the military, police or civilian component of a United Nations operation,

(*b*) is, in his or her capacity as an official or expert on mission of the United Nations, a specialised agency of the United Nations or the International Atomic Energy Agency, present in an area where a United Nations operation is being conducted,

(*c*) is assigned, with the agreement of the competent organ of the United Nations, by a Government or intergovernmental organisation to carry out activities in support of the fulfilment of the mandate of a United Nations operation,

(*d*) is engaged by the Secretary-General of the United Nations or by a specialised agency or by the International Atomic Energy Agency to carry out such activities, or

(*e*) is deployed by a humanitarian non-governmental organisation or agency under an agreement with the Secretary-General of the United Nations or with a specialised agency or with the International Atomic Energy Agency to carry out such activities.

Criminal Justice (Safety of United Nations Workers) Act 2000, s 1(1)

"USE OF FORCE"

For the purposes of *sections 18* and *19*

(*a*) a person uses force in relation to another person or property not only when he or she applies force to, but also where he or she causes an impact on, the body of that person or that property;

(*b*) a person shall be treated as using force in relation to another person if—
(i) he or she threatens that person with its use, or
(ii) he or she detains that person without actually using it; and
(*c*) a person shall be treated as using force in relation to property if he or she threatens a person with its use in relation to property.

(2) *Sections 18* and *19* shall apply in relation to acts immediately preparatory to the use of force as they apply in relation to acts in which force is used.

(3) A threat of force may be reasonable although the actual use of force may not be.

(4) The fact that a person had an opportunity to retreat before using force shall be taken into account, in conjunction with other relevant evidence, in determining whether the use of force was reasonable.

Non-Fatal Offences Against the Person Act 1997, s 20(1)–(4)

V

"VEHICLE"

"vehicle" means any means of transportation of a United Nations worker.

Criminal Justice (Safety of United Nations Workers) Act 2000, s 3(2)

"VICINITY"

"vicinity", in relation to catering premises, means land within a reasonable distance, not exceeding 100 metres, of the premises.

Criminal Justice (Public Order) Act 2003, s 2(1)

"VIOLENT DISORDER"

Where—

(*a*) three or more persons who are present together at any place (whether that place is a public place or a private place or both) use or threaten to use unlawful violence, and
(*b*) the conduct of those persons, taken together, is such as would cause a person of reasonable firmness present at that place to fear for his or another person's safety,

then, each of the persons using or threatening to use unlawful violence shall be guilty of the offence of violent disorder.

(2) For the purposes of this section—

(*a*) it shall be immaterial whether or not the three or more persons use or threaten to use unlawful violence simultaneously;
(*b*) no person of reasonable firmness need actually be, or be likely to be, present at that place.

(3) A person shall not be convicted of the offence of violent disorder unless the person intends to use or threaten to use violence or is aware that his conduct may be violent or threaten violence.

Criminal Justice (Public Order) Act 1994, s 15(1)

W

"WATERWAY"

"waterway" means any route upon water used by any conveyance.

Non-Fatal Offences Against the Person Act 1997, s 14(2)

OFFENCES AGAINST THE STATE

A

"ACT"

"act" includes omission and a reference to the commission or doing of an act includes a reference to the making of an omission.

Criminal Justice (Terrorist Offences) Act 2005, s 3

"AGGREGATED DATA"

"aggregated data" means data that cannot be related to individual subscribers or users.

Criminal Justice (Terrorist Offences) Act 2005, s 61(1)

"APPLICABLE INSTRUMENT"

(4) In *subsection (3)*—

"applicable instrument" means—

(*a*) in relation to an act to which_section 9 *(1)* or *(2)* applies, the Hostage Convention as defined in section 8,

(*b*) in relation to an act to which section 10 *(1)*, *(2)* or *(3)* applies, the Terrorist Bombing Convention as defined in section 8, (*c*) in relation to an act to which section 11 *(1)* or *(2)* applies, the Internationally Protected Persons Convention as defined in section 8, and

(*d*) in relation to an act to which section 13 *(1)* or *(2)* applies, the Terrorist Financing Convention as defined in section 12.

Criminal Justice (Terrorist Offences) Act 2005, s 43(4)

B

"BANK"

"bank" means the holder of a licence under the Central Bank Act, 1971, and the persons specified in section 7 (4) of that Act and any other financial institution.

Offences Against the State(Amendment) Act 1985, s 1(1)

(4) Subsection (1) of this section shall not apply in relation to the Agricultural Credit Corporation, Limited, the Industrial Credit Company, Limited, the Post Office Savings Bank, a trustee savings bank certified under the Trustee Savings Banks Acts, 1863 to 1965, a building society, an industrial and provident society, a friendly society, a credit union, an investment trust company or the manager under a unit trust scheme in respect of the carrying on of the business of the scheme.

Central Bank Act 1971, s 7(4)

"BUILDING"

In this section the word "building" includes a part of a building and also all outhouses, yards, and gardens within the curtilage of the building.

Offences Against the State Act 1939, s 25(5)

C

"CHEMICAL WEAPONS"

"chemical weapons" means—

(*a*) toxic chemicals and their precursors, except where intended for—

(i) peaceful purposes,

(ii) purposes relating to protection against toxic chemicals, or

(iii) law enforcement purposes within the State,

as long as the types and quantities are consistent with such purposes;

(*b*) munitions and devices specifically designed to cause death or other harm through the toxic properties of those toxic chemicals defined in *paragraph (a)* of this definition which would be released as a result of the employment of such munitions and devices; or

(*c*) any equipment specifically designed for use directly in connection with the employment of those munitions or devices.

Chemical Weapons Act 1997, s 2

"CLOSING ORDER"

(1) Whenever an officer of the Gárda Síochána not below the rank of chief superintendent is satisfied that a building is being used or has been used in any way for the purposes, direct or indirect, of an unlawful organisation, such officer may make an order (in this section referred to as a closing order) that such building be closed for the period of **[Twelve]** months from the date of such order.

(2) Whenever a closing order has been made an officer of the Gárda Síochána not below the rank of chief superintendent may—

(*a*) extend the operation of such closing order for a farther period not exceeding **[Twelve]** months from the expiration of the period mentioned in such closing order;

(*b*) terminate the operation of such closing order.

(3) Whenever a closing order has been made or has been extended, any person having an estate or interest in the building to which such closing order relates may apply to the High Court, in a summary manner on notice to the Attorney-General, for such order as is hereinafter mentioned, and on such application the High Court, if it is satisfied that, having regard to all the circumstances of the case, the making or the extension (as the case may be) of such closing order was not reasonable, may make an order quashing such closing order or the said extension thereof, as the case may be.

(4) Whenever and so long as a closing order is in operation, the following provisions shall have effect, that is to say:—

(*a*) it shall not be lawful for any person to use or occupy the building to which such closing order relates or any part of such building;

(*b*) any member of the Gárda Síochána not below the rank of inspector may take all such steps as he shall consider necessary or expedient to prevent such building or any part thereof being used or occupied in contravention of this sub-section;

(*c*) every person who uses or `occupies such building or any part of such building in contravention of this sub-section shall be guilty of an offence under this section and shall be liable on summary conviction thereof to imprisonment for a term not exceeding three months.

(5) In this section the word "building" includes a part of a building and also all outhouses, yards, and gardens within the curtilage of the building.

"(6) Whenever a closing order has been extended, a member of the Gárda Síochána not below the rank of chief superintendent may extend the operation of such closing order for a further period or periods each of which shall not exceed 12 months, but a closing order shall not be in operation for more than three years.".

Offences Against the State Act 1939, s 25 amended and subsection 6 inserted by Criminal Law Act 1976, s 4

D

"DATA"

"data" means communications data.

Criminal Justice (Terrorist Offences) Act 2005, s 61(1)

"DATA RETENTION REQUEST"

"data retention request" means a request made under section 63 for the retention of traffic data or location data or both.

Criminal Justice (Terrorist Offences) Act 2005, s 61

(1) Subject to *subsections (2)* and *(4)*, the Garda Commissioner may request a service provider to retain, for a period of 3 years, traffic data or location data or both for the purposes of—

(*a*) the prevention, detection, investigation or prosecution of crime (including but not limited to terrorist offences), or

(*b*) the safeguarding of the security of the State.

(2) The data retention request must be made in writing.

(3) Traffic data and location data that are in the possession of a service provider on the passing of this Act and that were retained by the service provider for the purposes specified in *subsection (1)* are deemed to have been the subject of a data retention request, but only if the 3 year retention period for the data has not elapsed before the passing of this Act.

(4) For the purposes of this Part, the 3 year retention period begins—

(*a*) in the case of traffic data or location data referred to in *subsection (3)*, on the date before the passing of this Act on which the data were first processed by the service provider, or

(*b*) in the case of any other traffic data or location data, on the date on or after the passing of this Act on which the data were first so processed.

(5) Notwithstanding any other enactment or instrument, a service provider shall retain, for the purposes and the period specified in *subsection (1)*, the data specified in a data retention request made to the provider.

(6) Nothing in this section shall be taken as requiring a service provider to retain aggregated data or data that have been made anonymous.

Criminal Justice (Terrorist Offences) Act 2005, s 63

"DECLARATION OF LEGALITY"

(1) Any person (in this section referred to as the applicant) who claims to be a member of an organisation in respect of which a suppression order has been made may, at any time within thirty days after the publication of such order in the *Iris Oifigiúil*, apply to the High Court in a summary manner on notice to the Attorney-General for a declaration (in this Act referred to as a declaration of legality) that such organisation is not an unlawful organisation.

(2) Where, on an application under the foregoing sub-section of this section, the High Court, after hearing such evidence as may be adduced by the applicant or by the Attorney-General, is satisfied that the organisation to which such application relates is not an unlawful organisation, it shall be lawful for the High Court to make a declaration of legality in respect of such organisation.

(3) The High Court shall not make a declaration of legality unless the applicant for such declaration either—

(*a*) gives evidence in support of the application and submits himself to cross-examination by counsel for the Attorney-General, or

(*b*) satisfies the High Court that he is unable by reason of illness or other sufficient cause to give such evidence and adduces in support of the application the evidence of at least one person who submits himself to cross-examination by counsel for the Attorney-General.

(4) Whenever, on an application under this section, the High Court, or the Supreme Court on appeal from the High Court, makes a declaration of legality in respect of an organisation, the suppression order relating to such organisation shall forthwith become null and void, but without prejudice to the validity of anything previously done thereunder.

(5) Where the High Court makes a declaration of legality, it shall be lawful for that court, on the application of the Attorney-General, to suspend the operation of the next preceding sub-section of this section in respect of such declaration until the final determination of an appeal by the Attorney-General to the Supreme Court against such declaration, and if the High Court so suspends the said sub-section, the said sub-section shall only come into operation in respect of such declaration if and when the Supreme Court affirms the order of the High Court making such declaration.

(6) Whenever an application for a declaration of legality is made under this section and is refused by the High Court, or by the Supreme Court on appeal from the High Court, it shall not be lawful, in any prosecution of the applicant for the offence of being a member of the organisation to which such application relates, to give in evidence against the applicant any of the following matters, that is to say:—

(*a*) the fact that he made the said application, or
(*b*) any admission made by him or on his behalf for the purposes of or during the hearing of the said application, or
(*c*) any statement made in the oral evidence given by him or on his behalf (whether on examination in chief, cross examination, or re-examination) at the hearing of the said application, or
(*d*) any affidavit made by him or on his behalf for the purposes of the said application.

Offences Against the State Act 1939, s 20

"DESIGNATED JUDGE"

"designated judge" means the person designated under section 8 of the Act of 1993.

Criminal Justice (Terrorist Offences) Act 2005, s 61(1)

(1) The President of the High Court shall from time to time after consultation with the Minister invite a person who is a judge of the High Court to undertake (while serving as such a judge) the duties specified in this section and, if he accepts the invitation, the Government shall designate him for the purposes of this Act.

(2) A person designated under this section (referred to in this Act as "the designated judge") shall hold office in accordance with the terms of his designation and shall have the duty of keeping the operation of this Act under review, of ascertaining whether its provisions are being complied with and of reporting to the Taoiseach—

(*a*) at such intervals (being intervals of not more than twelve months) as the designated judge thinks desirable in relation to the general operation of the Act, and
(*b*) from time to time in relation to any matters relating to the Act which he considers should be so reported.

(3) For the purpose of his functions under this Act, the designated judge—

(*a*) shall have power to investigate any case in which an authorisation has been given, and

(*b*) shall have access to and may inspect any official documents relating to an authorisation or the application therefor.

(4) The designated judge may, if he thinks it desirable to do so, communicate with the Taoiseach or the Minister on any matter concerning interceptions.

(5) Every person who was concerned in, or has information relevant to, the making of the application for, or the giving of, an authorisation, or was otherwise concerned with the operation of any provision of this Act relating to the application or authorisation, shall give the designated judge, on request by him, such information as is in his possession relating to the application or authorisation.

(6) If the designated judge informs the Minister that he considers that a particular authorisation that is in force should not have been Oven or (because of circumstances arising after it had been given) should be cancelled or that the period for which it was in force should not have been extended or further extended, the Minister shall, as soon as may be, inform the Minister for Transport, Energy and Communications and shall then cancel the authorisation.

(7) The Taoiseach shall cause a copy of a report under *subsection (2)* of this section together with a statement as to whether any matter has been excluded therefrom in pursuance of *subsection (8)* of this section to be laid before each House of the Oireachtas.

(8) If the Taoiseach considers, after consultation with the designated judge, that the publication of any matter in a report under *subsection (2)* of this section would be prejudicial to the prevention or detection of crime or to the security of the State, the Taoiseach may exclude that matter from the copies of the report laid before the Houses of the Oireachtas.

Interception of Postal Packets and Telecommunications Messages (Regulation) Act 1993, s 8

"DIRECTIVE"

"Directive" means Directive 2002/58/EC of the European Parliament and of the Council of 12 July 2002 concerning the processing of personal data and protection of privacy in the electronic communications sector.

Criminal Justice (Terrorist Offences) Act 2005, s 61(1)

"DISCLOSURE REQUEST"

"disclosure request" means a request under section 64 for the disclosure of traffic data or location data retained in accordance with section 63 (5).

Criminal Justice (Terrorist Offences) Act 2005, s 61(1)

"DISPOSAL ORDER"

(1) Subject to *subsection (2)*, where an interlocutory order has been in force for not less than 7 years in relation to funds, the High Court may, on application by a member of the Garda Síochána, make an order directing that all or, if appropriate, a specified part of the funds be transferred, subject to such terms and conditions as the Court may specify, to the Minister for Finance or such other person as the Court may determine.

(2) Subject to *subsections (6)* and *(8)*, the Court shall make a disposal order in relation to any funds that are the subject of an application under *subsection (1)* unless it is satisfied that the funds are not funds that had been used or were intended for use in committing or facilitating the commission of an offence under *section 6* or *13*.

(3) The applicant shall give notice of an application under this section to—

(*a*) the respondent unless the Court is satisfied that it is not reasonably possible to ascertain the respondent's whereabouts, and

(*b*) such other (if any) persons as the Court may direct.

(4) A disposal order operates to deprive the respondent of any rights to the funds to which the order relates and on the making of the order the funds are transferred to the Minister for Finance or other person determined by the Court.

(5) The Minister for Finance may dispose of any funds transferred to him or her under this section and any proceeds of the disposition and any money transferred to that Minister under this section shall be paid into and disposed of by him or her for the benefit of the Exchequer.

(6) In proceedings under *subsection (1)*, before deciding whether to make a disposal order, the Court shall give any person claiming ownership of the funds an opportunity to be heard by the Court and to show cause why the order should not be made.

(7) On application by the respondent or, if the respondent's whereabouts cannot be ascertained, on the Court's own initiative, the Court may, if it considers it appropriate to do so in the interests of justice, adjourn the hearing of an application under *subsection (1)* for such period not exceeding 2 years as it considers reasonable.

(8) The Court shall not make a disposal order if it is satisfied that there would be a serious risk of injustice.

Criminal Justice (Terrorist Offences) Act 2005, s 16

22C.—(1) Subject to subsection (2), where an interim order has been in force for not less than 12 months in relation to specified property, the High Court may, on application by the Minister, make an order authorising the Minister to dispose of the property as he sees fit.

(2) Subject to subsection (4), the Court shall make a disposal order in relation to any property that is the subject of an application under subsection (1) unless it is satisfied that the property is not the property of an unlawful organisation.

(3) The Minister shall give notice of an application under this section to—

(*a*) the respondent unless the Court is satisfied that it is not reasonably possible to ascertain the respondent's whereabouts, and
(*b*) such other (if any) persons as the Court may direct.

(4) Before deciding whether to make a disposal order under subsection (1), the Court shall give any person claiming ownership of the specified property an opportunity to be heard by the Court and to show cause why the order should not be made.

(5) On application by the respondent or, if the respondent's where abouts cannot be ascertained, on the Court's own initiative, the Court may, if it considers it appropriate to do so in the interests of justice, adjourn the hearing of an application under subsection (1) for such period not exceeding 2 years as it considers reasonable.

Offences Against the State Act 1939, s 22c inserted by the Criminal Justice (Terrorist Offences) Act 2005, s 51

"DOCUMENT"

the word "document" includes a book and also a newspaper, magazine, or other periodical publication, and also a pamphlet, leaflet, circular, or advertisement;

["and also—

(*a*) any map, plan, graph or drawing,
(*b*) any photograph,
(*c*) any disc, tape, sound track or other device in which sounds or other data (not being visual images) are embodied so as to be capable (with or without the aid of some other equipment) of being reproduced therefrom, and
(*d*) any film, microfilm, negative, tape or ether device in which one or more visual images are embodied (whether with or without sounds or other data) so as to be capable (as aforesaid) of being reproduced therefrom and a reproduction or still reproduction of the image or images embodied therein whether enlarged or not and whether with or without sounds or other data".].

Offences Against the State Act 1939, s 2 amended by Offences Against the State (Amendment) Act 1972, s 5

E

"EUROJUST"

"Eurojust" means the body established by Council Decision of 28 February 2002[2] setting up Eurojust with a view to reinforcing the fight against serious crime.

European Arrest Warrant Act 2003, s 2

"EUROPEAN ARREST WARRANT"

"European arrest warrant" means a warrant, order or decision of a judicial authority of a Member State, issued under such laws as give effect to the Framework Decision in that Member State, for the arrest and surrender by the State to that Member State of a person in respect of an offence committed or alleged to have been committed by him or her under the law of that Member State.

European Arrest Warrant Act 2003, s 2

"EUROPEAN COMMUNITIES"

"European Communities" has the same meaning as it has in the European Communities Act 1972.

European Arrest Warrant Act 2003, s 2

"the European Communities" means the European Economic Community, the European Coal and Steel Community and the European Atomic Energy Community.

European Communities Act 1972, s 1(1)

"EXPLOSIVE"

"explosive" means an explosive within the meaning of the Explosives Act, 1875, and any other substance or thing that is an explosive substance within the meaning of the Explosive Substances Act, 1883.

Offences Against the State (Amendment) Act 1998, s 1

This Act shall apply to gunpowder and other explosives as defined by this section.

The term 'explosive' in this Act—

(1) Means gunpowder, nitro-glycerine, dynamite, guncotton, blasting powders, fulminate of mercury or of other metals, coloured fires, and every other substance, whether similar to those above mentioned or not, used or manufactured with a view to produce a practical effect by explosion or a pyrotechnic effect; and

(2) Includes fog-signals, fireworks, fuzes, rockets, percussion caps, detonators, cartridges, ammunition of all descriptions, and every adaptation or preparation of an explosive as above defined.

Explosives Act 1875, s 3

(1) In this Act, unless the context otherwise requires,—

The expression 'explosive substance' shall be deemed to include any materials for making any explosive substance; also any apparatus, machine, implement, or materials used, or intended to be used, or adapted for causing, or aiding in causing, any explosion in or with any explosive substance; also any part of any such apparatus, machine, or implement.

Explosive Substances Act 1883, s 9

"EXPLOSIVE OR OTHER LETHAL DEVICE"

In this section "explosive or other lethal device" means any of the following:

(*a*) an explosive weapon or device that is designed, or has the capability, to cause death, serious bodily injury or substantial material damage;
(*b*) an incendiary weapon or device that is designed, or has the capability, to cause death, serious bodily injury or substantial material damage;
(*c*) a weapon or device that is designed, or has the capability, to cause death, serious bodily injury or substantial material damage through the release, dissemination or impact of any of the following:
  (i) a toxic chemical as defined in the Chemical Weapons Act 1997;
  (ii) a microbial or other biological agent;
  (iii) a toxin, whatever its origin or method of production;
  (iv) a substance having an effect similar to the effect of anything referred to in any of *subparagraphs (i)* to *(iii)*;
  (v) ionising radiation or a radioactive substance, as defined in the Radiological Protection Act 1991.

Criminal Justice (Terrorist Offences) Act 2005, s 10(9)

F

"FIREARM"

"firearm" has the same meaning as it has in the Firearms Acts, 1925 to 1990.

Offences Against the State (Amendment) Act 1998, s 1

(1) In the *Firearms Acts, 1925* to *1990*, "firearm" means—

(*a*) a lethal firearm or other lethal weapon of any description from which any shot, bullet or other missile can be discharged;
(*b*) an air gun (which expression includes an air rifle and an air pistol) or any other weapon incorporating a barrel from which metal or other slugs can be discharged;
(*c*) a crossbow;
(*d*) any type of stun gun or other weapon for causing any shock or other disablement to a person by means of electricity or any other kind of energy emission;
(e) a prohibited weapon as defined in section 1 (1) of the Firearms Act, 1925;
(*f*) any article which would be a firearm under any of the foregoing paragraphs but for the fact that, owing to the lack of a necessary component part or parts, or to any other defect or condition, it is incapable of discharging a shot, bullet or other missile or of causing a shock or other disablement (as the case may be);
(*g*) save where the context otherwise requires, any component part of any article referred to in any of the foregoing paragraphs and, for the purposes of this definition, the following articles shall be deemed to be such component parts as aforesaid.
  (i) telescope sights with a light beam, or telescope sights with an electronic light amplification device or an infra-red device, designed to be fitted to a firearm specified in *paragraph (a), (b), (c)* or *(e)*, and
  (ii) a silencer designed to be fitted to a firearm specified in *paragraph (a), (b)* or *(e)*.

(2) The following provisions are hereby repealed:

(*a*) the definition of "firearm" in section 1 (1) of the Firearms Act, 1925, and in section 1 of the Firearms (Proofing) Act, 1968, and
(*b*) section 2 of the Firearms Act, 1964, and section 2 of the Firearms Act, 1971.

Firearms and Offensive Weapons Act 1990, s 4

"FRAMEWORK DECISION"

"Framework Decision" means the Framework Decision on Combating Terrorism adopted by the Council of the European Union at Luxembourg on 13 June 2002, the text of which is set out for convenience of reference in—

(*a*) *Part 1* of *Schedule 1*, in the case of the Irish language text, and
(*b*) *Part 2* of *Schedule 1*, in the case of the English language text.

Criminal Justice (Terrorist Offences) Act 2005, s 4

"FUNDS"

"funds" means—

(*a*) assets of every kind, whether tangible or intangible, movable or immovable, however acquired, and
(*b*) any legal document or instrument in any form, including electronic or digital, evidencing title to, or any interest in, any asset, including, but not limited to, a bank credit, traveller's cheque, bank cheque, money order, share, security, bond, draft and letter of credit.

Criminal Justice (Terrorist Offences) Act 2005, s 12

G

"GARDA COMMISSIONER"

"Garda Commissioner" means the Commissioner of the Gárda Síochána.

Criminal Justice (Terrorist Offences) Act 2005, s 61

H

"HOSTAGE CONVENTION"

"Hostage Convention" means the International Convention against the Taking of Hostages adopted by resolution 34/146 of the General Assembly of the United Nations on 17 December 1979, the English language text of which is set out for convenience of reference in *Schedule 3*.

Criminal Justice (Terrorist Offences) Act 2005, s 8

"HOSTAGE" SEE THE

I

"IMPRISONMENT"

"imprisonment" includes detention in Saint Patrick's Institution and a place of detention provided under section 2 of the Prisons Act 1970, and "prison" shall be construed accordingly.

Criminal Justice Act 2006, s 87

"IMPRISONMENT"

"imprisonment" includes—

(*a*) detention in Saint Patrick's Institution, and
(*b*) detention in a place provided under section 2 of the Prisons Act 1970,

and "sentence of imprisonment" shall be construed accordingly.

Criminal Justice Act 2006, s 98

"INCRIMINATING DOCUMENT"

the expression "incriminating document" means a document of whatsoever date, or bearing no date, issued by or emanating from an unlawful organisation or appearing to be so issued or so to emanate or purporting or appearing to aid or abet any such organisation or calculated to promote the formation of an unlawful organisation.

Offences Against the State Act 1939, s 2

"INTERIM ORDER"

If satisfied on application *ex parte* by a member of the Gárda Síochána that a person is in possession or control of funds that are being used or may be intended for use in committing, or facilitating the commission of, an offence under section 6 or *13*, the High Court may make an order prohibiting the person, any other specified person or any other person having notice of the order from—

(*a*) disposing of or otherwise dealing with all or, where appropriate, a specified part of the funds during such period, not exceeding 40 days, as may be specified by the Court, or
(*b*) diminishing the value of the funds during that period.

(2) An interim order—

(*a*) may contain such provisions, conditions and restrictions as the Court considers necessary or expedient, and

(3) On application by the respondent or any other person claiming ownership of the funds specified in an interim order that is in force, the Court may discharge or, as may be appropriate, vary the order if satisfied that those funds or a part of them are not funds that are being used or may be intended for use in committing or facilitating the commission of an offence under *section 6* or *13*.

(4) On application by a member of the Gárda Síochána or any other person, the Court may vary an interim order to such extent as may be necessary to permit—

(*a*) the enforcement of any order of a court for the payment by the respondent of any sum, including any sum in respect of costs,
(*b*) the recovery by a county registrar or sheriff of income tax due by the respondent pursuant to a certificate issued by the Collector-General under section 962 of the Taxes Consolidation Act 1997, together with the fees and expenses provided for in that section, or
(*c*) the institution of proceedings for, or relating to, the recovery of any other sum owed by the respondent.

(5) *Subsection (4)* is not to be construed to limit the generality of section 6 of the Act of 1996 as made applicable by *section 20* of this Act.

(6) On application at any time by a member of the Gárda Síochána, the Court shall discharge an interim order.

(7) Subject to *subsections (3)*, *(6)* and *(11)*, an interim order continues in force until the end of the period specified by the Court and then lapses unless an application for an interlocutory order in respect of any of the funds concerned is brought during that period.

(8) If an application for an interlocutory order is brought within the period allowed under *subsection (7)*, the interim order lapses on—

(*a*) the determination of the application,
(*b*) the expiry of the ordinary time for bringing an appeal against the determination, or
(*c*) if such appeal is brought, the determination or abandonment of the appeal or any further appeal or the expiry of the ordinary time for bringing any further appeal,

whichever is the latest.

(9) Notice of an application under *subsection (3)* for the discharge or variation of an interim order shall be given by the respondent or other person making the application to—

(*a*) the member of the Garda Síochána who applied for the interim order, and
(*b*) such other (if any) persons as the Court may direct.

(10) Notice of an application under *subsection (4)* for the variation, or under *subsection (6)* for the discharge, of an interim order shall be given by the applicant to—

(*a*) the respondent unless the Court is satisfied that it is not reasonably possible to ascertain the respondent's whereabouts, and
(*b*) such other (if any) persons as the Court may direct.

(11) Where a forfeiture order, or a confiscation order, under the Act of 1994 relates to any funds that are the subject of an interim order that is in force—

(*a*) the interim order is discharged, if it relates only to the funds that are the subject of the forfeiture order or the confiscation order, as the case may be, and
(*b*) the interim order is varied by the exclusion from it of the other funds, if it relates to other funds in addition to the funds that are the subject of the forfeiture order or the confiscation order, as the case may be.

Criminal Justice (Terrorist Offences) Act 2005, s 14

"INTERIM ORDER"

The Minister may apply *ex parte* to the High Court for an interim order under subsection (2) in respect of specified property where the Minister is of the opinion that it—

(*a*) is the property of an unlawful organisation, whether or not the property is in the possession or control of that organisation, and
(*b*) is forfeited to and vested in the Minister by virtue of section 22.

(2) On application under subsection (1), the Court may issue an interim order prohibiting any of the following from disposing of or otherwise dealing with the property specified in the order or from diminishing its value:

(*a*) any person in possession or control of the property;
(*b*) any person having notice of the order;
(*c*) any other person specified in the order.

(3) An interim order—

(*a*) may contain such provisions, conditions and restrictions as the Court considers necessary or expedient, and
(*b*) shall provide for notice of the order to be given to—

(i) any person named in the order, and
(ii) any other person who is or appears to be affected by it, unless the Court is satisfied that it is not reasonably possible to ascertain the person's whereabouts.

(4) On application by the respondent or any other person claiming ownership of any property specified in an interim order that is in force under this section, the Court may discharge or vary the order, as it considers appropriate, if it is shown to the Court's satisfaction that the property is not the property of an unlawful organisation.

(5) On application at any time by the Minister, the Court shall discharge an interim order.

(6) Subject to subsections (4) and (5), an interim order continues in force until the expiry of 12 months from the date of its making and then lapses, unless an application for a disposal order in respect of any property specified in the interim order is brought during that period.

(7) If an application for a disposal order is brought within the period allowed under subsection (6), the interim order lapses on—

(*a*) the determination of the application,
(*b*) the expiry of the ordinary time for bringing an appeal against the determination, or
(*c*) if such appeal is brought, the determination or abandonment of the appeal or any further appeal or the expiry of the time for bringing any further appeal,

whichever is the latest.

(8) Notice of an application under subsection (4) shall be given by the respondent or other person making the application to—

(*a*) the Minister, and
(*b*) any person to whom the Court directs that notice of the application be given.

(9) Notice of an application under subsection (5) shall be given by the Minister to—

(*a*) the respondent, unless the Court is satisfied that it is not reasonably possible to ascertain the respondent's whereabouts, and
(*b*) any person to whom the Court directs that notice of the application be given.

Offences Against the State Act 1939, s 22B inserted by the Criminal Justice (Terrorist Offences) Act 2005, s 51

"INTERLOCUTORY ORDER"

If, on application by a member of the Garda Síochána, it appears to the High Court on evidence tendered by the applicant that a person is in possession or control of funds that were being used or may be intended for use in committing or facilitating the commission of an offence under section 6 or *13*, the Court shall, subject to *subsection (2)* of this section, make an order prohibiting the respondent, any other specified person or any other person having notice of the order from—

(*a*) disposing of or otherwise dealing with all or, where appropriate, a specified part of the funds, or
(*b*) diminishing the value of the funds,

unless the Court is satisfied, on evidence tendered by the respondent or any other person, that the funds are not being used or intended for use in committing or facilitating the commission of an offence under *section 6* or *13*.

(2) The Court shall not make an interlocutory order if it is satisfied that there would be a serious risk of injustice.

(3) Evidence tendered by the applicant for an interlocutory order may consist of or include evidence admissible by virtue of *section 18*.

(4) An interlocutory order—

(*a*) may contain such provisions, conditions and restrictions as the Court considers necessary or expedient, and
(*b*) shall provide for notice of the order to be given to the respondent and any other person who appears to be or is affected by it unless the Court is satisfied that it is not reasonably possible to ascertain their whereabouts.

(5) On application by the respondent or any other person claiming ownership of the funds concerned, the Court may discharge or, as may be appropriate, vary an order that is in force if satisfied that—

(*a*) the funds concerned, or a part of them, are not funds that are being used or may be intended for use in committing or facilitating the commission of an offence under *section 6* or *13*, or
(*b*) the order causes any other injustice.

(6) On application by a member of the Garda Síochána or any other person, the Court may vary an interlocutory order to such extent as may be necessary to permit—

(*a*) the enforcement of any order of a court for the payment by the respondent of any sum, including any sum in respect of costs,
(*b*) the recovery by a county registrar or sheriff of income tax due by the respondent pursuant to a certificate issued by the Collector-General under section 962 of the Taxes Consolidation Act 1997, together with the fees and expenses provided for in that section, or
(*c*) the institution of proceedings for, or relating to, the recovery of any other sum owed by the respondent.

(7) *Subsection (6)* is not to be construed to limit the generality of section 6 of the Act of 1996 as made applicable by *section 20* of this Act.

(8) On application at any time by a member of the Garda Síochána, the Court shall discharge an interlocutory order.

(9) Subject to *subsections (5)*, *(6)* and *(12)*, an interlocutory order continues in force until—

(*a*) the determination of an application for a disposal order in relation to the funds concerned,
(*b*) the expiry of the ordinary time for bringing an appeal from that determination, or
(*c*) if such an appeal is brought, the determination or abandonment of the appeal or any further appeal or the expiry of the ordinary time for bringing any further appeal,

whichever is the latest.

(10) Notice of an application under *subsection (1)* for an interlocutory order or of an application under *subsection (6)* for the variation, or under *subsection (8)* for the discharge, of an interlocutory order shall be given by the applicant to—

(*a*) the respondent unless the Court is satisfied that it is not reasonably possible to ascertain the respondent's whereabouts, and
(*b*) any other person to whom the Court directs that notice be given.

(11) Notice of an application under *subsection (5)* to discharge or vary an interlocutory order shall be given by the respondent or other person making the application to—

(*a*) the member of the Garda Síochána who applied for the interlocutory order, and
(*b*) such other (if any) persons as the Court may direct.

(12) Where a forfeiture order, or a confiscation order, under the Act of 1994 relates to any funds that are the subject of an interlocutory order that is in force—

(*a*) the interlocutory order is discharged, if it relates only to the funds that are the subject of the forfeiture order or the confiscation order, as the case may be, and
(*b*) the interlocutory order is varied by the exclusion from it of the other funds, if it relates to other funds in addition to the funds that are the subject of the forfeiture order or the confiscation order, as the case may be.

Criminal Justice (Terrorist Offences) Act 2005, s 15

"INTERNATIONAL PROTECTED PERSONS CONVENTION"

"Internationally Protected Persons Convention" means the Convention on the Prevention and Punishment of Crimes against Internationally Protected Persons, including Diplomatic Agents, adopted by resolution 3166 of the General Assembly of the United Nations on 14 December 1973, the English language text of which is set out for convenience of reference in *Schedule 4*.

Criminal Justice (Terrorist Offences) Act 2005, s 8

"INTERNATIONALLY PROTECTED PERSON"

In this section "internationally protected person" means, in relation to an offence under *subsection (1)* or *(2)*—

(*a*) a person who, at the time of the commission of the offence—
- (i) is a Head of State, a member of a body that performs the functions of a Head of State under the constitution of a state, a Head of Government or a Minister for Foreign Affairs, and
- (ii) is outside the territory of the state in which he or she holds office,

(*b*) a person who does not fall within *paragraph (a)* and who, at the time of the commission of the offence—
- (i) is a representative or official of a state or an official or agent of an international organisation of an intergovernmental character, and
- (ii) is entitled under international law to protection from attack on his or her person, freedom or dignity,

or

(*c*) a person who, at the time of the commission of the offence—
- (i) is a member of the family of a person mentioned in *paragraph (a)* and is accompanying him or her, or
- (ii) is a member of the family and of the household of a person mentioned in *paragraph (b)*.

Criminal Justice (Terrorist Offences) Act 2005, s 11(7)(a)(b)(c)

"IRISH SHIP"

"Irish ship" has the same meaning as in section 9 of the Mercantile Marine Act 1955.

Criminal Justice (Terrorist Offences) Act 2005, s 3

The following ships shall be known as Irish ships and shall, subject to subsection (3) of section 18 of this Act, be entitled to wear the proper national colours and assume national character—

(*a*) State-owned ships;
(*b*) ships which are wholly owned by persons being citizens of Ireland (hereinafter referred to as Irish citizens) or Irish bodies corporate and are not registered under the law of another country;
(*c*) other ships registered or deemed to be registered under this Act.

Mercantile Marine Act 1955, s 9

"ISSUING STATE"

"issuing state" means, in relation to a European arrest warrant, a Member State designated under section 3, a judical authority of which has issued that European arrest warrant.

European Arrest Warrant Act 2003, ss 2 & 3

M

"MEMBER OF THE GARDA SÍOCHÁNA"

"member of the Garda Síochána" means a member of the Garda Síochána not below the rank of Chief Superintendent.

Criminal Justice (Terrorist Offences) Act 2005, s 12

"MEMBERS OF ANY UNLAWFUL ORGANISATION"

"members of any unlawful organisation" includes members of such an organisation whose identities are unknown to the Garda Síochána.

Offences Against the State (Amendment) Act 1998, s 8(4)

"MOTOR VEHICLE"

Motor vehicle.

"motor vehicle" means a mechanically propelled vehicle (including a bicycle and tricycle) which derives its motive power from an internal combustion engine or from an electric motor, and includes any vehicle which is designed, constructed and suitable for traction on a road by a mechanically propelled vehicle.

SI No 17/1968, art 4 Customs (Land Frontier) Regs 1968

"MOTOR VEHICLE PASS"

Motor vehicle pass.

"motor vehicle pass" means a pass issued by the Revenue Commissioners on an approved form in respect of a motor vehicle owned and registered in the State.

SI No 117/1968, art 4

O

"OFFENCE"

the word "offence" includes treason, felonies, misdemeanours, and statutory and other offences.

Offences Against the State Act 1939, s 2

"ORGANISATION"

the word "organisation" includes associations, societies, and other organisations or combinations of persons of whatsoever nature or kind, whether known or not known by a distinctive name.

Offences Against the State Act 1939, s 2

P

"PRESCRIBED PERIOD" SEE UNDER THE

"PROCESSING"

"processing" has the same meaning as in the Data Protection Acts 1988 and 2003.

Criminal Justice (Terrorist Offences) Act 2005, s 61(1)

"'processing', of or in relation to information or data, means performing any operation or set of operations on the information or data, whether or not by automatic means, including—

(*a*) obtaining, recording or keeping the information or data,
(*b*) collecting, organising, storing, altering or adapting the information or data,
(*c*) retrieving, consulting or using the information or data,
(*d*) disclosing the information or data by transmitting, disseminating or otherwise making it available, or
(e) aligning, combining, blocking, erasing or destroying the information or data.

Data Protection Act 1988, s 1 substituted by Data Protection (Amendment) Act 2003, s 2(a)(v)

"PROPERTY"

'property' does not include moneys held in a bank.

Offences Against the State Act 1939, s 22A inserted by Criminal Justice (Terrorist Offences) Act 2005, s 51

"PROPERTY OF UNLAWFUL ORGANISATION"

For the removal of doubt, it is hereby declared that section 22 of the Principal Act applies and always applied to property ["or any other form of property"] of an unlawful organisation acquired by it at any time while a suppression order under section 19 of that Act in respect of it is or was in force as well as to the property of the organisation immediately upon the making of the suppression order.

(2) Moneys held by any person for the use or benefit of, or for use for the purposes of, an unlawful organisation in respect of which a suppression order under section 19 of the Principal Act is in force shall be deemed, for the purposes of this Act and sections 22 and 23 of The Principal Act, to be the property of the organisation, and this Act and those sections shall apply and have effect accordingly.

Offences Against the State (Amendment) Act 1985, s 8(2) as amended by Criminal Justice (Terrorist Offences) Act 2005, s 55

"PUBLIC MEETING"

In this section the expression "public meeting" includes a procession and also includes (in addition to a meeting held in a public place or on unenclosed land) a meeting held in a building or on enclosed land to which the public are admitted, whether with or without payment.

Offences Against the State Act 1939, s 27(5)

R

"REFEREE"

"Referee" means the holder of the office of Complaints Referee under the Act of 1993.

Criminal Justice (Terrorist Offences) Act 2005, s 61

There shall stand established the office of Complaints Referee and the holder of the office shall be known as the Complaints Referee and is referred to in this section as "the Referee". There shall stand established the office of Complaints Referee and the holder of the office shall be known as the Complaints Referee and is referred to in this section as "the Referee".

Interception of Postal Packets and Telecommunications Regulations Act 1993, s 9(2)(a)

"RELEVANT PROVISION"

"relevant provision" means—

(*a*) in relation to the Hostage Convention, Article 5(1),
(*b*) in relation to the Terrorist Bombing Convention, Article 6(1) or (2),
(*c*) in relation to the Internationally Protected Persons Convention, Article 3(1), and
(*d*) in relation to the Terrorist Financing Convention, Article 7(1) or (2).

Criminal Justice (Terrorist Offences) Act 2005, s 43(4)

"RESPONDENT"

"respondent" means—

(*a*) a person in respect of whom an application for an interim order or an interlocutory order has been made, or

(*b*) a person in respect of whom an interim order or an interlocutory order has been made,

and includes a person who, but for this Act, would become entitled on the death of a person referred to in *paragraph (a)* or *(b)* to any funds to which such an order relates (being an order that is in force and is in respect of that person).

Offences Against the State Act 1939, s 22a inserted by Criminal Justice (Terrorist Offences) Act 2005, s 51

"respondent" means—

(*a*) a person in respect of whom an application for an interim order or an interlocutory order has been made, or

(*b*) a person in respect of whom an interim order or an interlocutory order has been made,

and includes a person who, but for this Act, would become entitled on the death of a person referred to in *paragraph (a)* or *(b)* to any funds to which such an order relates (being an order that is in force and is in respect of that person).

Criminal Justice (Terrorist Offences) Act 2005, s 12

S

"SCHEDULE OFFENCES"

Whenever while this Part of this Act is in force the Government is satisfied that the ordinary courts are inadequate to secure the effective administration of justice and the preservation of public peace and order in relation to offences of any particular class or kind or under any particular enactment, the Government may by order declare that offences of that particular class or kind or under that particular enactment shall be scheduled offences for the purposes of this Part of this Act.

(2) Whenever the Government has made under the foregoing sub-section of this section any such declaration as is authorised by that sub-section, every offence of the particular class or kind or under the particular enactment to which such declaration relates shall, until otherwise provided by an order under the next following sub-section of this section, be a scheduled offence for the purposes of this Part of this Act.

(3) Whenever the Government is satisfied that the effective administration of justice and the preservation of public peace and order in relation to offences of any particular class or kind or under any particular enactment which are for the time being scheduled offences for the purposes of this Part of this Act can be secured through the medium of the ordinary courts, the Government may by order declare that offences of that particular class or kind or under that particular enactment shall, upon the making of such order, cease to be scheduled offences for the purposes of this Part of this Act.

Offences Against the State Act 1939, s 36

"SECRET SOCIETY"

In this section the expression "secret society" means an association, society, or other body the members of which are required by the regulations thereof to take or enter into, or do in fact take or enter into, an oath, affirmation, declaration or agreement not to disclose the proceedings or some part of the proceedings of the association, society, or body.

Offences Against the State Act 1939, s 16(2)

"SEDITIOUS DOCUMENT"

the expression "seditious document" includes—

(*a*) a document consisting of or containing matter calculated or tending to undermine the public order or the authority of the State, and

(*b*) a document which alleges, implies, or suggests or is calculated to suggest that the government functioning under the Constitution is not the lawful government of the State or that there is in existence in the State any body or organisation not functioning under the Constitution which is entitled to be recognised as being the government of the country, and

(*c*) a document which alleges, implies, or suggests or is calculated to suggest that the military forces maintained under the Constitution are not the lawful military forces of the State, or that there is in existence in the State a body or organisation not established and maintained by virtue of the Constitution which is entitled to be recognised as a military force, and

(*d*) a document in which words, abbreviations, or symbols referable to a military body are used in referring to an unlawful organisation.

Offences Against the State Act 1939, s 2

In this section "serious offence" has the same meaning as it has in *section 8*.

Offences Against the State (Amendment) Act 1998, s 9(3)

"SERIOUS OFFENCE"

"serious offence" means an offence which satisfies both of the following conditions:

(*a*) it is an offence for which a person of full age and capacity and not previously convicted may, under or by virtue of any enactment, be punished by imprisonment for a term of 5 years or by a more severe penalty, and

(*b*) it is an offence that involves loss of human life, serious personal injury (other than injury that constitutes an offence of a sexual nature), false imprisonment or serious loss of or damage to property or a serious risk of any such loss, injury, imprisonment or damage,

and includes an act or omission done or made outside the State that would be a serious offence if done or made in the State.

Offences Against the State (Amendment) Act 1998, s 8(4)

"serious offence" means an offence for which a person may be punished by imprisonment for a term of 4 years or more.

Criminal Justice Act 2006, s 70(1)

"SERVICE PROVIDER"

"service provider" means a person who is engaged in the provision of a publicly available electronic communications service by means of fixed line or mobile telephones.

Criminal Justice (Terrorist Offences) Act 2005, s 61(1)

"SHIP"

"ship" includes any vessel used in navigation.

Criminal Justice (Terrorist Offences) Act 2005, s 3(1)

"STRUCTURED GROUP"

"structured group" means a group that—

(*a*) is not randomly formed for the immediate commission of a single offence, and

(*b*) does not need to have formally defined roles for its members, continuity of its membership or a developed structure.

Criminal Justice Act 2006, s 70(1)

"SUPPRESSION ORDERS"

(1) If and whenever the Government are of opinion that any particular organisation is an unlawful organisation, it shall be lawful for the Government by order (in this Act referred to as a suppression order) to declare that such organisation is an unlawful organisation and ought, in the public interest, to be suppressed.

(2) The Government may by order, whenever they so think proper, amend or revoke a suppression order.

(3) Every suppression order shall be published in the *Iris Oifigiúil* as soon as conveniently may be after the making thereof

(4) A suppression order shall be conclusive evidence for an purposes other than an application for a declaration of legality that the organisation to which it relates is an unlawful organisation within the meaning of this Act.

Offences Against the State Act 1939, s 19

T

"TERRITORY OF THE STATE"

"territory of the State" includes a vessel registered in the State.

Criminal Justice (Illicit Traffic by Sea) Act 2003, s 1(1)

"TERRORIST ACTIVITY"

"terrorist activity" means an act that is committed in or outside the State and that—

(*a*) if committed in the State, would constitute an offence specified in *Part 1* of *Schedule 2*, and

(*b*) is committed with the intention of—
  (i) seriously intimidating a population,
  (ii) unduly compelling a government or an international organisation to perform or abstain from performing an act, or
  (iii) seriously destabilising or destroying the fundamental political, constitutional, economic or social structures of a state or an international organisation.

Criminal Justice (Terrorist Offences) Act 2005, s 4

"TERRORIST BOMBING CONVENTION"

"Terrorist Bombing Convention" means the International Convention for the Suppression of Terrorist Bombings adopted by resolution 52/164 of the General Assembly of the United Nations on 15 December 1997, the English language text of which is set out for convenience of reference in *Schedule 5*.

Criminal Justice (Terrorist Offences) Act 2005, s 8

"TERRORIST FINANCING CONVENTION"

"Terrorist Financing Convention" means the International Convention for the Suppression of the Financing of Terrorism adopted by resolution 54/109 of the General Assembly of the United Nations on 9 December 1999, the English language text of which is set out for convenience of reference in *Schedule 7*.

Criminal Justice (Terrorist Offences) Act 2005, s 12

"TERRORIST GROUP"

"terrorist group" has the same meaning as in the Framework Decision.

Criminal Justice (Terrorist Offences) Act 2005, s 4

"TERRORIST LINKED ACTIVITY"

"terrorist-linked activity" means an act—

(*a*) that is committed in or outside the State and that—
  (i) if committed in the State, would constitute an offence specified in *Part 2* of *Schedule 2*, and
  (ii) is committed with a view to engaging in a terrorist activity,

or

(*b*) that is committed in or outside the State and that—
  (i) if committed in the State, would constitute an offence specified in *Part 3* of *Schedule 2*, and
  (ii) is committed with a view to engaging in a terrorist activity or with a view to committing an act that, if committed in the State, would constitute an offence under section 21 or 21A of the Act of 1939.

Criminal Justice (Terrorist Offences) Act 2005, s 4

"THE HOSTAGE"

Subject to *subsections (3)* to *(5)*, a person is guilty of the offence of hostage-taking if he or she, in or outside the State—

(*a*) seizes or detains another person ("the hostage"), and
(*b*) threatens to kill, injure or continue to detain the hostage,

in order to compel a state, an international intergovernmental organisation, a person or a group of persons to do, or abstain from doing, any act.

Criminal Justice (Terrorist Offences) Act 2005, s 9(1)(a)

"THE PRESCRIBED PERIOD"

In this section "the prescribed period" means—

(*a*) the period of 14 days from the end of the preliminary examination referred to in *subsection (5)*, or
(*b*) where the accused waives a preliminary examination, the period of 14 days from the date of the waiver, or
(*c*) where the accused, on being sent forward for sentence, changes his or her plea to one of not guilty, the period of 14 days from the date on which he or she does so, or
(*d*) where the accused is brought before a Special Criminal Court for trial under section 47 of the Act of 1939, such period as is fixed by the Court when the Court fixes the date of trial.

Offences Against the State (Amendment) Act 1998, s 3(7)

"THE WITNESS"

Without prejudice to *subsection (1)*, in any such proceedings the accused shall not without the leave of the court call any other person (in this section referred to as "the witness") to give such evidence unless—

(*a*) the notice under that subsection includes the name and address of the witness or, if the name or address is not known to the accused at the time he or she gives the notice, any information in his or her possession which might be of material assistance in finding the witness,

(*b*) if the name or the address is not included in that notice, the court is satisfied that the accused, before giving the notice, took and thereafter continued to take all reasonable steps to secure that the name or address would be ascertained,

(*c*) if the name or the address is not included in that notice, but the accused subsequently discovers the name or address or receives other information which might be of material assistance in finding the witness, he or she gives notice forthwith of the name, address or other information, as the case may be, and

(*d*) if the accused is notified by or on behalf of the prosecution that the witness has not been traced by the name or at the address given, he or she gives notice forthwith of any such information which is then in his or her possession or, on subsequently receiving any such information, gives notice of it forthwith.

Offences Against the State (Amendment) Act 1998, s 3(2)

"TOXIC CHEMICAL"

"toxic chemical" means any chemical which through its chemical action on life processes can cause death, temporary incapacitation or permanent harm to humans or animals, including all such chemicals regardless of their origin or of their method of production, and regardless of whether they were produced in facilities, in munitions or elsewhere.

Chemical Weapons Act 1997, s 2

"TREASONABLE DOCUMENT"

the expression "treasonable document" includes a document which relates directly or indirectly to the commission of treason.

Offences Against the State Act 1939, s 2

"TRIABLE PERSON"

(8) In this section 'triable person' means a person sent or sent forward for trial to, or charged before or transferred under this Act to, a Special Criminal Court.

Offences against the State Act 1939, s 49(8) amended and inserted by Criminal Justice (Terrorist Offences) Act 2005, s 53

U

"UNLAWFUL ORGANISATION"

In order to regulate and control in the public interest the exercise of the constitutional right of citizens to form associations, it is hereby declared that any organisation which—

(*a*) engages in, promotes, encourages, or advocates the commission of treason or any activity of a treasonable nature, or

(*b*) advocates, encourages, or attempts the procuring by force, violence, or other unconstitutional means of an alteration of the Constitution, or

(*c*) raises or maintains or attempts to raise or maintain a military or armed force in contravention of the Constitution or without constitutional authority, or.

(*d*) engages in, promotes, encourages, or advocates the commission of any criminal offence or the obstruction of or interference with the administration of justice or the enforcement of the law, or

(*e*) engages in, promotes, encourages, or advocates the attainment of any particular object, lawful or unlawful, by violent, criminal, or other unlawful means, or

(*f*) promotes, encourages, or advocates the non-payment of moneys payable to the Central Fund or any other public fund or the non-payment of local taxation,

shall be an unlawful organisation within the meaning and for the purposes of this Act, and this Act shall apply and have effect in relation to such organisation accordingly.

Offences Against the State Act 1939, s 18

W

"WITNESS" SEE UNDER THE

ORGANISED CRIME

A

"ACT"

"act" includes omission and a reference to the commission or doing of an act includes a reference to the making of an omission.

Criminal Justice Act 2006, s 70

"ACTIVITIES"

(b) references to activities include reference to—
  (i) Activities carried on outside the state, and
  (ii) Activities that do not constitute an offence or offences.

Criminal Justice Act 2006, s 71(A)(1)(B) inserted by Criminal Justice (Amendment) Act 2009, s 5

B

"BROADCAST"

'broadcast' means the transmission, relaying or distribution by wireless telegraphy, cable or the internet of communications, sounds, signs, visual images or signals, intended for direct reception by the general public whether such communications, sounds, signs, visual images or signals are actually received or not.

Offences against the state Act 1939, s 30(4BA)(f) amended by Criminal Justice (Amendment) Act 2009, s 21(1)(b)

Criminal Justice (Drug Trafficking) Act 1996, s 3A(h) inserted by Criminal Justice (Amendment) Act 2009, s 22(1)(b)

Criminal Justice Act 2007, s 50(4A)(h) inserted by Criminal Justice (Amendment) Act 2009, s 23(2)(a)

"CONSPIRACY"

Subject to *subsections (2)* and *(3)*, a person who conspires, whether in the State or elsewhere, with one or more persons to do an act—

(*a*) in the State that constitutes a serious offence, or
(*b*) in a place outside the State that constitutes a serious offence under the law of that place and which would, if done in the State, constitute a serious offence,

is guilty of an offence irrespective of whether such act actually takes place or not.

(2) *Subsection (1)* applies to a conspiracy committed outside the State if—

(*a*) the offence, the subject of the conspiracy, was committed, or was intended to be committed, in the State or against a citizen of Ireland,
(*b*) the conspiracy is committed on board an Irish ship,
(*c*) the conspiracy is committed on an aircraft registered in the State, or
(*d*) the conspiracy is committed by an Irish citizen or a [person ordinarily resident in the state] stateless.

(3) *Subsection (1)* shall also apply to a conspiracy committed outside the State in circumstances other than those referred to in *subsection (2)*, but in that case the Director of Public Prosecutions may not take, or consent to the taking of, proceedings for an offence under *subsection (1)* except in accordance with *section 74 (3)*.

(4) A person charged with an offence under this section is liable to be indicted, tried and punished as a principal offender.

Criminal Justice Act 2006, s 71(2)(d) amended by Criminal Justice (Amendment) Act 2009, s 4(a)(b)

"CRIMINAL ORGANISATION"

"'criminal organisation' means a structured group, however organised, that has as its main purpose or activity the commission or facilitation of a serious offence.

Criminal Justice Act 2006, s 70(1) substituted by Criminal Justice (Amendment) Act 2009, s 3(1)(a)

D

"DIRECTS"

'directs', in relation to activities, means—

(i) controls or supervises the activities, or
(ii) gives an order, instruction or guidance, or makes a request, with respect to the carrying on of the activities;

(*b*) references to activities include references to—
(i) activities carried on outside the State, and
(ii) activities that do not constitute an offence or offences.

Criminal Justice Act 2006, s 71(A)(1) inserted by Criminal Justice (Amendment) Act 2009, s 5(1)(a)

Offences against the State (Amendment) Act 1998, s 6 (1)(a) and (d) substituted by Criminal Justice (Amendment) Act 2009, s 25

"DOCUMENT OR OTHER RECORD"

In subsection (4) 'document or other record' includes, in addition to a document or other record in writing—

(*a*) a disc, tape, sound-track or other device in which information, sounds or signals are embodied so as to be capable (with or without the aid of some other instrument) of being reproduced in legible or audible form,
(*b*) a film, tape or other device in which visual images are embodied so as to be capable (with or without the aid of some other instrument) of being reproduced in visual form, and
(*c*) a photograph.".

Criminal Justice Act 2006, s 71B(5) inserted by Criminal Justice (Amendment) Act 2009, s 7

E

"EXPERTISE"

In subsection (1) 'expertise' means experience, specialised knowledge or qualifications.

Criminal Justice Act 2006, s 71B(2) inserted by Criminal Justice (Amendment) Act 2009, s 7

H

"HOME"

In this section 'home', in relation to the offender, means his or her sole or main residence or, if he or she has no such residence, his or her most usual place of abode or, if he or she has no such abode, the place which he or she regularly visits.".

Criminal Justice Act 2007, s 26A(11) inserted by Criminal Justice (Amendment) Act 2009, s 14

I

"IRISH SHIP"

"Irish ship" has the meaning it has in section 9 of the Mercantile Marine Act 1955.

Criminal Justice Act 2006, s 70(1)

The following ships shall be known as Irish ships and shall, subject to subsection (3) of section 18 of this Act, be entitled to wear the proper national colours and assume national character—

(*a*) State-owned ships;
(*b*) ships which are wholly owned by persons being citizens of Ireland (hereinafter referred to as Irish citizens) or Irish bodies corporate and are not registered under the law of another country;
(*c*) other ships registered or deemed to be registered under this Act.

Mercantile Marine Act 1955, s 9

O

"OFFENDER, THE"

(1) Where, on or after the commencement of a scheme under subsection (10), a person (other than a person under the age of 18 years), in this section referred to as ' the offender ', is convicted on indictment of—

(a) an offence under Part 7 of the Act of 2006, or
(b) an offence (other than an offence referred to in paragraph (*a*)) specified in Schedule 2 that has been committed as part of, or in furtherance of, the activities of a criminal organisation,

Where a person (other than a person under the age of 18 years), in this section referred to as 'the offender', is convicted on indictment of—

(*a*) an offence under Part 7 of the Act of 2006, or
(*b*) an offence (other than an offence referred to in paragraph (*a*)) specified in Schedule 2 that has been committed as part of, or in furtherance of, the activities of a criminal organisation.

Criminal Justice Act 2006, s 26A(1) inserted by Criminal Justice (Amendment) Act 2009, s 14

"ORDINARILY RESIDENT IN THE STATE"

For the purposes of the references in sections 71(2)(*d*) and 74(1)(*b*)(i) to a person's being ordinarily resident in the State, a person shall be taken to be so resident, on the date of the commission of the offence to which section 71(1) or 74(1), as the case may be, applies, if, for the 12 months immediately preceding that date, the person has his or her principal place of residence in the State.".

Criminal Justice Act 2006, s 70(3) inserted by Criminal Justice (Amendment) Act 2009, s 3(2)

"ORGANISED CRIME"

A person is guilty of an offence if, with knowledge of the existence of the organisation referred to in this subsection, the person participates in or contributes to any activity (whether constituting an offence or not)—

(*a*) intending either to—
 (i) enhance the ability of a criminal organisation or any of its members to commit, or
 (ii) facilitate the commission by a criminal organisation or any of its members of, a serious offence,

or

(*b*) being reckless as to whether such participation or contribution could either—
 (i) enhance the ability of a criminal organisation or any of its members to commit, or
 (ii) facilitate the commission by a criminal organisation or any of its members of, a serious offence.

(2) A person guilty of an offence under this section shall be liable on conviction on indictment to a fine or imprisonment for a term not exceeding 15 years or both.

(3) The reference in subsection (1) to the commission of a serious offence includes a reference to the doing of an act in a place outside the State that constitutes a serious offence under the law of that place and which act would, if done in the State, constitute a serious offence.

(4) In proceedings for an offence under this section it shall not be necessary for the prosecution to prove—

(*a*) that the criminal organisation concerned or any of its members actually committed, as the case may be—
  (i) a serious offence in the State, or
  (ii) a serious offence under the law of a place outside the State where the act constituting the offence would, if done in the State, constitute a serious offence,

(*b*) that the participation or contribution of the defendant actually—
  (i) enhanced the ability of the criminal organisation concerned or any of its members to commit, or
  (ii) facilitated the commission by it or any of its members of, a serious offence,

or

(*c*) knowledge on the part of the defendant of the specific nature of any offence referred to in subsection (1)(a) or (b).

(5) In determining whether a person participates in or contributes to an activity referred to in subsection (1), the court may consider, inter alia, whether the person—

(*a*) uses a name, word, symbol or other representation that identifies, or is associated with, the criminal organisation concerned, or
(*b*) receives any benefit from the criminal organisation concerned.

(6) In proceedings for an offence under this section, it shall be presumed, until the contrary is shown, that the participation or contribution (the 'relevant act') of the defendant referred to in subsection (1) was engaged in or made with the state of mind on the defendant's part referred to in paragraph (*a*) or (*b*) of that subsection if the circumstances under which the relevant act was committed—

(*a*) involved either—
  (i) the possession by the defendant, whilst in the presence of one or more other persons, of any article or item referred to in the Table to this section, or
  (ii) there being present in (or, in the case of a false registration plate referred to in paragraph 8 of that Table, present in or affixed to) any vehicle—
    (I) the use of which appears connected with the relevant act, and

(II) of which the defendant and one or more other persons were occupants on or about the date of commission of the relevant act,

any such article or item,

and

(*b*) those circumstances are such as give rise to a reasonable suspicion that the defendant's state of mind was as aforesaid at the time of the relevant act's commission.

Table

1. Any balaclava, boiler suit or other means of disguise or impersonation, including any article of Garda uniform or any equipment supplied to a member of the Garda Síochána or imitation thereof.

2. Any firearm (within the meaning of section 1 of the Firearms Act 1925), ammunition for a firearm or device that appears to the ordinary observer so realistic as to make it indistinguishable from a firearm.

3. Any knife to which section 9(1) of the Firearms and Offensive Weapons Act 1990 applies, weapon of offence within the meaning of section 10(2) of that Act or weapon to which section 12 of that Act applies.

4. Any implement for burglary or other article or item for gaining access to any premises or other structure without the permission of the owner or occupier thereof, including any key or card that has been stolen or any access code unlawfully procured.

5. Any plan of any premises or other structure unrelated to any lawful activity, trade or purpose being pursued or engaged in by one or more of the persons referred to in subsection (6)(*a*).

6. Any controlled drug (within the meaning of the Misuse of Drugs Act 1977).

7. Any substantial amounts, in cash, of any currency unrelated to any lawful activity, trade, transaction or purpose being pursued or engaged in by one or more of the persons referred to in subsection (6)(*a*).

8. Any false vehicle registration plate, that is to say, any plate purporting to be a plate for a mechanically propelled vehicle registered under section 131 of the Finance Act 1992 and displaying an identification mark other than that duly assigned by the Revenue Commissioners under Chapter IV of Part II of that Act and regulations thereunder.

9. Any article or item for making a counterfeit of any currency note or coin or making a counterfeit or otherwise for making a forgery of any credit or debit card.

10. Any article or item for making copies of any work, being an article or item of a design enabling, and held in circumstances indicating that it would likely be used for,

the making, on a substantial scale, of infringing copies (within the meaning of Part II of the Copyright and Related Rights Act 2000) of the work without the copyright owner's consent.

11. Any other article or item prescribed for the purposes of subsection (6).".

Criminal Justice Act 2006, s 72 substituted by Criminal Justice (Amendment) Act 2009, s 6

"OTHER OFFENCE, THE"

If at any time during the detention of a person pursuant to this section a member of the Garda Síochána, with reasonable cause, suspects that person of having committed an offence (the 'other offence') referred to in subsection (1) of this section, being an offence other than the offence to which the detention relates, and—

(*a*) the member of the Garda Síochána then in charge of the Garda Síochána station, or

(*b*) in case the person is being detained in a place of detention, other than a Garda Síochána station, an officer of the Garda Síochána not below the rank of inspector who is not investigating the offence to which the detention relates or the other offence, has reasonable grounds for believing that the continued detention of the person is necessary for the proper investigation of the other offence, the person may continue to be detained in relation to the other offence as if that offence was the offence for which the person was originally detained, but nothing in this subsection authorises the detention of the person for the other offence for any period longer than that which is authorised by or under the other provisions of this section.".

Offences against the State Act 1939, s 30(3A) inserted by Criminal Justice (Amendment) Act 2009, s 20(1)(a)

P

"PUBLISH"

'publish' means publish, other than by way of broadcast, to the public or a portion of the public.

Offences against the state Act 1939, s 30(4BA)(f) inserted by Criminal Justice (Amendment) Act 2009, s 21(1)(b)

Criminal Justice (Drug Trafficking) Act 1996, s 3A(h) inserted by Criminal Justice (Amendment) Act 2009, s 22(1)(b)

Criminal Justice Act 2007, s 50(4A)(h) inserted by Criminal Justice (Amendment) Act 2009, s 23(2)(c)

R

"RELEVANT ACT"

(6) In proceedings for an offence under this section, it shall be presumed, until the contrary is shown, that the participation or contribution (the 'relevant act') of the defendant referred to in subsection (1) was engaged in or made with the state of mind on the defendant's part referred to in paragraph (*a*) or (*b*) of that subsection if the circumstances under which the relevant act was committed—

(*a*) involved either—

(i) the possession by the defendant, whilst in the presence of one or more other persons, of any article or item referred to in the Table to this section, or

(ii) there being present in (or, in the case of a false registration plate referred to in paragraph 8 of that Table, present in or affixed to) any vehicle—

(I) the use of which appears connected with the relevant act, and

(II) of which the defendant and one or more other persons were occupants on or about the date of commission of the relevant act,

any such article or item,

and

(*b*) those circumstances are such as give rise to a reasonable suspicion that the defendant's state of mind was as aforesaid at the time of the relevant act's commission.

Table

1. Any balaclava, boiler suit or other means of disguise or impersonation, including any article of Garda uniform or any equipment supplied to a member of the Garda Síochána or imitation thereof.

2. Any firearm (within the meaning of section 1 of the Firearms Act 1925), ammunition for a firearm or device that appears to the ordinary observer so realistic as to make it indistinguishable from a firearm.

3. Any knife to which section 9(1) of the Firearms and Offensive Weapons Act 1990 applies, weapon of offence within the meaning of section 10(2) of that Act or weapon to which section 12 of that Act applies.

4. Any implement for burglary or other article or item for gaining access to any premises or other structure without the permission of the owner or occupier thereof, including any key or card that has been stolen or any access code unlawfully procured.

5. Any plan of any premises or other structure unrelated to any lawful activity, trade or purpose being pursued or engaged in by one or more of the persons referred to in subsection (6)(*a*).

6. Any controlled drug (within the meaning of the Misuse of Drugs Act 1977).

7. Any substantial amounts, in cash, of any currency unrelated to any lawful activity, trade, transaction or purpose being pursued or engaged in by one or more of the persons referred to in subsection (6)(*a*).

8. Any false vehicle registration plate, that is to say, any plate purporting to be a plate for a mechanically propelled vehicle registered under section 131 of the Finance Act 1992 and displaying an identification mark other than that duly assigned by the Revenue Commissioners under Chapter IV of Part II of that Act and regulations thereunder.

9. Any article or item for making a counterfeit of any currency note or coin or making a counterfeit or otherwise for making a forgery of any credit or debit card.

10. Any article or item for making copies of any work, being an article or item of a design enabling, and held in circumstances indicating that it would likely be used for, the making, on a substantial scale, of infringing copies (within the meaning of Part II of the Copyright and Related Rights Act 2000) of the work without the copyright owner's consent.

11. Any other article or item prescribed for the purposes of subsection (6).".

Criminal Justice Act 2006, s 72 substituted by Criminal Justice (Amendment) Act 2009, s 6

S

"SERIOUS OFFENCE"

(*b*) 'serious offence' means an offence for which a person may be punished by imprisonment for a term of 4 years or more.

Offences against the State (Amendment) Act 1998, s 6(1)(b) substituted by Criminal Justice (Amendment) Act 2009, s 25

"STRUCTURED GROUP"

" 'structured group' means a group of 3 or more persons, which is not randomly formed for the immediate commission of a single offence, and the involvement in which by 2 or more of those persons is with a view to their acting in concert in relation to the commission of an offence; for the avoidance of doubt, a structured group may exist notwithstanding the absence of all or any of the following:

(*a*) formal rules or formal membership, or any formal roles for those involved in the group;
(*b*) any hierarchical or leadership structure;
(*c*) continuity of involvement by persons in the group.".

Criminal Justice Act 2006, s 70(1) substituted by Criminal Justice (Amendment) Act 2009, s 3(1)(b)

U

"UNLAWFUL ORGANISATION"

(c) 'unlawful organisation' means an organisation in respect of which a suppression order has been made under section 19 of the Act of 1939.

Offences against the State (Amendment) Act 1998, s 6(1)(c) substituted by Criminal Justice (Amendment) Act 2009, s 24

PRACTICE AND PROCEDURE GENERAL

O

P

R

S

A

"A DIRECTION"

"a direction" means a direction given by the Minister under section 2 of the Criminal Justice Act 1960 authorising the release of a person from prison (within the meaning of that section) for a temporary period.

Criminal Justice Act 2006, s 98

"ABUSER"

"abuser" means an individual believed by a person who has authority or control over that individual to have seriously harmed or sexually abused a child or more than one child.

Criminal Justice Act 2006, s 176(1)

"ACTING DIRECTOR"

(2) (*a*) In the event of the incapacity through illness of the Director, the Taoiseach may appoint a person who shall be known as the Acting Director of Public Prosecutions and who is referred to in this Act as the Acting Director and the Acting Director shall perform all the functions conferred on the Director by this Act.

(*b*) No Acting Director shall be appointed to hold office for a term in excess of 12 months.

(*c*) The Acting Director shall hold office upon such terms and conditions as may be determined by the Taoiseach after consultation with the Minister for the Public Service.

Prosecution of Offences Act 1974, s 9

"ADULT AND ADULT RELATIVE"

"adult" means a person not below the age of eighteen years and

"adult relative" shall be construed accordingly.

SI No 119/1987, art 2(1)

"ALERT"

alert' means an alert entered in the SIS for the arrest and surrender, on foot of a European arrest warrant, of the person named therein.

European Arrest Warrant Act 2003, s 2(1) inserted by the Criminal Justice (Miscellaneous Provisions) Act 2009, 4(A)

"ANTI-SOCIAL BEHAVIOUR"

(2) For the purposes of this Part, a person behaves in an anti-social manner if the person causes or, in the circumstances, is likely to cause, to one or more persons who are not of the same household as the person—

(*a*) harassment,
(*b*) significant or persistent alarm, distress, fear or intimidation, or
(*c*) significant or persistent impairment of their use or enjoyment of their property.

Criminal Justice Act 2006, s 113(2)

"APPROPRIATE ADULT"

In Regulations 12(8) and 18(1) "appropriate adult", in relation to a person in custody, means—

(*a*) in case the person is married and his spouse is an adult and is readily available, his spouse, and
(*b*) in any other case, his parent or guardian or, where a parent or guardian is not readily available, an adult relative or some other responsible adult, as may be appropriate, in attendance at the station pursuant to subparagraph (b) or (c) of Regulation 13(2).

SI No 119/1987, art 2(3)

"APPROVED MEDICAL OFFICER"

"approved medical officer" means a consultant psychiatrist (within the meaning of the Mental Health Act 2001).

Criminal Law (Insanity) Act 2006, s 1

"consultant psychiatrist" means a consultant psychiatrist who is employed by a health board or by an approved centre or a person whose name is entered on the division of psychiatry or the division of child and adolescent psychiatry of the Register of Medical Specialists maintained by the Medical Council in Ireland.

Mental Health Act 2001, s 2(1)

"ARRESTABLE OFFENCE"

See below "Offence".

"ARRESTED PERSON"

"arrested person" means a person who is taken on arrest to, or arrested in, a station.

SI No 119/1987, art 2(1)

"ARTICLE"

"article" includes a substance, document or any thing.

Criminal Justice Act 2006, s 183(5)

"AUDIO RECORDING"

"audio recording" includes a recording, on any medium, from which sound may by any means be produced, and cognate words shall be construed accordingly.

Criminal Justice Act 2006, s 15

"AUTHORISED PERSON"

"authorised person" means a person who is appointed in writing by the Minister, or a person who is one of a class of persons which is prescribed, to be an authorised person for the purposes of this Part.

Criminal Justice Act 2006, s 98

"2005 COUNCIL DECISION"

"2005 Council Decision" means Council Decision 2005/671/JHA of 20 September 2005 on the exchange of information and co-operation concerning terrorist offences.

Criminal Justice (Mutual Assistance) Act 2008, s 2(1)

B

"BEHAVIOUR WARNING"

(1) Subject to *subsection (5)*, a member of the Garda Síochána may issue a behaviour warning to a person who has behaved in an anti-social manner.

(2) The behaviour warning may be issued orally or in writing and, if it is issued orally, it shall be recorded in writing as soon as reasonably practicable and a written record of the behaviour warning shall be served on the person personally or by post.

(3) The behaviour warning or, if it is given orally, the written record of it shall—

(*a*) include a statement that the person has behaved in an anti-social manner and indicate what that behaviour is and when and where it took place,

(*b*) demand that the person cease the behaviour or otherwise address the behaviour in the manner specified in the warning, and

(*c*) include notice that—

(i) failure to comply with a demand under *paragraph (b)*, or

(ii) issuance of a subsequent behaviour warning,

may result in an application being made for a civil order.

(4) The member of the Garda Síochána referred to in *subsection (1)* may require the person to give his or her name and address to the member for purposes of the behaviour warning or the written record of it.

(5) A behaviour warning may not be issued more than one month after the time that—

(*a*) the behaviour took place, or

(*b*) in the case of persistent behaviour, the most recent known instance of that behaviour took place.

(6) Subject to *subsection (7)*, a behaviour warning remains in force against the person to whom it is issued for 3 months from the date that it is issued.

(7) If an application is made under *section* 115 in respect of the person, the behaviour warning remains in force against the person until the application is heard or otherwise determined by the District Court.

Criminal Justice Act 2006, s 114

"BORSTAL" (discontinued)

On the commencement of this Act, the use of the term "Borstal" shall be discontinued and, accordingly, references in any statute or instrument made under statute to a Borstal Institution or to Borstal Institutions shall thenceforth be construed as references to Saint Patrick's Institution.

Criminal Justice Act 1960, s 12

"BROADCAST"

"broadcast" means the transmission, relaying or distribution by wireless telegraphy of communications, sounds, visual images or signals, intended for reception by the public generally or a section of it, whether the broadcast is so received or not, and cognate words shall be construed accordingly.

Criminal Justice Act 2006, s 181(11)

'broadcast' means the transmission, relaying or distribution by wireless telegraphy of communications, sounds, signs, visual images or signals, intended for direct reception by the general public whether or not such communications, sounds, signs, visual images or signals are actually received.

Criminal Procedure Act 1967, s 4J(5) inserted by the Criminal Justice Act 1999, s 9

C

"CAUTION"

(*a*) caution the person being interviewed in the following terms:

"You are not obliged to say anything unless you wish to do so but whatever you say will be taken down in writing and may be given in evidence. As you are aware this interview is being taped and the tape may be used in evidence",

and,

(*b*) state all of the following:
   (i) the name and rank of that member and the name and rank of any other member or members then present;

(ii) the name and status of any other person present;
(iii) the name of the person being interviewed;
(iv) the date, time of commencement of the recording and the location of the station; and
(v) that the person being interviewed has been given a notice pursuant to regulation 5 (2).

SI No 74/97, art 6(2)(a)

"CENTRAL AUTHORITY OF THE STATE"

The Minister shall be the Central Authority in the State for the purposes of this Act.

(2) The Minister may, by order, designate such persons as he or she considers appropriate to perform such functions of the Central Authority in the State as are specified in the order and different persons may be so designated to perform different functions of the Central Authority in the State.

(3) For so long as an order under *subsection (2)* remains in force, a reference in this Act to the Central Authority in the State shall, insofar as it relates to the performance of a function specified in the order, be construed as a reference to the person designated by the order to perform the function concerned.

(4) The Minister shall, by notice in writing, inform the General Secretariat of the Council of the European Union of the making of an order under this section and of the names of the persons designated under the order.

(5) The Minister may, by order, amend or revoke an order under this section (including an order under this subsection).

(6) The Central Authority in the State shall, in each year, prepare a report on the operation, in the preceding year, of *Part 2*, and shall cause copies of each such report to be laid before both Houses of the Oireachtas as soon as may be after it is so prepared.

European Arrest Warrant Act 2003, s 6

"CENTRAL MENTAL HOSPITAL" SEE THE

"CHIEF GOVERNOR OF IRELAND"

Lord Lieutenant' shall include any other 'Chief Governor or Governors of *Ireland*.

Petty Sessions (Ireland) Act 1851, xliv

"CHILD"

"child" means a person under 18 years of age, except where the context otherwise requires.

Criminal Justice Act 2006, s 176(1)

"CIRCUIT COURT"

On the commencement of this Act, a Court of First Instance, which shall be called An Chúirt Chuarda (The Circuit Court) shall stand established.

(2) The Circuit Court shall be constituted of the following judges—

(*a*) a judge, who shall be styled "Uachtarán na Cúirte Cuarda" ("The President of the Circuit Court"), and
(*b*) such number of ordinary judges (each of whom shall be styled "Breitheamh den Chúirt Chuarda" ("Judge of the Circuit Court")) as may from time to time be fixed by Act of the Oireachtas.

Courts (Establishment and Constitution) Act 1961, s 4

"CIVIL ORDER"

(1) On application made in accordance with this section, the District Court may make an order (a "civil order") prohibiting the respondent from doing anything specified in the order if the court is satisfied that—

(*a*) the respondent has behaved in an anti-social manner,
(*b*) the order is necessary to prevent the respondent from continuing to behave in that manner, and
(*c*) having regard to the effect or likely effect of that behaviour on other persons, the order is reasonable and proportionate in the circumstances.

(2) The court may impose terms or conditions in the civil order that the court considers appropriate.

(3) An application for a civil order may only be made by a senior member of the Garda Síochána and shall be made—

(*a*) on notice to the respondent, and
(*b*) in the district court district in which the respondent resides at the time.

(4) Before making the application, the senior member of the Garda Síochána must be satisfied that either or both of the following conditions have been met:

(*a*) the respondent has been issued a behaviour warning and has not complied with one or more of the demands of that warning;
(*b*) the respondent has been issued 3 or more behaviour warnings in less than 6 consecutive months.

(5) The respondent in an application under *subsection (1)* may not at any time be charged with, prosecuted or punished for an offence if the act or omission that constitutes the offence is the same behaviour that is the subject of the application and is to be determined by the court under *subsection (1) (a)*.

(6) Unless discharged under *subsection (7)*, a civil order remains in force for no more than the lesser of the following:

(*a*) two years from the date the order is made;
(*b*) the period specified in the order.

(7) The court may vary or discharge a civil order on the application of the person subject to that order or a senior member of the Garda Síochána.

(8) An applicant under *subsection (7)* shall give notice of the application—

(*a*) if the applicant is the person subject to the civil order, to a senior member of the Garda Síochána in the Garda Síochána district in which the applicant resides, or
(*b*) if the applicant is a senior member of the Garda Síochána, to the person who is the subject of the civil order.

(9) The standard of proof in proceedings under this section is that applicable to civil proceedings.

(10) The jurisdiction conferred on the District Court by this section may be exercised as follows:

(*a*) in respect of *subsections (1)* and *(2)*, by a judge of the District Court for the time being assigned to the district court district in which the respondent resides at the time the application is made;
(*b*) in respect of subsection (7), by a judge of the District Court for the time being assigned to the district court district in which the person subject to the civil order resides at the time the application is made.

Criminal Justice Act 2006, s 115(1)

"CIVIL SERVICE" SEE THE

"CLINICAL DIRECTOR"

"clinical director" has the meaning assigned to it by the Mental Health Act 2001, and, where an approved medical officer is duly authorised by a clinical director to perform his or her functions under this Act, the officer shall, in relation to those functions, be deemed, for the purposes of this Act, to be a clinical director.

Criminal Justice (Insanity) Act 2006, s 1

(1) The governing body of each approved centre shall appoint in writing a consultant psychiatrist to be the clinical director of the centre.

(2) Nothing in this section shall be construed as preventing a consultant psychiatrist from being the clinical director of more than one approved centre.

Mental Health Act 2001, s 71

"COMMISSIONER" SEE THE

"COMPANY"

In this section—

"company" means any company which may be wound up under the Companies Acts 1963 to 2006.

Criminal Justice (Mutual Assistance) Act 2008, s 43(3)

"COMPETENT PERSON"

"competent person" means a person employed by a public authority and includes an immigration officer who is deemed to have been appointed as such an officer under section 3 of the Immigration Act 2004.

Criminal Justice Act 2006, s 18(1)

"COMPLAINANT"

'Complainant' shall include 'Informant' or 'Prosecutor.

Petty Sessions (Ireland) Act 1851, xliv

"COMPLAINT"

the Word 'Complaint' shall include 'Information.'

Petty Sessions (Ireland) Act 1851, xliv

"COUNCIL DECISION"

'Council Decision' means Council Decision 2007/533/JHA of 12 June 2007 on the establishment, operation and use of the second generation Schengen Information System.".

European Arrest Warrant Act 2003, s 2(1) inserted by Criminal Justice (Miscellaneous Provisions) Act 2009, s 4(B)

Criminal Justice (Miscellaneous Provisions) Act 2009, s 21(1)

"CONSUL"

In this Regulation "consul" means, in relation to a foreign national, the diplomatic or consular representative of that person's own country either in the State or accredited to the State on a non- residential basis, or a diplomatic or consular representative of a third country which may formally or informally offer consular assistance to a national of a country which has no resident representative in the State.

SI No 119/87, s 14(6)

"CONVENTION"

"Convention" means the Convention for the Protection of Human Rights and Fundamental Freedoms done at Rome on the 4th day of November, 1950, as amended by Protocol No. 11 done at Strasbourg on the 11th day of May, 1994.

European Arrest Warrant Act 2003, s 37(2)

"CONVENTION COUNTRY"

For the purposes of the amendments to this Act effected by Part 2 of the Extradition (European Union Conventions) Act 2001, 'Convention country' means—

(*a*) a country designated under section 4(1) of that Act, or
(*b*) in such provisions of this Act as are specified in an order under subsection (1A) (inserted by section 52 of the *European Arrest Warrant Act 2003)* of section 4 of the Extradition (European Union Conventions) Act 2001, a country designated by that order, to which the provisions so specified apply.".

Extradition Act 1965, s 3(19) substituted by European Arrest Warrant Act 2003, s 47(b)

"COUNCIL FRAMEWORK DECISION" SEE THE

"COUNTRY"

"'country' includes territories for whose external relations the country concerned is responsible.".

Extradition Act 1965, s 3 inserted by European Arrest Warrant Act 2003, s 47(a)

"COUNTY"

the Word 'County' shall be deemed to include 'County of a City,' 'County of a Town,' or 'Riding of a County,' as the Case may be;

"county" means an administrative county.

Juries Act 1976, s 2

"COURT"

"the Court" means the Court of Criminal Appeal but, in sections 2 to 5 and 7, as modified by section 6, also includes the Courts-Martial Appeal Court.

Criminal Procedure Act 1993, s 1

"COURT OF CRIMINAL APPEAL"

For the purpose of hearing and determining any particular appeal cognisable by the Court of Criminal Appeal, the Court of Criminal Appeal shall be summoned in accordance with directions to be given by the Chief Justice, and the Court shall be duly constituted if it consists of not less than three judges—

(*a*) of whom one shall be either—
  (i) the Chief Justice, or
  (ii) an ordinary judge of the Supreme Court nominated by the Chief Justice, and
(*b*) of whom the other two shall be either—
  (i) two ordinary judges of the High Court nominated by the Chief Justice, or
  (ii) the President of the High Court, if nominated by the Chief Justice and willing to act, and one ordinary judge of the High Court nominated by the Chief Justice,

but any other available judge or judges of the Supreme Court or the High Court may, at the request of the Chief Justice, attend as a member or members of the Court.

Courts (Establishment and Constitution) Act 1961, s 3(2)

"CRIMINAL LUNATIC"

"criminal lunatic" means a person who is detained in a district mental hospital or in the Central Mental Hospital by warrant, order or direction of the Government or the Minister or under the provisions of section 91 of the Army Act, 1881, or of the Defence Act, 1954, and, if he is undergoing a sentence of penal servitude or imprisonment, or of detention in Saint Patrick's Institution, whose sentence has not expired.

Criminal Justice Act 1960, s 3(1)

"CRIMINAL MATTERS"

"criminal matters" includes criminal proceedings and applications for any order of certiorari, mandamus, prohibition or other State side order or injunction with respect to criminal proceedings or any other proceedings connected with criminal proceedings or any matter arising thereout and also includes cases stated, certifications by an Attorney General under section 29 of the Courts of Justice Act, 1924, references under section 34 of the Criminal Procedure Act, 1967, and applications and other proceedings arising out of criminal proceedings.

Prosecution of Offences Act 1974, s 1

"CUSTODY"

"custody" means custody in a Garda Síochána station.

SI No 119/87, s 2

"CUSTODY RECORD"

"custody record" means a record kept under regulation 6 of the Custody Regulations.

SI No 74/97, art 2

"custody record" means a record kept under Regulation 6;

(1) A record (in these Regulations referred to as the custody record) shall be kept in respect of each person in custody.

(2) The member in charge shall record or cause to be recorded in the custody record as soon as practicable such information as is required to be recorded by these Regulations. Each entry in the record shall be signed or initialled by the member making it.

(3) Where a person in custody is transferred to another station, the member in charge of the station from which he is transferred shall send with him the custody record relating to him, or a copy of it, to the member in charge of that other station.

(4) Without prejudice to the responsibility of any other member for the accuracy and completeness of any entry which he has made in a custody record, the member in charge shall be responsible for the accuracy and completeness of all entries made in the custody record while he is the member in charge.

(5) Paragraph (2) does not apply to a record referred to in Regulation 10(5) or paragraph (10) or (11) of Regulation 12.

SI No 119/87, s 2, reg 6

"CUSTODY REGULATIONS" SEE THE

D

"DATE OF APPLICANTS RELEASE FROM PRISON"

"date of the applicant's release from prison" means the date on which the applicant's sentence of imprisonment for the purposes of *section* 90 *(3)* expires or, as the case may be, his or her remission from the sentence begins.

Criminal Justice Act 2006, s 93(10)

"DESIGNATED CENTRE"

(1) The Central Mental Hospital is hereby designated as a centre (in this Act referred to as a "designated centre") for the reception, detention and care or

treatment of persons or classes of persons committed or transferred thereto under the provisions of this Act.

(2) The Minister for Health and Children by order may after consultation with the Mental Health Commission established under section 32 of the Act of 2001, designate a psychiatric centre as a centre (in this Act referred to as a "designated centre") for the reception, detention and, where appropriate, care or treatment of persons or classes of persons committed or transferred thereto under the provisions of this Act.

(3) Part 4 of the Act of 2001 shall apply to any person who is detained in a designated centre under this Act.

(4) In this section, "psychiatric centre" means a hospital or in-patient facility in which care or treatment is provided for persons suffering from a mental disorder within the meaning of the Act of 2001.

Criminal Law (Insanity) Act 2006, s 3

"DIPLOMATIC OFFICER"

"diplomatic officer" means a member of the staff of a diplomatic mission of a foreign State having diplomatic rank.

Criminal Justice Act 1990, s 3(3)

"DIRECTOR OF PUBLIC PROSECUTIONS"

(1) There is hereby established the office of Director of Public Prosecutions and the holder of the office shall be known as the Director of Public Prosecutions and is referred to subsequently in this Act as the Director.

(2) The Director shall be appointed by the Government.

(3) (*a*) A person shall not be appointed to be the Director unless at the date of his appointment he is a practising barrister or a practising solicitor and has practised as a barrister or as a solicitor for at least ten years.

(*b*) For the purposes of this subsection, service for any, period in a position in the Civil Service for appointment to which practice as a barrister or a solicitor was a necessary qualification, shall be deemed to be practise as a barrister or a solicitor, as the case may be for that period and a person, while holding such a position, shall be deemed to be a practising barrister or a practising solicitor, as the case may be.

(4) The Director shall be a civil servant in the Civil Service of the State.

(5) The Director shall be independent in the performance of his functions.

(6) The Attorney General and the Director shall consult together from time to time in relation to matters pertaining to the functions at the Director.

(7) (*a*) (i) There shall be a committee consisting of
(I) the Chief Justice,
(II) the Chairman of the General Council of the Bar of Ireland,
(III) the President of the Incorporated Law Society,
(IV) the Secretary to the Government, and
(V) the Senior Legal Assistant in the Office of the Attorney General.
(ii) In the case of any of the persons aforesaid signifying at any time his unwillingness or inability to act for any period as a member of the, committee the Taoiseach may, after consultation with the Attorney General, appoint another person to be a member of the committee in his place for that period.

(*b*) The committee established by this subsection shall, whenever so requested by the Taoiseach, select candidates for appointment to the office of Director and shall inform the Taoiseach of the candidates selected and of their suitability for such appointment.

(*c*) The Government shall not appoint a person to be the Director unless the person was selected or amongst those selected by the committee aforesaid pursuant to a request under paragraph (*b*) of this subsection in relation to that appointment, but—
(i) if the candidate is unable to select a suitable candidate pursuant to a particular request under that paragraph, or
(ii) if the Government decide not to, appoint to, be the Director any of the candidates selected by the committee pursuant to a particular request under that paragraph.

then either—

(I) the Government shall appoint a person to be the Director who was selected or amongst those selected by the committee pursuant to a previous request (if any) under that paragraph in relation to that appointment or
(II) the Taoiseach shall make a further request to the committee under that paragraph and the Government shall appoint a person to be the Director who was selected or amongst those selected by the committee pursuant to that request or pursuant to another request under that paragraph in relation to that appointment.

(*d*) The Taoiseach may, after consultation with the Attorney General, make regulations for the purposes of this subsection.

(8) (*a*) The Director shall hold office upon such terms and conditions as may be determined by the Taoiseach after consultation with the Minister for the Public Service.

(*b*) (i) The Taoiseach shall, after consultation with the Minister for the Public Service, make a scheme for the grant of superannuation benefits for the Director.

(ii) The scheme shall fix the time and conditions of retirement of the Director.

(iii) The Taoiseach may, after consultation with the Minister for the Public Service, make a scheme amending a scheme under this subsection.

(iv) A scheme under this subsection shall be carried out in accordance with its terms.

(v) Every scheme under this subsection shall be laid before each House of the Oireachtas as soon as may be after it is made and, if either House, within the next twenty-one days on which that House has sat after the scheme is laid before it, passes a resolution annulling the scheme, the scheme shall be annulled accordingly, but without prejudice to the validity of anything previously done thereunder.

(9) (*a*) The Director may be removed from office by the Government after consideration by them of the report of a committee under paragraph (*b*) of this subsection.

(*b*) Whenever the Government so request, a committee appointed by them and consisting of the Chief Justice, a Judge of the High Court nominated, by the Chief Justice, and the Attorney General shall—

(i) investigate the condition of health, either physical or mental, of the Director, or

(ii) inquire into the conduct (whether in the execution of his office or otherwise) of the Director, either generally or on a particular occasion,

and, in either case, with particular reference to such matters as may be mentioned in the request and the committee may conduct the investigation or inquiry in such manner as it thinks proper, whether by examination of witnesses or otherwise, and in particular may conduct any proceedings in camera and for this purpose shall have all such powers, rights and privileges as are vested in a Judge of the High Court on the occasion of an action and, upon the conclusion of the investigation or inquiry, the committee shall report the result thereof to the Government.

(10) There shall be employed in the office of the Director so many officers and servants as the Taoiseach shall, with the sanction of the Minister for the Public Service, from time to time determine and all such officers and servants shall hold notice on such terms and conditions as the Minister for the Public Service shall prescribe.

(11) The power of appointing a person to be an officer or servant of the Director shall be vested in the Taoiseach.

Prosecution of Offenders Act 1974, s 2

In this section "Director of Public Prosecutions" includes a person for the time being exercising the functions of that office.

Criminal Justice Act 1999, s 31(3)

"DISQUALIFICATION" (JURY)

A person shall be disqualified for jury service if on conviction of an offence in any part of Ireland—

(*a*) he has at any time been sentenced to imprisonment or penal servitude for life or for a term of five years or more or to detention under section 103 of the Children Act, 1908, or under the corresponding law of Northern Ireland, or

(*b*) he has at any time in the last ten years—

   (i) served any part of a sentence of imprisonment or penal servitude, being, in the case of imprisonment, a sentence for a term of at least three months, or

   (ii) served any part of a sentence of detention in Saint Patrick's Institution or in a corresponding institution in Northern Ireland, being a sentence for a term of at least three months.

Juries Act 1976, s 8

"DISTRICT"

"district" means a Garda Síochána district.

SI No 119/1987, art 2

"DISTRICT COURT"

On the commencement of this Act, a Court of First Instance, which shall be called An Chúirt Dúiche (The District Court), shall stand established.

(2) The District Court shall be constituted of the following judges—

(*a*) a judge who shall be styled "Uachtaráin na Cúirte Dúiche" ("The President of the District Court"), and (*b*) such number of other judges (each of whom shall be styled "Breitheamh den Chúirt Dúiche ("Justice of the District Court")) as may from time to time he fixed by Act of the Oireachtas.

Courts (Establishment and Constitution) Act 1961, s 5

"DISTRICT MENTAL HOSPITAL"

the expression "district mental hospital" means a mental hospital provided under section 21 of this Act by a mental hospital authority.

Mental Treatment Act 1945, s 3

"DOCTOR"

"doctor" means a registered medical practitioner.

SI No 119/1987, art 2

"DOCUMENT"

In sections 13 and 14 of the Act of 1939, "document" does not include any of the things specified in the amendment of the definition of "document" made by section 5 of the Offences against the State (Amendment) Act, 1972.

Criminal Law Act 1976, s 14

the word "document" includes a book and also a newspaper, magazine, or other periodical publication, and also a pamphlet, leafl et, circular, or advertisement;

["and also—

(*a*) any map, plan, graph or drawing,
(*b*) any photograph,
(*c*) any disc, tape, sound track or other device in which sounds or other data (not being visual images) are embodied so as to be capable (with or without the aid of some other equipment) of being reproduced therefrom, and
(*d*) any fi lm, microfi lm, negative, tape or ether device in which one or more visual images are embodied (whether with or without sounds or other data) so as to be capable (as aforesaid) of being reproduced therefrom and a reproduction or

still reproduction of the image or images embodied therein whether enlarged or not and whether with or without sounds or other data".].

Offences Against the State Act 1939, s 2 amended by Offences Against the State (Amendment) Act 1972, s 5

"document" includes—

(*a*) a map, plan, graph, drawing, photograph or record, or
(*b*) a reproduction in permanent legible form, by a computer or other means (including enlarging), of information in non-legible form.

Criminal Justice Act 2006, s 183(5)

"DOMESTIC WARRANT"

"domestic warrant" means a warrant (other than a European arrest warrant) issued, for the arrest of a person, by a court in the State.

European Arrest Warrant Act 2003, s 31

E

"ELECTRONIC RECORDING"

"electronic recording" includes—

(*a*) a record of an oral communication made on tape, and
(*b*) a record, made on tape, of a series of visual images appearing as a moving picture whether or not including an accompanying soundtrack.

SI No 74/1997, art 2

"EQUIPMENT"

"equipment" means electronic recording equipment that has been provided to and installed in Garda Síochána stations for the purpose of recording interviews to which these Regulations apply.

SI No 74/1997, art 2

"EVIDENCE IN SUPPORT OF AN ALIBI"

In this section—

"evidence in support of an alibi" means evidence tending to show that by reason of the presence of the accused at a particular place or in a particular area at a particular time he was not, or was unlikely to have been, at the place where the offence is alleged to have been committed at the time of its alleged commission.

Criminal Justice Act 1984, s 20(8)

"EXECUTING STATE"

In this section "executing state" means, in relation to a European arrest warrant, a Member State (a judicial authority of which has ordered the arrest and surrender to the State, pursuant to the European arrest warrant, of a person in respect of whom that warrant was issued).

European Arrest Warrant Act 2003, s 28(5)

ALSO

European Arrest Warrant Act 2003, s 36(2)

"EXPLOSIVE"

"explosive" means an explosive within the meaning of the Explosives Act 1875 and any other substance or thing that is an explosive substance within the meaning of the Explosive Substances Act 1883.

Criminal Justice Act 2007, s 2

The expression 'explosive substance' shall be deemed to include any materials for mak-ing any explosive substance; also any apparatus, machine, implement, or materials used, or intended to be used, or adapted for causing, or aiding in causing, any explosion in or with any explosive substance; also any part of any such apparatus, machine, or implement.

Explosive Substances Act 1883, s 9

The term 'explosive' in this Act—

(1) Means gunpowder, nitro-glycerine, dynamite, guncotton, blasting powders, fulminate of mercury or of other metals, coloured fires, and every other substance, whether similar to those above mentioned or not, used or manufactured with a view to produce a practical effect by explosion or a pyrotechnic effect; and

(2) Includes fog-signals, fireworks, fuzes, rockets, percussion caps, detonators, cartridges, ammunition of all descriptions, and every adaptation or preparation of an explosive as above defined.

Explosives Act 1875, s 3

"EXTRADITION"

"extradition" means the surrender of a person under the provisions of Part II to a country in relation to which that Part applies.

Extradition Act 1965, s 3(1)

"EXTRADITION AGREEMENT"

"extradition agreement" has the meaning assigned to it by subsection (1) of section 8.

Extradition Act 1965, s 3(1)

"EXTRADITION PROVISIONS"

In this section "extradition provisions" has the same meaning as it has in the Act of 1965.

European Arrest Warrant Act 2003, s 30(4)

"extradition provisions" means the provisions of an extradition agreement or of an order under section 8 applying Part II otherwise than in pursuance of an extradition agreement.

Extradition Act 1965, s 3(1)

.—(1) Where by any international agreement or convention to which the State is a party an arrangement (in this Act referred to as an extradition agreement) is made with another country for the surrender by each country to the other of persons wanted for prosecution or punishment or where the Government are satisfied that reciprocal facilities to that effect will be afforded by another country, the Government may by order apply this Part in relation to that country.

Extradition Act 1965, s 8(1)

F

"FINE"

In this section "fine" includes any compensation, costs or expenses in addition to a fine ordered to be paid.

Criminal Justice Act 2006, s 195(3)

"FRAMEWORK DECISION"

"Framework Decision" means Council Framework Decision of 13 June 2002 on the European arrest warrant and the surrender procedures between Member States, the text of which—

(*a*) in the Irish language, is set out in *Part A* of the *Schedule*, and
(*b*) in the English language, is set out in *Part B* of the *Schedule*.

European Arrest Warrant Act 2003, s 2(1)

"FUNCTIONS"

"functions" includes powers and duties, and references to the performance of functions include, as respects powers and duties, references to the exercise of the powers and the carrying out of the duties.

European Arrest Warrant Act 2003, s 2(1)

G

"GOVERNOR"

"governor" includes, in relation to a prisoner, a person for the time being performing the functions of governor.

Criminal Justice Act 2006, s 98

H

"HIGH COURT"

(1) On the commencement of this Act, the Court of First Instance referred to in Article 34 of the Constitution as An ArdChúirt" (The High Court) shall stand established.

(2) The High Court shall be constituted of the following judges—

(*a*) the president thereof, who shall be styled "Uachtarán na hArd-Chúirte" ("The President of the High Court"), and

(*b*) such number of ordinary judges (each of whom shall be styled "Breitheamh den ArdChúirt" ("Judge of the High Court")) as may from time to time be fixed by Act of the Oireachtas.

(3) The Chief Justice shall be ex officio an additional judge of the High Court.

(4) The President of the Circuit Court shall be ex officio an additional judge of the High Court.

(5) (*a*) Where, owing to the illness of a judge of the High Court or for any other reason, a sufficient number of judges of the High Court is not available for the transaction of the business of that Court or, on account of the volume of business to be transacted in the High Court or for any other reason arising from the state of business in that Court, it is expedient to increase temporarily the number of judges available for the purposes of the High Court, the Chief Justice, at the request of the President of the High Court, may request any ordinary judge of the Supreme Court to sit in the High Court as an additional judge thereof, and every ordinary judge of the Supreme Court so requested shall sit in the High Court.

(*b*) Whenever an ordinary judge of the Supreme Court sits in the High Court in pursuance of this subsection, he shall be an additional judge of the High Court for all the purposes of that Court.

Courts (Establishment and Constitution) Act 1961, s 2

"HOME ADDRESS"

In this section—

"home address", in relation to any person, means the address of his or her sole or main residence or, if he or she has no such residence, his or her most usual place of abode or, if he or she has no such abode, the place which he or she regularly visits.

Criminal Justice Act 2006, s 92(11)

"HORSE"

the Word 'Horse' shall include any other Animal of any Kind commonly used or employed in drawing any kind of Carriage.

Summary Jurisdiction (Ir) Act 1851, s xxv

I & J

"IMPRISONMENT"

"imprisonment" includes—

(*a*) detention in Saint Patrick's Institution,
(*b*) detention in a place provided under section 2 of the Prisons Act 1970, and
(*c*) detention in a place specified under section 3 of the Prisons Act 1972,

and "prison" and "sentence of imprisonment" shall be construed accordingly.

Criminal Justice Act 2007, s 24(1)

"imprisonment" includes penal servitude and detention in Saint Patrick's Institution.

Criminal Justice Act 1984, s 3

"imprisonment" includes detention in Saint Patrick's Institution.

Criminal Justice Act 1993, s 1(1)

"INDICTMENT"

In the Construction of this Act the Word 'Indictment' shall be understood to include 'Information,' 'Inquisition,' and 'Presentment,' as well as Indictment and also any 'Plea,' 'Replication,' or other Pleading, and any Nisi Prius Record.

Criminal Procedure Act 1851, s xxx

"INFORMATION"

In this section "information" includes—

(*a*) a document or record, and
(*b*) information in non-legible form.

Criminal Justice Act 2006, s 182(7)

"INFORMATION IN NON LEGIBLE FORM"

"information in non-legible form" includes information on microfilm, microfiche, magnetic tape or disk.

Criminal Evidence Act 1992, s 2(1)

"INJURED PARTY"

Subject to the provisions of this section, on conviction of any person of an offence, the court, instead of or in addition to dealing with him in any other way, may, unless it sees reason to the contrary, make (on application or otherwise) an order (in this Act referred to as a "compensation order") requiring him to pay compensation in respect of any personal injury or loss resulting from that offence (or any other offence that is taken into consideration by the court in determining sentence) to any person (in this Act referred to as the "injured party") who has suffered such injury or loss.

Criminal Justice Act 1993, s 6(1)

"INTOXICATION"

"intoxication" means being under the intoxicating influence of any alcoholic drink, drug, solvent or any other substance or combination of substances.

Criminal Law (Insanity) Act 2006, s 1

"ISSUING JUDICIAL AUTHORITY"

"issuing judicial authority" means, in relation to a European arrest warrant, the judicial authority in the issuing state that issued the European arrest warrant concerned.

European Arrest Warrant Act 2003, s 2(1)

"JUDGE"

"trial judge" and "judge", in relation to proceedings before a Special Criminal Court, means a member of that Court, and the references in *subsections (2) (a)* and *(5) (a)* to an accused person being sent forward for trial include, where appropriate, references to such a person being charged before that Court.

Criminal Justice Act 2006, s 181(11)

"JUDICIAL AUTHORITY"

"judicial authority" means the judge, magistrate or other person authorised under the law of the Member State concerned to perform functions the same as or similar to those performed under section 33 by a court in the State.

European Arrest Warrant Act 2003, s 2(1)

A court may, upon an application made by or on behalf of the Director of Public Prosecutions, issue a European arrest warrant in respect of a person—

(*a*) where it is satisfied upon reasonable grounds that—
- (i) a domestic warrant was issued for the arrest of that person but was not executed, and
- (ii) the person is not in the State,

And

(*b*) where—
- (i) the person would, if convicted of the offence concerned, be liable to a term of imprisonment of 12 months or more than 12 months, or
- (ii) a term of imprisonment of not less than 4 months has been imposed on the person in respect of the offence concerned and the person is required to serve all or part of that term of imprisonment.

(2) A European arrest warrant shall, in so far as is practicable, be in the form set out in the Annex to the Framework Decision and shall specify—

(*a*) the name and the nationality of the person to whom it relates,
(*b*) the name, address, fax number and e-mail address of—
(i) the District Court Office for the district in which the District Court was sitting when it issued the European arrest warrant,
(ii) the Circuit Court Office of the county in which the Circuit Criminal Court was sitting when it issued the European arrest warrant,
(iii) the Central Office of the High Court, or
(iv) the Registrar of the Special Criminal Court,

as may be appropriate,

(*c*) the offence to which the European arrest warrant relates including a description thereof,
(*d*) that a conviction, sentence or detention order is immediately enforceable against the person, or that a domestic warrant for his or her arrest has been issued in respect of that offence,
(e) the circumstances in which the offence was committed or is alleged to have been committed, including the time and place of its commission or alleged commission, and the degree of involvement or alleged degree of involvement of the person in the commission of the offence, and
(*f*) (i) the penalties to which the person named in the European arrest warrant would, if convicted of the offence to which the European arrest warrant relates, be liable,
(ii) where the person named in the European arrest warrant has been convicted of the offence specified therein and a sentence has been imposed in respect thereof, the penalties of which that sentence consists, and
(iii) where the person named in the European arrest warrant has been convicted of the offence specified therein but has not yet been sentenced, the penalties to which he or she is liable in respect of the offence.

(3) Where it is not practicable for the European arrest warrant to be in the form set out in the Annex to the Framework Decision, the European arrest warrant shall, in addition to containing the information specified in *subsection (2)*, include such other information as would be required to be provided were it in that form.

(4) For the avoidance of doubt, a European arrest warrant may be issued in respect of one or more than one offence.

(5) In this section "court" means—

(*a*) the court that issued the domestic warrant to which *subparagraph (i)* of section 33 *(1)(a)* applies, or
(*b*) the High Court.

European Arrest Warrant Act 2003, s 33

K

"KEEPER OF A BROTHEL"

"keeper of a brothel" means a person referred to in section 11 (which relates to brothel keeping) of the Criminal Law (Sexual Offences) Act, 1993.

Children Act 2001, s 249(4)

A person who—

(*a*) keeps or manages or acts or assists in the management of a brothel,
(*b*) being the tenant, lessee, occupier or person in charge of a premises, knowingly permits such premises or any part thereof to be used as a brothel or for the purposes of habitual prostitution, or
(*c*) being the lessor or landlord of any premises or the agent of such lessor or landlord, lets such premises or any part thereof with the knowledge that such premises or some part thereof are or is to be used as a brothel, or is wilfully a party to the continued use of such premises or any part thereof as a brothel,

shall be guilty of an offence.

Criminal Law (Sexual Offences) Act 1993, s 11

L

"LAWFUL AUTHORITY"

In this section "lawful authority" means the authority of—

(*a*) a court in any proceedings involving the relocated witness, or
(*b*) a member of the Garda Síochána not below the rank of chief superintendent.

Criminal Justice Act 1999, s 40(4)

"LEGAL REPRESENTATIVE"

"legal representative" means a practising barrister or a practising solicitor.

Criminal Law (Insanity) Act 2006, s 1

"LORD LIEUTENANT"

Lord Lieutenant' shall include any other 'Chief Governor or Governors of *Ireland.*

Petty Sessions (Ireland) Act 1851, xliv

"LOSS"

"loss" means any matter (including mental distress resulting from the death and funeral expenses) for which damages could be awarded in respect of the death by virtue of Part V of the Civil Liability Act, 1961.

Criminal Justice Act 1993, s 6(12)(a)

M

"MALICE"

Where a person kills another unlawfully the killing shall not be murder unless the accused person intended to kill, or cause serious injury to, some person, whether the person actually killed or not.

(2) The accused person shall be presumed to have intended the natural and probable consequences of his conduct; but this presumption may be rebutted.

Criminal Justice Act 1964, s 4

"MANDATORY TERM OF IMPRISONMENT"

"mandatory term of imprisonment" includes, in relation to an offence, a term of imprisonment imposed by a court under an enactment that provides that a person who is guilty of the offence concerned shall be liable to a term of imprisonment of not less than such term as is specified in the enactment.

Criminal Justice Act 2006, s 98

"MARKET VALUE"

"'market value' means, in relation to land, the price that would have been obtained in respect of the unencumbranced fee simple were the land to have been sold on the open market, in the year immediately preceding the bringing of the proceedings concerned, in such manner and subject to such conditions as might reasonably be calculated to have resulted in the vendor obtaining the best price for the land.".

Courts (Supplemental Provisions) Act 1961, s 2 inserted by the Civil Liability and Courts Act 2004, s 45(1)

"MASTER TAPE"

"master tape" means the tape of an interview to which these Regulations apply on which the interview is recorded and which is sealed in accordance with these Regulations before it leaves the presence of the person being interviewed and is any one of the tapes used in the equipment.

SI No 74/1997, art 2

"MEMBER"

"member" means a member of the Garda Síochána.

SI No 74/1997, art 2

"member" means a member of the Garda Síochána.

SI No 119/1987, art 2

"member" means a member of the Garda Síochána.

Criminal Justice (Miscellaneous Provisions) Act 1997, s 1(1)

"MEMBER IN CHARGE"

In these Regulations "member in charge" means the member who is in charge of a station at a time when the member in charge of a station is required to do anything or cause anything to be done pursuant to these Regulations.

SI No 119/1987, art 4(1)

"member in charge" means a member of the Garda Síochána who is in charge of a Garda Síochána station at a time when the member in charge of a station is required to do anything or cause anything to be done pursuant to this Act.

Children Act 2001, s 3

"member in charge" has the meaning assigned to it by regulation 4 of the Custody Regulations.

SI No 74/1997, art 2

"MEMBER OF THE FAMILY"

In this subsection "member of the family" means wife, husband, father, mother, grandfather, grandmother, stepfather, stepmother, son, daughter, grandson, granddaughter, stepson, stepdaughter, brother, sister, half-brother, half-sister, a person who is the subject of, or in whose favour there is made, an adoption order under the Adoption, Act 1952 and 1964.

Prosecution of Offences Act 1974, s 6(2)(b)

"MEMBER STATE"

"Member State" means a Member State of the European Communities (other than the State) or Gibraltar.

European Arrest Warrant Act 2003, s 2(1)

"MENTAL DISORDER"

"mental disorder" includes mental illness, mental disability, dementia or any disease of the mind but does not include intoxication;

In this Act "mental disorder" means mental illness, severe dementia or significant intellectual disability where—

(*a*) because of the illness, disability or dementia, there is a serious likelihood of the person concerned causing immediate and serious harm to himself or herself or to other persons, or

(*b*) (i) because of the severity of the illness, disability or dementia, the judgment of the person concerned is so impaired that failure to admit the person to an approved centre would be likely to lead to a serious deterioration in his or her condition or would prevent the administration of appropriate treatment that could be given only by such admission, and

(ii) the reception, detention and treatment of the person concerned in an approved centre would be likely to benefit or alleviate the condition of that person to a material extent.

(2) In *subsection (1)*—

"mental illness" means a state of mind of a person which affects the person's thinking, perceiving, emotion or judgment and which seriously impairs the mental function of the person to the extent that he or she requires care or medical treatment in his or her own interest or in the interest of other persons;

"severe dementia" means a deterioration of the brain of a person which significantly impairs the intellectual function of the person thereby affecting thought, comprehension and memory and which includes severe psychiatric or behavioural symptoms such as physical aggression;

"significant intellectual disability" means a state of arrested or incomplete development of mind of a person which includes significant impairment of intelligence and social functioning and abnormally aggressive or seriously irresponsible conduct on the part of the person.

Mental Health Act 2001, s 3

"MONIES"

'monies' means coins and notes in any currency, bank drafts, postal orders, certificates of deposit and any other similar instruments easily convertible into money.".

Criminal Justice Act 2006, s 183A(5) inserted by Criminal Justice Act 2007, s 46

"MONTH"

the Word 'Month' shall mean 'Calendar Month.'

Petty Sessions (Ireland) Act 1851, s xliv

N

"NEWLY DISCOVERED FACT"

In subsection (1) "newly-discovered fact" means—

(*a*) where a conviction was quashed by the Court on an application under section 2 or a convicted person was pardoned as a result of a petition under section 7, or has been acquitted in any re-trial, a fact which was discovered by him or came to his notice after the relevant appeal proceedings had been finally determined or a fact the significance of which was not appreciated by the convicted person or his advisers during the trial or appeal proceedings, and

(*b*) where a conviction was quashed by that Court on appeal, a fact which was discovered by the convicted person or came to his notice after the conviction to which the appeal relates or a fact the significance of which was not appreciated by the convicted person or his advisers during the trial.

Criminal Procedure Act 1993, s 9(6)

"NOLLE PROSEQUI"

At the trial of a prisoner on indictment at the prosecution of the Attorney-General of Saorstát Eireann a *nolle prosequi* may be entered at the instance of the Attorney-General of Saorstát Eireann at any time after the indictment is preferred to the jury and before a verdict is found thereon, and every such *nolle prosequi* shall be in the following form, that is to say:—

On the .... day of ...., 19......., at the trial of A.B. on the prosecution of the Attorney-General of Saorstát Eireann on an indictment for .... the said Attorney-General in his proper person (or by his counsel) stated to the court that he would not further prosecute the said A. B. on the said indictment, where upon it was ordered by the court that the said A. B. be discharged of and from the indictment aforesaid.

Criminal Justice (Administration) Act 1924, s 12

O

"OATH"

the Word 'Oath' shall include, 'Affirmation' or 'solemn Declaration,' as the Case may be.

Petty Sessions (Ireland) Act 1851, s xliv

"OFFENCE"

(1) In this section, except where the context otherwise requires, 'offence' means, in relation to a person to whom a European arrest warrant applies, an offence (other than an offence specified in the European arrest warrant in respect of which the person's surrender is ordered under this Act) under

the law of the issuing state committed before the person's surrender, but shall not include an offence consisting, in whole, of acts or omissions of which the offence specified in the European arrest warrant consists in whole or in part.

European Arrest Warrant Act 2003, s 22(1) substituted by the Criminal Justice (Terrorist Offences) Act 2005, s 80

(1) In this section, except where the context otherwise requires—

'offence' means, in relation to a person to whom a European arrest warrant applies, an offence under the law of a Member State (other than the issuing state) committed before the person's surrender to the issuing state under this Act; and.

European Arrest Warrant Act 2003, s 23(1) substituted by the Criminal Justice (Terrorist Offences) Act 2005, s 81

"offence" means an arrestable offence as defined in section 2 of the Criminal Law Act, 1997.

Criminal Justice Act 1999, s 42(1)

"arrestable offence" means an offence for which a person of full capacity and not previously convicted may, under or by virtue of any enactment, be punished by imprisonment for a term of five years or by a more severe penalty and includes an attempt to commit any such offence.

Criminal Law Act 1997, s 2

"OFFENDER"

"offender" means a person in respect of whom a restriction on movement order is, or may be, made under *section* 101.

Criminal Justice Act 2006, s 98

Where a person (other than a person under the age of 18 years) (in this section referred to as "*the offender*") is convicted on indictment of an offence specified in Schedule 2, the court shall consider whether it is appropriate to make an order or orders under this section in relation to the offender for the purpose of monitoring the offender after release from prison or for the purpose of protecting any person.

Criminal Justice Act 2007, s 26

"ORAL EVIDENCE"

'oral evidence' includes—

(i) any evidence given through a live television link pursuant to Part III of the Criminal Evidence Act, 1992, or section 39 of the *Criminal Justice Act, 1999*, or

(ii) a videorecording of any evidence given through a live television link pursuant to that Part or section in proceedings under section 4F **[or**

"(iii) any other videorecording, or an audiorecording, which may be admitted by the trial court as evidence of any fact stated in it.".]

Criminal Procedure Act 1967, s 4E(5)(b) inserted by Criminal Justice Act 1999, s 9 as amended by Criminal Justice Act 2006, s 20

"ORDER"

the Word 'Order' shall include 'Conviction.

Petty Sessions (Ireland) Act 1851, s xliv

P

"PATIENT"

"patient", in *sections* 12, 13 and 14, means a person detained in a designated centre pursuant to this Act.

Criminal Law (Insanity) Act 2006, s 1

"PERSON IN CHARGE"

"person in charge" means—

(*a*) in relation to a criminal lunatic detained in a district mental hospital, the resident medical superintendent thereof, and

(*b*) in relation to a criminal lunatic detained in the Central Mental Hospital, the Resident Physician and Governor thereof.

Criminal Justice Act 1960, s 3(1)

"PLACE"

"place" includes any building or part of a building, vehicle, vessel, aircraft or hovercraft and any other place whatsoever.

Criminal Justice Act 1984, s 3

place' means a physical location and includes—

(*a*) a dwelling, residence, building or abode,
(*b*) a vehicle, whether mechanically propelled or not,
(*c*) a vessel, whether sea-going or not,
(*d*) an aircraft, whether capable of operation or not, and
(e) a hovercraft.".

Criminal Justice (Miscellaneous Provisions) Act 1997, s 10(6) substituted by the Criminal Justice Act 2006, s 6

In this section "place" includes a ship or other vessel, an aircraft, a railway wagon or other vehicle, and a container used for the transporting of goods.

European Arrest Warrant Act 2003, s 25(7)

"place" includes premises.

Criminal Justice (Mutual Assistance) Act 2008, s 61

"POLICE"

"police" means, in relation to the first-mentioned place in *subsection (1)*, any police force in that place, or a member thereof, whether that force is organised at a national, regional or local level.

Criminal Justice Act 2006, s 95(9)

"POTENTIAL JUROR"

In this section, "potential juror" means a person who, at the time an offence under this section is alleged to have been committed, has been summoned for jury service but has not been empanelled as a juror to serve on a particular jury.

Criminal Justice Act 1999, s 41(2)

"PRESCRIBED"

"prescribed" means prescribed by regulations made by the Minister under this Act.

Criminal Justice Act 2006, s 87

"PRISON OFFICER"

"prison officer" includes any member of the staff of a prison and any person having the custody of, or having duties in relation to the custody of, a person detained in a prison.

Criminal Justice Act 1990, s 3(3)

"PRISON"

"prison" means any place for which rules or regulations may be made under the Prisons Acts, 1826 to 1980, section 7 of the Offences against the State (Amendment) Act, 1940, section 233 of the Defence Act, 1954, section 2 of the Prisoners of War and Enemy Aliens Act, 1956, or section 13 of the Criminal Justice Act, 1960.

Criminal Justice Act 1990, s 3(3)

"prison" means a place of custody administered by the Minister for Justice, Equality and Law Reform.

Criminal Justice Act 1999, s 42(1)

In this Act "prison" includes Saint Patrick's Institution (within the meaning of the Criminal Justice Act, 1960).

Criminal Law (Jurisdiction) Act 1976, s 1(1)

"prison" includes Saint Patrick's Institution, any place provided under section 2 of the Prisons Act, 1970, any place in which persons are kept in military custody pursuant to section 2 of the Prisons Act, 1972, or any place specified to be used as a prison under section 3 of that Act, and "governor" and "prison officer" shall be construed accordingly.

Criminal Law Act 1976, s 1

"prison" means a place of custody administered by the Minister.

Criminal Law (Insanity) Act 2006, s 1

"PRISONER"

"prisoner" means a person who is in prison on foot of a sentence of imprisonment, on committal awaiting trial, on remand or otherwise.

Criminal Justice Act 1999, s 42(1)

"prisoner" means a person who is in prison on foot of a sentence of imprisonment, on committal awaiting trial, on remand or otherwise.

Criminal Law (Insanity) Act 2006, s 1

"PROBATION AND WELFARE OFFICER"

In this section, 'probation and welfare officer' means a person appointed by the Minister to be—

(*a*) a welfare officer,
(*b*) a probation officer, or
(*c*) a probation and welfare officer.

Criminal Justice Act 1960, s 2(10) substituted by the Criminal Justice (Temporary Release of Prisoners) Act 2003, s 1

"probation and welfare officer" means a person appointed by the Minister to be—

(a) a probation officer,
(b) a welfare officer, or
(c) a probation and welfare officer.

Criminal Justice Act 2006, s 98

"PROBATION AND WELFARE SERVICE"

"probation and welfare service" means those officers of the Minister assigned to perform functions in the part of the Department of State for which the Minister is responsible commonly known by that name.

Criminal Justice Act 2006, s 98

"PROCEEDINGS"

"proceedings" includes proceedings under section 4E (application by accused for dismissal of charge) of the Act of 1967 where oral evidence (within the meaning of subsection (5) of that section) is given.

Criminal Justice Act 2006, s 15

"PROCURATOR FISCAL"

In this section "Procurator Fiscal" includes a Depute.

Criminal Justice Act 1999, s 32(3)

"PROTOCOLS TO THE CONVENTION"

"Protocols to the Convention" means the following protocols to the Convention, construed in accordance with Articles 16 to 18 of the Convention:

(*a*) the Protocol to the Convention done at Paris on the 20th day of March, 1952;
(*b*) Protocol No. 4 to the Convention securing certain rights and freedoms other than those already included in the Convention and in the First Protocol thereto done at Strasbourg on the 16th day of September, 1963;
(*c*) Protocol No. 6 to the Convention concerning the abolition of the death penalty done at Strasbourg on the 28th day of April, 1983.

European Arrest Warrant Act 2003, s 37(2)

"PSYCHIATRIC CENTRE"

In this section, "psychiatric centre" means a hospital or in-patient facility in which care or treatment is provided for persons suffering from a mental disorder within the meaning of the Act of 2001.

Criminal Law (Insanity) Act 2006, s 3(4)

"PUBLIC AUTHORITY"

"public authority" means—

(*a*) a Minister of the Government,
(*b*) the Commissioners of Public Works in Ireland,
(*c*) a local authority within the meaning of the Local Government Act 2001,
(*d*) the Health Service Executive,
(*e*) a harbour authority within the meaning of the Harbours Act 1946,
(*f*) a board or other body (not being a company) established by or under statute,
(*g*) a company in which all the shares are held by, or on behalf of, or by directors appointed by, a Minister of the Government, or
(*h*) a company in which all the shares are held by a board or other body referred to in *paragraph (f)* , or by a company referred to in *paragraph (g)*.

Criminal Justice Act 2006, s 18(1)

"PUBLISH"

"publish" means publish, other than by way of broadcast, to the public generally or a section of it.

Criminal Justice Act 2006, s 181(11)

R

"RECOGNIZANCE"

Every recognizance entered into by way of bail before a District Justice or a Justice of the District Court or a Peace Commissioner shall be in the following form, or in such similar form as the circumstances may require:—

Be it remembered that on the .... day of ...., in the year of our Lord .... A. B., of..................... (labourer), C. D., of .... (grocer), and E. F., of .... (butcher), personally came before me the undersigned, a District Justice in Saorstát Eireann (or a Justice of the District Court of Saorstát Eireann or a Peace Commissioner) for the District of ...., and severally acknowledged themselves to owe to Saorstát Eireann the several sums following, that is to say, the said A. B. the sum of ...., and the said C. D. and E. F. the sum of .... each, to be made and levied of their several goods and chattels, lands and tenements respectively, to the use of the Minister for Finance of Saorstát Eireann, if he the said A. B. fail in the condition endorsed. Taken and acknowledged the day and year first above mentioned, at .... before me, ...

The condition of the within-written recognizance is such, that whereas the said A. B. was this day charged before me, the Justice *or* Peace Commissioner within mentioned for that (etc., as in the warrant); if, therefore, the said A. B. will appear at the next sitting of the District Court (*or* of the Circuit Court, *or* of the High Court *or* of the Central Criminal Court, as the case may be) to be holden in and for the District (*or* as the case may be) and there surrender himself into the custody of the keeper of the (common gaol) there, and plead to such charge or indictment as may be preferred against him, and take his trial upon the same, and not depart the said Court without leave, then the said recognizance to be void, or else to stand in full force and virtue.

Criminal Justice (Administration) Act 1924, s 13

"RELEVANT DATE"

"relevant date" means the date of conviction for the drug trafficking offence concerned.

Criminal Justice Act 2006, s 87

"RELEVANT PLACE"

In *subsection (5)*, "relevant place" means any place which, on or after the commencement of this section, is a designated centre.

Criminal Law (Insanity) Act 2006, s 17(6)

"RELOCATED WITNESS"

In this section "relocated witness" means any person who intends to give or has given evidence in proceedings for an offence and who as a consequence has moved residence, under any programme operated by the Garda Síochána for the protection of witnesses, to any place, whether within or outside the State.

Criminal Justice Act 1999, s 40(3)

"REMAND INSTITUTION"

"remand institution" means an institution (other than a prison) whose use for the purposes of this Act has been approved of by the Minister.

Criminal Justice Act 1960, s 1

"REMISSION FROM THE SENTENCE"

"remission from the sentence" means, in relation to the sentence imposed on a person, the remission which the person may earn from the sentence under the rules or practice whereby prisoners generally may earn remission of sentence by industry and good conduct.

Criminal Justice Act 2006, s 87

"remission from the sentence" means, in relation to the sentence imposed on a person, the remission which he or she may earn from that sentence under the rules or practice whereby prisoners generally may earn remission of sentence by industry and good conduct.

Criminal Justice Act 2007, s 24(1)

"REQUESTER"

Where a person (in this section referred to as 'the requester') has had records taken in pursuance of powers conferred by section 6 or 6A of this Act or section 12 of the Act of 2006, and proceedings for an offence to which section 4 applies—

(*a*) are not instituted against the requester within the period of twelve months from the date of the taking of the records, and the failure to institute such proceedings within that period is not due to the fact that he or she has absconded or cannot be found, or

(*b*) have been so instituted and—

(i) the requester is acquitted,

(ii) the charge against the requester in respect of the offence concerned is dismissed under section 4E of the Criminal Procedure Act 1967, or

(iii) the proceedings are discontinued,

he or she may request the Commissioner to have the records concerned destroyed or their use limited.

Where a person (in this section referred to as 'the requester') has had records taken in pursuance of powers conferred by section 6 or 6A of this Act or section 12 of the Act of 2006, and proceedings for an offence to which section 4 applies—

(*a*) are not instituted against the requester within the period of twelve months from the date of the taking of the records, and the failure to institute such proceedings within that period is not due to the fact that he or she has absconded or cannot be found, or

(*b*) have been so instituted and—

(i) the requester is acquitted,

(ii) the charge against the requester in respect of the offence concerned is dismissed under section 4E of the Criminal Procedure Act 1967, or

(iii) the proceedings are discontinued,

he or she may request the Commissioner to have the records concerned destroyed or their use limited.

Criminal Justice Act 1984, s 8(1) substituted by the Criminal Justice Act 2007, s 49

"REVENUE OFFENCE"

In this section "revenue offence" means, in relation to an issuing state, an offence in connection with taxes, duties, customs or exchange control.

European Arrest Warrant Act 2003, s 38(3)

"REVIEW BOARD"

On the establishment day there shall stand established a board to be known as An Bord Athbhreithnithe Meabhair-Shláinte (An Dlí Coiriúil) or, in the English Language, the Mental Health (Criminal Law) Review Board (in this Act referred to as "the Review Board") to perform the functions conferred on it by or under this Act.

(2) The Review Board shall be independent in the exercise of its functions under this Act and shall have regard to the welfare and safety of the person whose detention it reviews under this Act and to the public interest.

(3) The provisions of Schedule 1 shall have effect in relation to the Review Board.

Criminal Law (Insanity) Act 2006, s 11

"ROAD"

the Word 'Road' shall include 'Highway' or other public Thoroughfare, and 'Street' shall include any Lane or Passage in any Town.

Summary Jurisdiction (Ireland) Act 1851, s XXV

S

"SCHENEGEN CONVENTION"

"'Schengen Convention' means the Convention implementing the Schengen Agreement of 14 June 1985 between the Governments of the States of the Benelux Economic Union, the Federal Republic of Germany and the French Republic on the gradual abolition of checks at their common borders done at Schengen on 19 June 1990 and includes any amendment to or modification of that Convention whether before or after the passing of this Act but does not include the Council Decision.

European Arrest Warrant Act 2003, s 2(1) inserted by Criminal Justice (Miscellaneous Provisions) Act 2009, s 4(d)

Criminal Justice (Miscellaneous Provisions) Act 2009, s 21(1)

"SENIOR MEMBER OF THE GARDA"

"senior member of the Garda Síochána" means a member of the Garda Síochána not below the rank of a superintendent.

Criminal Justice Act 2006, s 113

"SENTENCE"

"sentence" includes a sentence of imprisonment and any other order made by a court in dealing with a convicted person other than—

(*a*) an order under section 17 of the Lunacy (Ireland) Act, 1821, or section 2 (2) of the Trial of Lunatics Act, 1883, or
(*b*) an order postponing sentence for the purpose of obtaining a medical or psychiatric report or a report by a probation officer.

Criminal Justice Act 1993, s 1(1)

"sentence" includes a sentence of imprisonment and an order postponing sentence.

Criminal Justice Act 2006, s 87

"SENTENCING COURT"

"sentencing court" means the court referred to in *section 2 (1)*.

Criminal Justice Act 1993, s 1(1)

If it appears to the Director of Public Prosecutions that a sentence imposed by a court (in this Act referred to as the "sentencing court") on conviction of a person on indictment was unduly lenient, he may apply to the Court of Criminal Appeal to review the sentence.

Criminal Justice Act 1993, s 2(1)

"SERIOUS HARM"

"serious harm" means injury which creates a substantial risk of death or which causes permanent disfigurement or loss or impairment of the mobility of the body as a whole or of the function of any particular member or organ.

Criminal Justice Act 2006, s 176(1)

"SEXUAL ABUSE"

"sexual abuse" means an offence under paragraphs 1 to 13 and 16(*a*) and (*b*) of the Schedule to the Sex Offenders Act 2001.

Criminal Justice Act 2006, s 176(1)

"SHIP"

"ship" includes any boat or other vessel.

Criminal Law (Jurisdiction) Act 1976, s 10(3)

"SIS"

'SIS' means the system referred to in Title IV of the Schengen Convention or, as appropriate, the system established under Chapter 1 of the Council Decision.".

European Arrest Warrant Act 2003, s 2(1) inserted by Criminal Justice (Miscellaneous Provisions) Act 2009, s 4(d)

"SPECIAL COURT"

"special court" means a special court established under Article 38.3.1° of the Constitution.

Criminal Law (Insanity) Act 2006, s 1

"SPECIFIED DATE"

the date (in this section referred to as the "specified date") on which it proposes to pass sentence should the person contravene a condition of the order, being a date that falls not later than 6 months after the making of the order, and.

Criminal Justice Act 2006, s 100(3)(A)

"STATE AUTHORITY"

"State authority" means any authority being—

(*a*) a Minister of State, or
(*b*) the Commissioners of Public Works in Ireland, or
(*c*) the Irish Land Commission, or
(*d*) the Revenue Commissioners, or
(e) the Attorney General.

Courts (Supplemental Provisions) Act 1961, s 2

"STATEMENT"

"statement" means a statement the making of which is duly proved and includes—

(*a*) any representation of fact, whether in words or otherwise,
(*b*) a statement which has been videorecorded or audiorecorded, and
(*c*) part of a statement.

Criminal Justice Act 2006, s 15

"STATION"

"station" means a Garda Síochána station.

SI No 119 of 1987, art 2

"station" means a Garda Síochána station to which these Regulations apply.

SI No 74/1997, art 2

"STATUTE"

the word "statute" means any statute being—

(*a*) a pre-union Irish statute, or
(*b*) a British statute, or
(*c*) a Saorstát Éireann statute, or
(*d*) an Act of the Oireachtas (whether passed before or after this Act).

Statutory Instruments Act 1947, s 1(1)

"STATUTORY DECLARATION"

"statutory declaration" includes a statutory declaration made under *section* 17 or *18*.

Criminal Justice Act 2006, s 15

17.— (1) A person who makes a statement to a member of the Garda Síochána during the investigation of an arrestable offence (not being a person who is at that time suspected by any such member of having committed it) may make a statutory declaration that the statement is true to the best of the person's knowledge and belief.

(2) For the purposes of section 1(1)(*d*) of the Statutory Declarations Act 1938 a member of the Garda Síochána may take and receive a statutory declaration made under *subsection (1)*.

(3) Instead of taking and receiving such a statutory declaration the member may take the person's statement on oath or affirmation and for that purpose may administer the oath or affirmation to him or her.

Criminal Justice Act 2006, s 17

(2) A person who makes a statement to a competent person in the course of the performance of the competent person's official duties may make a statutory declaration that the statement is true to the best of the person's knowledge and belief.

(3) For the purposes of section 1(1)(*d*) of the Statutory Declarations Act 1938 a competent person may take and receive a statutory declaration made under *subsection (2)*.

Criminal Justice Act 2006, s 18

"STATUTORY INSTRUMENT"

the expression "statutory instrument" means an order, regulation, rule, scheme or bye-law made in exercise of a power conferred by statute.

Statutory Instruments Act 1947, s 1(1)

"STREET"

and 'Street' shall include any Lane or Passage in any Town.

Summary Jurisdiction (Irl) Act 1851, xxv

"SUPERINTENDANT"

"superintendent" means a superintendent of the Garda Síochána and, in relation to a district, means a superintendent who is in charge of the district and includes an inspector of the Garda Síochána who is in charge of the district in the superintendent's absence.

SI No 119/1987, s 2

T

"TAPE"

"tape" means any magnetic tape or other recording medium on which an electronic recording may be made or copied.

SI No 74/1997, art 2

"TELECOMMUNICATIONS MESSAGES"

"telecommunications message" have the meanings that they have respectively in the Act of 1983, but, for the avoidance of doubt, it is hereby declared that the latter expression includes a telegram.

Interception of Postal Packets and Telecommunications Messages (Regulation) Act 1993, s 1

"THE ACTING DIRECTOR"

"the Acting Director" has the meaning assigned to it by section 9 of this Act.

Prosecution of Offences Act 1974, s 1

In the event of the office of Director being vacant, the Taoiseach may appoint a person to be Director until such time as an appointment is made under section 2 of this Act.

(*b*) A person appointed under this subsection shall hold office upon such terms and conditions as may be determined by the Taoiseach after consultation with the Minister for the Public Service.

(2) (*a*) In the event of the incapacity through illness of the Director, the Taoiseach may appoint a person who shall be known as the Acting Director of Public Prosecutions and who is referred to in this Act as the Acting Director and the Acting Director shall perform all the functions conferred on the Director by this Act.

(*b*) No Acting Director shall be appointed to hold office for a term in excess of 12 months.

(*c*) The Acting Director shall hold office upon such terms and conditions as may be determined by the Taoiseach after consultation with the Minister for the Public Service.

Prosecution of Offences Act 1974, s 9

"THE CENTRAL MENTAL HOSPITAL"

"the Central Mental Hospital" means the Central Criminal Lunatic Asylum established in pursuance of the Central Criminal Lunatic Asylum (Ireland) Act, 1845.

Criminal Justice Act 1960, s 1

Criminal Lunatic Asylum (Ireland) Act 1845

The Central Mental Hospital is hereby designated as a centre (in this Act referred to as a "designated centre") for the reception, detention and care or treatment of persons or classes of persons committed or transferred thereto under the provisions of this Act.

Criminal Law (Insanity) Act 2006, s 3

"THE CIVIL SERVICE"

"the Civil Service" has the meaning assigned to it by the Civil Service Commissioners Act, 1956.

Prosecution of Offences Act 1974, s 1

"the Civil Service" means the Civil Service of the Government and the Civil Service of the State.

Civil Service Commissioners Act 1956, s 2(1)

"THE COMMISSIONER"

"the Commissioner" means the Commissioner of the Garda Síochána.

Criminal Justice (Joint Investigation Teams) Act 2004, s 1(1)

"THE COUNCIL FRAMEWORK DECISION"

"the Council Framework Decision" means the Framework Decision of 13 June 2002 of the Council of the European Union on joint investigation teams[1], the text of which is for convenience of reference set out—

(*a*) in *Part 1* of the *Schedule* to this Act, in the case of the Irish language text, and
(*b*) in *Part 2* of that *Schedule*, in the case of the English language text.

Criminal Justice (Joint Investigation Teams) Act 2004, s 1(1)

"THE CUSTODY REGULATIONS"

"the Custody Regulations" means the Criminal Justice Act, 1984 (Treatment of Persons in Custody in Garda Síochána Stations) Regulations, 1987 (S.I. No. 119 of 1987).

SI No 74/1997, art 2

"THE DEFENCE FORCES"

"the Defence Forces" means the Permanent Defence Force within the meaning of the Defence Act, 1954.

Criminal Law Act 1976, s 1

the expression "the Defence Forces" means the defence forces to be raised and maintained under this Act.

The Defence Act 1954, s 2(1)

"THE DIRECTOR"

"the Director" has the meaning assigned to it by section 2 of this Act.

Prosecution of Offences Act 1974, s 1(1)

There is hereby established the office of Director of Public Prosecutions and the holder of the office shall be known as the Director of Public Prosecutions and is referred to subsequently in this Act as the Director.

Prosecution of Offences Act 1974, s 1(1)

"THE PRESCRIBED PERIOD"

the definition of "prescribed period":

"(*c*) where the accused, on being sent forward for sentence, changes his plea to not guilty, the period of fourteen days after the accused is, in accordance with section

13(4)(*b*) of the Criminal Procedure Act, 1967, served with the documents referred to in section 4B(1) of that Act, or".

Criminal Justice Act 1984, s 20(8)d as substituted by Criminal Justice Act 1999, s 16(3)

"THE STATEMENT"

Where a person has been sent forward for trial for an arrestable offence, a statement relevant to the proceedings made by a witness (in this section referred to as "the statement") may, with the leave of the court, be admitted in accordance with this section as evidence of any fact mentioned in it if the witness, although available for cross-examination—

(*a*) refuses to give evidence,
(*b*) denies making the statement, or
(*c*) gives evidence which is materially inconsistent with it.

(2) The statement may be so admitted if—

(*a*) the witness confirms, or it is proved, that he or she made it,
(*b*) the court is satisfied—
  (i) that direct oral evidence of the fact concerned would be admissible in the proceedings,
  (ii) that it was made voluntarily, and
  (iii) that it is reliable,

and

(*c*) either—
  (i) the statement was given on oath or affirmation or contains a statutory declaration by the witness to the effect that the statement is true to the best of his or her knowledge or belief, or
  (ii) the court is otherwise satisfied that when the statement was made the witness understood the requirement to tell the truth.

(3) In deciding whether the statement is reliable the court shall have regard to—

(*a*) whether it was given on oath or affirmation or was videorecorded, or
(*b*) if *paragraph (a)* does not apply in relation to the statement, whether by reason of the circumstances in which it was made, there is other sufficient evidence in support of its reliability,

and shall also have regard to—

(i) any explanation by the witness for refusing to give evidence or for giving evidence which is inconsistent with the statement, or
(ii) where the witness denies making the statement, any evidence given in relation to the denial.

(4) The statement shall not be admitted in evidence under this section if the court is of opinion—

(*a*) having had regard to all the circumstances, including any risk that its admission would be unfair to the accused or, if there are more than one accused, to any of them, that in the interests of justice it ought not to be so admitted, or

(*b*) that its admission is unnecessary, having regard to other evidence given in the proceedings.

(5) In estimating the weight, if any, to be attached to the statement regard shall be had to all the circumstances from which any inference can reasonably be drawn as to its accuracy or otherwise.

(6) This section is without prejudice to sections 3 to 6 of the Criminal Procedure Act 1865 and section 21 (proof by written statement) of the Act of 1984.

Criminal Justice Act 2006, s 16(1)

"THIRD COUNTRY"

"third country" means a country other than the State or a Member State.

European Arrest Warrant Act 2003, s 2(1)

"TRIAL JUDGE"

"trial judge" and "judge", in relation to proceedings before a Special Criminal Court, means a member of that Court, and the references in *subsections (2) (a)* and *(5) (a)* to an accused person being sent forward for trial include, where appropriate, references to such a person being charged before that Court.

Criminal Justice Act 2006, s 181(11)

"TRUE COPY"

"true copy" shall be read in accordance with section 12 *(7)*.

European Arrest Warrant Act 2003, s 2(1)

For the purposes of this Act, a document shall be deemed to be a true copy of an original document if it has been certified as a true copy of the original document by—

(*a*) the issuing judicial authority, or

(*b*) an officer of the central authority of the issuing state duly authorised to certify it as a true copy.

and where the seal of the issuing judicial authority or the central authority of the issuing state has been affixed to the document, judicial notice shall be taken of that seal.

European Arrest Warrant Act 2003, s 12(7)

V

"VEHICLE"

"vehicle" includes a railway train or any other railway vehicle.

Criminal Law (Jurisdiction) Act 1976, s 10(3)

"VIDEO RECORDING"

"videorecording" includes a recording, on any medium, from which a moving image may by any means be produced, together with the accompanying soundrecording, and cognate words shall be construed accordingly.

Criminal Justice Act 2006, s 15

W

"WITNESS ORDER"

In this section, 'witness order' means an order made under subsection (1).

Criminal Procedure Act 1967, s 4k(4) inserted by Criminal Justice Act 1999, s 9

The trial court may, in relation to the trial of the accused, make an order requiring a person whose statement of evidence was served on the accused or whose deposition was taken to—

(*a*) attend before the trial court and give evidence at the trial of the accused, and
(*b*) produce to that court any document or thing specified in the order.

Criminal Procedure Act 1967, s 4k(1) inserted by Criminal Justice Act 1999, s 9

"WITNESS SUMMONS"

In this section, 'witness summons' means a summons issued under subsection (1).

Criminal Procedure Act 1967, s 4L(4) inserted by Criminal Justice Act 1999, s 9

On application by the prosecutor or the accused, a summons may be issued out of the trial court requiring the person to whom the summons is directed to—

(*a*) attend before the trial court and give evidence at the trial of the accused, and
(*b*) produce to that court any document or thing specified in the summons,

unless the court is satisfied that the person proposed to be summoned cannot give any material evidence or, as the case may be, produce any document or thing likely to be material evidence.

Criminal Procedure Act 1967, s 4L(1) inserted by Criminal Justice Act 1999, s 9

"WORKING COPY"

"working copy" means any tape, that is not the master tape, used in the equipment.

SI No 74/97, art 2

Y

"YEAR AND A DAY"

In this section, "the 'year and a day' rule" means the rule of law that an act or omission is conclusively presumed not to have caused a person's death if more than a year and a day elapsed between the act or omission and the death.

(2) The "year and a day" rule is hereby abolished for all purposes, including—

(*a*) for the purposes of offences involving the death of a person, and
(*b*) for the purpose of determining whether a person committed suicide.

(3) *Subsection (2)* does not affect the continued application of the "year and a day" rule to any case where the act or omission, or the last of the acts or omissions, that caused the death occurred before the day on which this Act is passed.

Criminal Justice Act 1999, s 38

SEXUAL OFFENCES

A

"A RAPE OFFENCE"

'a rape offence' means any of the following, namely, rape, attempted rape, burglary with intent to commit rape, aiding, abetting, counselling and procuring rape, attempted rape or burglary with intent to commit rape, and incitement to rape and, other than in sections 2 (2) and 8 of this Act, rape under section 4, attempted rape under section 4, aiding, abetting, counselling and procuring rape under section 4 or attempted rape under section 4 and incitement to rape under section 4.

Rape Act 1981, s 1 as amended by Criminal Law Rape (Amendment) Act 1990, s 12

"A SEXUAL ASSAULT OFFENCE"

'a sexual assault offence' means a rape offence and any of the following, namely, aggravated sexual assault, attempted aggravated sexual assault, sexual assault, attempted sexual assault, aiding, abetting, counselling and procuring aggravated sexual assault, attempted aggravated sexual assault, sexual assault or attempted sexual assault, incitement to aggravated sexual assault or sexual assault and conspiracy to commit any of the foregoing offences.".

Rape Act 1981, s 1 as amended by Criminal Law Rape (Amendment) Act 1990, s 12

"AGGRAVATED SEXUAL ASSAULT"

(1) In this Act "aggravated sexual assault" means a sexual assault that involves serious violence or the threat of serious violence or is such as to cause injury, humiliation or degradation of a grave nature to the person assaulted.

Criminal Law Rape (Amendment) Act 1990, s 3(1)

"APPLICANT"

"applicant" means the person referred to in *subsection (1)*.

Sex Offenders Act 2001, s 11(10)

A person who, by reason of *sections* 7 and *8*, is subject to the requirements of this Part for a period of an indefinite duration may apply to the court for an order discharging the person from the obligation to comply with those requirements on the ground that the interests of the common good are no longer served by his or her continuing to be subject to them.

Sex Offenders Act 2001, s 11(1)

"applicant" means a member of the Garda Síochána not below the rank referred to in *section 16* who has applied to the court for the making of a sex offender order and, in relation to such an order that is in force, means any member of the Garda Síochána.

Sex Offenders Act 2001, s 15

"AUDIO REPRESENTATION"

"audio representation" includes—

(*a*) any such representation by means of tape, computer disk or other thing from which such a representation can be produced, and

(*b*) any tape, computer disk or other thing on which any such representation is recorded.

Child Trafficking and Pornography Act 1998, s 2

B

"BROTHER"

In this Act the expressions 'brother' and 'sister,' respectively, include half-brother and half-sister, and the provisions of this Act shall apply whether the relationship between the person charged with an offence under this Act and the person with whom the offence is alleged to have been committed, is or is not traced through lawful wedlock.

Punishment of Incest Act 1908, s 3

C

"CHILD"

"child" means a person under the age of 17 years.

Child Trafficking and Pornography Act 1998, s 2

'child' means a person under the age of 17 years.

Criminal Law (Sexual Offences) Act 1993, s 6(4) inserted by Children Act 2001, s 250 substituted by Criminal Law (Sexual Offences) (Amendment) Act 2007, s 2

"child" means a person who is less than 18 years of age.

Sex Offenders Act 2001, s 25

"CHILD PORNOGRAPHY"

"child pornography" means—

(*a*) any visual representation—
  (i) that shows or, in the case of a document, relates to a person who is or is depicted as being a child and who is engaged in or is depicted as being engaged in explicit sexual activity,
  (ii) that shows or, in the case of a document, relates to a person who is or is depicted as being a child and who is or is depicted as witnessing any such activity by any person or persons, or
  (iii) whose dominant characteristic is the depiction, for a sexual purpose, of the genital or anal region of a child,

(*b*) any audio representation of a person who is or is represented as being a child and who is engaged in or is represented as being engaged in explicit sexual activity,

(*c*) any visual or audio representation that advocates, encourages or counsels any sexual activity with children which is an offence under any enactment, or

(*d*) any visual representation or description of, or information relating to, a child that indicates or implies that the child is available to be used for the purpose of sexual exploitation within the meaning of *section 3*,

irrespective of how or through what medium the representation, description or information has been produced, transmitted or conveyed and, without prejudice to the generality of the foregoing, includes any representation, description or information produced by or from computer-graphics or by any other electronic or mechanical means but does not include—

(I) any book or periodical publication which has been examined by the Censorship of Publications Board and in respect of which a prohibition order under the Censorship of Publications Acts, 1929 to 1967, is not for the time being in force,

(II) any film in respect of which a general certificate or a limited certificate under the Censorship of Films Acts, 1923 to 1992, is in force, or

(III) any video work in respect of which a supply certificate under the Video Recordings Acts, 1989 and 1992, is in force;

"document" includes—

Child Trafficking and Pornography Act 1998, s 2

"COMPLAINANT"

'complainant' means a person in relation to whom a sexual assault offence is alleged to have been committed.

Criminal Law (Rape) Act 1981, s 1(1) as substituted by Criminal Law (Rape) (Amendment) Act 1990, s 12

"CONSULTANT PSYCHIATRIST"

In this section and in section 19C of this Act 'consultant psychiatrist' has the same meaning as in the Mental Health Act 2001.

Courts-Martial Appeals Act 1983, s 19B(6) inserted by Defence (Amendment) Act 2007, Sch 4, Pt 1

"CONTRACT OF EMPLOYMENT"

"contract of employment" means—

(*a*) a contract of service or apprenticeship, or
(*b*) any other contract whereby an individual agrees with another person, who is carrying on the business of an employment agency within the meaning of the Employment Agency Act, 1971, and is acting in the course of that business, to do or perform personally any work or service for a third person (whether or not the third person is a party to the contract),

whether the contract is express or implied and if express, whether it is oral or in writing.

Sex Offenders Act 2001, s 25

"CONVICTION"

"conviction" (other than in *sections 12, 22, 26(8)* and *33*) includes a finding of guilty but insane and "convicted" and cognate expressions shall be construed accordingly.

Sex Offenders Act 2001, s 2

"COURT"

"court" means any court exercising criminal jurisdiction and includes court-martial.

Sex Offenders Act 2001, s 2

D

"DATE OF THE APPLICANTS RELEASE FROM PRISON"

"date of the applicant's release from prison" means the date on which the applicant's sentence of imprisonment referred to in *section 8 (3)* expires or, as the case may be, his or her remission from the sentence begins.

Sex Offenders Act 2001, s 11(10)

"DISTRIBUTES"

In this section "distributes", in relation to child pornography, includes parting with possession of it to, or exposing or offering it for acquisition by, another person, and the reference to "distributing" in that context shall be construed accordingly.

Child Trafficking and Pornography Act 1998, s 5(2)

"DOCUMENT"

"document" includes—

(*a*) any book, periodical or pamphlet, and
(*b*) where appropriate, any tape, computer disk or other thing on which data capable of conversion into any such document is stored.

Child Trafficking and Pornography Act 1998, s 2

H

"HOME ADDRESS"

"home address", in relation to any person, means the address of his or her sole or main residence or, if he or she has no such residence, his or her most usual place of abode or, if he or she has no such abode, the place which he or she regularly visits.

Sex Offenders Act 2001, s 10(11)

L

"LOITERING"

A member of the Garda Síochána who has reasonable cause to suspect that a person is loitering in a street or public place in order to solicit or importune another person or other persons for the purposes of prostitution may direct that person to leave immediately that street or public place.

(2) A person who without reasonable cause fails to comply with a direction under *subsection (1)* shall be guilty of an offence and shall be liable on summary conviction to a fine not exceeding—

(*a*) £250, in the case of a first conviction,
(*b*) £500, in the case of a second conviction, or
(*c*) £500 or to imprisonment for a term not exceeding 4 weeks or to both, in the case of a third or any subsequent conviction.

(3) In this section "loitering" includes loitering in a motor vehicle.

Criminal Law (Sexual Offences) Act 1993, s 8(3)

M

"MAN"

In this Act "man" and "woman" include respectively a male and a female person of any age; but this does not affect any rule of law by virtue of which a male person is treated by reason of his age as being incapable of committing an offence of any particular kind.

Criminal Law (Rape) Act 1981, s 1(3)

"MENTALLY IMPAIRED"

In this section "mentally impaired" means suffering from a disorder of the mind, whether through mental handicap or mental illness, which is of such a nature or degree as to render a person incapable of living an independent life or of guarding against serious exploitation.

Criminal Law (Sexual Offences) Act 1993, s 5(5)

P

"PERSON IN AUTHORITY"

"person in authority" means—

(*a*) a parent, step-parent, guardian, grandparent, uncle or aunt of the victim,
(*b*) any person who is, for the time being, in *loco parentis* to the victim, or
(*c*) any person who is, for the time being, responsible for the education, supervision or welfare of the victim.

Criminal Law (Sex Offences) Act 2006, s 1

"PHOTOGRAPHIC REPRESENTATION"

"photographic representation" includes the negative as well as the positive version.

Child Trafficking and Pornography Act 1998, s 2

"PLACE"

In this section "place" includes any dwelling, any building or part of a building and any vehicle, vessel or structure.

Child Trafficking and Pornography Act 1998, s 7(6)

"POLICE"

"police" means, in relation to the first-mentioned place in *subsection (1)*, any police force in that place, or a member thereof, whether that force is organised at a national, regional or local level.

Sex Offenders Act 2001, s 13(6)

"PRINCIPAL OFFENCE" SEE UNDER THE

"PROBATION AND WELFARE OFFICER"

"probation and welfare officer" means a person appointed by the Minister to be a probation and welfare officer or to be a welfare officer or probation officer.

Sex Offenders Act 2001, s 27

"PROBATION AND WELFARE SERVICE"

"probation and welfare service" means the probation and welfare service of the Department of Justice, Equality and Law Reform.

Sex Offenders Act 2001, s 27

"PROSTITUTE"

In this Act and in any other enactment, whether passed before or after this Act, a reference to a prostitute includes a reference to a male person who is a prostitute and a reference to prostitution shall be construed accordingly.

Criminal Law (Sexual Offences) Act 1993, s 1(4)

"PUBLIC PLACE"

"public place" means any place to which the public have access whether as of right or by permission and whether subject to or free of charge.

Criminal Law (Sexual Offences) Act 1993, s 1

Q

"QUALIFYING PERIOD"

"qualifying period" means—

(*a*) a period of 7 days, or
(*b*) 2 or more periods, in any period of 12 months, which (taken together) amount to 7 days.

Criminal Justice Act 2006, s 92(11)

"qualifying period" means—

(*a*) a period of 7 days, or
(*b*) 2 or more periods, in any period of 12 months, which (taken together) amount to 7 days.

Sex Offenders Act 2001, s 10(11)

R

"RAPE UNDER SECTION 4"

In this Act "rape under *section 4*" means a sexual assault that includes—

(*a*) penetration (however slight) of the anus or mouth by the penis, or
(*b*) penetration (however slight) of the vagina by any object held or manipulated by another person.

(2) A person guilty of rape under *section 4* shall be liable on conviction on indictment to imprisonment for life.

(3) Rape under *section 4* shall be a felony.

Criminal Law (Rape) Amendment Act 1990, s 4

"RELEVANT DATE"

In this Part, "relevant date" means the date of conviction for the sexual offence concerned.

Sex Offenders Act 2001, s 6

"RELEVANT WORK"

In this section "relevant work" means work or a service (including State work or a service) a necessary and regular part of which consists, mainly, of the person referred to in *subsection (3), (5)* or *(6)* having unsupervised access to, or contact with, a child or children or a mentally impaired person or persons.

Sex Offenders Act 2001, s 26

"REMISSION FROM THE SENTENCE"

"remission from the sentence" means, in relation to the sentence imposed on a person, the remission which the person may earn from the sentence under the rules or practice whereby prisoners generally may earn remission of sentence by industry and good conduct.

Sex Offenders Act 2001, s 2

"RESPONDENT"

"respondent" means a person in respect of whom an application for a sex offender order has been made or in respect of whom such an order has been made.

Sex Offenders Act 2001, s 15

S

"SENTENCE"

"sentence" includes a sentence of imprisonment and any other order made by a court in dealing with a convicted person, including—

(*a*) an order under section 2(2) of the Trial of Lunatics Act, 1883, and
(*b*) an order postponing sentence.

Sex Offenders Act 2001, s 2

"SENTENCE INVOLVING POST RELEASE SUPERVISION"

"sentence involving post-release supervision" shall be construed in accordance with *section 29 (1)*;

(1) A court may impose on a sex offender in respect of the sexual offence concerned a sentence involving post-release supervision, that is to say a sentence which consists of—

(*a*) the imposition of a sentence of imprisonment for a specified term (whether in addition to the imposition of a fine or not), and
(*b*) a provision that during a specified period ("the supervision period") commencing on the date of the offender's release from prison, the offender

shall be under the supervision of a probation and welfare officer and requiring the offender to comply with such conditions as are specified in the sentence for securing that supervision.

Sex Offenders Act 2001, s 7(1)

"SEX OFFENDER"

"sex offender" means a person who, after the commencement of this Part, is convicted of a sexual offence for which, in the opinion of the court before which the person appears, the appropriate sentence is, apart from the provisions of this Part, one of imprisonment for any term (whether in addition to the imposition of a fine or not).

Sex Offenders Act 2001, s 27(1)

"SEX OFFENDERS ORDER"

If, on application to it in that behalf by a member of the Garda Síochána not below the rank of Chief Superintendent, it appears to the court, on evidence tendered by the applicant, that the conditions specified in *subsection (2)* are satisfied in respect of the respondent, the court may make an order (in this Act referred to as a "sex offender order") prohibiting the respondent from doing one or more things specified in the order.

(2) The conditions mentioned in *subsection (1)* are that—

(*a*) the respondent has been convicted, before or after the commencement of this Part, either—

(i) in the State of a sexual offence, or

(ii) in a place outside the State of an offence and the act constituting that offence would, if done in the State, constitute a sexual offence (within the meaning of this Act) under the law of the State,

and

(*b*) the respondent has, at a time referred to in *subsection (3)*, acted on one or more occasions in such a way as to give reasonable grounds for believing that an order under this section is necessary to protect the public from serious harm from him or her.

(3) The time mentioned in *paragraph (b)* of *subsection (2)* is any time subsequent to the date of the respondent's release from prison or, as the case may be, the date on which the sentence imposed on the respondent in respect of the offence referred to in that subsection otherwise ceases to be in force, being in either case a time after the commencement of this Part.

(4) A sex offender order shall contain only such prohibitions on the respondent's doing a thing or things as the court considers necessary for the purpose of protecting the public from serious harm from the respondent.

(5) References in this section to protecting the public from serious harm from the respondent shall be construed as references to protecting a member or members of the public from death or serious personal injury, whether physical or psychological, which would be occasioned if the respondent were to commit a sexual offence at a time subsequent to the making of the application under this section.

(6) A sex offender order shall continue in force until the expiration of—

(*a*) 5 years from the date of notification of its making being given to the respondent, or
(*b*) such longer period as the court may provide for in the order.

(7) For so long as a sex offender order is in force, *Part 2* shall have effect as if—

(*a*) the respondent were subject to the requirements of that Part, and
(*b*) "relevant date" (within the meaning of that Part) were the date on which notification of the making of the sex offender order has been given to the respondent.

(8) *Subsection (7)* shall not operate to prevent a respondent's remaining subject to the requirements of *Part 2*, on the date that the sex offender order concerned ceases to be in force, if, by reason of the operation of *section 7* and *8* (including those sections as applied by *section 13*), he or she would remain so subject to those requirements.

(9) The reference in *subsection (3)* to the date of the respondent's release from prison is a reference to the date on which the sentence of imprisonment imposed on the respondent in respect of the offence referred to in *subsection (2)* (if such be the sentence imposed) expires or, as the case may be, the respondent's remission from the sentence begins.

Sex Offenders Act 2001, s 16

"SEXUAL ACT"

"sexual act" means—

(*a*) an act consisting of—
  (i) sexual intercourse, or
  (ii) buggery,

between persons who are not married to each other, or

(*b*) an act described in section 3(1) or 4(1) of the Act of 1990.

Criminal Law (Sexual Offences) Act 2006, s 1

"SEXUAL ASSAULT"

The offence of indecent assault upon any male person and the offence of indecent assault upon any female person shall be known as sexual assault.

Criminal Law (Rape) (Amendment) Act 1990, s 2(1)

"SEXUAL INTERCOURSE"

"sexual intercourse" shall be construed in accordance with section 1(2) of the Act of 1981.

Criminal Law (Sexual Offences) Act 2006, s 1

In this Act references to sexual intercourse shall be construed as references to carnal knowledge as defined in section 63 of the Offences against the Person Act, 1861, so far as it relates to natural intercourse (under which such intercourse is deemed complete on proof of penetration only).

Criminal Law (Rape) Act 1981, s 1(2)

"SEXUAL OFFENCES"

"sexual offence" shall be construed in accordance with section 3.

Sex Offenders Act 2001, s 2

(1) Each of the offences referred to in the *Schedule* shall, subject to *subsections (2)* and *(3)*, be a sexual offence for the purposes of this Act.

(2) An offence referred to in—

(*a*) *paragraph 2* of the *Schedule* (sexual assault or indecent assault),
(*b*) *paragraph 5* of the *Schedule* (incest by males),
(*c*) *paragraph 6* of the *Schedule* (incest by females of or over 17 years of age), or
(*d*) *paragraph 18, 19* or *20* of the *Schedule* in so far as it relates to an offence referred to in *paragraph (a), (b)* or *(c)*,

shall not be a sexual offence for the purposes of this Act if—

(i) the victim of or, as the case may be, the other party to the offence was aged, at the date of the offence's commission, 17 years or more, and
(ii) the person guilty of the offence has not, in respect of the offence, been sentenced to any punishment involving deprivation of liberty for a limited or

unlimited period of time or been made subject to any measure involving such deprivation of liberty.

(3) An offence referred to in—

(*a*) *paragraph 8* of the *Schedule* (defilement of girl between 15 and 17 years of age),
(*b*) *paragraph 11* of the *Schedule* (buggery of persons under 17 years of age),
(*c*) *paragraph 12* of the *Schedule* (gross indecency with males under 17 years of age), or
(*d*) *paragraph 18, 19* or *20* of the *Schedule* in so far as it relates to an offence referred to in *paragraph (a), (b)* or *(c)*,

shall not be a sexual offence for the purposes of this Act if—

(i) the victim of or, as the case may be, the other party to the offence was aged, at the date of the offence's commission, 15 years or more but less than 17 years, and
(ii) the person guilty of the offence was aged, at that date, not more than 3 years older than that victim or other party.

Sex Offenders Act 2001, s 3

Sexual Offences for Purposes of Act

1. Rape.

2. Sexual assault (whether the offence of which the person was convicted was known by that name or by the name "Indecent assault upon a female person" or "Indecent assault upon a male person").

3. Aggravated sexual assault (within the meaning of section 3 of the Act of 1990).

4. Rape under section 4 of the Act of 1990.

5. An offence under section 1 of the Act of 1908 (incest by males).

6. An offence under section 2 of the Act of 1908 (incest by females of or over 17 years of age).

7. An offence under section 1 of the Act of 1935 (defilement of girl under 15 years of age).

8. An offence under section 2 of the Act of 1935 (defilement of girl between 15 and 17 years of age).

9. The offence of buggery with a person or with an animal referred to in section 61 of the Act of 1861.

10. The offence of an attempt to commit such buggery referred to in section 62 of the Act of 1861.

Sexual Offences

11. An offence under section 3 of the Act of 1993 (buggery of persons under 17 years of age).

12. An offence under section 4 of the Act of 1993 (gross indecency with males under 17 years of age).

13. An offence under section 11 of the Criminal Law Amendment Act, 1885 (acts of gross indecency).

14. An offence under section 5 of the Act of 1993 (protection of mentally impaired persons).

15. An offence under section 4 of the Act of 1935 (defilement of mentally impaired females).

16. An offence under any of the following provisions of the Child Trafficking and Pornography Act, 1998—

(*a*) section 3 (child trafficking and taking, etc., child for sexual exploitation),
(*b*) section 4 (allowing child to be used for child pornography),
(*c*) section 5 (producing, distributing, etc., child pornography),
(*d*) section 6 (possession of child pornography).

17. An offence under section 2 of the Sexual Offences (Jurisdiction) Act, 1996 (sexual offences committed outside the State).

18. An offence consisting of attempting to commit an offence referred to in any of *paragraphs 1* to *17* of this Schedule (other than such an offence that itself consists of an attempt to do a particular act).

19. An offence consisting of aiding, abetting, counselling, procuring or inciting the commission of an offence referred to in any of *paragraphs 1* to *18* of this Schedule.

20. An offence consisting of conspiracy to commit an offence referred to in any foregoing paragraph of this Schedule.

Sex Offenders Act 2001, sched

"SISTER"

In this Act the expressions 'brother' and 'sister,' respectively, include half-brother and half-sister, and the provisions of this Act shall apply whether the relationship between the person charged with an offence under this Act and the person with whom the offence is alleged to have been committed, is or is not traced through lawful wedlock.

Punishment of Incest Act 1908, s 3

"SOLICITS OR IMPORTUNES"

"solicits or importunes" includes soliciting or importuning from or in a motor vehicle, and cognate words shall be construed accordingly.

Criminal Law (Sexual Offences) Act 1993, s 1(1)

"STATE WORK OR A SERVICE"

"State work or a service" means work done or a service performed by a person who—

(*a*) holds office under, or is otherwise in the service of the State (including as a civil servant, within the meaning of the Civil Service Regulation Act, 1956),
(*b*) is a member of the Garda Síochána or the Defence Forces,
(*c*) is an officer or servant of a local authority for the purposes of the Local Government Act, 1941, or
(*d*) is an officer or servant of a harbour authority, health board or vocational education committee.

Sex Offenders Act 2001, s 25

"STREET"

"street" includes any road, bridge, lane, footway, subway, square, court, alley or passsage, whether a thoroughfare or not, which is for the time being open to the public; and the doorways, entrances and gardens abutting on a street and any ground or car-park adjoining and open to a street, shall be treated as forming part of a street.

Criminal Law (Sexual Offences) Act 1993, s 1

"SUPERVISION PERIOD"

A court may impose on a sex offender in respect of the sexual offence concerned a sentence involving post-release supervision, that is to say a sentence which consists of—

(*a*) the imposition of a sentence of imprisonment for a specified term (whether in addition to the imposition of a fine or not), and

(*b*) a provision that during a specified period ("the supervision period") commencing on the date of the offender's release from prison, the offender shall be under the supervision of a probation and welfare officer and requiring the offender to comply with such conditions as are specified in the sentence for securing that supervision.

Sex Offenders Act 2001, s 29(1)(a) and (b)

(2) The aggregate of the sentence of imprisonment referred to in *subsection (1)(a)* and the supervision period shall not exceed the duration of the maximum term of imprisonment that may be imposed in respect of the sexual offence concerned.

(3) The term of the sentence of imprisonment referred to in *subsection (1)(a)* shall not be less than the term the court would have imposed if it had considered the matter apart from the provisions of this Part.

(4) In determining the period to be specified as the supervision period, the matters to which the court shall have regard shall include the matters referred to in *paragraphs (a)* to *(d)* of *section 28 (2)*.

(5) The reference in this section to the date of the offender's release from prison is a reference to the date on which the offender's sentence of imprisonment referred to in *subsection (1)(a)* expires or, as the case may be, the offender's remission from the sentence begins.

Sex Offenders Act, 2001, s 29(2)–(5)

"SUPERVISION PERIOD CONDITIONS"

A court may impose on a sex offender in respect of the sexual offence concerned a sentence involving post-release supervision, that is to say a sentence which consists of—

(*a*) the imposition of a sentence of imprisonment for a specified term (whether in addition to the imposition of a fine or not), and

(*b*) a provision that during a specified period ("the supervision period") commencing on the date of the offender's release from prison, the offender shall be under the supervision of a probation and welfare officer and requiring the offender to comply with such conditions as are specified in the sentence for securing that supervision.

Sex Offenders Act 2001, s s 27(1), 29(1)(b) or 30

V

"VISUAL REPRESENTATION"

"visual representation" includes—

(*a*) any photographic, film or video representation, any accompanying sound or any document,
(*b*) any copy of any such representation or document, and
(*c*) any tape, computer disk or other thing on which the visual representation and any accompanying sound are recorded.

Child Trafficking and Pornography Act 1998, s 2

W

"WOMAN"

In this Act "man" and "woman" include respectively a male and a female person of any age; but this does not affect any rule of law by virtue of which a male person is treated by reason of his age as being incapable of committing an offence of any particular kind.

Criminal Law (Rape) Act 1981, s 1(3)

SURVEILLANCE

A

"ACT OF 1993"

"Act of 1993" means the Interception of Postal Packets and Telecommunications Messages (Regulation) Act 1993.

Criminal Justice (Surveillance) Act 2009, s 1

"ARRESTABLE OFFENCE"

"arrestable offence" has the meaning it has in section 2 (as amended by section 8 of the Criminal Justice Act 2006) of the Criminal Law Act 1997.

Criminal Justice (Surveillance) Act 2009, s 1

"arrestable offence" means an offence for which a person of full capacity and not previously convicted may, under or by virtue of any enactment, **[or the common law]** be punished by imprisonment for a term of five years or by a more severe penalty and includes an attempt to commit any such offence.

Criminal Law Act 1997, s 2 as amended by the Criminal Justice Act 2006, s 8

"AUTHORISATION"

"authorisation" means an authorisation for the carrying out of surveillance issued under *section 5* or varied or renewed under *section 6*.

Criminal Justice (Surveillance) Act 2009, s 1

(1) An application under *section 4* for an authorisation and under *section 6* for a variation or renewal of an authorisation—

(*a*) shall be made *ex parte* and shall be heard otherwise than in public, and
(*b*) may be made to a judge assigned to any district court district.

(2) Subject to *subsection (4),* the judge shall issue such authorisation as he or she considers reasonable, if satisfied by information on oath of the superior officer concerned that—

(*a*) the requirements specified in *subsection (1), (2)* or *(3)*, as the case may be, of *section 4* are fulfilled, and
(*b*) to do so is justified, having regard to the matters referred to in *section 4(5)* and all other relevant circumstances.

(3) An information on oath of a superior officer specifying the grounds for his or her belief that the surveillance is necessary for the purpose of preventing the commission of arrestable offences referred to in *section 4(1)(b)*, or the commission of revenue offences referred to in *section 4(3)(b)*, need not specify a particular arrestable offence or a particular revenue offence, as the case may be, in respect of which the authorisation is being sought.

(4) The judge shall not issue an authorisation if he or she is satisfied that the surveillance being sought to be authorised is likely to relate primarily to communications protected by privilege.

(5) An authorisation may impose such conditions in respect of the surveillance authorised as the judge considers appropriate.

(6) An authorisation shall be in writing and shall specify—

(*a*) particulars of the surveillance device that is authorised to be used,
(*b*) the person who, or the place or thing that, is to be the subject of the surveillance,
(*c*) the name of the superior officer to whom it is issued,
(*d*) the conditions (if any) subject to which the authorisation is issued, and
(*e*) the date of expiry of the authorisation.

(7) An authorisation may authorise the superior officer named in it, or any member of the Garda Síochána, any member of the Defence Forces or any officer of the Revenue Commissioners designated by that superior officer, accompanied by any other person whom he or she considers necessary, to enter, if necessary by the use of reasonable force, any place for the purposes of initiating or carrying out the authorised surveillance, and withdrawing the authorised surveillance device, without the consent of a person who owns or is in charge of the place.

(8) An authorisation shall expire on the day fixed by the judge that he or she considers reasonable in the circumstances and that is not later than 3 months from the day on which it is issued.

(9) Subject to any conditions imposed by the judge under *subsection (5)*, an authorisation shall have effect both within the district court district to which the judge is assigned and in any other part of the State.

Criminal Justice (Surveillance) Act 2009, s 5

"AUTHORISED PERSON"

In this section—

"authorised person" means—

(*a*) a person referred to in section 62(4)(*a*) of the Garda Síochána Act 2005,
(*b*) the Minister for Defence,
(*c*) the Minister for Finance, and
(*d*) a person the disclosure to whom is—
 (i) authorised by the Commissioner of the Garda Síochána, the Chief of Staff of the Defence Forces or a Revenue Commissioner, or
 (ii) otherwise authorised by law.

Criminal Justice (Surveillance) Act 2009, s 13(4)

(i) the Minister
(ii) the Attorney General,
(iii) the Director of Public Prosecutions,
(iv) the Chief State Solicitor,
(v) the Criminal Assets Bureau,
(vi) the Comptroller and Auditor General,
(vii) the Ombudsman Commission or an officer of the Commission,
(viii) the Garda Síochána Inspectorate or an officer of the Inspectorate,
(ix) the Revenue Commissioners, or
(x) a member of either of the Houses of the Oireachtas where relevant to the proper discharge of the member's functions.

Garda Síochána Act 2005, s 62(4)(A)

C

"COMPLAINTS PROCEDURE"

(1) A person who believes that he or she might be the subject of an authorisation or an approval under *section 7* or *8* may apply to the Referee for an investigation into the matter.

(2) A superior officer who makes a report under *section 7(11)* or *8(9)*, or receives a report under *section 7(12)* or *8(10)*, may apply to the Referee for an investigation into a matter if he or she believes that such an investigation would be in the interests of justice.

(3) If an application is made under this section (other than one that the Referee considers to be frivolous or vexatious), the Referee shall investigate—

(*a*) whether an authorisation was issued or an approval was granted as alleged in the application, and
(*b*) if so, whether there has been a relevant contravention.

(4) If, after investigating the matter, the Referee concludes that there has been a relevant contravention, the Referee shall—

(*a*) notify the applicant, and any other person whose interests are materially affected by the relevant contravention, in writing of that conclusion, and
(*b*) make a report of his or her findings to the Taoiseach.

(5) In the circumstances referred to in *subsection (4)*, the Referee may also, if he or she is of opinion that the relevant contravention was material and that to do so would be justified in the circumstances, by order do one or more of the following things:

(*a*) direct—
  (i) the quashing of the authorisation or the reversal of the approval, and
  (ii) the destruction of the written record of approval concerned, the report under *section 7(11)* or *8(9)* concerned, and any information or documents obtained as a result of the authorisation or approval;
(*b*) make a recommendation for the payment of such sum, not exceeding 5,000, specified in the order by way of compensation to the person who was the subject of the authorisation or approval;
(*c*) report the matter and any recommendation under *paragraph (b)* to—
  (i) the Garda Síochána Ombudsman Commission, in the case of a contravention by the Garda Síochána,
  (ii) the Minister for Defence, in the case of a contravention by the Defence Forces,
  (iii) the Minister for Finance, in the case of a contravention by the Revenue Commissioners;
(*d*) report the matter and any recommendation under *paragraph (b)* to the judge designated under *section 12*.

(6) If the Referee is of opinion that, in all the circumstances, it would not be in the public interest to—

(*a*) notify, under *subsection (4)(a)*, the applicant or the other person, if any, of a conclusion that there has been a relevant contravention,
(*b*) direct the quashing, reversal or destruction under *subsection (5)(a)*, or
(*c*) make a recommendation for the payment of a sum by way of compensation under *subsection (5)(b)*, he or she shall decline to do so.

(7) If, after investigating the matter, the Referee concludes that there has not been a relevant contravention, the Referee shall give notice in writing to the applicant stating only that there has been no such contravention.

(8) A decision of the Referee under this section is final.

(9) A relevant contravention that is not material does not of itself constitute a cause of action at the suit of a person who was the subject of the authorisation or approval concerned.

(10) A person in charge of a Garda Síochána station within the meaning of section 99(10) of the Garda Síochána Act 2005, a place under the control of the Defence Forces or the Revenue Commissioners or any other place in which documents relevant to an investigation under this section are kept shall ensure that the Referee has access to those places, and to the authorisations, written records of approval, reports and other relevant documents that the Referee may request.

(11) The Referee—

(*a*) may, on his or her own initiative, and
(*b*) shall, where a case has been referred to him or her by the designated judge under *section 12(8)*, investigate whether there has been a relevant contravention and this section (other than *subsection (7)*) shall apply to such an investigation as if the references to "the applicant" in *subsections (4)* and (6) were to "the person who was the subject of the authorisation or approval".

(12) In this section—

"Referee" means the holder of the office of Complaints Referee under the Act of 1993;

"relevant contravention" means a contravention of a provision of *sections 4* to *8*.

Criminal Justice (Surveillance) Act 2009, s 11

D

"DOCUMENT"

"document" includes—

(*a*) any book, record or other written or printed material in any form, and
(*b*) any recording, including any data or information stored, maintained or preserved electronically or otherwise than in legible form.

Criminal Justice (Surveillance) Act 2009, s 1

J

"JUDGE"

"judge" means a judge of the District Court.

Criminal Justice (Surveillance) Act 2009, s 1

M

"MEMBER"

"member" means an officer, non-commissioned officer, private or seaman of the Defence Forces.

Defence (Amendment) Act 1990, s 1

"MEMBER OF THE DEFENCE FORCES"

"member of the Defence Forces" means a member of the Defence Forces within the meaning of section 1 of the Defence (Amendment) Act 1990, other than a member of the Reserve Defence Force within the meaning of the Defence Act 1954.

Criminal Justice (Surveillance) Act 2009, s 1

"MEMBER OF THE GARDA SÍOCHÁNA"

"member of the Garda Síochána" means a member of the Garda Síochána within the meaning of section 3 of the Garda Síochána Act 2005, other than a person referred to in paragraph (*b*) of that definition.

Criminal Justice (Surveillance) Act 2009, s 1

"member", in relation to the Garda Síochána, means—

(*a*) a member of any rank (including the Garda Commissioner) appointed under *Part 2* or under an enactment repealed by this Act, and

(*b*) a reserve member, but does not include a member of the civilian staff of the Garda Síochána.

Garda Siochana Act 2005, s 3

"MINISTER"

"Minister" means the Minister for Justice, Equality and Law Reform.

Criminal Justice (Surveillance) Act 2009, s 1

O

"ORGANISED CRIME"

"organised crime" has the meaning it has in Part 7 of the Criminal Justice Act 2006.

Criminal Justice (Surveillance) Act 2009, s 15(4)

A person who, for the purpose of enhancing the ability of a criminal organisation to commit or facilitate—

(*a*) a serious offence in the State, or
(*b*) in a place outside the State, a serious offence under the law of that place where the act constituting the offence would, if done in the State, constitute a serious offence,

knowingly, by act—

(i) in a case to which *paragraph (a)* applies, whether done in or outside the State, and
(ii) in a case to which *paragraph (b)* applies, done in the State, on board an Irish ship or on an aircraft registered in the State,

participates in or contributes to any activity of the organisation is guilty of an offence.

(2) In proceedings for an offence under *subsection (1)*, it shall not be necessary for the prosecution to prove that—

(*a*) the criminal organisation concerned actually committed a serious offence in the State or a serious offence under the law of a place outside the State where the act constituting the offence would, if done in the State, constitute a serious offence, as the case may be,
(*b*) the participation or contribution of the person concerned actually enhanced the ability of the criminal organisation concerned to commit or facilitate the offence concerned, or
(*c*) the person concerned knew the specific nature of any offence that may have been committed or facilitated by the criminal organisation concerned.

(3) In determining whether a person participates in or contributes to any activity of a criminal organisation, the court may consider, *inter alia*, whether the person—

(*a*) uses a name, word, symbol or other representation that identifies, or is associated with, the organisation, or
(*b*) receives any benefit from the organisation.

(4) For the purposes of this section, facilitation of an offence does not require knowledge of a particular offence the commission of which is facilitated, or that an offence actually be committed.

Criminal Justice Act 2006, s 72

P

"PLACE"

"place" includes—

(*a*) a dwelling or other building,
(*b*) a vehicle, whether mechanically propelled or not,
(*c*) a vessel, whether sea-going or not,
(*d*) an aircraft, whether capable of operation or not, and
(*e*) a hovercraft.

Criminal Justice (Surveillance) Act 2009, s 1

R

"REFEREE"

In this section—

"Referee" means the holder of the office of Complaints Referee nder the Act of 1993.

Criminal Justice (Surveillance) Act 2009, s 11(12)

(2) (*a*) There shall stand established the office of Complaints Referee and the holder of the office shall be known as the Complaints Referee and is referred to in this section as "the Referee".

(*b*) A person appointed to be the Referee shall be a judge of the Circuit Court, a judge of the District Court or a person who is for the time being a practising barrister, or a practising solicitor, of not less than 10 years' standing.
(*c*) The Referee shall be appointed by the Taoiseach, shall hold office for a term of 5 years and, subject to the provisions of this subsection, shall be eligible for reappointment as the Referee.
(*d*) Subject to the provisions of this subsection, the terms and conditions, including terms and conditions relating—
  (i) except in a case where the Referee is a judge of the Circuit Court or a judge of the District Court, to remuneration, and
  (ii) to allowances for expenses,

upon which the Referee shall hold office shall be such as may be determined by the Minister, with the consent of the Minister for Finance, at the time of his appointment or reappointment.

(e) The Referee may at any time resign his office as the Referee by letter sent to the Taoiseach and the resignation shall take effect on and from the date of receipt of the letter.
(*f*) The Referee may be removed from office by the Taoiseach but only for stated misbehaviour or incapacity and upon resolutions passed by Dáil Éireann and by Seanad Éireann calling for his removal.

Interception of Postal Packets and Telecommunications Messages (Regulation) Act 1993, s 9(2)

"RELEVANT CONTRAVENTION"

"relevant contravention" means a contravention of a provision of *sections 4* to *8*.

Criminal Justice (Surveillance) Act 2009, s 11(12)

"RELEVANT MINISTER"

"relevant Minister" means—

(*a*) the Minister, in relation to approvals granted by a superior officer of, and documents and information in the custody of, the Garda Síochána,
(*b*) the Minister for Defence, in relation to approvals granted by a superior officer of, and documents and information in the custody of, the Defence Forces, and
(*c*) the Minister for Finance, in relation to approvals granted by a superior officer of, and documents and information in the custody of, the Revenue Commissioners.

Criminal Justice (Surveillance) Act 2009, s 1

"RELEVANT PERSON"

"relevant person" means a person who is or was—

(*a*) a member of the Garda Síochána, a member of the Defence Forces or an officer of the Revenue Commissioners,
(*b*) a reserve member of the Garda Síochána within the meaning of the Garda Síochána Act 2005,
(*c*) a member of the Reserve Defence Force within the meaning of the Defence Act 1954,
(*d*) a member of the civilian staff of the Garda Síochána or of the Defence Forces, or
(*e*) engaged under a contract or other arrangement to work with or for the Garda Síochána, the Defence Forces or the Revenue Commissioners.

Criminal Justice (Surveillance) Act 2009, s 13(4)

"REVENUE OFFENCE"

"revenue offence" means an offence under any of the following provisions that is an arrestable offence:

(*a*) section 186 of the Customs Consolidation Act 1876;
(*b*) section 1078 of the Taxes Consolidation Act 1997;
(*c*) section 102 of the Finance Act 1999;
(*d*) section 119 of the Finance Act 2001;
(*e*) section 79 (inserted by section 62 of the Finance Act 2005) of the Finance Act 2003;
(*f*) section 78 of the Finance Act 2005.

Criminal Justice (Surveillance) Act 2009, s 1

S

"SUPERIOR OFFICER"

"superior officer" means—

(*a*) in the case of the Garda Síochána, a member of the Garda Síochána not below the rank of superintendent;

(*b*) in the case of the Defence Forces, a member of the Defence Forces not below the rank of colonel; and
(*c*) in the case of the Revenue Commissioners, an officer of the Revenue Commissioners not below the rank of principal officer.

Criminal Justice (Surveillance) Act 2009, s 1

"SURVEILLANCE"

"surveillance" means—

(*a*) monitoring, observing, listening to or making a recording of a particular person or group of persons or their movements, activities and communications, or
(*b*) monitoring or making a recording of places or things, by or with the assistance of surveillance devices.

Criminal Justice (Surveillance) Act 2009, s 1

"SURVEILLANCE DEVICE"

"surveillance device" means an apparatus designed or adapted for use in surveillance, but does not include—

(*a*) an apparatus designed to enhance visual acuity or night vision, to the extent to which it is not used to make a recording of any person who, or any place or thing that, is being monitored or observed,
(*b*) a CCTV within the meaning of section 38 of the Garda Síochána Act 2005, or
(*c*) a camera, to the extent to which it is used to take photographs of any person who, or any thing that, is in a place to which the public have access.

Criminal Justice (Surveillance) Act 2009, s 1

T

"TERRORIST ACTIVITY"

"terrorist activity" and "terrorist-linked activity" have the meanings they have in section 4 of, and Schedule 2 to, the Criminal Justice (Terrorist Offences) Act 2005.

"terrorist activity" means an act that is committed in or outside the State and that—

(*a*) if committed in the State, would constitute an offence specified in *Part 1* of *Schedule 2*, and
(*b*) is committed with the intention of—

(i) seriously intimidating a population,
(ii) unduly compelling a government or an international organisation to perform or abstain from performing an act, or
(iii) seriously destabilising or destroying the fundamental political, constitutional, economic or social structures of a state or an international organisation;

"terrorist-linked activity" means an act—

(*a*) that is committed in or outside the State and that—
(i) if committed in the State, would constitute an offence specified in *Part 2* of *Schedule 2*, and
(ii) is committed with a view to engaging in a terrorist activity,

Or

(*b*) that is committed in or outside the State and that—
(i) if committed in the State, would constitute an offence specified in *Part 3* of *Schedule 2*, and
(ii) is committed with a view to engaging in a terrorist activity or with a view to committing an act that, if committed in the State, would constitute an offence under section 21 or 21A of the Act of 1939.

Criminal Justice (Terrorist Offences) Act 2005, s 4

SCHEDULE 2

Offences for purposes of Definitions of "Terrorist Activity" and "Terrorist-Linked Activity"

SECTION 4

PART 1

(Paragraph (a) of definition of "terrorist activity")

Common law offences

1. The following common law offences:
(*a*) murder;
(*b*) manslaughter;
(*c*) rape.

Non-fatal offences against the person

2. An offence under any of the following provisions of the Non-Fatal Offences against the Person Act 1997:

(*a*) section 3 (assault causing harm);
(*b*) section 4 (assault causing serious harm);

(*c*) section 6 (syringe and other attacks);
(*d*) section 12 (poisoning);
(*e*) section 13 (endangerment);
(*f*) section 14 (endangering traffic);
(*g*) section 15 (false imprisonment).

Offence of torture

3. Any offence under section 2 of the Criminal Justice (United Nations Convention Against Torture) Act 2000.

Sexual offences

4. An offence under any of the following provisions of the Criminal Law (Rape) (Amendment) Act 1990:

(*a*) section 2 (sexual assault);
(*b*) section 3 (aggravated sexual assault);
(*c*) section 4 (rape under section 4).

Criminal damage

5. Any offence under section 2 (damaging property) of the Criminal Damage Act 1991.

Malicious damage

6. An offence under any of the following provisions of the Malicious Damage Act 1861:

(*a*) section 35 (maliciously obstructing railways);
(*b*) section 36 (obstructing engines or carriages on railways);
(*c*) section 37 (damaging telegraphs);
(*d*) section 48 (removing or concealing buoys, etc.).

Offences relating to aircraft and vehicles

7. An offence under any of the following provisions:

(*a*) section 11 of the Air Navigation and Transport Act 1973 (unlawful seizure of aircraft);
(*b*) section 3 of the Air Navigation and Transport Act 1975 (unlawful acts against the safety of aviation);
(*c*) section 10 of the Criminal Law (Jurisdiction) Act 1976 (unlawful seizure of vehicles, etc.).

Offences relating to explosives

8. An offence under any of the following provisions of the Explosive Substances Act 1883:

(*a*) section 2 (causing explosion likely to endanger life or damage property);
(*b*) section 3 (making or possessing, etc., explosives with intent to endanger life or property);
(*c*) section 4(1) (making or possessing explosives in suspicious circumstances).

Offences relating to firearms and other weapons

9. An offence under any of the following provisions:

(*a*) section 2 of the Firearms Act 1925 (restrictions on possession, use and carriage of firearms);
(*b*) section 10 of the Firearms Act 1925 (restrictions on manufacture and sale of firearms);
(*c*) section 15 of the Firearms Act 1925 (possessing firearms or ammunition with intent to endanger life or cause serious injury to property);
(*d*) section 26 of the Firearms Act 1964 (possessing firearms while taking vehicle without authority);
(e) section 27 of the Firearms Act 1964 (using firearms to resist arrest or aid escape);
(*f*) section 27A of the Firearms Act 1964 (possessing firearms or ammunition in suspicious circumstances);
(*g*) section 27B of the Firearms Act 1964 (carrying firearms with criminal intent).

Offences relating to chemical weapons, nuclear material and other dangerous substances

10. An offence under any of the following provisions:

(*a*) section 3 of the Chemical Weapons Act 1997 (chemical weapons);
(*b*) section 4 of the Chemical Weapons Act 1997 (possession of listed toxic chemicals and precursors);
(*c*) section 38 of the Radiological Protection Act 1991 (offences relating to nuclear material);
(*d*) section 61 of the Post Office Act 1908 (prohibition of placing injurious substances in or against post office letter boxes);
(e) section 63(1)(a) of the Post Office Act 1908 (prohibition of sending dangerous substances by post).

Offences under this Act

11. An offence under any of the following provisions of this Act:

(*a*) section 9 (offence of hostage-taking);
(*b*) section 10 (offence of terrorist bombing);
(*c*) section 11 (offences against internationally protected persons).

PART 2

(Paragraph (a)(i) of definition of "terrorist-linked activity")

Aggravated burglary and robbery

12. An offence under any of the following provisions of the Criminal Justice (Theft and Fraud Offences) Act 2001:

(*a*) section 13 (aggravated burglary);
(*b*) section 14 (robbery).

Blackmail, extortion, etc.

13. Any offence under section 17 (blackmail, extortion and demanding money with menaces) of the Criminal Justice (Public Order) Act 1994.

PART 3

(Paragraph (b)(i) of definition of "terrorist-linked activity")

Forgery Offences

14. An offence under any of the following provisions of the Criminal Justice (Theft and Fraud Offences) Act 2001 in so far as that offence relates to an instrument within the meaning of paragraph (*a*), (e), (*f*), (*j*), (k), (*l*), (*m*), (*n*), (*o*) or (*p*) of the definition of "instrument" in section 24 of that Act:

(*a*) section 25 (forgery);
(*b*) section 26 (using a false instrument);
(*c*) section 27 (copying false instrument);
(*d*) section 28 (using copy of false instrument);
(e) section 29 (custody or control of certain false instruments, etc.).

Criminal Justice (Terrorist Offences) Act 2005 Schedule 2, Parts 1, 2 & 3

"TRACKING DEVICE"

"tracking device" means a surveillance device that is used only for the purpose of providing information regarding the location of a person, vehicle or thing.

Criminal Justice (Surveillance) Act 2009, s 1

W

"WRITTEN RECORD OF APPROVAL"

"written record of approval" means a written record of approval prepared by a superior officer under *section 7(6)* or *8(6)*.

Criminal Justice (Surveillance) Act 2009, s 1

A superior officer who approves the use of a surveillance under this section shall, as soon as practicable and, in any case, not later that 8 hours after the surveillance has been approved, prepare a written record of approval of that surveillance.

Criminal Justice (Surveillance) Act 2009, s 7(6)

A superior officer who approves the use of a tracking device under this section shall, as soon as practicable and, in any case, not later that 8 hours after the surveillance has been approved, prepare a written record of approval of the use of then tracking device.

Criminal Justice (Surveillance) Act 2009, s 8(6)